WAR, TERROR & PEACE
IN THE QUR'AN AND IN ISLAM:
INSIGHTS FOR MILITARY & GOVERNMENT LEADERS

T. P. SCHWARTZ-BARCOTT

June 2004: All Rights Reserved

The Army War College Foundation Press
Copyright 2004 by Timothy Philip Schwartz-Barcott
All rights reserved. Permission to reproduce any element of this work may be requested through the
Army War College Foundation Press, 122 Forbes Avenue, Carlisle, PA 17013.
ISBN 0-970-96822-1
Manufactured in the United States of America
First Edition

PERMISSIONS AND AUTHORIZATION TO EXCERPT:

Every attempt has been made by the author to secure the appropriate permissions for
material reproduced in this book. If there has been any oversight, we will be glad to try to rectify
the situation if written requests are made to the author in a timely manner.

Arabic script and translations by Najih Lazar.

Excerpts from *Bravo Two Zulu* by Andy McNab, copyright © 1993, reprinted by permission of
Random House U.K. and Bantam Press, a division of Transworld Publishers Ltd. London, England.

Mohammed by Maxime Rodinson. English translation copyright © 1971 by Anne Carter. Originally
published in French as *Mahomet* by Club Francais du Livre. Second (revised) edition published by
Editions du Seuil, 1968. Reprinted by permission of Georges Borchardt, Inc. for Editions du Seuil.

"Good Kills" copyright © April 20, 2003 by Peter Maass. This article originally appeared in *(The)
New York Times Magazine*. Reprinted by permission of the author.

Excerpts from *My Jihad* by Aukai Collins. Copyright © 2002 by Aukai Collins. Reprinted by
permission of The Lyons Press, an imprint of Globe Pequot Press, Guilford, CT.

Excerpts from *Jihad in the West*, by Paul Fregosi. Amherst, NY: Prometheus Books. Copyright ©
1998 by Paul Fregosi. Reprinted with permission.

Excerpts from *The Meaning of the Glorious Koran* Translated by Mohammed Marmaduke
Pickthall, copyright © 1953 by New American Library, used by permission of Dutton Signet,
a division of Penguin Group (USA), Inc.

Excerpts from John L. Esposito, *Islam: The Straight Path*, 3rd Edition, (paperback) 1998, used by
permission of Oxford University Press.

Excerpts from *Foreign Affairs*, reprinted by permission of *Foreign Affairs*, Vol. 81 #3, May/June
2002, reprinted by permission of the Council of Foreign Relations, Inc. www.foreignaffairs.org.

Excerpts from Ahmed Rashid, *Taliban: Militant Islam, Oil & Fundamentalism in Central Asia*,
reprinted by permission of Yale University Press. Copyright © 2000.

Excerpts from *Faith Beyond Belief: A Journey to Freedom, by David Eberly*, Copyright © 2002,
reprinted by permission of Brandy lane Publishing, Inc.

Photos of Istanbul residents and of the 1979 Peace Treaty by permission of AP/WORLDWIDE
PHOTOS. Photo of Arab volunteer unit courtesy of REUTERS/Goran Tomasevic Photo by GORAN
TOMASEVIC. Photo of U.S. soldier confronting Iraqi citizen with Qur'an courtesy of REUTERS/
Radu Sigheti.

Icon of 3 birds drinking water, Jerusalem, 14th Century, as rendered by Alan Greco
of Alan Greco Design, Inc.

DEDICATION

To all people who try their best to bring
more peace, understanding, health, and happiness
to all people throughout the world.

TABLE OF CONTENTS

LIST OF FIGURES, MAPS, AND TABLES

DETAILED TABLE OF CONTENTS

ACKNOWLEDGEMENTS

Many people and organizations assisted me in preparing this book. It is not possible to acknowledge all of them. Nor are any of them responsible for any errors, oversights, or misrepresentations that might be found in this book. These are mine alone, and they are unintentional, I assure you.

Very helpful to me were some of the reference librarians and staff at the libraries of Brown University, the Naval War College, Newport, RI, the University of Rhode Island, and Providence College.

Among the people who were willing to be interviewed and identified about war, terror, and peace in the Qur'an and in the history of Islam were Najih Lazar, Professor Muhammad Qasim Zaman of the Islamic Studies Department, Brown University, and Professor Mohammed Sharif, University of Rhode Island. People who informed me about recent and current combat operations in the Middle East include General Anthony C. Zinni USMC (Ret.), Colonel Thomas Greenwood USMC, Lt. Colonel Kerry Knowles USMC (Ret.), Chris Seiple, 1st Lieutenant Rye Schwartz-Barcott USMC, and Gunnery Sergeant Julio Chang USMC.

Alan Greco of Alan Greco Design provided first rate and friendly service in designing the covers, figures, maps, and artwork. Pat Chaney of One On One PC always was willing and able to provide superb yet cheerful technical assistance on all matters involving electronic word and data processing as well as a keen eye for glitches in composition. Their combination of creativity, attention to details, and sheer technical competence is outstanding.

Among the people who read and commented on at least one chapter of drafts of the manuscript were General Anthony C. Zinni USMC (Ret.), Lt. General Bernard Trainor, USMC (Ret.), Colonel Walter P. Lang USA (Ret.), Colonel Michael M. Smith USAF, Colonel John Glasgow USMC (Ret.), Lt. Colonel Kerry Knowles USMC (Ret.), Lt. Colonel Ray Stewart USMC (Ret.), Professor Gerhard Lenski of the University of North Carolina, Professor Robin M. Williams, Jr. of Cornell University and the University of California, Irvine, Professor Richard Kohn of the University of North Carolina, Chapel Hill, Professor Adeed Dawisha of Miami University, Professor Louis Hicks of St. Mary's College, Chris Seiple, President of the Institute for Global Engagement, and several reviewers who prefer to remain anonymous. Readers of parts of early drafts also included Najih Lazar, George Roberts Coulter, and Denise Schwartz.

At the Army War College Foundation, Colonel Stephen P. Riley USA (Ret.) and Colonel Zane Finkelstein USA (Ret.) were able to see the importance of this work when some others were unable or unwilling to do so. Colonel Riley then mustered some of the the resources to get it published with the help of an amiable staff including Colonel Walt Woods USMC (Ret.), Colonel Richard Willis USA (Ret.), Anne Woods, Judy Nunez, and Rebecca Bremer. Pat Moran, Colonel Edward Skender USA (Ret.) and Cathy Craley at Stackpole Books were instrumental in getting it done on schedule.

Intellectually, this work reflects a long-standing debt that I will always have to several outstanding thinkers and mentors, Gerhard E. Lenski, Emeritus Professor of the University of North Carolina, and Kai T. Erikson, Emeritus Professor of Yale University, among them. Both of these fine men encouraged me to think and to feel deeply about the human beings and the human societies that I study, even when few others seem to care.

Timely, critical comments by 1st Lieutenant Rye Schwartz-Barcott USMC were especially valuable because of his familiarity with current issues in international relations and military operations in combat zones. Professor Donna Schwartz-Barcott read through the entire manuscript and offered many useful suggestions for improving it in many places. For years she also supported in many other ways my often odd and inconvenient hours working on the manuscript, starting on the day of the infamous passenger jet attacks on the World Trade Center in New York and the Pentagon in Washington, DC, September 11, 2001. So much has changed in the world since then — but not her support and companionship. For this I am most grateful.

PREFACE

My first Vietnam experience as a young second lieutenant, in 1967, convinced me that we were missing a critical consideration in understanding the nature of that conflict, the actions of the enemy, and the plight of the people. As a language trained advisor to the Vietnamese Marines, I was immersed in the society and culture and came away from that tour of duty with a different perspective on the war than that of many of my contemporaries. Most of them saw the conflict from a purely military view inside U.S. units fighting there. In many experiences since then, I have seen the flaw in not taking culture and history into account in our analysis of what we face. We must go beyond the traditional order of battle estimates to a deeper understanding of what confronts us. This is especially important in the cultural conflicts we seem to face since the end of the Cold War.

Tim Schwartz-Barcott has produced a remarkable work that analyzes the cultural, religious, and historical aspects that influence decisions and actions taken by the enemy we face today. It is an insightful tool in helping us understand the nature of this current conflict and in interpreting and predicting actions of the enemy. For decision makers in this conflict, this is a vital guide to analyzing these challenges.

General Anthony C. Zinni, USMC (Ret.)
Former Commander in Chief , United States Central Command.
Co-author, *Battle Ready*.

Members of an Arab volunteer unit hold weapons and the Koran during exercises in a military base near Baghdad March 12, 2003. REUTERS/Goran Tomasevic

FOREWORD

"For Muslims the Quran is the book of God. It is the eternal, uncreated, literal word of God sent down from heaven, revealed one final time to the Prophet Muhammad as a guide for humankind."

— John Esposito, *Islam: The Straight Path*

"The movement adopted the slogan: 'The Qur'an is our constitution. The Prophet is our Guide; Death for the glory of Allah is our greatest ambition.'"

— Peter Marsden, *The Taliban: War, Religion and the New Order in Afghanistan* (referring to the Muslim Brotherhood)

Probably like you and a lot of other people, I have had to reconsider what I know about Islam and people who commit violence in the name of Islam in light of the terrorist attacks on the World Trade Center, the Pentagon, and so many related (and unrelated) acts of violence since then. Only three days after the attacks, President Bush addressed the nation and told us that Islam is a religion of peace and that Muslims are peaceful people. Spokespersons for Muslim communities throughout the U.S. echoed similar sentiments and disavowed as Muslims anyone who would approve of these attacks. At the same time, however, network television transmitted live coverage of joyous celebrations of the attacks in the streets of Cairo, Beirut, Baghdad, Kabul, and other cities in the Middle East. Rapidly developing news stories told us that many of the planners and perpetrators of the attacks were, or had been, devout Muslims who recited passages from Islam's holiest book, *al-Qur'an (The Koran)*[1] five times a day, each day of their adult lives, as required of all people who practice Islam. Copies were found in their abandoned apartments and automobiles. Their alleged leader, Osama bin Laden, was reported to quote often from the Qur'an while inciting his minions to conduct holy war, *Jihad*, against the "infidels of the West." Photos were published of al-Qaeda and Taliban soldiers holding aloft both their Kalashnikov rifles and their Qur'ans while dancing in victory circles, exhorting each other and threatening doom on their distant enemies. A famous videotape was broadcasted throughout the World showing bin Laden at a sit-down dinner in Afghanistan with a visiting Saudi shaykh. They quoted from the Qur'an as they celebrated the attacks of 9-11-2001.

"Fight them, Allah will torture them, with your hands he will torture them. He will deceive them and he will give you victory. Allah will forgive the believers, he is knowledgeable about everything."[2]

I found myself asking whether this verse really is in the Qur'an. If so, is it an isolated verse that was being quoted "out of context," a verse that is incompatible with most or all of the other verses in the Qur'an? Did bin Laden use this verse or other verses in the Qur'an to motivate and instruct the terrorists? Could proponents of violence be doing the same thing in the West Bank, Gaza, Egypt, Somalia, Kenya, Syria, Iraq, Iran, Pakistan, Malaysia, and even in the United States? Are there other verses in the Qur'an that can help us to understand how and why its proponents wage war as they do, and to anticipate how they might wage war in the future, or defer to making peace?

Suddenly it dawned on me that I had never read the Qur'an thoroughly, let alone conscientiously and objectively, although I had some familiarity with it over the last four decades and with Muslims and Islam. I had taken undergraduate courses in the history and philosophy of world religions, including Islam, and in military history, where limited attention was given to some of the great battles (that included a few of the many sieges of Constantinople (Istanbul) between what were conveniently called "Christian" and "Moslem" armies). Later, as an infantry and ground reconnaissance officer in the United States Marine Corps in Vietnam, 1965-66, I had firsthand opportunities to witness how and why men and women fight when they serve in the armed forces of several very different nations. Their political and military leaders tried to motivate and control their combatants with very different incentives, threats, and appeals to ideologies. Since then, as a sociologist and college instructor, I have tried to stay abreast of issues about Arab societies and Islam, along with other societies and religions, in order to be reasonably informed about these topics while teaching courses, attending conferences, and writing research reports. Occasionally I have had discussions with some of my Muslim students about their religious beliefs and their perceptions of world affairs. While volunteering to teach English writing skills to prisoners at a local state prison, I have read and discussed passages of the Qur'an with some of the young men who had converted to Islam and were eager to share their faith with me. On visits to countries in the

Middle East I had conversations about current events with Muslims from several walks of life. Muhammad was mentioned much more than the Qur'an. Walking in and around the minarets and mosques of Cairo and Jerusalem at noon and evening prayers, I was struck by the religiosity of some of the worshippers and the seeming nonchalance of many others. Even more memorable was the sheer quantity of shocking evidence, in the forms of ancient ruins and recently burned and bombed-out apartments and automobiles, of how violence and religious fervor have been aggravating each other for centuries in the Middle East. This was far beyond what I had witnessed as a Marine Corps infantry officer in the Far East during the Vietnam War era.

Clearly, then, it was time to read the Qur'an in its entirety, and as objectively as possible. I started by spending afternoons in the extensive Islamic literature collection of the Rockefeller Library at Brown University, leafing through the dozens of editions of Qur'ans, Qur'an commentaries, and concordances. Soon it became apparent that there were many verses in the Qur'an about war and peace that were difficult to find without a very careful and systematic reading, in part because the indexes to the editions were woefully incomplete, as were the concordances. Furthermore, most of the commentaries had their own very limited and usually biased points of view or they were so focused that they missed many of the verses that dealt with war and peace. Phone calls and E-mail correspondence with some leading Islamic scholars in the U.S. also revealed that many commentators had limited if not biased knowledge of what the Qur'an's verses say, literally, about war and peace. There was a lot of wishful thinking, selective perception, and denial about what is and is not in the Qur'an. Surely there are many books in English about Islam but few if any address peace, terror, and war in the Qur'an in a systematic and objective manner. No one seems to have focused on the Qur'an as a sourcebook of ideas, motivations, and justifications for peace, terror, and war. This book is meant to fill these needs.

My purposes here are to:

1. Accurately and fairly summarize what the Qur'an has to say about war and peace.

2. Re-consider some of the key events in the military history of Islamic fighters and groups in light of the Qur'an.

3. Evaluate a variety of interpretations of the Qur'an regarding these topics.

4. Then suggest a set of reasonable policies and procedures for military and government leaders who are dealing with Qur'an-oriented people and organizations — not only adversaries — but also allies, neutrals, and members of the armed forces.

In doing these things, this book also encourages readers to think anew, objectively and inclusively, about so many of the categorical statements that government officials, religious leaders, and academicians have made about Islam, Muslims, and the Qur'an, particularly since September 2001.

This book is <u>not</u> an assessment or a critique of the morality of the Qur'an, of Muhammad, of Islam, or of any other religion, ethnic group, nationality, or nation. Nor is it a new military history of Islam (although Chapters 3-5 provide new analyses of more than 225 famous battles and wars which involved Muslim combatants between 624 and 2004 A.D.). There is a vast and accomplished literature that has done some of these things. Primarily, this book is intended to be an objective and useful exposition and commentary on what the Qur'an has to say about war and peace. It also shows how these sayings can enlighten our understanding of why some hostile people and organizations are behaving as they do. Perhaps we can reduce their hostility and their destructiveness if we understand them more thoroughly and objectively.

The questions that will be answered in this book include:

1. What does the Qur'an say, literally and specifically, in its more than 6,000 verses, about peace and war between Muslims and non-Muslims?

2. How could these statements about peace and war be used by literalists and opportunists to sustain or make peace and to wage war and other hostilities between Muslims and non-Muslims?

3. What evidence is there that the statements in the Qur'an about war and peace have had significant influence on the combat behaviors of Muslims and in the history of Muslim warfare?

4. Given the statements in the Qur'an about war and peace, and in light of the history of Muslim warfare, what kinds of preparations and actions should government and military leaders take now, in order to minimize the likelihood of

future hostilities with Muslim states, organizations, groups, and people, and to optimize the likelihood of favorable outcomes in the event that new hostilities occur?

The introductory chapter that follows this Foreword reviews some of the many recent provocative claims about how the Qur'an is provoking and sustaining many Arab terrorists and hostile regimes in the Middle East. For readers who might want a little refresher on the Qur'an, the chapter then describes the Qur'an, how it was produced, and some of the reasons why it is so important to so many Muslims — arguably more influential to many Muslims than the Torah and the Bible are to Jews and Christians. It addresses the often heard objections by some scholars and clerics that the Qur'an can only be understood and appreciated in Arabic, and by native-born Muslims who are raised in Islamic communities and are intensively educated about the Qur'an. It also discusses the popular objection of some scholars and zealots that no passage of the Qur'an can be understood alone and without taking into account its historical and literary contexts. Even if these objections are valid, they often are irrelevant when, as is so common in the contemporary era, considerable numbers of people with power are not trying to *understand* the Qur'an. Quite the contrary. Their purpose is to *use* the Qur'an, and specific verses of the Qur'an, so selectively as to legitimate their own violent schemes and to recruit, motivate, and instruct others according to their purpose. In all likelihood this is exactly what Osama bin Laden and the Saudi shaykh were doing at dinner when they quoted the Qur'an (in the passage presented a few pages ago). Many other people are doing the same thing throughout the World. Saddam Hussein of Iraq comes immediately to mind. Contexts of documents like the Qur'an are important to people such as these only when these people give importance to them. Literalists and opportunists are categories of people who often ignore contexts, or twist them to suit their own purposes. They are likely to continue to do so, especially now that the terrorist attacks of 9-11-2001 have become so galvanizing, definitive, influential, and unforgettable to so many leaders and citizens throughout the World — at least until ways are found to neutralize these uses (or misuses) of the Qur'an.

Chapter 1 ends with a brief description of the methods that I have used in order to find all of the relevant verses in the Qur'an regarding war and peace, and to analyze those verses as objectively as possible so that we can develop ways to accommodate or react to them in morally responsible and lawful ways.

Chapter 2 is the heart of this book. It presents more than one hundred passages from the Qur'an, categorized according to topics that are crucial to government and military leaders, that define war and peace and instruct believers on how to behave accordingly. I encourage you to move directly to this chapter and read these Qur'anic passages for yourself. Then ask yourself how you would react to them, especially if you and many of your friends were physically healthy, underemployed, marginalized males, ages fifteen to fifty, who were increasingly frustrated and angry about what you believe are grave injustices and humiliations to you and your people by outsiders who seem to rebuke and violate these same passages.

Chapters 3, 4, and 5 review and interpret more than 225 of the most famous wars and battles during Muhammad's life and in Muslim military history since then. The purpose is to determine how closely the battles correspond to passages in the Qur'an about peace, terror, and war. Chapter 3 focuses on Muhammad's life as a military commander and on six of the most consequential battles that he led or authorized during his life. Chapter 4 presents new and objective analysis of 214 of the most famous "Muslim" battles and wars between Muhammad's death in 632 and 1984. Chapter 5 provides original interpretations of nine of the most consequential wars since 1984 that have involved Muslim combatants, including the U.S. led invasions and occupations of Afghanistan in 2001 and Iraq in 2003. The purpose of these chapters is <u>not</u> to look for contradictions or violations of Qur'anic commandments, but rather to enable us to understand more fully how proponents of the Qur'an and of Muslim military traditions behaved in past battles so that government and military leaders can prepare to sustain peace and make war appropriately, if necessary, in the future. These chapters, along with Chapter 6, can also serve to provide "context" for readers who feel that the many Qur'anic passages in Chapter 2 are not sufficiently comprehensible as they stand.

Chapter 7 summarizes and expands on the many insights that are specified in Chapters 1-6. It also offers dozens of suggestions about how leaders in government and the military can use our growing knowledge of the Qur'an and its proponents to help sustain peace, defuse terrorism, and if necessary, wage war in effective and just ways. This chapter advances the proposition that the Qur'an can become an ally in war and in peace, in many ways, if we will let it. For this is one of my hopes: that *the Qur'an, along with other holy books that continue to be so important to so many people in the modern world, can become a greater force in sustaining international peace in the decades ahead.*

The Epilogue offers conciliatory encouragements to all of us — Muslims and non-Muslims, leaders and followers, young and old — that can lead to greater peace and understanding for all of us. These encouragements are derived from the many insights about war, terror, and peace in the Qur'an and in Islam that are presented in Chapters 1-7.

---

[1] As a sign of respect and sensitivity to Islam and Muslims, I will use the Islamic word Qur'an (short for al-Qur'an), rather than the spelling that was popularized by the British more than a century ago, except when I present quotations by other authors who use other spellings.

[2] "Bin Laden on Tape: We Calculated in Advance," *The Providence Journal*, December 14, 2001, p. A17 (quoting from the Associated Press).

وَعِبَادُ ٱلرَّحْمَٰنِ ٱلَّذِينَ يَمْشُونَ عَلَى ٱلْأَرْضِ
هَوْنًا وَإِذَا خَاطَبَهُمُ ٱلْجَاهِلُونَ قَالُوا سَلَٰمًا

"The faithful slaves of the Beneficient

are they who walk upon the Earth modestly,

and when the foolish ones address them, answer,

'Peace.'"

– Al-Qur'an 25:63

CHAPTER ONE

APPROACHING THE QUR'AN AND ITS PROPONENTS

IMAGES OF THE QUR'AN IN CURRENT CONFLICTS

Let us first consider a few images of the Qur'an and of Islam in newspaper articles about violent events in the Middle East.

"Muslim Cleric Issues Call for Jihad Against U.S."

(June 7, 2003) "BAGHDAD, Iraq — The imam at one of Baghdad's largest mosques urged more than a thousand listeners yesterday to wage a jihad, or religious war, against U.S. occupying forces in Iraq. Speaking at Friday prayer services, Imam Mouaid al-Ubaidi denounced the Americans as 'invaders' and 'aggressors' and implicitly praised recent guerrilla attacks against U.S. soldiers as self-defense by people being 'strangled'.... In his sermon, Ubaidi deplored the deaths of two Iraqis in a shootout last Sunday with U.S. soldiers within a few hundred feet of the Abu Hanifa mosque in which he spoke. He openly encouraged listeners to resist the occupying forces with whatever means they have. His voice rising in power and anger, the cleric recited a poem from the Quran to defend those who attack U.S. forces. 'How can you blame a person who is being strangled if he hurts the person who is strangling him? How can you blame the person who is being oppressed who hurts the person who is oppressing him?'"[1]

"Suicide Bomber Kills 15 in Israel"

(March 5, 2003) "The bomber was identified as Mahmoud Hamdan Kawasme, a 20-year old from the West Bank city of Hebron. In an Arabic letter that was tightly folded to survive the blast, Kawasme said that the destruction of the World Trade Center was foretold in the Koran, the sacred text of Islam. The letter extolled the 'miracles of the Koran,' and urged readers to pass the news. 'A sort of will, if you like,' Israeli foreign ministry spokesman Jonathan Peled said."[2]

1

As shown in these excerpts from newspaper articles, a recurring image in the mass media is that the Qur'an is (or was) very prominent in the lives of many violence-oriented people including Osama bin Laden, Saddam Hussein, Colonel Muammar al-Qaddafi, Yassar Arafat, some Muslim clerics, and many members of militant Islamic organizations throughout the Middle and Far East. Captioned photographs in the newspapers often have shown soldiers of al-Qaeda, the Taliban, and the PLO in "victory circles," thrusting their Qur'ans and Kalashnikov rifles towards the heavens as they exhort each other to defeat their enemies. Other photographs and articles reveal copies of the Qur'an, a training manual, and a "hijacking letter" of instruction that exhort their readers to commit violence with passages from the Qur'an and with references to famous battles that Muhammad commanded. These items were among the personal effects that were left behind in the automobiles and apartments of the hijackers who crashed the jet airplanes into the World Trade Center and the Pentagon on September 11, 2001.[3]

Mounting evidence also shows that Osama bin Laden and his supporters used the Qur'an to justify the terrorist attacks. In a widely televised version of a translated videotape, Osama and a shaykh from Saudi Arabia are having a sit-down dinner at a remote location in Afghanistan in November 2001. They are discussing how Osama planned the attacks on the World Trade Center. Osama paraphrases several verses from the Qur'an by way of explaining his actions, saying, "I was ordered to fight the people until they say there is no god but Allah, and his prophet Muhammad." The shaykh then quotes another verse from the Qur'an, translated as follows: "Fight them, Allah will torture them, with your hands, he will torture them. He will deceive them and he will give you victory. Allah will forgive the believers, he is knowledgeable about everything."[4]

There have been many other published accounts about the importance of the Qur'an to Osama. Reuters reported that, twice in his speech on al-Jazeera television, November 3, 2001, Osama referred to the Qur'an as "God's book" and as "Islam's holy book." He also referred to the West, the U.S., and the United Nations, as waging "...a war of annihilation. Rise in support of your religion, Islam is calling you. Your support for us makes us stronger." Khaled Abon El Fadl, a professor of Islamic law at U.C.L.A., analyzed Osama's speeches and determined that, "bin Laden heavily focused on the Koranic verses about fighting oppression," and that he "cited Koranic verses conveying God's permission for victims of injustice to throw-off the yoke of oppression."[5]

Beyond the possible influence of the Qur'an on Osama bin Laden and the planning and execution of the terrorist attacks, there is considerable evidence that the Qur'an often plays a prominent role in political events in many parts of the Muslim world including Iran, Libya, Iraq, Somalia, and Pakistan. Especially since the Islamic revolution in Iran under the Ayatollah Khomeini in 1979, the Qur'an has often been quoted publicly by many government leaders in the Middle East, from reformists to fundamentalists, and by their antagonists outside of government, as a way of legitimizing armed violence against each other. Peter Marsden claims that many of the contemporary references to the Qur'an by political leaders in the Middle East and Far East can be traced back to a youth movement called "The Muslim Brotherhood" that began in Egypt in 1928. It considers all Islam to originate out of only two sources, the Qur'an and the prophetic tradition. The movement adopted the slogan: "The Qur'an is our constitution. The Prophet is our Guide; Death for the glory of Allah is our greatest ambition."[6] Even the leaders of supposedly secular regimes often resort to invoking passages from the Qur'an.

Journalist Mark Bowden, whose account of the disastrous U.S. peacekeeping mission in Somalia in 1993 became famous through the book (and movie) *Black Hawk Down*, published a detailed article on Saddam Hussein based on interviews with a number of Saddam's former confidants who had escaped to the West. They told Bowden that Saddam resorts to public pronouncements from the Qur'an whenever it suits his purpose. Bowden wrote that "...in a heartwarming demonstration of his religious feelings, Hussein donated blood — a pint at a time for three years — so that a calligrapher could handcraft a 600-page copy of the Koran, every word written in the dictator's precious bodily fluid.... It is now on display in a Baghdad museum." Bowden also claims that "Because he has come so far, he feels anointed by destiny. Everything that he does is, by definition, the right thing to do.... In recent years, in his speeches, he has begun using passages and phrases from the Koran, speaking the words as if they are his own. In the Koran, Allah says, "If you thank me, I will give you more."[7]

The Qur'an is important in recent events in Pakistan where, among many other events, several of the people who planned the capture and execution of the late reporter for *The Wall Street Journal*, Daniel Pearl, justified their actions by quoting the Qur'an. Ironically, the country's President, General Parviz Muzsharif, has also used the Qur'an to legitimize actions by his government. On May 25, 2002, in the middle of escalating tensions and a military buildup between

India and Pakistan over border disputes about Kashmir, Pakistan's chief of state, General Muzsharif, was attending a religious ceremony in Islamabad celebrating the "glory of the Qur'an" and the birthday of Muhammad. He stopped the ceremony briefly and announced over national television that Pakistan had just successfully test-fired a medium range missile that was capable of carrying nuclear warheads at least 150 kilometers.[8]

Of course, these images of the Qur'an in the mass media do not establish that the Qur'an is a primary cause of violence or war — nor is this a purpose, theme, or finding of this book. Rather, these mass media images only indicate that the Qur'an often is present in the daily lives of some of the people who have perpetrated infamous violent events, and that these people have referred to both the Qur'an and to violence and warfare in favorable ways. Sometimes they claim that passages in the Qur'an compel violent actions that include war. This is the reason why this book focuses on those passages in the Qur'an that might be of special interest to its proponents who are also interested in war and peace, for whatever reasons. For background, it can be useful to first consider the nature of the Qur'an and some of the reasons why it is so important to so many people.

THE QUR'AN AS A HOLY BOOK

Reduced to basic statistics, the Qur'an is a book of about 80,000 words organized into more than 6,000 verses in 114 chapters (called *sura* or *surah* in Arabic). Among Muslims it is widely regarded as all of the sacred revelations from Allah (often translated as "God" in English) to Muhammad that occurred in the last twenty-two years of his life, 610-632 A.D.[9] The first of the revelations are believed to have occurred to Muhammad when he was forty years old and in his customary place of retreat, a cave on Mt. Hira outside of Mecca during Ramadan, "the month of heat," in 610. In *The Meaning of the Glorious Koran*, Mohammed Marmaduke Pickthall provides a standard rendition of the event.

> "He was asleep or in a trance when he heard a voice say: 'Read!' He said: 'I cannot read.' The voice again said, 'Read!' Muhammad went outside where he was met by the angel Gabriel, who told him, 'O Muhammad! Thou art Allah's messenger, and I am Gabriel.'"

Pickthall then explains the sacred nature of the Qur'an this way.

"The words which came to him when in a state of trance are held
sacred by the Muslims and are never confounded with those
which he uttered when no physical change was apparent in him.
The former are the Sacred Book; the latter the *Hadith* or *Sunnah*
of the Prophet. And because the angel of Mt. Hira bade him 'Read'
— insisted on his 'Reading' though he was illiterate — the Sacred
Book is known as *Al-Qur'an*, 'The Reading,' the Reading of the
man who knew not how to read."[10]

Others regard the Qur'an to be a compilation of mystical sayings
attributed to Muhammad by his relatives, friends, and followers. They
were recorded during his lifetime by various followers and then assembled and collated, more or less in the current form, by some of his devo-
tees in the years immediately after his death in 632. Still others, including the late, noted scholar of Islam, John Wansbrough, have concluded
that the content of the Qur'an had not been finalized until at least two
hundred years after Muhammad's death. He found evidence that, like
the Christian Bible and the Jewish Tanahk, the Qur'an was the product
of a long period of composition after Muhammad's death.[11]

In contemporary English language translations of the Qur'an,
there is some variability in the order and numbering of the verses,
but not much. Generally it is organized by the length of the chapters,
from longest to shortest, although there are some exceptions. A long-
established, mainstream translation by a broadly-educated, devout,
voluntary convert to Islam, such as Mohamed Marmaduke Pickthall,
presents a version of the Qur'an that has one hundred-fourteen chapters with varying numbers of verses (from two hundred verses in
chapter 3 to only three verses in chapter 108). The chapter titles often
are enigmatic and poetic rather than denotative (i.e. " Smoke," "The
Wind-Curved Sandhills"). They apparently emerged through a
process of debate and consensus among early Islamic scholars who
often selected as chapter titles distinctive and captivating words and
phrases from within the chapters. Regarding war, only a few of the
chapter titles have obvious relevance: "Spoils of War" (chapter 8),
"The Troops" (49), "The Ranks" (61); while others may or may not
pertain to war: "Victory" (48), "The Overwhelming" (88), "The
Overthrowing" (81), "Those Who Set the Ranks" (37), "The Cleaving"
(82), "The Sundering" (84), "Power" (97), "The Calamity" (101),
"Rivalry in Worldly Increase" (102), "The Jinn" (72), "The
Disbelievers" (109), "The Romans" (30) "The Children of Israel" (17),
and "The Thunder" (13). As it turns out, all of these chapters have at

least a few verses that deal with armed conflict between Muslims and non-Muslims, as do many other chapters in the Qur'an whose titles are not obviously related to war, such as "The Clans" (33), a chapter that is often remarkably violent and boastful about how the Muslims under Muhammad first confounded and then defeated an army of united clans from Mecca at the "Battle of the Trench" outside of Medina.[12] However, none of these chapters, or any chapters in the Qur'an, are restricted to the topic of warfare. In fact, a strong case can be made that warfare does not dominate the majority of the verses in any chapter in the Qur'an, even the chapters that refer to Muhammad's most famous battles (Badr, Uhud, and "The Trench").

Regarding peace, none of the titles of the one hundred-fourteen chapters include the word "peace" or any of its obvious synonyms. The chapter title that comes closest is "The Unity" (112), although this might not refer to unity between or among nations so much as to unity among Muslims, a personal, spiritual condition, or many other possibilities. Other chapter titles that *might* imply peaceful relations are "Mankind" (114 — the last chapter), "The Beneficent" (60), "The Clans" (33), "Solace" (94), and "Small Kindnesses" (107).

The verses within the chapters vary considerably in style, form, and content. Some verses have hundreds of words and cover many topics. Others only have four words and one subject, such as verse 3 of chapter 114: "The God of Mankind." The verses take on many different forms, including:

- Descriptions and explanations of the creation of the heavens, Earth, and humankind, of the lives of the prophets Abraham, David, and Jesus Christ, of ancient battles between Arabs and Jews, and reinterpretations of Biblical versions of these topics

- Prayers and praises to Allah and descriptions of Allah's powers and preferences

- Poetic verses that rhapsodize about the heavens, nature, and other topics

- General principles for organizing and operating Islamic societies

- Prescriptions, proscriptions and admonitions from Allah to Muhammad, to all believers, to various categories of disbelievers (particularly to Jews and Christians), to polytheists, and to idolaters

- Repudiations of the beliefs and behaviors of disbelievers, idolaters and other miscreants

- Specific guidelines from Allah and from Muhammad to believers regarding appropriate daily behaviors, interpersonal relations, rituals, and civic obligations such as paying taxes

- Justifications for the actions of Allah, Muhammad, and believers

- Brief descriptions, explanations and interpretations of a number of monumental political events before and during Muhammad's life including his escape from Mecca and the truce of Hudaybiya, and some of the military battles that he commanded

- Promises, exhortations, and congratulations to believers who fought and will fight in the cause of Allah against non-believers, as well as complaints, and condemnations of cowards and other miscreants who have failed and will fail to fight for Allah's cause

WHY IS THE QUR'AN SO IMPORTANT?

With all of these attributes, it is not hard to understand why the Qur'an has become the most enduring and influential book ever published in Arabic. It is also widely believed to be the first book published in Arabic and the first book widely distributed through all Arab-speaking lands. Not surprisingly, it became the basis for much of Arab scholarship and literature since then. For believers, it presents the words and thoughts of Allah, as recited to Muhammad, and as such, it is the one true and final source of all Islamic beliefs and practices. It provides general principles and specific rules for many of the events and problems that believers face in the course of their lives. It is also required recitation each day for each and every Muslim — a requirement that apparently is obeyed by many, if not all Muslims.

> "To memorize it, as many Muslims have ceremoniously done, and perhaps even to quote from it, as every Muslim does daily in his formal prayers and otherwise, is to enter into some sort of communion with ultimate reality.... The outsider who would understand the religion of Islam must bear constantly in mind that Muslims do not read the Koran and conclude that it is divine; they believe it to be divine, and then they read it."[13]

As I understand the protocol, most Muslim sects require each of their members to pray five times each day while prostrate, facing Mecca. The prayers must include recitations from memory of at least two surahs (chapters) from the Qur'an in Arabic. One of these chapters must be the first surah ("The Opening") in the Qur'an. It is presented here for familiarization and because it is so frequent in the daily recitations of Muslims, even though it does not obviously deal with peace or war.

"Praise be to Allah, Lord of the Worlds,
The Beneficient, the Merciful.
Owner of the Day of Judgment,
Thee (alone) we worship; Thee (alone) we ask for help.
Show us the straight path,
The path of those whom Thou hast favored;
Not (the path) of those who earn Thine anger
nor of those who go astray."[14]

Additional chapters can be selected according to the preferences of the individual reciter or the Imam or prayer leader, if a group of believers is praying together. Often the second chapter that is recited is a short and easily memorized chapter (such as # 112 — "The Unity") because many Muslims are not familiar with the longer and more intricate chapters.[15] However, John Esposito, a noted scholar of Islam, has indicated that many Muslims (especially Muslims highly literate in Arabic) often use a much more random procedure in selecting a second reading, and one that leads them to read and have faith in any of the 6,000 verses in the Qur'an. He says that its format "enables a believer, however brief one's schedule, to simply open the text at random and start reciting at the beginning of any paragraph, since each bears a truth to be learned and remembered."[16] If Esposito is correct about this, then every paragraph, including those that deal with the topics of peace, terror, and war, have considerable likelihood of being recited by quite a large number of Muslims each day. Many Muslims would recite paragraphs about these and other topics more than a few times in the course of their lives if they abide by the Islamic practice of reciting from the Qur'an at least five times each day.

In addition to the Qur'an's spiritual power, for many readers it is said to possess unparalleled beauty, majesty, and imagery in its literary style. It is said to be so rhythmic and poetic that even the most illiterate and uneducated believers can remember long passages that have been recited to them. Pickthall comments on this attribute this way:

"It is a fact that the Koran is marvelously easy for believers to commit to memory. Thousands of people in the East know the whole Book by heart. The translator, who finds great difficulty in remembering well-known English quotations accurately, can remember page after page of the Koran in Arabic with perfect accuracy."[17]

Besides having descriptive and instructive qualities, the Qur'an is said to be highly inspirational and evocative. For some readers its verses can have double and triple meanings. It can be read and reacted to at many different levels of understanding, especially in Arabic, the way it is supposed to be recited by or to all believers, even if they do not understand Arabic. Thus, some people read it and understand it more deeply and discursively than others. These spiritual, philosophical, and metaphysical qualities have special appeal to clerics, scholars and poets, whereas the Qur'an's passages about many topics in international relations are attracting a much wider range of readers, especially in the last few years. These topics include violent conflict between believers and Jews, Christians, and people of other religions, religious persecution, minority-majority group relationships, encroachment on Muslim lands and holy places by non-Muslims, warfare, annihilation of the civilian communities of adversaries, truces, prisoners of war, and accommodations for non-believers in Muslim communities.

New and widespread interest in the Qur'an's treatment of these topics has occurred for a number of reasons including what Islamic scholar James Piscatori has called "the fragmentation of religious authority." This has resulted from the forces of modernization and globalization, including sudden growth in urbanization, secularization, access to television, radio, videos, and cheap paperback editions of the Qur'an into many different languages and dialects. Piscatori explains it this way:

"...these social and political changes have also contributed to a fragmentation of religious authority whereby, to put it crudely, the meaning of scripture no longer needs to be interpreted by a religious establishment but, rather, lies in the eye of the beholder. Many Muslims would vehemently insist that the centuries-long development of Islamic jurisprudence and Koranic exegesis provides definitive guidance to the faithful. But this tradition now confronts the proliferation of modern-educated individuals, who have direct access to the basic religious texts and question why they should automatically defer to the religious class."[18]

Piscatori then explains how this fragmentation spawns radicals such as Osama bin Laden.

> "It has thus become difficult to say with reassuring finality what is Islamic and what is not. This shifting of goalposts and the ease with which individuals can presume to invoke and defend Muslim tradition have allowed Osama bin Laden to claim to speak on behalf of Islam. Radicalization, therefore, appears to have emerged as much from distinctly modern conditions as from the prior experience of inauspicious Muslim-Western encounters.[19]

Fragmentation of religious authority also makes it much easier for many people to ignore historical and literary context of specific passages in any book, — the Bible, the Torah, and the Qur'an included — and to select passages that interest them because these passages are congruent with their beliefs, biases, and motives. Of special importance are people who focus upon the exact wording of certain passages and attribute meaning to them as eternally valid facts or imperatives, rather than as metaphors, figures of speech, suggestions, or provocations. Henceforth I will refer to people who react like this as *literalists*. I will use the term *opportunists* to refer to people who emphasize passages literally in order to justify their own actions and to recruit and manipulate others.

CONSIDERING VIOLENCE-ORIENTED OPPORTUNISTS AND LITERALISTS[20]

There is a growing body of evidence showing that persuasive, violence-oriented opportunists can deftly recruit and indoctrinate into violence people who are literalists. They can also convert appreciable numbers of people who are marginalized, chronically frustrated and depressed males, ages 15-50, into violence-oriented literalists, under certain conditions, and at least for periods of several days, weeks, or months. Noted terrorist expert Harvey Kushner described how this has happened in refugee camps in the West Bank of Israel and in the Gaza strip under the direction of terrorist organizations including Hamas:

> "The potential bombers attend classes in which trained Islamic instructors focus on the verses of the Qur'an and the Hadith, the sayings of the Prophet Muhammad that form the basis of Islamic law and idealize the glory of dying for Allah. Students are promised

an afterlife replete with gold palaces, sumptuous feasts, and virgin brides. Students are also told that their martyrdom guarantees that 70 of their relatives and friends will gain entry to heaven."[21]

After extensive indoctrination about scriptures and the use of explosives, selected combatants are prepared for their missions with verses from the Qur'an.

"The suicide bombers leave for their missions directly from their mosques, after having completed many days of chanting the relevant scriptures aloud with their spiritual handlers. A favorite verse reads: 'Think not of those who are slain in Allah's way as dead. No, they live on and find their sustenance in the presence of their Lord.' The bombers' frenzied mantras are said to create a strong, albeit pleasurable, belief that they will sit with Allah. So strong is this belief that the bomber is able to walk among his enemy without exhibiting the slightest anxiety."[22]

The document that was referred to earlier in this chapter, "Military Studies in the Jihad Against Tyrants," (that was found by FBI agents in the personal effects of the hijackers who crashed jet airplanes into the World Trade Center and the Pentagon) provides another example of how violence-prone opportunists use the Qur'an and references to some of the famous battles in Muslim military history.[23] References to the Qur'an, passages from the Qur'an, and references to famous battles led by Muhammad, are interspersed throughout the document's one hundred-eighty pages of instructions on "kidnapping and assassination using rifles, pistols, explosives, poisons, and cold steel." For example, page 154 instructs the terrorists: "When undertaking any assassination using a knife, the enemy must be struck in one of these lethal spots: anywhere in the rib cage, both or one eye, the pelvis (under target's navel), the area directly above the genitals, the axon (back of the head), the end of the spinal column directly above the person's buttocks." Page 152 identifies some cases of failed and successful bombings. "Some of the brothers in Egypt tried to blow up the motorcade of the former Minister of the Interior's vehicle (ZIB) by putting 200 kilograms of TNT in a pick-up truck." Along with instructions like these the manual quotes entire verses from the Qur'an five times and partial verses at least ten times as ways to exhort readers to spy, assassinate, bomb and carry out other missions of violence.

"The youth came to prepare themselves for Jihad [holy war], commanded by the majestic Allah's order in the holy Koran. [Koranic
verse]: 'Against them make ready your strength to the utmost of
your power, including steeds of war, to strike terror into (the
hearts of) the enemies of Allah and your enemies, and others
besides whom ye may not know, but whom Allah doth know.'"[24]

Five battles are mentioned by name from the entire history of
Muslim warfare: Badr (four times), the Trench (Khandak, twice),
Uhud, Hudaybiya, and Honein (Hunayn). Four of these were led by
Muhammad and are referred to at various places in the Qur'an. No
battles after Muhammad's death are mentioned.[25] Most of these references to Muhammad's battles are used to encourage the use of spies
by Muslim commanders in order to know the enemy's size, capabilities, and intentions. Other references mention that it is all right to
beat and kill "hostages" (prisoners of war) in order to extract useful
information.

"The prophet — Allah bless and keep him — called on the people,
who then descended on Badr. They were met by Kureish camels
carrying water. Among their takers was a young black [slave] man
belonging to the Al-Hajjaj clan. They took him [as hostage]. The
companions of the prophet — Allah bless and keep him — started
asking him about Abou Sofian and his companions. He first said,
'I know nothing about Abou Soufian but I know about Abou Jahl,
Atba, Sheiba, and Omaya Ibn Khalaf.' But when thy beat him he
said, 'O yes, I will tell you. This is the news of Abou Soufian....'"[26]

"In the Honein attack, after one of the spies learned about the
Muslims kindness and weakness then fled, the prophet — Allah
bless and keep him — permitted [shedding] his blood and said,
'Find and kill him.' Salma Ibn Al-Akwaa followed, caught, and
killed him."[27]

"After the Badr attack, the prophet — Allah bless and keep him —
showed favor to some hostages, like the poet Abou Izza, by
exchanging most of them for money. The rest were released for
providing services and expertise to the Muslims."[28]

Not all references to Muhammad and his battles portray
Muhammad as violent and bellicose.

"In his attacks, the prophet — Allah bless and keep him — would find out the enemy's intention. In the Hodaibiya [*sic*] [battle] days, though he did not want war, he exercised caution by sending a special 40 man reconnaissance group, headed by A'kkaha Ibn Mohsen Al-Azda. One of that group's forerunners found a man who led them to the enemy's livestock. They captured 200 camels from that livestock and brought them to Madina."[29]

Appendix B of this document contains a letter translated into English that is called "Full Text of Hijacking Letter." This letter was "found at three different locations used by suspected terrorists in the 11 September 2001 attacks. One letter was found in Mohammad Atta's suitcase left at the airport, one in Nawaf Alhazmi's vehicle at Dulles International Airport, and one at crime scene [*sic*] in Stony Creek Township, PA, where a fourth commercial jet crashed."[30]

The letter tells the hijackers how to behave on the night before the mission. Among other things, they are to read two chapters of the Qur'an and reflect on their meanings.

"The Last Night:

1. Make an oath to die and renew your intentions. Shave excess hair from the body and wear cologne. Shower.
2. Make sure you know all aspects of the plan well, and expect the responses, or a reaction, from the enemy.
3. Read al-Tabby and Anvil [traditional war chapters from the Qur'an] and reflect on their meanings and remember all of the things that God has promised for the martyrs.

....

12. Bless your body with some verses of the Quran [done by reading verses into one's hands and then rubbing the hands over things over whatever is to be blessed], the luggage, clothes, the knife, your personal effects, your ID, your passport, and all your papers."[31]

The Qur'an is mentioned by name four more times in the six-page letter. Verses from the Qur'an are quoted at least eight more times. They include the following exhortations:

"So remember God, as He said in His book: 'Oh Lord, pour your patience upon us and make our feet steadfast and give us victory over the infidels.'

When the confrontation begins, strike like champions who do not want to go back to this world. Shout, 'Allah Akbar,' because this strikes fear in the hearts of the nonbelievers. God said: 'Strike above the neck, and strike at all of their extremities.'

Then implement the way of the prophet in taking prisoners. Take prisoners and kill them. As Almighty God said: 'No prophet should have prisoners until he has soaked the land with blood. You want the bounties of this world [in exchange for prisoners] and God wants the other world [for you], and God is all-powerful, all-wise.'"[32]

More recently, evidence was captured by U.S. Special Forces troops in al-Qaeda safe houses in Kabul, in March 2002, that indicates that the Qur'an was used extensively in the military training of thirty-nine recruits.[33] All of the recruits were unmarried. Most of them came from impoverished, peasant families in Afghanistan, Pakistan, and several other countries where, as children, they had memorized a few passages from the Qur'an in their native languages. Several had studied the Qur'an extensively in madrassas before joining al-Qaeda, and several had supposedly memorized all of it. Several of the recruits had been associated with fundamentalist groups in their native countries. The evidence indicated that these recruits had been trained for months in a camp in Rishkan, about twenty miles south of Kabul. The "walls are still painted with Koranic verses and slogans involving the jihad. 'All the Christians, Jews and infidels have joined hands against Afghanistan,' one poster claimed." Training documents advocated an "Islamic fervor" in the camp. Training materials and pamphlets were printed in Arabic, and in many other languages, and emphasized passages of the Qur'an about the necessity of waging jihad against foreign enemies throughout the world. One pamphlet depicted an anti-American scene and urged readers to "Fight until there is no discord and all of religion is for God." Military instruction drew heavily from religious doctrine. Abandoned notes of a student in a class on ambush tactics read, "Without a sign from the leader you should not retreat, because the Koran says 'Do not retreat; in time of war there is no death. My only power is the power of Allah.'"

Besides Osama bin Laden and others mentioned so far in this chapter who might have associated the Qur'an with violence, let us now consider the cases of three others. Naji is a former Taliban soldier in Afghanistan. Mullah Mohammed Omar was once the spiritual and military leader of the Taliban. Aukai Collins is a native-born U.S. citizen who converted to Islam and voluntarily became a Muslim soldier in Afghanistan, Kosovo, Chechneya, and other countries, before he became disillusioned with random terrorism, became an FBI informant, and published his memoirs, *My Jihad.*

THE CASE OF NAJI: ONCE A TALIBAN SOLDIER IN AFGHANISTAN[34]

The New York Times journalist Michael Finkel spent several days conversing with a former Taliban soldier named Naji in Afghanistan in November 2001 as the war raged between his former Taliban comrades and infantry of the Northern Alliance, supported by U.S. led coalition air and ground forces. Naji was born about 1976, one of ten children in a poor peasant family of Tajik Muslims. When he was about 13 the Soviets invaded and the schools in his province were closed. His father sent him to live with an uncle who lived in Pakistan, where he could attend a free Muslim madrassa school.

> "Naji's family was Muslim, but at the madrasa he learned a new form of Islam. Here, he was schooled in a puritan interpretation of Islamic law — a version that preached that music and dancing were anti-Islamic; that women should not work or attend school; that card playing and kite flying and most athletic pursuits were impure. Naji memorized large portions of the Koran. He studied the sayings of the Prophet Muhammad."

After six years of study, his teachers surprised him when they told him that he was destined to become a soldier. "I was told that foreigners had overtaken my country; that non-Muslims were controlling Afghanistan. I was told that because I am educated I had to join the Taliban, and purify my country." Naji was sent to Kandahar where he and other Taliban recruits were trained in Taliban ideology under the new leader of the Taliban, Mullah Omar. "You were pulled to him like a magnet. I was ready to give my life for him." Naji was then armed with a Kalashnikov rifle and sent off to war against the Soviets with the other recruits. After the Soviets withdrew, the Taliban fought against other Afghan tribes in order to consolidate their hold on power. Naji became disenchanted with how the Taliban destroyed villages and abused ordinary Afghan people who could not defend themselves. He slowly came to realize that "This is not how Islam works." He also felt he was treated as a second-class citizen by the Taliban, who were predominantly Pashtun, because he was a member of the Tajik minority. While fighting against the Northern Alliance resistance in northeast Afghanistan, he was proselytized by Ali, a Tajik fighter for the Northern Alliance who was the son of his father's good friend from their home province. In October 2001, U.S. warplanes dropped leaflets on his unit's position that showed photos of Taliban soldiers burning houses of Afghan people. Then U.S. planes bombed his unit for several nights. Naji worked out a scheme that allowed him to be captured by Ali and the Northern Alliance forces. Within two days he was fighting with them and living in Ali's house in Taloqan. His Taliban phase was over.

Naji's case suggests that a number of opportunists, including Mullah Omar, used verses from the Qur'an repeatedly in order to convert Naji and many others into Taliban fighters. Naji said that he was required to memorize large portions of the Qur'an in the madrassa and that, later in his indoctrination, Mullah Omar had great influence over him, convincing him to fight for the Taliban cause. Let us now consider the case of Mullah Omar, whose status, living or dead, is still uncertain at the time of this writing.

MULLAH MUHAMMAD OMAR: SELF-PROCLAIMED CALIPH OF THE FORMER TALIBAN GOVERNMENT[35]

Mohammed Omar had a mercurial but brief career as the leader of the Taliban in Afghanistan from about 1997 until December 2001, as best as we can tell from journalistic accounts. During this time he was instrumental in changing (some would say eliminating) many of the institutions in the country by creating a police state based on the indoctrination of thousands of young soldiers like Naji. Omar was born in 1959 to a family of landless, uneducated peasants of the Hotak tribe of Pashtuns in a small village near Kandahar. He studied the Qur'an at village madrassas until the Soviets invaded and his father died, leaving him to fend for his mother and extended family. Eventually, failing to find gainful employment, Omar opened a small madrassa of his own, taught a very fundamentalist version of the Qur'an, and became increasingly incensed about violations of sacred scriptures that he thought he saw everywhere about him, not only by the Soviet invaders but also by many of the Afghan warlords who battled among themselves for power and spoils. In time, Omar took up arms, recruited combatants of his own, and resorted to violence in order to avenge violations of Qur'anic law, as he understood them.

"There is now an entire factory of myths and stories to explain how Omar mobilized a small group of Taliban against the rapacious Kandahar warlords. The most credible story, told repeatedly, is that in the spring of 1994 Singesar neighbours came to tell him that a commander had abducted two teenage girls, their heads had been shaved and they had been taken to a military camp and repeatedly raped. Omar enlisted some 30 Talibs who had only 16 rifles between them and attacked the base, freeing the girls and hanging the commander from the barrel of a tank. They captured quantities of arms and ammunition. 'We were fighting against Muslims who had gone wrong. How could we remain quiet when we could see crimes being committed against women and the poor?' Omar said later."[36]

Anwer Sher, a retired Pakistani general who helped the Taliban rise to power recalled that "Mullah Omar had been a lower-level commander, but he was a man of character, with the Koran in one hand and the gun in the other. They sent their people to the commanders and elders and said: 'Are you with us or against us.'" Soon, Omar's prestige grew to the point that he emerged as the leader of the Taliban, demanding that his followers fight only for the purpose of creating a just Islamic society as envisioned in the Qur'an. "Scarred and blinded in his right eye during combat against Soviet invaders in the 1980s, he came to believe about a decade ago that he had been called upon by God to purge Afghanistan of sin and violence, to make it a pure Islamic state." By 1996 Omar came to see himself as a successor to the Prophet Muhammad.

"Omar literally cloaked himself in the trappings of the Prophet Mohammed. On April 4, 1996, as the Taliban neared total control, he was moved by zeal to unseal a shrine in Kandahar that held a cloak believed to have belonged to the Prophet, the founder of Islam.... He lifted it in the air as he stood on a rooftop, displaying it to a crowd of followers. The event was caught on videotape, one of the very few times that he was ever photographed. He placed the cloak, which only the Prophet was said to have worn, upon his own shoulders. And at that moment, he declared himself the commander of the faithful, the leader of all Islam. No one had claimed that title since the Fourth Caliph, more than 1,000 years ago."[37]

Shortly after this, Osama bin Laden moved to Afghanistan with his al-Qaeda security forces. He befriended Omar and became a major financier of Taliban military operations.

"He flattered and praised Omar, encouraging his belief that Afghanistan was the center of a new religious empire that reached around the world, according to officials familiar with the relationship. As recently as last January, at the wedding of his son, bin Laden, in the course of a long speech on the subject of holy war, implied that Omar was 'the new caliph,' the supreme ruler of all Muslims and the rightful successor to the Prophet."[38]

These accounts indicate that Omar and bin Laden often responded to the Qur'an both as literalists and as opportunists, using it to persuade others to fight as soldiers against their enemies throughout the world. They also established many military camps in Afghanistan that trained a new generation of jihadists, many of whom had been recruited from many other countries, including the U.S., with the idea of eventually spreading jihad throughout the world. Besides Naji, another of the trainees in their camps was an American, Aukai Collins.

AUKAI COLLINS: AMERICAN JIHADIST[39]

Aukai Collins is a native-born U.S. citizen in his late twenties who converted to Islam while he was serving a long sentence in a detention center of the California Youth Authority in 1993 for a series of robberies and auto thefts. Prior to this Collins had a turbulent upbringing, with early and frequent exposure to marital strife between his parents, and exposure to drug dealing, guns, and parental neglect. Incarcerated, he resisted pressure on him to join white supremacist gangs, and gradually gravitated towards a calm and collected Muslim inmate named Kesacee, who introduced him to the Qur'an.

"After we talked for a while, I asked him about his book. He told me that it was the Qur'an, and that I could touch it if I washed my hands. This was obviously unusual, but I was impressed by his respect for this book.... The next day Kesacee brought me some small books and pamphlets about Islam. The small book was called *Qur'anic Verses*. It was just a small paperback book with selected *ayat*, or verses, from the Qur'an. I took the books back to my cell and found that the *ayat* were practical, interesting, and logical. But beyond these observations I had no desire to look any further into Islam."[40]

During the next week Collins had conversations with Kesacee that increased his interest in Islam. Yet, his conversion took him by surprise.

"One of the other things that impressed me about the Muslims was that they never proselytized. The religion seemed to pretty much speak for itself. But, as I sat there and listened on that Saturday, I had a sense that I wanted to convert. Just before the class finished I told Kesacee. He seemed quite pleased and went to tell the Imam. The Imam asked me to come up in front of everybody. I wasn't exactly sure what becoming a Muslim entailed, but I was pleased when I found out how simple it was. The Imam explained the basic tenets of Islam and told me to repeat after him: '*Ashadu Allah illaha ilalallah, wa ashadu ana Muhammador rasulallah.*' I bear witness that there is no God except God, and I bear witness that Muhammad is His messenger. That brief statement would change the rest of my life."[41]

After his release from the detention center Collins joined a mosque in San Diego. He grew increasingly interested in the Qur'an's commandments regarding jihad as they could be applied to what he understood to be the oppression of Muslims in Bosnia.

"For a jihad to be declared, any given situation must meet several criteria as stipulated in the Holy Qur'an. To put it simply, when a Muslim land is being attacked and Muslims are being killed there is the need for jihad. In this case it becomes a duty for all able-bodied Muslims to come to the aid of the people being attacked. But even then jihad has many rules. It is forbidden to kill noncombatants. Crops and trees cannot be destroyed, and livestock cannot be killed. It is even forbidden to destroy the houses of worship of other faiths, and Muslims cannot force a person to convert to Islam."[42]

Noticing Collin's interest in jihad, a fellow Muslim at the mosque suggested that Collins travel to Bosnia and join in the jihad against Serb attacks on Muslim communities.

"This was exhilarating: not only would I be able to help the
Muslims of Bosnia but I would also complete my own faith. Jihad
is the highest act of faith in Islam. The prophet Muhammad,
peace and blessings be upon him, said that if a Muslim dies without making jihad, or at least having had the intentions to make it,
then he dies with a form of hypocrisy in his heart."[43]

Turned back from the Bosnia border for lack of a visa, Collins
eventually found his way to Pakistan and Afghanistan, where he was
trained in the mujahideen camps financed by Osama bin Laden, and
where the Qur'an was recited often each day by many of his comrades.

"The camp woke up about half an hour before the *azan*, then
salaat (prayer) was performed about fifteen minutes after the call.
I had just finished my ablution when the *azan* started. Prayer
occurs five times a day, according to Islamic custom, and it was an
especially important part of the daily routine for the
mujahideen.... When the *azan* sounded over the loudspeakers, the
seemingly deserted camp came to life. Mujahideen streamed out
of the tents and mud shacks all over the camp to create a sort of
rush-hour traffic headed toward the mosque. Some walked and
chatted in little groups, while others made their way alone. Once
inside, the mosque looked like any other mosque in the world,
with one important exception. Muslims usually empty their pockets when they pray, and before prayer you'll usually see a little
pile of car keys or a cell phone next to each person. Here, however, it was an AK-47 or perhaps an old Russian SKS rifle. Some men
sat quietly and recited the Qur'an while others said optional
prayers before the *Salaatul Fajr*. Fifteen minutes or so after the
call to prayer the Imam would get up and everyone would perform *Salaatul Fajr*. The camp would be quiet for at least an hour
or so afterward. Many of the mujahideen sat in groups of three or
four to recite verses from the Qur'an."[44]

Other than for the rituals related to the five daily prayers,
Collins found life in the camps to be disorganized and boring. Most
of his comrades were poorly trained, poorly equipped, and indifferent about actually fighting. One of his few close friends was another
foreigner who was intent of waging jihad aggressively against enemies of Islam. This fellow, Ahmed Omar Saeed Sheikh, was a
Pakistani who had been born and raised in the United Kingdom. He
adopted the *nom de guerre* of Umar and was fond of listening to tape

recordings of the Qur'an throughout the day. Collins and Umar taught themselves how to use all of the various weapons in the camp, many of which had been stolen, purchased, or captured as booty from Soviet soldiers. They rehearsed ambushes and sought out contact against Soviet patrols, often alarming their own camp commander with their independence and unruly manners. Both of them grew frustrated by the lack of combat to the point that Umar decided to leave camp in 1994 so that he could participate in a hostage-capture operation across the border in Kashmir against the Indian army. Collins decided not to go with Umar because he did not believe that hostage-taking was an aggressive or appropriate form of jihad. Years later, Collins learned that Umar had participated in a famous hijacking of an aircraft in India and that Umar was on trial in Karachi, Pakistan, for the kidnapping and murder of the late *Wall Street Journal* reporter, Daniel Pearl.

Frustrated, Collins quit the mujahideen camp in Afghanistan in order to relocate to a combat zone where he would be allowed to actively engage in jihad each day — but not terrorism against civilians. Kosovo and Chechneya provided these opportunities in abundance for him. He participated in raids against enemy installations and ambushes against enemy patrols, killed several Russian soldiers with his rifle and grenades. He witnessed his fellow mujahideen mutilate the bodies of Russian corpses and capture, torture and execute Russian POWs.

"None of the four Russian soldiers said a word. Their uniforms were covered with dirt and blood. Each had already been beaten to some degree or another, and the one who'd apparently committed the worst atrocities couldn't see out of his right eye, which was swollen shut. They just stood there and looked for all the world like four eerie, breathing cadavers. The field commander finished his sentence. 'In the name of Allah I sentence you to death on this day in the Republic of Chechneya for your crimes against the Chechen people.' He nodded to a burly Chechen fighter standing off to the side, who casually took the first soldier by the arm and led him between the pit and the other three soldiers. The soldier made no attempt to fight or struggle. 'Get on your knees,' the burly fighter told him. When the Russian complied, the Chechen kicked him on his shoulder and the soldier fell over on his side. The fighter straddled him and pulled a large curved knife from a sheath on his belt. He pulled the soldier's head back by his filthy

21

hair and ran the knife back and forth over his neck in a ghastly sawing motion. Bright red blood squirted out as the Russian's throat was severed. His legs kicked a few times, and he grasped one of the Chechen's arms. A noise came from his throat as his last breath escaped through his gaping neck. Then the Chechen simply let the soldier's head flop onto the ground. It was tilted so far back now that it was almost completely severed."[45]

While attacking a Russian outpost, Collins tripped enemy booby traps and suffered severe wounds to his legs. He barely survived. Then he was evacuated out of Chechneya for a series of surgeries. During recuperation he returned to the U.S. in order to raise money for his next adventure and to try to help support his wives and dependents in the U.S., Chechneya, and Pakistan. This led to his becoming an anti-terrorism "consultant" to the FBI. One assignment had Collins infiltrate some of the Arab terrorist cells that were located around Scottsdale, Arizona so that their members could acquire weapons at local gun shows to be smuggled back to the Middle East and take lessons at local flight schools that would prepare them for the attacks on the Pentagon and World Trade Center in 2001.

"I was still working for the Bureau at this time and reporting to Andy regularly. Both the FBI and Andy were fully aware of all the Arabs whom Ghareeb and I had contact with, including the scrawny little guy, whose name is widely known now: Hani Hanjoor. Hani Hanjoor would get his pilot's license in 1999 and would fly an American Airlines plane into the Pentagon. They were hardly 'deep-cover sleepers,' as the FBI is calling them now. They lived very openly, and although I had no idea what some of them would eventually do, they made no secrets about what they thought or believed."[46]

As in so many of his other adventures, Collins eventually became disillusioned with the FBI and CIA. He returned to Chechneya in 1999 on his own in order to renew his life as a jihadist. There he joined a platoon of *Nokche Bores* ("Chechen Wolves") in the defense of Grozny and witnessed much of its destruction. Despite extraordinary deprivations there, Collins found that his comrades had remarkable resilience because of their Islamic faith and their attention to the Qur'an, even after months of Russian air, gas, and artillery attacks on the front lines.

"Prayer time always gave me strength in Chechneya. The Russians had come to destroy Chechneya because of its Islamic faith, but even in the worst conditions we stopped to fulfill our commitments to that faith five times a day.... As we started to pray I heard the rapid *whoomph whoomph* of Grad missiles as they left their launchers. Moments later the earth began to erupt around us as the missiles impacted almost on top of us. I had an almost uncontrollable urge to run for the cover of the trenches, but the Imam didn't stop his recitation of the Qur'an. You are not allowed to stop praying before the Imam signals the end of prayer. As the dirt rained down on us from the explosions of the missiles, the Imam raised his voice so that we could hear him over the deafening explosions that threatened to consume us. As he calmly called out the last words to signal the end of the prayer, all of the guys jumped into the trenches with an unusual serenity. No one moved with the sense of urgency that you would expect of people who were under a rocket barrage. 'What was that all about?' I asked one of the guys while kneeling in the trench. 'They do that every time we break for prayer,' he replied. 'But we haven't lost anyone yet. Allah truly is the protector.'"[47]

Collins was intent on fighting in Grozny not only to end religious persecution of Muslims but also in order to achieve eternal paradise through martyrdom. Neither occurred. The Chechen Minister of Health convinced Collins that he would be of greater value to the Chechen people if he returned to the U.S. and established a supply line for bringing badly needed medical supplies to the Muslim fighters and civilians. Collins ends his memoir by reporting that he is doing this now while residing in the U.S. and working in "overseas security."

In reviewing this case of Aukai Collins, there is considerable evidence that he was often a literalist regarding passages in the Qur'an about waging jihad, although he does not identify many of the passages that were important to him. Collins only mentions two instances in the training camps where he quoted passages of the Qur'an to his comrades in an effort to encourage them to continue with their preparations for war. In neither of these instances does he seem to be so much an opportunist as he was simply sharing with others his belief in the passages of the Qur'an taken literally. Throughout his memoir Collins continually emphasizes that he only became a jihadist in order to stop religious persecution and violence against Muslims in the Muslim world. Yet, he also repeatedly admits that he has had a long-

standing fascination with guns and fighting that predated his conversion to Islam. He also admits that, to his own amazement, he loves
war, despite the damages that he has suffered in war, and that he is
one of the very few veteran combatants who still love combat.
Voluntarily returning to fight in Chechneya in 1999, he becomes
euphoric on his first patrol behind enemy lines:

> "After a while the fear passed and I felt almost exhilarated to be
> back in my element. Anyone who's ever been there would know
> the feeling. Walking through the brush with your weapon at the
> ready, you're aware of every sound and movement. Everything
> becomes sharper and clearer.... This was it! I was back in the sad-
> dle again. In Chechneya I'd loved to walk point and had even lost
> my leg to it, but here I was again. Most fools love war until they
> experience it. On that day I realized that I was among the strange
> few who knew war and loved it nonetheless."[48]

TO WHOM IS THE QUR'AN IMPORTANT REGARDING PEACE AND WAR?

Literalists and opportunists are not the only people who might be
very interested in, and influenced by, passages in the Qur'an about
peace and war. Because the Qur'an is available in inexpensive paperback books, audiotapes, and compact disks, translated into many of
the modern languages in the world (and increasingly available in
inexpensive bilingual editions in which the verses in Arabic are printed on one side of a page opposite the comparable verses in the native
language or dialect of the reader),[49] people from most nations and
religions can be influenced by the Qur'an if they take the time to
become familiar with it. In fact, one of the premises of this book is that
learning what the Qur'an says about peace and war can contribute to
international understanding, peacekeeping, and more humane conduct in wars, if and when wars occur. Chapter 7 elaborates on this
premise in considerable detail and provides suggestions for achieving
these goals. For the moment, however, let us assume the "obvious"
position that the Qur'an is, or is supposed to be, particularly important
on the topics that it addresses, including peace and war, to all people
who practice Islam — all Muslims. Who, besides Naji, Mullah Omar,
Aukai Collins, and the other Muslims mentioned so far in this book, is
familiar with the Qur'an on war and peace? Surely we don't want to
assume that all people who practice Islam, or any other religion, for

that matter, can read that religion's holy book, or that they do read it, can understand it, try to obey it, or actually do obey it. In fact, some contemporary scholars of Islam estimate that many Muslims are only minimally familiar with specific verses in the Qur'an. This is especially true of older Muslims in rural areas of the poorest nations where Islam prevails. They only know by heart enough of the verses to be able to recite the obligatory daily prayers in Arabic. Often they do not really understand the meanings of the Arabic words and verses even though they can recite them and they are spiritually moved by the recitations. "Ordinary Muslims are not drilled in every chapter and verse of the Qur'an."[50]

At the same time, however, we should also keep in mind that the World's population of Muslims is growing relatively fast and that Islam is a growing religion in many areas of the world. It is also becoming more diverse in terms of levels of formal education and growing middle classes in many of the Muslim nations that have stable governments and growing economies. Yet, we might also keep in mind the fact that, despite significant and often contentious differences within Islam, between Sunnis and Shi'ites, and among dozens of other sects, subcultures, cults, and schools of thought, all practicing Muslims are expected to pray from the Qur'an at least five times a day, and to revere the entire Qur'an as being the actual words of Allah — definitive, immutable, unconditional, final, and eternal. While Muslims are obliged to recite the Qur'an in Arabic, the increasing availability of inexpensive paperback translations and bi-lingual "side-by-side" editions make it much easier for readers who do not understand Arabic to recite the Qur'an in Arabic and still have considerable understanding of the conceptual meanings of the verses, if not the style, nuance, rhythm, and mysticism of the verses and the entire Qur'an.[51]

> "There is a striking unity or similarity of sentiment and attitudes
> among all the Muslims both within themselves and vis-a-vis the
> non-Muslim world, thus justifying the concept 'Muslim World.'...
> Five times a day Muslims must publicly and collectively say daily
> prayers including the first sura of the Koran followed, in some
> units, by another passage from the Koran."[52]

Given so much daily exposure to the Qur'an, it would not be surprising to find that many adult Muslims who have some formal schooling and live in urban areas possess at least a fair familiarity with some of the Qur'an's passages about peace and war. Excluding pre-school children, this would probably mean that at least 500,000,000 of the World's estimated 1,155,109,000 Muslims have some knowledge of the Qur'an on peace and war.[53] A conventional geographical image of the primary "Muslim World" in given in Map 1-1. It depicts those nations whose populations are over 50% Muslim (dark shade) and those nations whose populations are between 50%-30% Muslim (diagonal shade). As shown in Map 1-1, at least forty-two nations have more than 50% Muslim population. These include the European nation, Albania, dozens of nations in the Middle East and Africa, and three nations in the Far East (Malaysia, Brunei, and Indonesia).

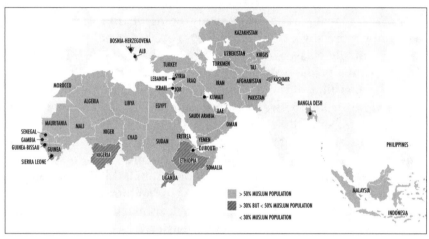

MAP 1-1
NATIONS WITH LARGE MUSLIM POPULATIONS

Only three of these nations have Islamic state governments: Iran, Saudi Arabia, and Sudan. Afghanistan was a nominal Islamic state under Mullah Muhammad Omar from 1997 until about November 2001 (the U.S. and allied invasion), although the government was never recognized by the United Nations. The nations with 50%-30% Muslim population include Guinea-Bissau, Sierre Leone, Nigeria, Uganda, Ethiopia, Bosnia-Herzegovina, and Kashmir.

Figure 1-1 identifies the six nations with the largest percentages of Muslim populations. Indonesia leads these nations by having 184 million Muslims in the early 1990s.

Figure 1-2 is a bar graph that shows Muslims as numbers and percentages of regional populations in 1990. Notice that the largest

Figure 1-1

COUNTRIES WITH THE LARGEST MUSLIM POPULATIONS

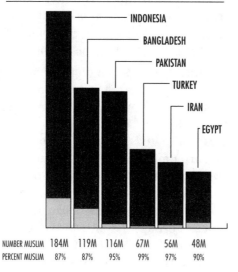

	INDONESIA				
		BANGLADESH			
			PAKISTAN		
				TURKEY	
					IRAN
					EGYPT

NUMBER MUSLIM	184M	119M	116M	67M	56M	48M
PERCENT MUSLIM	87%	87%	95%	99%	97%	90%

Figure 1-2

MUSLIMS AS A PERCENTAGE OF REGIONAL POPULATIONS, 1990

20% of the world's population are followers of Islam — more than one billion people.

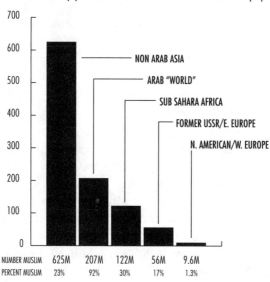

NON ARAB ASIA				
ARAB "WORLD"				
SUB SAHARA AFRICA				
FORMER USSR/E. EUROPE				
N. AMERICAN/W. EUROPE				

NUMBER MUSLIM	625M	207M	122M	56M	9.6M
PERCENT MUSLIM	23%	92%	30%	17%	1.3%

27

number (625 million) of the World's Muslims lived in non-Arab Asia, whereas the Arab world only accounted for about 207 million Muslims, although those Muslims accounted for 92% of the population in the Arab world. Notice also that about 56 million Muslims lived in the former USSR and East Europe, while about 9.6 million Muslims lived in North America and West Europe in 1990.

Statistics from the 2000 census indicate that there were about 5.8 million Muslims living in the United States, considerably more than in many countries that are predominantly Muslim, such as Libya, Qatar, Kuwait, Lebanon, and Jordan. A noted scholar on the topic of Islam, John Esposito, has estimated that more than one million of the Muslims in the U.S. are native-born U.S. citizens who have converted to Islam, that more than 500,000 Muslims live in and around Chicago, that Islam is the fastest growing religion in the U.S., and that, contrary to popular belief, significant numbers of Muslims have resided here since colonial times. Perhaps twenty percent of the slaves were Muslim. It is estimated that more than 4,000 Muslims serve in the U.S. armed forces and more than 40,000 Muslims are employed in other departments and agencies of the U.S. government.[54]

Overall, this geographic and demographic review of the Muslim world encourages us to consider that each day the Qur'an's passages on peace and war could be of great interest to more than 500,000,000 Muslims in many nations of the modern world, including many of the more than five million in the United States. The Qur'an might be expected to be the most often read and recited book in at least 42 nations of the world in which the majority of the populations are Muslim. Surely, the Qur'an could be most influential in the official affairs of the governments of Saudi Arabia, Iran, and The Sudan, because they are Islamic states whose constitutions are based on the Qur'an and on Qur'anic law.

Geographically and demographically, Islam's influence, and probably the Qur'an's influence as well, is likely to expand considerably during the next few decades because of high rates of natural increase (i.e. birth rates minus death rates) and high rates of emigration by Muslims from the primary Muslim world to the non-Muslim world. Of course there are many other factors involved in a projection such as this. The main point to be kept in mind, however, is that there are plenty of reasons to expect that the pronouncements about peace and war in the Qur'an are disseminated far, wide, deep, and on a daily basis to a growing population and area in the contemporary world.

HOLY BOOKS AS SOURCES OF GUIDANCE ON PEACE AND WAR

Books that are considered holy such as the Bible, Qur'an, and Talmud were not composed and published for advocating warfare or for instructing their believers on how to conduct warfare. Nor has their purpose been to establish international peace on earth among all people of all nations so much as to provide guidance as to how their believers could find individual spiritual peace and live in greater harmony with their neighbors in their immediate community. Therefore, it should not be surprising to find that the subjects of international peace and warfare are not dealt with systematically in the holy books. Nonetheless, there are a considerable number of passages scattered about in the holy books about all of these topics. Often the passages refer to historical events that were particularly important to those who founded and developed the religion. Of course, religions and religious training vary considerably in terms of the latitude that they allow their followers in knowing the contents of the holy books and in behaving according to commandments in the holy books. Some religions, sects within the religions, and religious schools and congregations are much more orthodox, fundamentalist, conservative or liberal than others.

Keeping this in mind, and striving to be as objective as possible, please consider for a moment how we might behave if we were persons such as Naji, Omar, or Aukai, or if we were at an impressionable age, in a chronically agitated or depressed state of mind, and in the company of many other peers who were like us in these regards. How might we react to the following passages from the holy books of three different religions if passages like the following were recited to us and to our friends each day in appealing ways by charismatic leaders who captivate us with their promises of wondrous rewards if we obey these passages — and warn us of eternal doom if we do not.

FIRST READING

"When thou comest nigh until a city to fight against it, then proclaim peace unto it.

And it shall be, if it make thee answer of peace, and open unto thee, then it shall be, that all the people that is found therein shall be tributaries unto thee, and they shall serve thee. And if it will make no peace with thee, but will make war against thee, then

29

thou shall it besiege. And when the lord thy God hath delivered it into thine hands, thou shalt smite every male thereof with the edge of the sword.... And the women, and the little ones, and the cattle, and all that is in the city, even all the spoil thereof, shalt thou take unto thyself; and thou shalt eat the spoil of thine enemies, which the Lord thy God hath given thee."[55]

SECOND READING

"When you approach a town to attack it, you shall offer it terms of peace. If it responds reasonably and lets you in, all the people present there shall serve you at forced labor. If it does not surrender to you, but would join battle with you, you shall lay siege to it: and when the Lord your God delivers it into your hand, you shall put all its males to the sword. You may, however, take as your booty the women, the children, the livestock, and everything in the town — all its spoil — and enjoy the use of the spoil of your enemy, which the Lord your God gives you. Thus you shall deal with all towns that lie very far from you; towns that do not belong to nations hereabout. In the towns of the latter peoples, however, which the Lord your God is giving you as a heritage, you shall not let a soul remain alive.... Only trees that you know do not yield food may be destroyed, you may cut them down for constructing siegeworks against the city that is waging war on you, until it has been reduced."[56]

THIRD READING

"And when We would destroy a township We send commandment to its folk who live at ease, and afterward they commit abomination therein, and so the Word (of doom) hath effect for it, and We annihilate it with complete annihilation. How many generations have we destroyed since Noah! And Allah sufficeth as Knower and Beholder of the sins of His slaves."[57]

These three readings, from the Bible, the Torah (Tanahk), and the Qur'an, respectively, are presented here for several reasons. They indicate the kinds of passages that might appeal to violence-prone literalists. They also indicate the kinds of material that opportunists can use to recruit, indoctrinate, and instruct violence-prone followers. These readings also display some rather obvious similarities among the holy books of Christianity, Judaism, and Islam regarding prescriptions for peace, war, and violence. All three passages allow their believers to capture enemy communities and, if the enemy resists, to commit considerable violence against enemy communities. Consider the likelihood that any one of these three passages could justify the use of violence or elicit violence by highly frustrated and angry people from any of these religious backgrounds. Also consider that, in the heat of actual combat, many fighters throughout history probably have behaved under severe stress according to a very few simple commandments that they have internalized, often subconsciously, through repetition over long periods of time. This is even more likely to be true when compelling social controls, norms, and other pressures are brought to bear upon them by their peers and superiors, if any are close-by at the time.

Holy books often are regarded by their proponents as the definitive sources for commandments about acceptable and unacceptable social behaviors, attitudes, and conditions. Therefore, it should not be entirely surprising to find that some proponents, and some people who seek to manipulate proponents, search through holy books for commandments about war and peace. It should also not be surprising to find that these people often select, retain, and refer to commandments about war and peace that are compatible with their preconceptions, their purposes, and their peers. With this in mind, would it really be surprising to find that the holy books have been used in these ways by more than a few political and military leaders and many of their followers? Might a list of such leaders include many of the caliphs who succeeded Muhammad, as well as Charles Martel, Charlmagne, the Papal leaders who commissioned the Christian Crusades, Suleiman, Khomeini, Quaddafi, Milosevic, Mullah Omar, Osama bin Laden, and Saddam Hussein, to name but a few?

For opportunists, and for almost anyone else who is so inclined, the literary and historical contexts of passages about war and peace in the holy books can be irrelevant. Opportunists probably do not care about or read adjacent passages. They do not worry about whether their uses of these passages are congruent with literary and historical contexts. This is because opportunists are not trying to understand these passages so much as they are trying to find a few passages, or just a few excerpts, phrases, or words, that are useful to them — that serve their political and military purposes. It is even possible that the less they know about the literary and historical contexts, the more likely that they can find at least a few passages that will suit their purposes, especially in a book that is as discursive, metaphorical, figurative, and evocative as the Qur'an. Opportunists do not want to be confronted by complexities, qualifications, and contradictions among different passages. They do not want to find anything that might discount the utility of a few powerful and seemingly unambiguous passages that compel them and their followers to take controversial and violent actions, or that excuse them for actions already taken.

This is also why a frequently heard objection of Qur'anic scholars is rather irrelevant when it is applied to people who want to use the Qur'an rather than understand it. Some scholars claim that the Qur'an can only be understood in Arabic, or better yet, in the traditional Arabic of Muhammad's time, because its meanings, rhythms, and metaphors are untranslatable from Arabic into other languages. While this might be true (and was said to be true in a quote from the translator, Mohammed Marmaduke Pickthall, that was presented a few pages ago), it also can be increasingly irrelevant in contemporary world affairs. This is because those proponents who comprehend only Arabic and are intent on using the Qur'an for political and military purposes can readily select and apply a few passages from the Qur'an that they believe will best serve their purposes. If they are opportunists who are intent on using these passages to recruit, motivate, or instruct others regarding war and peace, this might be relatively easy to do because many rank and file Qur'an adherents are illiterate, semi-literate, or they do not understand Arabic even though they have been trained to memorize, repeat, recite and pronounce passages of the Qur'an in Arabic.[58] These followers are unlikely to challenge opportunists and literalists who are literate in Arabic when they make use of passages about war and peace in the Qur'an. This same objection by some Islamic scholars also is increasingly irrelevant in the modern world because only a small and decreasing percentage (about 20%) of contemporary Muslims understand Arabic and because the Qur'an has been translated into most of the major languages. These translated versions are now readily available in inexpensive paperback books, audiotapes, and compact disks in most of the large urban areas throughout the world. This allows almost everyone who is literate in at least one modern language to select passages from the Qur'an in the language of their choice — and for whatever reason. Recall the three cases of the Qur'an's proponents that I presented a few pages ago: Naji, Mullah Omar, and Aukai Collins. None of them were Arabs. Nor were they fluent in Arabic. Yet, they were inspired and sustained by Qur'anic passages. In the case of Mullah Omar, he used Qur'anic passages with telling effect to recruit, train, and direct many Taliban soldiers in war.

In sum, while a thorough understanding of the Qur'an might require high literacy in traditional and modern Arabic language and a thorough understanding of its literary and historical contexts, the Qur'an is now so readily available in so many languages to so many people throughout the World, that almost any person in the World today who is literate in at least one national language can select a few passages from the Qur'an about war and peace that suits his or her preconceptions and purposes.[59]

To minimize the possibility that I have done this myself in writing this book, I have used a set of procedures derived from social science research methods that I have strived to practice for the past thirty years as a professional sociologist. Hopefully these procedures will make this research as objective, valid, and useful to others as possible.

FINDING PEACE AND WAR IN THE QUR'AN: SOME RESEARCH PROCEDURES

References to war and peace are scattered throughout the Qur'an in such a way that it is necessary to read the entire Qur'an, word by word, as carefully and objectively as possible in order to find all of the relevant passages. Then it is necessary to compare and contrast these passages very judiciously in order to detect repetitions, variations, and ambiguities. With this purpose in mind, I read three of the most well regarded English translations of the Qur'an before I selected as my primary source Pickthall's esteemed and long-established translation and commentary on the Qur'an, *The Meaning of the Glorious Koran*.[60] Using Pickthall's translation, I noted all verses that used the words "war," "terror," "peace," or any of their synonyms, such as "battle," "fight," "attack," "fear," "panic," "hate," "harmony," "friendship," and "understanding." I also noted all verses that mentioned behaviors or beliefs that involved peaceful or hostile relationships between believers and non-believers, their groups, communities, and societies. Then I compared these verses with the same verses in two other well-known translations of the Qur'an, by Ali and Arberry. To reduce the chance that I had missed any relevant verses from the more than 6,000 verses in the Qur'an, I also used *A Concordance of the Qur'an* by Kassis, and I read additional commentaries and interpretations by Ali and Haleem, among others. I also read several translated compilations of the Hadith (Sunnah), the second most important book in Islam. It is widely believed to consist of various recollections that Muhammad's followers shared with other followers regarding some of Muhammad's noteworthy behaviors, statements, and attitudes during his daily activities and some of his military battles.[61]

Next, in order to estimate the validity of Pickthall's translation of the Qur'an from Arabic into English, I asked several devout Muslims who are fluent in both Arabic and English languages to translate seven passages in the Qur'an from Arabic into English.[62] Then I read and compared interpretations of Qur'anic passages about war and peace that have been published by critical, moderate, and fundamentalist analysts of the Qur'an and of the military history of Islam. Their names and works are listed in the Bibliography. Chapter 6 reviews the interpretations of some of these analysts. I also spoke about these topics with several professors of Islamic studies and leaders in the Islamic communities in the U.S. However, I often found that most of the experts obviously had already made up their minds on these matters and that almost everyone had extreme or one-sided positions regarding the place of war and peace in the Qur'an and in Islam. There was little or no middle ground. Typically, the experts rarely quoted more than one or two of their favorite lines from the Qur'an and they seemed to be unaware or intolerant of passages that contradicted their favorite passages. Rarely, if ever, did they mention more than one or two of the more than one hundred passages from the Qur'an that follow in Chapter 2. Rarely did they acknowledge that various passages about war and peace in the Qur'an could actually be influencing how and why some people are engaging in warfare and in efforts to avoid warfare in the world today.

This is why I encourage you to read very carefully and objectively all of the passages that follow in Chapter 2. Then you will be able to make informed decisions about the many current issues that are addressed in this book. If your experience is like mine, your reward will be a much fuller and fresher familiarity than most people possess about peace, conflict, terror, and war in the Qur'an and in Islam.

---

[1] Edmund L. Andrews and Patrick E. Tyler. "Muslim Cleric Issues Call for Jihad against U.S." *The New York Times*, Saturday, June 7, 2003, p. 1. (as quoted in *The Providence Journal*, June 7, 2003. p. A-1).

[2] Megan K. Stack. "Suicide Bomber Kills 15 in Israel." *Los Angeles Times*, March 6, 2003, p. 1.

[3] "Military Studies in the Jihad Against Tyrants," translated as "Terrorist Training Manual," U.S. Department of Justice, Federal Bureau of Investigation, (Washington, DC: November, 2001). These items are discussed at length later in this chapter.

[4] Associated Press, "Bin Laden on Tape: We Calculated in Advance." Published in *The Providence Journal*, December 14, 2001, p. A17. By the way, I have not found the verb "torture" used in English translations of this verse. Usually the verb "fight" is used.

[5] Teresa Watanabe, *Los Angeles Times*, quoted in *The Providence Sunday Journal*, September 30, 2001, page B-1, "Understanding Islam."

[6] Peter Marsden, *The Taliban: War, Religion and the New Order in Afghanistan*, (London: ZED Books, Inc. 1998), p. 68.

[7] Mark Bowden, "Tales of the Tyrant," *The Atlantic Monthly*, May, 2002, pp. 35-51.

[8] WGBH, Boston, "Morning News," May 25, 2002.

[9] The material in this section about the Qur'an is distilled from the books by Esposito (1998), Hitti (1971), Pickthall (1955), and Rodinson (1971). As mentioned in the Foreword of this book, as a sign of respect and cultural sensitivity to Islam and Muslims, I use the Islamic word Qur'an (short for al-Qur'an), rather than the spelling that was popularized by the British more than a century ago, "Koran." The exception to this is when I present quotations from other authors who use a different spelling or term. However, I will use the Gregorian dating system rather than the Islamic dating system throughout this book because I assume that most readers are less familiar with the Islamic system, which begins with the year of Muhammad's flight (*hegira* or *hijrah*) from Mecca as zero, and corresponds to the year 622 A.D. in the Gregorian system.

[10] Pickthall, p. x.

[11] John Wansbrough, *Qur'anic Studies*, 1977, and his obituary in *The London Times*, June 28, 2002, p. 8.

[12] See Pickthall's commentary about chapter 33, The Clans," (1955: 299) and Chapter 6 of this book for a more detailed description of "The Battle of the Trench."

[13] *Encyclopedia Britannica, Volume 13*. 1973. p. 454.

[14] This is the first chapter, "The Opening," in the Qur'an as translated by Pickthall, p. 31. Notice that while this passage does not mention war and peace, it literally states that Allah has favored some people more than others, and that the people who do not follow the straight path of Allah have gone astray and have earned Allah's anger. In other words, the first and most popular chapter in the Qur'an each day introduces its readers to the attitudes of favoritism and anger from a divine source — Allah. This comment is made as an objective application of the method of content analysis in the social sciences — not as a moral judgment or as criticism of this chapter or of the Qur'an.

[15] Over the years, many Muslims from different walks of life have explained to me the norms regarding daily recitation of the Qur'an like this. For example, Professor Zaman, at Brown University, has told me that "...ordinary Muslims are not drilled in every verse and chapter of the Qur'an. Most of them can recite only a few of their favorites in Arabic. Often they do not know what the words really mean."

[16] Esposito, p. 21.

[17] Pickthall, p. 380. I have heard similar testimonies again and again from Islamic scholars and students of Arabic language. However, there are two verses in the Qur'an itself (chapter 59: verses 22 and 32) that suggests some skepticism about this matter. Both of them state, "...We have made the Qur'an easy to remember; but is there any that remembereth?")

[18] James Piscatori, "The Turmoil Within: The Struggle for the Future of the Islamic World," *Foreign Affairs*: Volume 81 No. 3, May/June 2002, p. 146.

[19] Piscatori, p. 146.

[20] For discussion about violence-oriented opportunists and literalists see Sprinzak, 2000; Finkel, 2001; Appleton and Marty, 2002. For a greater understanding, of the social origins and the religious beliefs and practices of contemporary religious militants and terrorists see David C. Rapoport, 1998; Walter Reich, 1998; and especially Jessica Stern, 2003.

[21] Harvey Kushner, "Suicide Bombers: Business as Usual," in Harvey W. Kushner (editor), *Essential Readings on Political Terrorism: Analyses of Problems and Prospects for the 21st Century,* Gordian Knot Books, 2002, p. 40.

[22] Kushner, p. 41

[23] "Military Studies in the Jihad Against Tyrants," translated as "Terrorist Training Manual," U.S. Department of Justice, Federal Bureau of Investigation, (Washington, DC: November, 2001), Appendix B in this document is called the "Full Text of Hijacking Letter." All quotations from these documents are presented in this book as they presented in these documents, despite the frequent errors in spelling, grammar, and syntax.

[24] "Military Studies...," p. 8. Notice the word "terror," and its context, in this excerpt from the Qur'an.

[25] The absence of references to battles after Muhammad's death supports the assertion by John Esposito (that is presented later in this book) that Muhammad's life was the normative period and that his battles are given the most emphasis in Islamic schools.

[26] "Military Studies...," p. 78.

[27] "Military Studies...," p. 79.

[28] "Military Studies...," p. 79.

[29] "Military Studies...," p. 76.

[30] "Military Studies...," Appendix B, p. 12.

[31] "Military Studies...," Appendix B, p. 13. Government and military leaders might note that terrorists are instructed to read two chapters of the Qur'an, in particular, on the night before executing their terrorist attacks: al-Tabby and Anuil. Relevant verses from these chapters of the Qur'an are examined in the next Chapter of this book.

[32] "Military Studies...," Appendix B, p. 16. Readers are advised to be skeptical of these translations of verses from the Qur'an. In Chapter 2, I present passages from the Qur'an that are somewhat similar to these translations but that differ in some crucial respects, namely that the comparable verses that I have found in respected English translations by Pickthall, Haleem, Ali, and Bell are generally *less* violent and absolute. This raises the prospect that the verses presented here in Chapter 1 either were translated poorly or that the original author of the verses, possibly Mohammed Atta or a religious scholar hired by him to draft this letter, was an opportunist who exaggerated the violence in the Qur'anic verses. Page 12 of the FBI's document offers a speculation about the author of the letter: "It was more than likely written by a religious scholar who had prior knowledge of the attacks."

[33] This material about the extensive use of materials from the Qur'an in the training camps of al-Qaeda recruits in Afghanistan is based on an article in *The Sunday New York Times,* "A Nation Challenged: Life in bin Laden's Army.," March 17, 2002, pp. 18-20.

[34] Naji's case is based on an article by Michael Finkel, "Naji's Taliban Phase: The Making and Unmaking of a Holy Warrior," in the *The Sunday New York Times,*

December 16, 2001, pp. 78-81.

[35] This case on Mullah Omar is based on a book by Ahmed Rashid, *Taliban: Islam, Oil, and the New Great Game in Central Asia*, pp. 22-27 and passim, and on an article in *The New York Times*, "Religion, War Are All Omar Knows," December 7, 2001, p. 4.

[36] Rashid, p. 25.

[37] *New York Times*, p. 4.

[38] *New York Times*, p. 4.

[39] This case is based on Aukai Collins, *My Jihad*. Collin's case is presented here in greater detail than the cases of Naji and Omar because far more is known about Collins and his experiences with Islam, the Qur'an, war, and peace that will be useful throughout the remainder of this book. Collin's case can also help guard against erroneous assumptions and conclusions that can follow from holding narrow stereotypes of Muslims.

[40] Collins, p. 142.

[41] Collins, p. 143.

[42] Collins, p. xi.

[43] Collins, p. 5.

[44] Collins, p. 24.

[45] Collins, p. 88.

[46] Collins, p. 30.

[47] Collins, p. 31.

[48] Collins, p. 203.

[49] This assessment is based on personal conversations that I have had with Najih Lazar of Narragansett, Rhode Island, and with other Muslims who are living in the United States. Mr. Lazar said that he has at least three editions of the Qur'an in his home. One edition is in Arabic. Another edition is in English. A third edition is "side-by-side" bilingual in Arabic and English.

[50] Professor Muhammad Qasim Zaman of the Islamic Studies Department, Brown University, Providence, Rhode Island. Personal communication, November 21, 2002. Additionally, I have also personally witnessed several instances of non-Arab Muslims reciting the obligatory first chapter of the Qur'an. Later, in conversations with me, they have told me that, while they are spiritually moved by these recitations, they do not know the meanings of the words and verses. This is not an impediment to their faith, however. Some of them even say that Muslims fluent in Arabic often tell them that it is sometimes easier to believe if you do not understand.

[51] This assertion is supported by personal conversations that I have had with a number of Muslims who are living in the United States including Mr. Najih Lazar of Narragansett, Rhode Island.

[52] "Islam." *Encyclopedia Britannica*, Volume 12. 1973, pp. 663-664.

[53] Statistical information here is based on the *World Almanac and Book of Facts, 2001*, (New York: World Almanac Books), pp. 689, 692. The statistical information and the basic forms of the figures are based on the *State of War and Peace Atlas*, compiled by Dan Smith. 1997, pp. 44-45.

[54] Esposito, p. 208.

[55] The *Holy Bible*. King James Version. Deuteronomy 20: 10-13, 24.

[56] *Tanakh. The Holy Scriptures*. The New JPS Translation According to the Traditional Hebrew Text. Philadelphia & Jerusalem: The Jewish Publication Society. 1985, pp. 20.10 and 20.11 from the chapters of the same numbers.

[57] Pickthall, *The Meaning of the Glorious Koran*, p. 205 (chapter 17, verses 16-17 of the Qur'an).

[58] Keep in mind that less than 20% of the Muslim in the contemporary world are Arabs, and that only about 40% of the adult Arabs who are Muslims are fully literate in Arabic (*The State of War and Peace Atlas*, pp. 44-45; the 2002 *World Almanac*, pp. 760-859). Testimony that many non-Arab Muslims have memorized Qur'anic passages in Arabic without understanding the words or their meanings comes from conversations that I have had with non-Arabic Muslims over the years. Often they will recite long passages from the Qur'an to me in Arabic, but will then say that they have no idea of how the words are written or what they mean.

[59] Of course it is also true that the Christian Bible and, perhaps less so, the Jewish Torah and Talmud are widely available in many nations and translated into many languages. However, passages about war and peace in the Bible, Torah, and Talmud might be less compelling to Christians and Jews because, among other reasons, the Bible and Torah are not considered by their adherents to be the final, definitive, and eternal word of God, and their adherents are not required to prostrate themselves in public, collective prayer ceremonies to recite passages from their holy books five times every day of their lives.

[60] Pickthall's translation was selected because it has withstood the "test of time" and is so widely respected and available in libraries throughout the world. Pickthall voluntarily converted to Islam, lived as a Muslim in Muslim societies for decades, and dedicated his life to explaining Islam and the Qur'an in the English language to all who are interested. He also was aware of the unique linguistic qualities of spoken and written Arabic and of the limitations of any translation of a document so historical, complex, and metaphorical as the Qur'an. In his Foreword he wrote:

> "The aim of this work is to present to English readers what Muslims the world over hold to be the meaning of the words of the Koran, and the nature of that Book, in not unworthy language and concisely, with a view to the requirements of English Muslims. It may be reasonably claimed that no Holy Scripture can be fairly presented by one who disbelieves its inspiration and its message; and this is the first English translation of the Koran by an Englishman who is a Muslim.... The Koran cannot be translated. That is the belief of old-fashioned Shaykhs and the view of the present writer. The Book is here rendered almost literally and every effort has been made to choose befitting language. But the result is not the Glorious Koran, that inimitable symphony, the very sounds of which move men to tears and ecstasy. It is only an attempt to present the meaning of the Koran — and peradventure something of the charm — in English. It can never take the place of the Koran in Arabic, nor is it meant to do so."

Like Pickthall, my purpose is to present the passages about war and peace in the Qur'an so as to reveal their literal meanings or to come as close as possible to the literal meanings. I am aware that some contemporary theories in semiotics and cultural studies, such as deconstructionism and post-modernism, question the possibility of "literal meaning" of text, especially of text as "deep" and connotative as the Qur'an. Nonetheless, Pickthall's translation is considered by contemporary scholars such as Michael Sells to be "extremely literal." See Michael Sells, *Approaching the Qur'an: The*

Early Revelations, (White Cloud Press, 2001), p. 215.

[61] My analysis of compilations of the Hadith is presented in Chapter 2. Generally I found the Hadith to reinforce, and at times extend, the Qur'an's pronouncements about how Muslims should behave toward non-Muslims regarding war.

[62] Very informative to me were these spontaneous translations of passages (i.e. passages numbered 11, 12, 37, 45, 56, 58, 114 in Chapter 2 of this book) of the Qur'an by devout, contemporary Muslims who are now living in the U.S. but who were born and raised in nations that are predominantly Muslim. Never did their translations contradict Pickthall's translations in ways that are substantively significant regarding war, terror, and peace, except that one translator, Najih Lazar, did not find the word "terror," or its synonyms, in the passages in which Pickthall translated an Arabic word into English as "terror."

CHAPTER TWO

THE QUR'AN'S PASSAGES ON PEACE, TERROR, AND WAR

This chapter presents all of the different, distinctive passages that I found in the Qur'an related to making peace and waging war between and among different nations. For easy reference I have organized these passages into conventional categories of common interest to military and government leaders in the U.S. including: the sources, nature, and importance of peace, treaties, the moral nature and causes of war, the enemies of Muslim armies, goals and general orders for battle, main themes and forms of Muslim warfare, motivations and justifications for Muslims fighting in combat against non-Muslims, behavioral prescriptions and proscriptions for Muslims in combat, spoils of war, treatment of enemy prisoners, and reasons to end warfare. Some verses are presented more than once, under several different categories, because these verses deal with more than one topic in complex ways that cannot be readily broken into separate units without sacrificing meaning. Often the passages that follow include several verses that surround a focal verse about war or peace. This is done in order to enhance understanding of that focal verse and to provide a sense of the literary, spiritual, and historical contexts of the Qur'an.

When reading the passages that follow, it can be helpful to keep in mind that the translator, Mohammed Marmaduke Pickthall, was a widely respected British scholar who converted to Islam, lived as a Muslim in Cairo for much of his life, dedicated his life to Islamic scholarship, and tried to present the most literal translations possible of the Qur'an from Arabic into English. I present the passages here with the same exact spelling, punctuation, capitalization, and grammar as Pickthall, realizing the highly idiosyncratic and at times perplexing style and content of the material.[1] It can also be useful to look for what might be similarities, ambiguities, and even contradictions between and among verses and passages, not only in your mind, but also in the minds of other readers and reciters — literalists and opportunists, in particular.

It can be very worthwhile to consider the extent to which these passages manifest what some scholars claim to be four general restrictive principles that can be found throughout the Qur'an: "right-eous intention," "proportionality," "discrimination," and "transgres-sion avoidance." According to Islamic scholar Muhammad Abdel Haleem,[2] righteous intention means that Muslims must fight "in the way of Allah," so that Allah's word is "uppermost" in their minds, rather than for other reasons such as revenge, booty, or self-aggran-dizement. Proportionality means "no more harm should be caused to them than they have caused." Discrimination means that only the enemy's combatants are to be fought. The transgressions to be avoid-ed by Muslim fighters are initiation of fighting, fighting those with whom a treaty has been concluded, surprising the enemy without first inviting them to make peace, destroying crops, and killing those who should be protected. Of course, anyone who has ever been in sus-tained combat probably knows that principles such as these are easi-er said than done. Readers might also notice some similarities between several of these purported Islamic principles of war and some of the legal principles of war that evolved out of Greek and Roman military tribunals, including the four "Basic Principles of the Law of War" that have been codified by the Hague and the Geneva Conventions: military necessity, humanity, proportionality, and dis-tinction.[3] These subjects will be considered in later chapters regard-ing the history of Muslim warfare and on policy implications for future wars that involve proponents of the Qur'an. When reading the Qur'anic passages in this chapter, however, readers are encouraged to consider whether these principles are frequently in evidence. Are these principles always compatible and unambiguous? Are there other principles besides these four that are implied in the passages? Let us first consider what the Qur'an has to say about the topic of peace between groups and nations.

PEACE

The word "peace" and its synonyms are not common in the Qur'an. References to peace are scattered about in various verses throughout the book, and they often deal with spiritual and existential peace of the individual Muslim "believer" rather than with peaceful relations between Muslim and non-Muslim groups or nations.

> 1. (446/97:3-5) "The Night of Power is better than a thou-sand months. The angels and the Spirit descend therein, by the permission of their Lord, with all decrees. (That night is) Peace until the rising of the dawn."

> 2. (440/89:27-28) "But ah! Thou soul at peace! Return unto thy Lord, content in His good pleasure!"

> 3. (263/25:63) "The (faithful) slaves of the Benificient are they who walk upon the earth modestly, and when the foolish ones address them answer: Peace."

At least one verse might be understood to assert that Allah is the source of all peace.

> 4. (394/59:23) "He is Allah, than [sic] whom there is no other God, the Sovereign Lord, the Holy One, Peace, the Keeper of Faith, the Guardian, the Majestic, the Compeller, the Superb, Glorified by Allah from all that they ascribe as partner (unto Him)."

There is also a verse that might imply that Allah summons, selects, and leads only certain people (believers) to the "abode of peace," which at some places in the Qur'an is referred to as a "straight path" — Islam.

> 5. (159/10:26) "And Allah summoneth to the abode of peace, and leadeth whom He will to a straight path."

Quite a few verses in the Qur'an emphasize the importance of peaceful relations between and among Muslims.

> 6. (369/49:10) "The believers are naught else than brothers. Therefore make peace between your brethren and observe your duty to Allah that haply ye may obtain mercy."

> 7. (53/2:224) "And make not Allah, by your oaths, a hindrance to your being righteous and observing your duty unto Him and making peace among mankind. Allah is Hearer, Knower."

> 8. (90/4:114) "There is no good in much of their secret conferences save (in) him who enjoineth almsgiving and kindness and peace-making among the people. Whoso doeth that, seeking the good pleasure of Allah, We shall bestow on him a vast reward."

> 9. (158/10:11) "Their prayer therein will be: Glory be to Thee, O Allah! And their greeting therein will be: Peace. And the conclusion of their prayer will be: Praise be to Allah, Lord of the Worlds!"

One passage stands out because it is so specific in instructing Muslims on how to mediate peace between other Muslims who are fighting.

> 10. (369/49:10) "And if two parties of believers fall to fighting, then make peace between them. And if one party of them doeth wrong to the other, fight ye that which doeth wrong till it return unto the ordinance of Allah; then, if it return, make peace between them justly, and act equitably. Lo! Allah loveth the equitable."

Often quoted is an inspiring verse in the Qur'an that does not use the word "peace" but seems to encourage tolerance and understanding among members of "mankind."[4] It suggests that all human beings, or at least all Muslims, originate from the same source and that Allah intentionally created gender, ethnic, and political differences to somehow encourage people to know one another and to realize that righteous behavior is the only basis for ranking one person higher than another.

> 11. (369/49:13) "Oh mankind! Lo! We have created you male and female and have made you nations and tribes that ye may know one another. Lo! The noblest of you, in the sight of Allah, is the best in conduct. Lo! Allah is Knower. Aware."

As far as mentioning peace in conjunction with waging war, two passages standout for their striking definitiveness. Both pertain to proper behavior for Muslims in the thick of battle. One prohibits Muslims from calling for peace while they are heavily engaged with the enemy and are winning, while the other encourages Muslims to be ready to accept the peace offerings by their adversaries at the same time.

> 12. (363/47:35) "So do not falter and cry out for peace when ye (will be) the uppermost, and Allah is with you, and He will not grudge (the reward of) your actions."

> 13. (143/8:61) "And if they incline to peace, incline thou also to it, and trust in Allah. Lo! He is the Hearer, the Knower."

TREATIES TO ESTABLISH TEMPORARY PEACE?

A number of verses specify rules for Muslims who enter into treaties with non-Muslims, and seem to emphasize how and why the treaties can be broken. They do not encourage treaty-making for purposes of creating or maintaining permanent peace so much as they indicate some of the obligations and vulnerabilities that Muslims incur through treaties.

> 14. (144/8:72) "Protect those with whom you have a treaty."

> 15. (145/9:4) "Excepting those of the idolaters with whom ye (Muslims) have a treaty, and who have since abated nothing of you right nor have supported anyone against you. (As for these), fulfill their treaty to them till their term. Lo! Allah loveth those who keep their duty (unto Him)."

> 16. (145/9:7) "How can there be a treaty with Allah and with His messenger for the idolaters save those with whom ye made a treaty at the Inviolable Place of Worship? So long as they are true to you, be true to them. Lo! Allah loveth those who keep their duty."

> 17. (145/9:12) "And if they break their pledges after their treaty (hath been made with you) and assail your religion, then fight the heads of disbelief — Lo! They have no binding oaths — in order that they may desist."

> 18. (143/8:58) "And if thou fearest treachery from any folk, then throw back to them (their treaty) fairly. Lo! Allah loveth not the treacherous."

> 19. (53/2:224) "And make not Allah, by your oaths, a hindrance to your being righteous and observing your duty unto Him and making peace among mankind. Allah is Hearer, Knower."

> 20. (201/16:92) "And be not like unto her who unravelleth
> the thread after she hath made it strong, to thin filaments,
> making you oaths a deceit between you because of a nation
> being more numerous than (another) nation. Allah only
> trieth you thereby, and He verily will explain to you on the
> Day of Resurrection that wherein ye differed."

Peace, then, is decidedly more prominent in the Qur'an as a sought-after individual, spiritual condition, a state of grace, and as a condition of non-hostility between two or more Muslim individuals or Muslim groups than as an esteemed condition of non-belligerence between a Muslim and a non-Muslim nation. In these forms, peace can be attained by believers of Islam only in one way — total surrender to the "straight path" of Islam ("total surrender" being a widely-accepted translation of the term "Islam"). One of the policy implications for today's government and military leaders (as discussed in Chapter 7) is to realize that the primary meanings of "peace" in the Qur'an are spiritual and intra-Muslim harmony. Some Muslims might believe that it is possible for them to have both types of harmony without having peaceful relations with non-Muslims, at least so long as non-Muslims do not interfere with the religious and communal lives of Muslims. Conceivably this could occur when relations between Muslim and non-Muslim nations are non-existent, indifferent, or even strained, or when a Muslim nation is engaged in external hostilities against one or more non-Muslim nations for reasons other than the religious persecution of Muslims. This could be the case in wars of religious, economic and political expansion by Muslim nations. Somewhat ironically, perhaps, most citizens of a Muslim nation might consider themselves to be at peace even if their nation is engaged in a brutal and bloody foreign war of expansion. Understandably then, appeals to citizens such as these to strive for peace might be futile and wasted.

It is also important to note that the Qur'an does not directly address the topics of international peace among all tribes and nations, how non-Muslim people regard peace, or whether peace can be an enduring condition in world affairs. Much more text and attention is given to the topic of war.

WAR: ITS MORAL NATURE, CAUSES, AND SOME GENERAL PROHIBITIONS

The Qur'an does not have much to say about the moral nature and causes of war, other than war that Muslims conduct in retaliation for religious persecution that they suffer. For purpose of contrast, consider some of the verses in a Christian Bible that often are identified as specifying the "causes of war."

> "From whence come wars and fightings among you? Come they not hence, even of your lusts that war in your members? Ye lust, and have not: ye kill, and desire to have, and cannot obtain: ye fight and war, yet ye have not, because ye ask not. Ye ask, and receive not, because ye ask amiss, that ye may consume it upon your lusts. Ye adulterers and adulteresses, know ye not that the friendship of the world is enmity with God? Whosoever therefore will be a friend of the world is the enemy of God."[5]

These Biblical verses assert that the "causes" of war really amount to one cause — human beings who lust after worldly material possessions and pleasures. Not mentioned are other factors that are frequently professed by religious leaders, philosophers, and historians, such as evil spirits, the devil, wrath of the gods, God's will, fear, hatred, revenge, various psychological and social pathologies, errors in political judgments, overpopulation, social inequalities, and so on.

In contrast to the Bible, consider some of the verses in the Qur'an that come closest to specifying the causes of war.

---

21. (124/7:30) "A party hath He led aright, while error hath just hold over (another) party, for lo! They choose the devils for protecting friends instead of Allah and deem that they are rightly guided."

---

22. (124/7:34) "And every nation hath its term, and when its term cometh, they cannot put if off an hour nor yet advance (it)."

---

23. (124/7:38) "He saith: Enter into the Fire among nations of the jinn[6] and humankind who passeth away before you. Every time a nation entereth, it curseth its sister (nation) till, when they have all been made to follow one another thither, the last of them saith unto the first of them: Our Lord! These

---

> led us astray, so give them double torment of the Fire. He saith: For each one there is double (torment), but ye know not."

> 24. (124/7:40) "Lo! They who deny Our revelation and scorn them, for them the gates of Heaven will not be opened nor will they enter the Garden until the camel goeth through the needle's eye. Thus do We requite the guilty."

According to Pickthall (1951: 32-33), the origin of the first wars among humans goes something like this in the Qur'an.[7] The current predicament of human beings on Earth originates in Adam and Eve being cast out of the Garden of Eden by Allah when they disobeyed him and were tempted into sin by Satan. They and their descendants fell into lives of sin, idolatry, and spiritual turmoil. Periodically Allah would make revelations to Abraham and other true prophets (the common ancestors of Muslims, Jews, and Christians) about how human beings could attain spiritual peace and salvation by willingly and totally surrendering (a common translation of the term "Islam") themselves to Allah and by following "the Straight Path" of righteous living. True Muslims ("believers") dedicate their lives to Allah and follow the Straight Path. Unfortunately, many more human beings are "disbelievers" who foolishly and wantonly refuse to follow Allah. Hypocrites only follow Allah when it is convenient and expeditious for them. Jews and Christians ("People of the Scripture") only accept some of Allah's rules and often violate them. Pagans ("idolaters") and polytheists have no understanding or appreciation of Allah. Out of these differences emerged differences among tribes, cities, and nations. Satan sows jealousy and other evils into some tribes and nations and deceives them into persecuting Muslims by attacking their communities, expelling them from their homes, excluding them from their holy places, and interfering with their practice of the "Five Pillars of Islam:" making the profession of faith (*shahada*), praying (*salat*) five times a day from the Qur'an, almsgiving (*zakat*), observing the fast during Ramadan, and pilgrimage to Mecca (*Hajj*) at least once in one's life, when possible.

As persecution becomes increasingly intolerable, Muslims are supposed to offer peaceful resolutions to the conflicts with their oppressors, and they are to consider emigrating to distant lands in order to escape the persecution.[8] However, if these efforts fail or they are impossible, Muslims are required by Allah to collectively launch armed retaliations against units of disbelievers who have persecuted them, and to fight according to Allah's rules, regardless of their own attitudes towards war and the likelihood of their own deaths. These collective, armed retaliations by Muslims under Muhammad's command clearly do constitute war in the Qur'an.[9]

> 25. 52/2:216) "Warfare is ordained for you, though it is hateful unto you: but it may happen that ye hate a thing which is good for you, and it may happen that ye love a thing which is bad for you. Allah knoweth, ye know not."

In these situations, most but not all Muslims are morally compelled to join into cohesive military units — ranks — in order to engage in battle against their tormenters. The Qur'an goes so far as to declare that Allah actually loves those who answer his call to battle in this way. The title of one chapter of the Qur'an (chapter 61) is translated as "The Ranks," — possibly underscoring the importance of fighting as a cohesive unit.

> 26. (397/61:4) "Lo! Allah loveth those who battle for His cause in ranks, as if they were a solid structure."

Still, there are several general prohibitions that believers must be mindful of before they engage in warfare against their persecutors. They must not initiate hostilities, fight during certain periods of time that are considered to be sacred unless they are attacked or persecuted during that period, and they must not attack pacifists, those who offer peace, those with whom believers have honorable treaties, those who "hold aloof," or those who seek refuge with the allies of believers.

> 27. (50/2:190) "Fight in the way of Allah against those who fight against you, but begin not hostilities. Lo! Allah loveth not aggressors."

> 28. (87/4:90) "Except those who seek refuge with a people between whom and you there is a covenant, or (those who) come unto you because their hearts forbid them to make war on you or make war on their own folk. Had Allah willed He could have given them power over you so that assuredly they would have fought you. So, if they hold aloof from you and wage not war against you and offer you peace, Allah alloweth you no way against them."

> 29. (52/2:217) "They question thee (O Muhammad) with regard to warfare in the sacred month, Say: Warfare therein is a great (transgression), but to turn (men) from the way of Allah; for persecution is worse than killing. And they will not cease from fighting against you till they have made you renegades from your religion, if they can. And whoso becometh a renegade and dieth in his disbelief: such are they whose works have fallen both in the world and the Hereafter. Such are rightful owners of the Fire: they will abide therein."

> 30. (146/9:6) "And if anyone of the idolaters seeketh thy protection (O Muhammad), then protect him so that he may hear the word of Allah, and afterward convey him to his place of safety. That is because they are a folk who know not."

WARTIME ENEMIES OF MUSLIM ARMIES

In the Qur'an the primary wartime enemies of Muslim armies are bands, tribes, coalitions, cities and nations of disbelievers, hypocrites, polytheists, and others who persecute Muslims, who are alleged to be plotting against Muslims, or who are objectionable in other ways. Qur'anic verses sometimes identify specific tribes of disbelievers that opposed Muhammad's armies during his lifetime, principally the Quraysh tribe of Arabs from Mecca (ironically Muhammad's own tribe at birth and his birthplace), as well as some groups of Jews and Christians in Mecca and in many other settlements including Medina, a polyglot oasis city that became the adopted home of Muhammad and of Islam during his life.

> 31. (140/8:19) "(O Qureysh!) If ye sought a judgment, now hath the judgment come unto you. And if ye cease (from persecuting the believers) it will be better for you, but if ye return (to the attack) We also shall return. And your host will avail you naught, however numerous it be, and (know) that Allah is with the believers (in His guidance)."

> 32. (394/59:11) "Hast thou not observed those who are hypocrites, (how) they tell their brethren who disbelieve among the people of the Scripture: If ye are driven out, we surely will go out with you, and we will never obey anyone

against you, and if ye are attacked we verily will help you. And Allah beareth witness that they verily are liars."

33. (394/59:14) "They will not fight against you in a body save in fortified villages or from behind walls. Their adversity among themselves is very great. Ye think of them as a whole whereas their hearts are divers. That is because they are a folk who have no sense."

Many of the verses of the Qur'an that deal with warfare describe, comment on, and try to explain aspects of one or more of the three famous battles between Muhammad's forces and the forces of the Quraysh and allies between 624-627 A.D.: Badr, Uhud, and "The Battle of the Trench." These battles are described in Chapter 4 in conjunction with Muhammad's life and the military history of Islam. Other verses refer to various armed expeditions that Muhammad sent against targets including merchant caravans and enclaves of Arab, Persian, and Byzantine opponents in cities as far away as Jerusalem and Damascus. In the case of the three famous battles against the Quraysh, the enemy armies were deceived by Satan's promise of victory into engaging Muhammad's armies in combat; but they suffer Allah's wrath on the battlefield after Satan abandons them, out of fear of Allah.

34. (142/8:48) "And when Satan made their deeds seem fair to them and said: No one of mankind can conquer you this day, for I am your protector. But when the armies came in sight of one another, he took flight, saying: Lo! I am guiltless of you. Lo! I see that which ye see not. Lo! I fear Allah. And Allah is severe in punishment."

GOALS AND THREE GENERAL ORDERS FOR MUSLIM IN BATTLE

Three short passages in the Qur'an come closest to constituting general orders for Muslim battle by suggesting the goals of war, preferred actions, attitudes, and beliefs for Muslim warriors. Notice that there are similarities and differences among the three passages on these matters. Also notice that there are many ambiguities or inconsistencies, even if the passages are taken literally as specific instructions.

> 35. (145/9:5) "Then, when the sacred months have passed,
> slay the idolaters wherever ye find them, and take them
> (captive), and besiege them, and prepare for them each
> ambush. But if they repent and establish worship and pay
> the poor-due, then leave their way free. Lo! Allah is
> Forgiving, Merciful."

This passage instructs believers to wait until sacred months have passed, but then they are to slay enemies who are "idolaters" wherever they are found, in addition to capturing their enemies, besieging them, and ambushing them. Taken literally, there would seem to be some contradiction or at least some ambiguity here. Are only "idolaters" (worshippers of idols) to be treated in these ways? Which enemy combatants are to be slain? Which ones are to be captured? Are they to be slain only if they resist being captured? Are they really to be slain wherever they are found, even if they are found in a mosque, on holy ground, or they are defenseless? Should they be ambushed first, if possible, and then besieged if they escape to defensive positions, or vice versa? One resolution to these questions might be for believers to understand that the Qur'an is allowing them to engage in all four combat behaviors (slay, take captives, besiege, and ambush) as they see fit. But if this is the case, then literalists and opportunists are left to make their own decisions, beyond the instructions in the Qur'an, because it is difficult if not impossible to perform all of these actions simultaneously and upon the same enemy combatants.

There also might be some ambiguity in the last two sentences of passage #35 regarding treatment of captives. There are three conditions for freeing captives: they must "repent," "establish worship," and "pay the poor-due" (i.e. a tax to support the poor people in Muslim communities). But what constitutes repentance? How can captives be expected to pay a tax if they are captives and all of their possessions have been taken from them? Also, does "leave their way free" actually mean allowing captives to do what they will, including return to their homeland or remain in Muslim communities? Perhaps other passages will clarify these matters.

> 36. (361/47:4) "Now when ye meet in battle those who
> disbelieve, then it is smiting of the necks until, when ye have
> routed them, then making fast of bonds, and afterward either
> grace or ransom till the war lay down its burdens. That (is
> the ordinance). And if Allah willed He could have punished

them (without you) but (thus it is ordained) that He may try
some of you by means of others. And those who are slain in
the way of Allah. He rendereth not their actions vain."

Taken literally, passage #36 instructs Muslim combatants on how
to deal with disbelievers (those who do not believe in Allah and Islam,
but who may or may not be idolaters) whom they "meet in battle."
Muslims are to smite the necks of their enemies, rout them, make fast
their bonds, and then try to "grace" (probably meaning to set them
free) or "ransom" them until the war ends (to "lay down its burdens").
This passage is similar to the previous passage, #35, in allowing
Muslim warriors to engage in a variety of behaviors towards the
enemy, but it also allows some additional and very specific behaviors
that were not mentioned in passage #35: smiting of necks, routing,
making fast the bonds of captives, and ransoming or releasing captives before the war is over.

Furthermore, passage #36 goes on to remind Muslims that Allah
could have punished the enemy without their assistance, but that battles allow Allah to try or test some Muslims. Those who are slain in
fighting his way will not die in vain. Passage #36 goes beyond passage
#35 in offering this as a motivation to Muslim warriors. Passages pre-
sented later in this chapter will show that many other motivations for
Muslim warriors are presented in the Qur'an.

The next passage, #37, adds instructions and possibly some ambiguities to the instructions in passages #35 and #36. One of its phrases,
"and slay them wherever ye find them," is among the most controversial in the Qur'an, especially when its context and the phrases around
it are ignored, as they often are.

37. (50/2:190-193) "Fight in the way of Allah against those
who fight against you, but begin not hostilities. Lo! Allah
loveth not aggressors. And slay them wherever ye find them,
and drive them out of the places whence they drove you out,
for persecution is worse than slaughter. And fight not with
them at the Inviolable Place of Worship until they first attack
you there, but if they attack you (there) then slay them. Such
is the reward of disbelievers. But if they desist, then lo! Allah
is Forgiving, Merciful. And fight them until persecution is no
more, and religion is for Allah. But it they desist, then let
there be no hostility except against wrongdoers."

Notice that this passage starts with a very direct command for Muslims to fight, but that at least two qualifications are specified. Muslims must "fight in the way of Allah," possibly meaning that they must fight as he would fight, if he fought, or that they must fight only for his goals, or that they must fight according to his instructions. Also, Muslims are not to begin the hostilities. Finally, they are to fight against those "who fight against you." Possibly this means that Muslims are not to attack defenseless people or those who refuse to fight, distinctions that could be extremely relevant in the light of contemporary events such as the terrorist attacks of 9-11-2001 and the threat of preemptive strikes. These subjects are discussed in Chapter 7 regarding prescriptions for military and government policies and actions. The phrase "Allah loveth not aggressors," reinforces the prohibition against Muslims being wartime aggressors, although it does not condemn aggressors or threaten them with punishment so much as it reminds them that they will not receive Allah's love. The third sentence, already commented on for its famous and controversial first phrase, also instructs Muslim combatants to drive-out the enemy from places that had been occupied by Muslims, and offers the rationalization that slaughtering the enemy in this way is less objectionable to Allah than is the persecution that the enemy inflicted on the Muslims to begin with. By the way, there is probably no better example of the danger and injustice of disregarding literary context than to quote the phrase "And slay them wherever ye find them" without noting that the surrounding phrases and verses mitigate the absoluteness of that phrase in several ways, especially by prohibiting Muslims from initiating hostilities and from slaughtering enemies who have not persecuted Muslims because of their religion.

The fourth and fifth sentences provide additional specificity regarding Muslim behaviors during combat. Muslims may attack and slay disbeliever enemies at the "Inviolable Place of Worship" (conceivably the holy mosque in Mecca, but possibly all Muslim holy places) but only if the enemy first attacks Muslims who are there. The last three sentences of passage #37 shift to the subject of ceasing the fighting, first saying that Allah will forgive the enemy and be merciful if "they desist." The passage continues by implying that "desist" means not only that the enemy must stop fighting Muslims in warfare, but that the enemy must also stop being "wrongdoers," must stop persecuting Muslims, and must allow that "religion is for Allah." Taken literally here, it is not clear whether this means that all persons of all religions must worship Allah, as would be the case if the enemy and all other nations converted to

Islam, or that Muslims are simply now free to practice Islam where and when they wish. As we will see, other Qur'anic passages that will be presented shortly seem to support both of these interpretations, a subject that will be addressed more fully in Chapter 6. However, it is worth noting that there are plenty of ambiguities in passage #37, just as there were ambiguities in passages #35 and #36. The final sentence of passage #37 seems to allow Muslim combatants to continue to fight even those enemy forces who desist in fighting the Muslims and also desist in religious persecution, if those forces are "wrongdoers" in other ways. Consider the possibility that contemporary literalists and opportunists might use passage #37 to legitimate their violence against a nation such as the United States by claiming that this is a nation of "wrongdoers," even is the nation is not actually waging war against Muslims or persecuting Muslims because of Islam.

Let us now turn to other passages in the Qur'an not only to learn about its instructions regarding other aspects of Muslim warfare but also to see whether other passages clarify the ambiguities that have been just been identified in passages #35, #36, and #37.

SOME THEMES AND FORMS OF MUSLIM WARFARE

DEFEND THE FAR BORDERS VIGOROUSLY

There is a noteworthy verse in chapter 8, "The Spoils of War," that instructs Muslims to vigorously defend their borders against known and unknown enemies and to invest heavily in this effort. It assures them that Allah will repay them and that their investment will not be in vain. Two translations of this verse are presented here, one from Ali, the other from Pickthall, respectively, because each verse has slightly different points of emphasis. As is the case in comparing most translations of the Qur'an, different translations do not contradict each other so much as they simply have slightly different styles, points of emphasis, and choices of words that are rather synonymous in English.

> 38. (Ali, 170/8:60) "And make ready for them whatever you can of armed force and of mounted pickets at the frontier, whereby you may frighten the enemy of Allah and your enemy and others besides them whom you know not, but Allah knows them. And whatever you spend in the way of Allah, it shall be repaid to you in full and you shall not be wronged."

> 39. (143/8:60) "Make ready for them all thou canst of (armed) force and of horses tethered, that thereby ye may dismay the enemy of Allah and your enemy, and others beside them whom ye know not. Allah knoweth them. Whatsoever ye spend in the way of Allah it will be repaid to you in full, and ye will not be wronged."

FIGHT IN THE WAY OF ALLAH

Besides passage #37, already discussed, there are a number of other passages that instruct Muslims to fight in the way of Allah, but they do so without emphasizing that Muslims should not be aggressors. Often there are slight differences among these verses in the form of additional instructions and comments, but they do not specify what is meant by the phrase "fight in the way of Allah." Literalists are left to ponder whether the word "way" means purpose, goals, methods, or particular tactics and behaviors that Muslim warriors should employ when engaged in combat.

> 40. (86/4:74) "Let those fight in the way of Allah who sell the life of this world for the other. Whoso fighteth in the way of Allah, be he slain or be he victorious, on him We shall bestow a vast reward."

> 41. (86/4:84) "So fight (O Muhammad) in the way of Allah — Thou art not taxed (with the responsibility for anyone) except for thyself—and urge on the believers. Peradventure Allah will restrain the might of those who disbelieve. Allah is stronger in might and stronger in inflicting punishments."

FIGHT THE ENEMY IN LIKE MANNER, RETALIATE, POSSIBLY FORGIVE

There are also verses in the Qur'an that instruct Muslims to retaliate "in like manner" against the enemy. Both Pickthall's and Ali's translations of one of these verses indicate that Muslims can attack during the "sacred month," if they were attacked during a "sacred month," and that Muslims can inflict the same kinds of punishments on the enemy as were inflicted on Muslims. These are two more examples of what scholars including Haleem refer to as the proportionality principle that they found throughout the Qur'an. Damage inflicted by Muslims in war should be proportionate to the damages that are inflicted upon them.[10]

> 42. (50/2:194) "The forbidden month for the forbidden month, and forbidden things in retaliation. And one who attacketh you, attack him in like manner as he attacked you. Observe your duty to Allah, and know that Allah is with those who ward off (evil)."

> 43. (Ali, 30/2:195) "The violation of a Sacred Month should be retaliated in the Sacred Month; and for all sacred things there is the law of retaliation. So, whoso transgresses against you, punish him for his transgression to the extent to which he has transgressed against you. And fear Allah and know that Allah is with those who fear Him."

It is not clear as to whether there could be considerable differences between these instructions to fight the enemy "in like manner" and the instructions in passages #40 and #41 to fight "in the way of Allah." For example, are Muslim combatants allowed to use mutilation and torture against enemies who mutilate and torture Muslims? The passages quoted so far in this Chapter do not convey an image of Allah as a deity who would condone torture or mutilation.

Regarding retaliation, its role in warfare often parallels its place in violent interpersonal conflicts, where its purposes can be to ward-off evil and to wreck violent personal revenge upon an enemy, as in Hammurabi's infamous code, "an eye for an eye." Retaliation can also take the form of a wronged party reducing the estate of a perpetrator in like amount (a slave destroyed or captured for a slave lost). Yet, while prescribed retaliation can be extremely vengeful and violent, apparently its use can be discretionary, rather than mandatory, at least when it involves other Muslims, depending on the original victim's sense of charity and forgiveness. It is not clear in the Qur'an as to whether the liberty of Muslims to withhold retaliation against other Muslims ("brothers") can be extended to non-Muslims who are wartime adversaries. This ambiguity could become very important if there are wars in the future between Muslim and non-Muslim forces (another topic to be addressed in Chapter 7 regarding government and military policies).

> 44. (48/2:178-179) "O ye who believe! Retaliation is prescribed for you in the matter of the murdered; the freeman for the freeman, and the slave for the slave, and the female for the female. And for him who is forgiven somewhat by

his (injured) brother, prosecution according to usage and payment unto him in kindness. This is an alleviation and a mercy from your Lord. He who transgresseth after this will have a painful doom. And there is life for you in retaliation, O men of understanding, that ye may ward off (evil)."

45. (100/5:45) "And We prescribed for them therein: The life for the life, and the eye for the eye, and the nose for the nose, and the ear for the ear, and the tooth for the tooth, and for wounds retaliation. But whoso forgoeth it (in the way of charity) it shall be expiation for him. Whoso judgeth not by that which Allah hath revealed: such are wrong-doers."

FIGHT IN CLOSED RANKS AS A SOLID UNIT

As previously mentioned, the Qur'an stresses the importance of Muslims fighting together in a cohesive unit. This theme is emphasized by the fact that a very famous chapter (61), "The Ranks," is named after a verse that promotes Muslim cohesiveness in battle. It is mentioned again here in order to underscore the fact that the Qur'an does not explicitly prescribe or proscribe Muslims fighting as self-appointed "free agents," alone, or in small cells, teams, squads, or other decentralized units. This can be an important consideration in light of the nature of many of the terrorist attacks in the world today (as discussed in Chapter 7).

46. (397/61:4) "Lo! Allah loveth those who battle for His cause in ranks, as if they were a solid structure."

ROUT THEM AND STRIKE FEAR IN THEIR SUPPORTERS

Translations by both Ali and Pickthall instruct Muslim combatants to not just defeat the enemy but to rout the enemy so decisively as to strike fear into them and their supporters.

47. (Ali, 170/8:58) "So, if thou catchest them in war, then by routing them strike fear in those that are behind them, that they may be admonished."

48. (143/8:57) "If thou comest on them in the war, deal with them so as to strike fear in those who are behind them, that haply they may remember."

49. (381/55:45-48) "The hosts will all be routed and will turn and flee." Nay, but the Hour (of doom) is their appointed tryst, and the Hour will be more wretched and more bitter (than their earthly failure). Lo! The guilty are in error and madness. On the day when they are dragged into the Fire upon their faces (it is said unto them): Feel the touch of hell."

INFLICT TERROR, AND MUCH MORE, ON DOMESTIC AND FOREIGN TARGETS

Before we consider what the Qur'an has to say about these topics, let us first consider a quotation attributed to Osama bin Laden that refers to some of these topics. This quotation was published in many mass media throughout the world on October 13, 2002, as proof that bin Laden is still alive and that he continues to advocate for violent events that will inflict terror on targets crucial to the U.S. economy until he is killed or there is an end to the injustice and aggression against Islam.

"The tape thought to be of bin Laden contained an anti-American message that is familiar from his previous video and audio messages. 'Let America increase the pace of this course of conflict or decrease it,' it says, 'we will retaliate in kind, God willing, and, as God is our witness, in the name of Islam we are preparing for you what would fill your hearts with terror, and they will target the hinges of your economy until you stop your injustice and aggression or either one of us dies first.'"[11]

Now turning to the Qur'an, it should not be surprising to learn that modern terms including "terrorism," "terrorist," and "terrorize" are not found in the Qur'an. Obvious synonyms, metaphors, and figures of speech for them are not to be found, either. However, the word "terror" is very much in evidence in the Qur'an, although occasionally the words "fear" and "panic" are used as alternatives, as is the case in phrases such as to "inflict terror," to "fill their hearts with fear," to "bring panic upon them." Different translators into English seem to prefer one of these three verbs to the other verbs.[12] For example, consider the same verse as presented in the translations by Ali and by Pickthall, respectively, according to the number that each of them assigned to the verse.

50. (Ali, 122/8:13) "When thy Lord revealed to the angels, saying, I am with you: so give firmness to those who believe. I will cast *terror* into the hearts of those who disbelieve. Smite, then, the upper parts of their necks, and smite off all finger-tips."

51. (139/8:12) "When thy Lord inspired the angels, (saying:) I am with you. So make those who believe stand firm. I will throw fear into the hearts of those who disbelieve. Then smite the necks and smite of them each finger."

Other passages threaten "terror," "torment," and "fire" on disbelievers — and without limiting these to combat situations in which disbelievers are the aggressors.

52. (140/8:13-14) "That is because they opposed Allah and His messenger. Whoso opposeth Allah and His messenger, (for him) lo! Allah is severe in punishment. That (is the award), so taste it, and (know) that for disbelievers is the torment of the Fire."

53. (74/3:151) "We shall cast *terror* into the hearts of those who disbelieve because they ascribe unto Allah partners, for which no warrant hath been revealed. Their habitation is the Fire, and hapless the abode of the wrong-doers."

While literalists and opportunists can readily disregard historical context, Pickthall explains that the preceding passage probably relates to the Muslim defeat at Uhud, whereas the following passage relates to the Muslim raids that followed their political victory at the Battle of the Trench. Muhammad ordered widespread attacks against several enclaves of Jewish tribes who were thought to have conspired with the Meccan army against the Muslims at the Battle of the Trench.[13] What we read here, however, is that terror is inflicted not just on the armed forces of the enemy who are in direct battle with Muslim forces, but also on other targets, including civilian populations in communities that are on foreign lands. Terror expands beyond the domestic battlefield through raids and surprise attacks on communities whose residents are asleep at night and even at noontime. Entire cities are sacked. Generations and entire tribes are annihilated in what possibly constitutes genocide in contemporary parlance.

54. (303/33:25-27) "And Allah repulsed the disbelievers in their wrath; they gained no good. Allah averted their attack from the believers. Allah is Strong, Mighty. And He brought those of the People of the Scripture who supported them down from their strongholds, and cast panic into their hearts. Some ye slew, and ye made captive some. And He caused you to inherit their land and their houses and their wealth, and land ye have not trodden. Allah is Able to do all things."

55. (237/21:43-44) "Or have they gods who can shield them from Us? They cannot help themselves nor can they be defended from Us. Nay, but We gave these and their fathers ease until life grew long for them. See they not how We visit the land, reducing it of its outlying parts? Can they then be the victors?"

56. (122/7:4-5) "How many a township have we destroyed! As a raid by night, or while they slept at noon, Our *terror* came unto them. No plea had they, when our *terror* came unto them, save that they said: Lo! We were wrong-doers."

57. (393/59:1-2) "In the name of Allah, the Beneficient, the Merciful. All that is in the heavens and all that is in the earth glorifieth Allah, and He is the Mighty, the Wise. He it is Who hath caused those of the People of the Scripture who disbelieved to go forth from their homes unto the first exile. Ye deemed not that they would go forth, while they deemed that their strongholds would protect them from Allah. But Allah reached them from a place whereof they recked [*sic*] not, and cast *terror* in their hearts so that they ruined their houses with their own hands and the hands of the believers. So learn a lesson, O ye who have eyes!"

58. (205/17:16-17) "And when We would destroy a township We send commandment to its folk who live at ease, and afterward they commit abomination therein, and so the Word (of doom) hath effect for it, and We annihilate it with complete annihilation. How many generations have we destroyed since Noah. And Allah sufficeth as Knower and Beholder of the sins of His slaves."

> 59. (236/21:11-15) "How many a community that dealt unjustly have We shattered, and raised up after them another folk! And, when they felt Our might, behold them fleeing from it! (But it was said unto them): Flee not, but return to that (existence) which emasculated you and to your dwellings, that ye may be questioned. They cried: Alas for us! Lo! We were wrongdoers. And this their crying ceased not till We made them as reaped corn, extinct."

> 60. (204-205/17:5-8) "So when the time for the first of the two came, We roused against you slaves of Ours of great might who ravaged (your) country, and it was a threat performed. Then we gave you once again your turn against them, and We aided you with wealth and children and made you more in soldiery, (Saying): If ye do good, ye do good for your own souls, and if ye do evil, it is for them (in like manner). So, when the time for the second (of the judgments) came (We roused against you others of Our slaves) to ravage you, and to enter the Temple even as they entered it the first time, and to lay waste all that they conquered with an utter wasting. It may be that your Lord will have mercy on you, but if ye repeat (the crime) We shall repeat (the punishment), and We have appointed hell a dungeon for the disbelievers."

By the way, it might be worth noting that passage #60 also admits that Muslims used "slaves of Ours of great might who ravaged (your) country." This raises the prospect that contemporary literalists and opportunists might find license to use mercenaries, prisoners, and combatants other than Muslims to conduct some attacks against their enemies.

Considering passages #50-60 as a whole in terms of the frequency and savagery of the violent actions that are described in them, is it so difficult to understand how some contemporary opportunists might use these passages to plan and to justify their acts of terrorism, warfare, and even genocide?

SUPPRESS DISSENT AMONG TROUBLESOME MUSLIMS AND ALLIES

There are also verses that might suggest to literalists that the Qur'an allows and encourages the suppression of dissent and pacifism among Muslims and their allies during times of war. For example, here is a passage that might be taken as a rebuke — or as even a threat of doom — by anyone who is faint-hearted about the subject of war. Could it be possible for some opportunists to use a verse like this to recruit soldiers and terrorists by calling into question their courage and mentioning to them that they can expect a terrible afterlife, if they refuse?

> 61. (362/47:20) "And those who believe, say; If only a Surah were revealed! But when a decisive Surah is revealed and war is mentioned therein, thou seest those in whose heart is a disease looking at thee with the look of men fainting unto death. Therefore woe unto them!"

Less frequent in the Qur'an, but hardly negligible, are verses that seem to promote slaughter and destruction of "hypocrites" (those who pretend to worship Allah but only do so out of convenience or for political purposes. This includes females, by the way). Often these verses appear to be referring to internal squabbles within a city occupied by Muslims, between one clan and another (thus the title of chapter 34, "The Clans"). Still, if such brutal treatment is prescribed for settling differences between Muslim clans over offenses such as being hypocritical, isn't it likely that opportunists could apply these passages to external armies and to non-Muslims? If it is permissible to treat Muslims so violently, then shouldn't non-Muslims be treated even more violently?

> 62. (306/34:60-61) "If the hypocrites, and those in whose hearts is a disease, and the alarmists in the city do not cease, We verily shall urge thee on against them, then they will be your neighbours in it but a little while. Accursed, they will be seized wherever found and slain with a (fierce) slaughter."

> 63.(306/34:73) "So Allah punisheth hypocritical men and hypocritical women, and idolatrous men and idolatrous women. But Allah pardoneth believing men and believing women, and Allah is Forgiving, Merciful."

Motivations And Justifications For Muslims Fighting In Combat

Many of the passages of the Qur'an, including some of the passages already presented in regards to the other categories, can be understood as providing motivations and justifications for Muslims fighting in combat against non-Muslims. Notice that there are many motivations besides the widely known and controversial one of gaining eternal paradise in the Garden of Eden for Muslims who die while fighting in "the way of Allah."

It Is Allah Who Is Killing Them And Is Responsible

> 64. (140/8:17) "Ye (Muslims) slew them not, but Allah slew them. And thou (Muhammad) threwest not when thou didst throw, but Allah threw, that He might test the believers in a fair test from Him. Lo! Allah is Hearer, Knower."

For The Cause Of Allah And To Oppose The Devil

> 65. (86/4:76) "Those who believe do battle for the cause of Allah; and those who disbelieve do battle for the cause of idols. So fight the minions of the devil. Lo! The devil's strategy is ever weak."

To Protect The Feeble People And Other Victims

> 66. (86/4:75) "How should ye not fight for the cause of Allah and of the feeble among men and of the women and the children who are crying: Our Lord! Bring us forth from out this town of which the people are oppressors! Oh, give us from Thy presence some protecting friend! Oh, give us from Thy presence some defender!"

Because You Have Been Wronged In Ways That Are Unacceptable To Allah

> 67. (244/22:39-40) "Sanction is given unto those who fight because they have been wronged; and Allah is indeed Able to give them victory; Those who have been driven from their homes unjustly only because they said: Our Lord is Allah—

> For had it not been for Allah's repelling some men by means
> of others, cloisters and churches and oratories and mosques,
> wherein the name of Allah is oft mentioned, would assuredly
> have been pulled down. Verily Allah helpeth one who
> helpeth Him. Lo! Allah is Strong, Almighty."

BECAUSE ALLAH WILL RESTRAIN THE MIGHT OF YOUR ENEMIES EVEN THOUGH THEY OUTNUMBER YOU

Enemy forces will often outnumber Muslim forces by a ratio of at least 2:1 and as much as 10:1 (as specified in passage #80, which follows in a few pages). And yet, the Muslims forces will prevail because the enemy forces lack "intelligence," and because Allah will restrain their might, if the Muslim forces fight steadfastly, obediently, and loyally.

> 68. (87/4:84) "So fight (O Muhammad) in the way of Allah—
> Thou art not taxed (with the responsibility for anyone)
> except for thyself—and urge on the believers. Peradventure
> Allah will restrain the might of those who disbelieve. Allah
> is stronger in might and stronger in inflicting punishment."

BECAUSE SOME ADVERSARIES BROKE TREATIES AND ASSAILED YOUR RELIGION

> 69. (145/9:12) "And if they break their pledges after their
> treaty (hath been made with you) and assail your religion,
> then fight the heads of disbelief—Lo! They have no binding
> oaths—in order that they may desist."

BECAUSE PARADISE IS A REWARD FOR MUSLIMS WHO FIGHT IN WAR FOR ALLAH

Paradise as a reward for Muslims who fight and die "in the way of Allah" probably is the most widely known and controversial content in the Qur'an. However, Esposito and some other scholars contend that Muhammad warned Muslims that paradise will be denied them if they fight only in order to attain paradise or if they intentionally let the enemy kill them.[14]

> 70. (86/4:74) "Let those fight in the way of Allah who sell
> the life of this world for the other. Whoso fighteth in the
> way of Allah, be he slain or be he victorious, on him We
> shall bestow a vast reward."

> 71. (155/9:111) "Lo! Allah hath bought from the believers
> their lives and their wealth because the Garden will be
> theirs; they shall fight in the way of Allah and shall slay and
> be slain. It is a promise which is binding on Him in the
> Torah and the Gospel and the Qur'an. Who fulfilleth His
> covenant better than Allah? Rejoice then in your bargain
> that ye have made, for that is the supreme triumph."

Notice that passage #71 also seems to reveal a belief that the
Jewish Torah and the Christian Gospel, and not just the Qur'an, also
promise eternal paradise to Jews and Christians who die while fighting
for their religions. Yet, Muslim warriors are more certain to gain this
reward because Allah favors them. If contemporary Muslim warriors
interpret passage #71 this way, then they might often be misunder-
standing the motives and purposes of Jewish and Christian adversaries.
Whether Muslim warriors would fight more or less aggressively, based
on such a belief, is open to speculation — and to scientific research.

BECAUSE COURAGE IN COMBAT PROVES TO ALLAH THAT YOU ARE A BELIEVER AND MAY ENABLE YOU TO BE A MARTYR ("WITNESS")[15]

> 72. (73/3:140-143) "If ye received a blow, the (disbelieving)
> people have received a blow the like thereof. These are
> (only) the vicissitudes which We cause to follow one anoth-
> er for mankind, to the end that Allah may know those who
> believe and may choose witnesses from among you; and
> Allah loveth not wrong-doers. And that Allah may prove
> those who believe, and may blight the disbelievers. Or
> deemed ye that ye would enter Paradise while yet Allah
> knoweth not those of you who really strive, nor knoweth
> those (of you) who are stedfast? And verily ye used to wish
> for death before ye met it (in the field). Now ye have seen it
> with your eyes!"

> 73. (388/67:19) "And those who believe in Allah and His
> messengers, they are the loyal; and the martyrs are with
> their Lord; they have their reward and their light; while as
> for those who disbelieve and deny Our revelations, they are
> owners of hell-fire."

BECAUSE THE BEHAVIORS AND BELIEFS OF SOME JEWS AND CHRISTIANS ARE BELLICOSE, SACRILEGIOUS, AND EVIL

Several passages promise rewards to Muslims who protect Muslim holy places from "unclean" people and from some, but not all, Jews and Christians who provoke war, commit abominations, and hold sacrilegious beliefs. While reading these passages, it is important to consider that the Qur'an does not routinely instruct Muslims to wage war on all Jews and Christians, but only upon some of their communities under certain circumstances. For example, passage #58, already presented, is one of many passages from chapter 17, titled "The Children of Israel," that admits that Muslims under Muhammad annihilated entire communities of Jews because "they commit abomination." Still, literalists and opportunists can readily ignore these qualifications and this historical context by focusing on only the most inflammatory phrases in passages such as these.

> 74. (147/9:28-30) "O ye who believe! The idolaters only are
> unclean. So let them not come near the Inviolable Place of
> Worship after this their year. If ye fear poverty (from the
> loss of their merchandise) Allah shall preserve you of His
> bounty if He will. Lo! Allah is Knower, Wise. Fight against
> such of those who have been given the Scripture as believe
> not in Allah nor the Last Day, and forbid not that which
> Allah hath forbidden by His messenger, and follow not the
> religion of truth, until they pay the tribute readily, being
> brought low. And the Jews say: Ezra is the son of Allah, and
> the Christians say: The Messiah is the son of Allah. That is
> their saying with their mouths. They imitate the saying of
> those who disbelieved of old. Allah (Himself) fighteth
> against them. How perverse are they?"

> 75. (102/5:62-66) "And thou seest many of them vying one
> with another in sin and transgression and their devouring
> of illicit gain. Verily evil is what they do. Why do not the
> rabbis and the priests forbid their evil-speaking and their

devouring of illicit gain? Verily evil is their handiwork. The
Jews say: Allah's hand is fettered. Their hands are fettered
and they are accursed for saying so. Nay, but both His
hands are spread out wide in bounty. He bestoweth as He
will. That which hath been revealed unto thee from thy
Lord is certain to increase the contumacy and disbelief of
many of them, and We have cast among them enmity and
hatred till the Day of Resurrection. As often as they light a
fire for war, Allah extinguisheth it. Their effort is for corruption in the land, and Allah loveth not corrupters. If only
the people of the Scripture would believe and ward off
(evil), surely We should remit their sins from them and
surely We should bring them into Gardens of Delight. If
they had observed the Torah and the Gospel and that which
was revealed unto them from their Lord, they would surely
have been nourished from above them and from beneath
their feet. Among them there are people who are moderate,
but many of them are of evil conduct."

Passage #75 has been presented in all of its length in order to
reinforce the facts that the Qur'an certainly has passages that could
be regarded by literalists and opportunists as anti-Semitic and anti-
Christian, but that the Qur'an does not always prescribe warfare,
and certainly not against all Jews and all Christians. "Among them
are people who are moderate." Contemporary government and military leaders would be well advised to keep this in mind in public
announcements and in making policy recommendations.

BECAUSE MUSLIMS WHO HELP IN CONQUERING OTHER RELIGIONS WILL HAVE THEIR SINS FORGIVEN AND WILL GAIN ETERNAL PARADISE

76. (398/61:9-13) "He it is who hath sent His messenger
with the guidance and the religion of truth, that He may
make it conqueror of all religion however much idolaters
may be averse. O ye who believe! Shall I show you a commerce that will save you from a painful doom? Ye should
believe in Allah and His messenger, and should strive for
the cause of Allah with your wealth and your lives. That is
better for you, if ye did but know. He will forgive you your
sins and bring you into Gardens underneath which rivers

> flow, and pleasant dwelling in Gardens of Eden. That is the
> supreme triumph. And (He will give you) another blessing
> which ye love: help from Allah and present victory. Give
> good tidings (O Muhammad) to believers."

Passages like #76 and #37, presented earlier, often fuel the ages-old and ongoing controversy as to whether the Qur'an prescribes warfare as a means for making Islam the only religion in the World or whether warfare should be used only to stop religious persecution of Muslims by non-Muslims. Notice that passage #75 does not include the word "war" and it does not explicitly prescribe war. However, its aggressive statements and use of the words "conqueror" and "victory" might tempt opportunists to use it as a battle cry for armed conflict that will not end until Islam prevails throughout the world.

SOME OTHER PRESCRIPTIONS AND PROSCRIPTIONS FOR MUSLIMS IN COMBAT

There are a number of other rather specific do's and don'ts for Muslims in combat in addition to the more general ones that are implicit in many of the Qur'anic verses that have already been presented. Collectively, these passages call for a considerable amount of discretion (called "discrimination" in Pickthall's translation) by Muslim warriors as to whom they should and should not attack, and the reasons for doing so. Notice, for instance, that passage #89 even uses the word "discriminate" and instructs Muslims to behave that way in peace and in war.

BE WILLING TO COMMIT YOUR WEALTH AND LIVES TO LONG EXPEDITIONS AGAINST DISTANT ENEMIES

Opportunists might ignore the fact that passages like the following often refer to specific expeditions that Muhammad ordered against distant cities such as Tabuk, on the trade route from Medina to Damascus. More worrisome is the possibility that opportunists will use passages like these to convince financiers to fund combat in distant foreign lands and persuade recruits to join in attacks in distant lands. Possibly this is what al-Qaeda strategist Dr. Ayman al-Zawahiri and others did with Osama bin Laden in the events that lead to the terrorist attacks of 9/11/2001 and, subsequently, while both of them participated in fighting in Afghanistan against the U.N. forces that were sent there in October 2001.[16]

> 77. (149/9:41-42) "Go forth, light-armed and heavy-armed,
> and strive with your wealth and your lives in the way of
> Allah! That is best for you if ye but knew. Had it been a
> near adventure and an easy journey they had followed thee,
> but the distance seemed too far for them. Yet will they
> swear by Allah (saying): If we had been able we would
> surely have set out with you. They destroy their souls, and
> Allah knoweth that they verily are liars."

BE STEADFAST, OBEDIENT, LOYAL, DESPITE BEING HEAVILY OUTNUMBERED

To be steadfast (spelled "stedfast" in Pickthall) probably is the most pronounced personal quality that is demanded of Muslim combatants, followed closely by obedience and loyalty to Allah, and a willingness to fight "harshly," even brutally, against enemy forces and their supporters, until religious persecution ends and Islam is free to flourish. The Qur'an informs its believers that these qualities are crucial because Muslim warriors will be greatly outnumbered by enemy forces. Predictably, the opposite qualities are disparaged: cowardice, retreating, and a conciliatory attitude in the form of premature calls for peace by the Muslims in the thick of battle. The Qur'an warns Muslim soldiers that the enemy will outnumber them by at least 2:1 or even 10:1. Yet Muslims will win if they are steadfast, obedient, loyal, and willing to fight "in the way of Allah" because Allah will intercede on their behalf once they display these qualities to him in battle. And besides this, the disbelievers lack "intelligence."

> 78. (73/3:146) "And with how many a prophet have there
> been a number of devoted men who fought (beside him).
> They quailed not for aught that befell them in the way of
> Allah, nor did they weaken, nor were they brought low.
> Allah loveth the stedfast."

> 79. (142/8:45-46) "O ye who believe! When ye meet an
> army, hold firm and think of Allah much, that ye may be
> successful. And obey Allah and His messenger, and dispute
> not one with another lest ye falter and your strength depart
> from you; but be stedfast! Lo! Allah is with the stedfast."

80. (143/8:65-66) "O Prophet! Exhort the believers to fight. If there be of you twenty stedfast they shall overcome two hundred, and if there be of you a hundred stedfast they shall overcome a thousand of those who disbelieve, because they (the disbelievers) are a folk without intelligence. Now hath Allah lightened your burden, for He knoweth that there is weakness in you. So if there be of you a stedfast hundred they shall overcome two hundred, and if there be of you a thousand (stedfast) they shall overcome two thousand by permission of Allah. Allah is with the stedfast."

81. (362/47:21) "Obedience and a civil word. Then, when the matter is determined, if they are loyal to Allah it will be well for them."

82. (362/47:31) "And verily We shall try you till We know those of you who strive hard (for the cause of Allah) and the stedfast and till We test your record."

FIGHT HARSHLY, THAT IS YOUR DUTY, POSSIBLY INCLUDING DEGRADATION, MUTILATION, AND ANNIHILATION OF THE ENEMY

83. (156/9:123) "O ye who believe! Fight those of the disbelievers who are near to you, and let them find harshness in you, and know that Allah is with those who keep their duty (unto Him)."

84. (99/5:33) "The only reward of those who make war upon Allah and His messenger and strive after corruption in the land will be that they will be killed or crucified, or have their hands and feet on alternate sides cut off, or will be expelled out of the land. Such will be their degradation in the world, and in the Hereafter theirs will be an awful doom."

85. (122/7:4-5) "How many a township have We destroyed! As a raid by night, or while they slept at noon, Our terror came unto them. No plea have they, when Our terror came unto them, save that they said: Lo! We were wrong doers."

Some violence-oriented opportunists might use passages #83-85 to compel their followers to terrorize, degrade, and mutilate individual enemy soldiers and prisoners. If so, these passages would reinforce the violent actions that are described in passages #50-60.

DON'T RETREAT OR ALLOW OTHERS TO DO SO

Retreating while engaged in combat is prohibited in many of the passages that have already been presented. It is also despised in enemy forces.

> 86. (140/8:15-16) "O ye who believe! When ye meet those who disbelieve in battle, turn not your backs to them. Whoso on the day turneth his back to them, unless manoeuvring for battle or intent to join a company, he truly hath incurred wrath from Allah, and his habitation will be hell, a hapless journey's-end."

> 87. (366/48:22) "And if those who disbelieve join battle with you they will take to flight, and afterward they will find no protecting friend or helper."

KILL THOSE WHO DON'T OFFER PEACE

> 88. (88/4:91) "Ye will find others who desire that they should have security from you, and security from their own folk. So often as they are returned to hostility they are plunged therein. If they keep not aloof from you nor offer you peace nor hold their hands, then take them and kill them wherever ye find them. Against such We have given you clear warrant."

DON'T KILL THOSE WHO OFFER PEACE JUST BECAUSE THEY DON'T BELIEVE IN ALLAH (DISCRIMINATION PRINCIPLE)

> 89. (88/4:94) "O ye who believe! When ye go forth (to fight) in the way of Allah, be careful to discriminate, and say not unto one who offereth you peace: "Thou are not a believer," seeking the chance profits of this like (so that ye may despoil him). With Allah are plenteous spoils. Even thus (as he now is) were ye before; but Allah hath since then been gracious unto you. Therefore, take care to discriminate. Allah is even Informed of what ye do."

72

Honor Those Who Are First To Fight; Reject Late-Comers

There is a status hierarchy among Muslim fighters. It honors the veterans who were first to fight and it discredits latecomers.

> 90. (388/62:10) "And what aileth you that ye spend not in the way of Allah, when unto Allah belongeth the inheritance of the heavens and the earth? Those who spent and fought before the victory are not upon a level (with the rest of you). Such are greater in rank than those who spent and fought afterwards. Unto each hath Allah promised good. And Allah is Informed of what ye do."

> 91. (152/9:83) "If Allah bring thee back (from the campaign) unto a party of them and they ask of thee leave to go out (to fight), then say unto them: Ye shall never more go out with me nor fight with me against a foe. Ye were content with sitting still the first time. So sit still, with the useless."

Reward And Protect Persecuted Refugees, Especially Those Who Fight

Protection should be provided for Muslim refugees who have been steadfast when victimized by enemy combatants. Honor should be bestowed upon Muslim refugees who retaliate against the enemy, even more if they suffer again because of it.

> 92. (202/16:110) "Then lo! The Lord—for those who become fugitives after they had been persecuted, and then fought and were stedfast—lo! Thy Lord afterward is (for them) indeed Forgiving, Merciful,..."

> 93. (246/23:58-60) "Those who fled their homes for the cause of Allah and then were slain or died, Allah verily will provide for them a good provision. Lo! Allah, He verily is Best of all who make provision. Assuredly He will cause them to enter by an entry that they will love. Lo! Allah verily is Knower, Indulgent. That (is so). And whoso hath retaliated with the like of that which he was made to suffer and then hath (again) been wronged, Allah will succour him. Lo! Allah verily is Mild, Forgiving."

> 94. (393/59:8-9) "And (it is) for the poor fugitives who have been driven out from their homes and their belongings, who seek bounty from Allah and help Allah and His messenger. They are the loyal. Those who entered the city and the faith before them love those who flee unto them for refuge, and find in their breasts no need for that which hath been given them, but prefer (the fugitives) above themselves though poverty become their lot. And whoso is saved from his own avarice—such are they who are successful."

DON'T SEND ALL BELIEVERS INTO BATTLE

Not all believers should go to the battle site. Some should stay behind to pray and to warn other citizens of the battle.

> 95. (156/9:122) "And the believers should not all go out to fight. Of every troop of them, a party only should go forth, that they (who are left behind) may gain sound knowledge in religion, and that they may warn their folk when they return to them, so that they may beware."

EXEMPT THE BLIND, LAME, AND SICK FROM COMBAT

While the blind, lame, and sick are exempted from fighting, although not prohibited from doing so, paradise is offered to all of those who heed the call to war of Allah and Muhammad. At the same time, the Qur'an threatens a "painful doom" on deserters and possibly even resisters and pacifists, depending on how literally readers take the phrase "whoso turneth back."

> 96. (366/48:17) "There is no blame for the blind, nor is there blame for the lame, nor is there blame for the sick (that they go not forth to war). And whoso obeyeth Allah and His messenger, He will make him enter Gardens underneath which rivers flow; and whoso turneth back, him will He punish with a painful doom."

SPOILS OF WAR: BOOTY, CAPTIVES, AND PRISONERS OF WAR

"Spoils of War" is the title of one of the longest chapters (chapter 8) in the Qur'an, although that chapter deals with many other topics besides spoils of war. Throughout the Qur'an there are many passages that promise steadfast Muslim warriors that their courageous efforts in warfare will reward them with many spoils of war: booty, captives and prisoners of war. It leaves considerable ambiguity as to how these are distinguished from each other and how they are to be acquired, distributed, and managed. While reading the following passages, it can help to keep in mind that many Arab and pastoral societies of Muhammad's time practiced slavery, bondage, polygamy, hostage-taking, raiding, looting, and plundering for commercial purposes. Booty was not necessarily limited to inanimate objects and livestock. Captives could and often did include any and all enemy warriors who surrendered, as well as support personnel, and all of the civilians in the camps of the enemy and their allies, including the elderly, handicapped, children and women — especially prized if they were young and sexually attractive. Enemy combatants who surrendered could be executed, enslaved, ransomed, or treated in many other ways. Their metal weapons and armor had high commercial value.

Some passages in the Qur'an remind Muslim warriors that they are to enjoy fully the spoils of war so long as they allot one-fifth "for Allah" and the "Messenger" (Muhammad). Some scholars interpret this to mean that one-fifth of the spoils of war is to be used by the Islamic State for the commonweal.[17]

> 97. (366/48:20) "Allah promiseth you much booty that ye will capture, and hath given you this in advance, and hath withheld men's hands from you, that it may be a token for the believers, and that He may guide you on a right path."

> 98. (144/8:69) "Now enjoy what ye have won, as lawful and good, and keep your duty to Allah. Lo! Allah is Forgiving, Merciful."

> 99. (141/8:41) "And know that whatever ye take as spoils of war, lo! A fifth thereof is for Allah, and for the Messenger, and for the kinsman (who hath need) and orphans and the needy and the wayfarer, if ye believe in Allah and that which We revealed unto Our slave on the Day of Discrimination, the day when the two armies met. And Allah is Able to do all things."

> 100. (366/48:15) "Those who were left behind will say,
> when ye set forth to capture booty: Let us go with you.
> They fain would change the verdict of Allah. Say (unto
> them, O Muhammad): Ye shall not go with us. Thus hath
> Allah said beforehand. Then they will say: Ye are envious of
> us. Nay, but they understand not, save a little."

Some verses are quite specific about what can constitute appropriate booty for Muslim combatants and what captured enemy resources can be pillaged and destroyed at the whim of the victors. One passage (#17) that was presented earlier discourages Muslims from rejecting peace initiatives from their enemies solely in order to be able to capture enemy possessions. Notice, also, that the following passage (#101) contains a prohibition against booty being misappropriated by rich Muslims as a commodity for commercial purposes.

> 101. (393/59:5-7) "Whatsoever palm-trees ye cut down or left
> standing on their roots, it was by Allah's leave, in order that
> he might confound the evil-livers. And that which Allah gave
> as spoil unto His messenger from them, ye urged not any
> horse or riding-camel for the sake thereof, but Allah giveth
> His messenger lordship over whom He will. Allah is Able to
> do all things. That which Allah giveth as spoil unto His mes-
> senger from the people of the townships, it is for Allah and
> His messenger and for the near of kin and the orphans and
> the needy and the wayfarer, that it become not a commodity
> between the rich among you. And whatsoever the messenger
> giveth you, take it. And whatsoever he forbiddeth, abstain
> (from it). And keep your duty to Allah. Lo! Allah is stern in
> reprisal."

PRISONERS OF WAR

The Qur'an indicates that prisoners should be firmly secured and then, eventually, they should be either ransomed, or, if they "repent," they might be converted to Islam, allowed to remain in Muslim communities as taxpaying residents, or freed.

102. (143/8:67-70) "It is not for any Prophet to have captives until he hath made slaughter in the land. Ye desire the lure of this world and Allah desireth (for you) the Hereafter, and Allah is Mighty, Wise. Had it not been for an ordinance of Allah which had gone before, and awful doom had come upon you on account of what ye took. Now enjoy what ye have won, as lawful and good, and keep your duty to Allah. Lo! Allah is Forgiving, Merciful. O Prophet! Say unto those captives who are in your hands: If Allah knoweth any good in your hearts He will give you better than that which hath been taken from you, and will forgive you. Lo! Allah is Forgiving, Merciful."

Two of the other passages that deal with the topic of prisoners of war were already presented in an earlier section on "Goals and Three General Orders for Muslim Battle." They are repeated here for convenience and to indicate some of the "ordinances" that the Qur'an imposes upon Muslim combatants who have captured enemy fighters.

103. (145/9:5) "Then, when the sacred months have passed, slay the idolaters wherever ye find them, and take them (captive), and besiege them, and prepare for them each ambush. But if they repent and establish worship and pay the poor-due, then leave their way free. Lo! Allah if Forgiving, Merciful."

104. (361/47:4) "Now when ye meet in battle those who disbelieve, then it is smiting of the necks until, when ye have routed them, then making fast of bonds, and afterward either grace or ransom till the war lay down its burdens. That (is the ordinance)..."

Nothing in the Qur'an explicitly proscribes or prescribes that Muslim combatants harass, abuse, torture, or execute enemy prisoners. However, there are many passages that righteously describe how Muslims have inflicted great pain, if not torture, on disbelievers in various situations that are not explicitly part of a particular battle. Is it possible that passages like these could be regarded by literalists and opportunists as justifications for them to torture prisoners of war?

105. (412/69:30-37) "(It will be said): Take him and fetter him
And then expose him to hell-fire
And then insert him in a chain whereof the length is seventy cubits.
Lo! he used not to believe in Allah the Tremendous,
And urged not on the feeding of the wretched,
Thereof hath he no lover here this day,
Nor any food save filth
Which none but sinners eat."

106. (413/69:43-52) "It is a revelation from the Lord of the Worlds.
And if he had invented false sayings concerning Us,
We assuredly had taken him by the right hand
And then severed his life-artery,
And not one of you could have held Us off from him."
And lo! it is a warrant unto those who ward off (evil).
And lo! We know that some among you will deny (it).
And lo! it is indeed an anguish for the disbelievers.
And lo! it is absolute truth.
So glorify the name of thy Tremendous Lord."

107. (243/22:19-22) "These twain (the believers and the disbelievers) are two opponents who contend concerning their Lord. But as for those who disbelieve, garments of fire will be cut out for them; boiling fluid will be poured down on their heads. Whereby that which is in their bellies, and their skins will be melted; And for them are hooked rods of iron. Whenever, in their anguish, they would go forth from thence they are driven back therein and (it is said unto them); Taste the doom of burning."

Taken literally, the behaviors described in passages #105-107 certainly sound like torture. However, it should be repeated that they are not explicitly directed at prisoners of war of Muslim military forces although they might apply to prisoners of war as well as to others who are objectionable to Muslims. We can only hope that literalists, opportunists, and others will not use passages like these against prisoners — or anyone else, for that matter.

Regarding spoils of war, then, the Qur'an paints a vivid picture of plenteous spoils of war for all Muslim combatants who persevere until the victory is complete. Included in the picture are many enemy prisoners of war, whose treatment by Muslim victors may or may not be compassionate, depending on which verses are followed, as well as on one's point of view. There seems to be a tacit assumption that most of the spoils of war will accrue from the homelands of the enemy forces rather than from possessions that the enemy discards while retreating from Muslim lands. The Qur'an makes no mention of Muslims who become prisoners or of Muslim property that becomes spoils of war by falling into enemy hands, probably because the Qur'an does not recognize Muslim defeats or the possibility of defeats. The assumption seems to be that Muslims have always won in war and they will continue to win handsomely in war because they will fight according to the dictates of Allah, with few if any exceptions.

ENDING A WAR

If we consider that a war usually consists of one or more armed violent battles between adversaries, then the Qur'an does not provide instructions as to how a Muslim armed force should end one discrete battle, other than to say (in passages already presented) that the enemy should be thoroughly routed, booty confiscated and enjoyed, and prisoners firmly secured. For ending an entire war, however, there are a number of relevant passages that specify one or more of the following conditions, some of which were mentioned previously in discussing "Goals and Three General Orders For Muslim Battles:" the enemy inclines to peace, an end of religious persecution of Muslims, religion for Allah, conqueror of all religion, tribute is paid, wrongdoers are punished or they cease to exist, enemies are brought low, the enemy desists, the enemy surrenders.

---

108. (143/8:61-62) "And if they incline to peace, incline thou also to it, and trust in Allah. Lo! He is the Hearer, the Knower. And if they would deceive thee, then lo! Allah is sufficient for thee. He it is Who supporteth thee with His help and with the believers."

---

109. (141/8:39) "And fight them until persecution is no more, and religion is all for Allah. But if they cease, then lo! Allah is Seer of what they do."

---

110. (147/9:28-29) "O ye who believe! The idolaters only are unclean. So let them not come near the Inviolable Place of Worship after this their year. If ye fear poverty (from the loss of their merchandise). Allah shall preserve you of His bounty if He will. Lo! Allah is Knower, Wise. Fight against such of those who have been given the Scripture as believe not in Allah nor the Last Day, and forbid not that which Allah hath forbidden by His messenger, and follow not the religion of truth, until they pay the tribute readily, being brought low."

111. (398/61:9-11) "He it is who hath sent His messenger with the guidance and the religion of truth, that He may make it conqueror of all religion however much idolaters may be averse. O ye who believe! Shall I show you a commerce that will save you from a painful doom? Ye should believe in Allah and His messenger, and should strive with your wealth and your lives. That is better for you, if ye did but know."

112. (366/49:16) "Say unto those of the wandering Arabs who were left behind: Ye will be called against a folk of mighty prowess,[18] to fight them until they surrender; and if ye obey, Allah will give you a fair reward; but if ye turn away as ye did turn away before, He will punish you with a painful doom."

Reading passage #112, and without considering its historical context, some readers might wonder whether this passage could be regarded as something of a call to arms by some alienated, contemporary proponents who are in exile from their homeland and who are angry at one or more nations of "mighty prowess." This passage calls on "wandering Arabs" to "fight them until they surrender." This condition could be very different from other conditions that are mentioned in passages of the Qur'an, such as fighting an enemy until religious persecution ends. In fact, the next passage (#113) seems to say that Muslims can continue fighting an enemy force who has "wrongdoers" even if "persecution is no more," "religion is for Allah," and the enemy has desisted.

113. (50/2:193) "And fight them until persecution is no more, and religion is for Allah. But if they desist, then let there be no hostility except against wrongdoers."

Taken literally, a passage like this raises the prospect that literalists and opportunists could believe that they are compelled by the Qur'an to continue to wage war against people whom they believe to be "wrongdoers" until there are no more wrongdoers, as vague as that word is in the Qur'an, and as troubling as that word might be to believers. Given ambiguities like these, is it really any wonder that war has been a frequent undertaking of various Muslim military leaders since Muhammad's time? Is it any wonder that some Muslims in the world today can claim that the Qur'an obligates their violence against at least some of the "disbelievers" in the world whom they consider to be "wrongdoers?"

MIRACLES, NATURE, TOXINS, AND AIR ATTACKS AS WAYS TO END WARS?

There are occasional passages in the Qur'an that attest that Allah occasionally saves his believers from precarious situations by allowing natural events such as sandstorms, hurricanes, plagues, and other phenomena to confound or destroy their enemies. In fact, one passage in the Qur'an might suggest to some adherents that Allah once allowed an airborne attack of toxic substances to defeat an overwhelming enemy force and end a war. Pickthall, a devout Muslim, has written that the following passage refers to a famous historical event that took place at Mecca, Muhammad's birthplace, in the year of his birth, about 571. Miraculously, Mecca and Muhammad's tribe, the Quraysh, were saved from near certain defeat by the Abyssinian ruler Abraha (whose army used an elephant during the siege) when his army was suddenly attacked by "flying creatures which pelted them with stones of baked clay."

> 114. (450/105:1-5) "In the name of Allah, the Benificient, the Merciful.
> Hast thou not seen how thy Lord dealt with the owners of the Elephant?
> Did He not bring their stratagem to naught,
> And send against them swarms of flying creatures,
> Which pelted them with stones of baked clay,
> And made them like green crops devoured (by cattle)?"

These verses constitute the entire chapter (#105) of the Qur'an. This chapter, named "The Elephant," is one of the most widely rec-

81

ognized chapters in the Qur'an among Muslims. This is because of its brevity, its appeal to Muslim children (who readily memorize and recite it to other children and adults), and its several fascinating, if not fantastic, allegations about a well-documented confrontation between two armies that had obvious consequences for the eventual emergence of Islam once Muhammad reached adulthood.[19]

Pickthall mentions two different interpretations of these "swarms of flying creatures." One interpretation contends that "an outbreak of smallpox in the camp" of the enemy is what really destroyed them. Another interpretation is that they were "insects carrying infection."[20] Is it possible that a Qur'anic passage such as this could suggest to some opportunists and other proponents of the Qur'an a hope for modern day miracles like this? Could a passage like this even be taken as an endorsement for the use of airborne attacks that would inflict toxic substances — smallpox, for instance — as last gasp ways to forestall defeat in battle or to win wars conclusively? Hopefully the answer is negative. Hopefully passages like this would not and will not be used in order to promote biological, chemical, or nuclear warfare. But, it might be prudent to at least consider the possibility and to try to reduce it. Chapter 7 suggests some of the ways to accomplish this.

While these observations might seem to be too speculative, morbid, and even a little paranoid, perhaps they are worth considering in light of some other facts about the content of the Qur'an and the history of Islamic warfare, including Muhammad's personal experiences as a warrior. The Qur'an has quite a few passages that testify to how Allah occasionally sends landslides, sandstorms, hurricanes, and other destructive forms of nature to punish people who disbelieve the Qur'an and Islam.[21] The Qur'an also has several verses that remind Muslims of the importance of assuring that their water and food supplies have not been tainted. In at least one instance, tainted water is used to torment a disbeliever.[22] In addition to these passages, there is another incident that involves poisoning and that is very famous in the history of Islam because Muhammad himself was one of the victims. While the incident is not portrayed explicitly in the Qur'an, it is often discussed and debated by educated Muslims and by scholars of Islam. Pickthall describes it this way:

> "In the seventh year of the Hijrah the Prophet led a cam-
> paign against Kheybar, the stronghold of the Jewish tribes
> in North Arabia, which had become a hornets' nest of his

enemies. The forts of Kheybar were reduced one by one....It was at Kheybar that a Jewess prepared for the Prophet poisoned meat, of which he only tasted a morsel without swallowing it, then warned his comrades that it was poisoned. One Muslim, who had already swallowed a mouthful, died immediately, and the Prophet himself, from the mere taste of it, derived the illness which eventually caused his death. The woman who had cooked the meat was brought before him. When she said that she had done it on account of the humiliation of her people, he forgave her."[23]

An even more specific and dramatic account of this poisoning is described by the noted scholar of Islam, Maxime Rodinson, who goes so far as to name the girl, Zaynab, who poisoned Muhammad:

"Another Jewish girl was less easily won. Her name was Zaynab; she had seen her father, uncle and husband killed. Ordered to prepare a roast lamb for the Prophet's dinner, she found out which part he liked best. It was the shoulder. She poisoned it, and the rest of the meat with it. Thinking that the first mouthful tasted strange, Muhammad spat it out; however Bishr, one of his Companions, swallowed the meat and died of it. The Prophet questioned Zaynab. 'You know what you have done to my people,' she replied. 'I said to myself: If he is a prophet, he will know [about the poison], and if he is an earthly king, I shall be rid of him.' Muhammad forgave her."[24]

Hopefully, knowledge about this famous incident of poisoning of Islam's second most revered figure would not and will not in any way suggest to opportunists that poison should be used against contemporary adversaries in order to somehow avenge the use of poison against Muhammad more than 1,300 year ago. Certainly, we can hope that retribution of this nature, and imitation of any poisoning, would be discouraged by the testimony that Muhammad forgave the person who poisoned him and who killed one of his comrades. These are matters worth pondering. These are the kinds of possible misuses of events in Islamic history that we should guard against. Other events in Islamic military history that might be used by some opportunists to provoke acts of violence in the future will be described in the chapters that follow.

AN ASIDE ON THE *HADITH*:
ISLAM'S SECOND MOST IMPORTANT BOOK

As mentioned several times in Chapter 1, the *Hadith* (also referred to as the *Sunnah* or the *Sunna*) is widely regarded as the second most important book in Islam, after the Qur'an. Purportedly it consists of "the words, the actions and the silent approval of Muhammad" in the course of his everyday life as recalled by some of his followers to other followers over the course of hundreds of years.[25] Some scholars believe that the Hadith is essential reading in order to understand the Qur'an and to carry out the commandments of Islam. Other scholars question the Hadith's historical authenticity. Paul Fregosi, while not an unbiased critic, claims that much of the Hadith has been challenged regarding its authenticity ever since it started. He claims that Muhammad himself had some of his followers punished for making false entries into the Hadith. It had grown to such excessive length scarcely one hundred years after Muhammad's death that one of its most venerated compilers, Imam al-Bukhari, had more than 590,000 of its 600,000 verses excised and destroyed as being apocryphal.[26]

For many readers the Hadith is less inspiring and less easy to use than is the Qur'an. It is very long, complex in its structure and internal references, and much less poetic and memorable in its style and imagery than is the Qur'an. Some editions and translations of the Hadith require nine volumes of more than eighty "books" and more than six thousand "chapters," some of which contain a profusion of rather disparate verses. By contrast, the Qur'an often is contained in one compact paperback volume or in one cassette audiotape. And so it is not surprising to find that the Hadith is much less popular than is the Qur'an in the daily lives of many Muslims. Unlike the Qur'an, the Hadith is not required recitation during the five daily prayers. It also is not so surprising that it is the Qur'an, not the Hadith, that has been quoted publicly by Muslim political and military leaders, including Osama bin Laden, Mullah Omar, and Saddam Hussein, to exhort their followers to do battle against non-Muslims (as quoted in Chapter 1). And it usually is the Qur'an, rather than the Hadith, that Muslim fighters hold aloft with their Kalashnikov rifles when they try to justify acts of violence against non-Muslims. Then too, it is the Qur'an – not the Hadith – that the perpetrators of the 9-11-2001 attack on the World Trade Center and the Pentagon left behind in their vehicles and in their apartments.

And yet, even if the Hadith is less common and less influential to

many Muslims than is the Qur'an, it still could be sufficiently influential to enough Muslims, particularly to powerful Muslim leaders, that
its directives regarding war, terror, and peace could be worth knowing, particularly if they contradict the Qur'an. Therefore it is worth
asking: Are the Hadith's directives similar to the Qur'an's directives
regarding war, terror, and peace?

With this question in mind, I read and analyzed a widely accepted version of the Hadith, Khan's "The Translation of the Meanings of
Sahih Al-Bukhari," Volumes 1-9, as well as Imam Nawawi's version,
Gardens of the Righteous, using the same procedures that I used to
read and analyze the Qur'an, as described in Chapter 1.[27]

WAR DIRECTIVES IN THE HADITH AND IN THE QUR'AN

I found that less than five percent of the Hadith's books, chapters,
and verses deal with war, terror, or peace between Muslim and non-
Muslim nations. Very noteworthy is the fact that almost all of this material deals with war, rather than with terror, or peace. Several of
Muhammad's most famous battles (that will be discussed in Chapter 3
of this book), including Badr, The Trench, and Hudaybiya, are recounted at some length in the Hadith. Book 53 ("The Book of Jihad") contains
many of the relevant passages about war, followed by Book 51 ("The
Book of Conditions"), Book 57 ("The Book of Al-Maghazi") and Book 80
("The Book of Punishments for those who Wage War Against Islam").
Even these books, however, have many chapters that do not obviously
deal with the subjects of war, terror, and peace. As with the Qur'an
itself, much of the Hadith deals with topics as diverse as personal
hygiene and clothing, Muslim social and sexual relations, feeding and
selling of livestock, teaching religion to slaves, observing fasts and holy
days, and behaving in the "way of Allah" in order to attain Paradise.

Regarding war, the Hadith's verses generally reinforce many of
the Qur'an's verses on some of the topics that have been analyzed here
in Chapter 2, such as the rules for distributing war booty, and guidelines for determining which members of the Muslim community
should and should not participate in military jihad. For example, verse
1206 of chapter 2, book 53 of the Hadith says that "...Allah guarantees
that He will admit the *Mujahid* in His Cause into Paradise if he is killed,
otherwise He will return him to his home safely with rewards and war
booty." This directive reinforces several passages of the Qur'an such as
passages #70 and 71 that are presented earlier in this Chapter regarding motivations for Muslims to fight and war booty, although the

Hadith verse also promises Muslims that they will be returned to their homes and that they will receive some war booty if they do not become martyrs by dying in battle in the cause of Allah. Another example of the Hadith reinforcing the Qur'an involves the proper motivation for Muslims to engage in military jihad. Verse 1218 of the Hadith states that: "Narrated Abu Musa: A man came to the Prophet and asked, 'A man fights for war booty; another fights for fame, and a third fights for showing off; which of them fights in Allah's Cause?' The Prophet said, 'He who fights that Allah's Word (i.e. Allah's Religion of Islamic Monotheism) be superior, fights in Allah's Cause.'" In doing so this passage in the Hadith reinforces the Qur'an's passages (#37, 40, and 41 that are presented earlier in this Chapter) that Muslims should fight for Allah's cause. However, the Hadith's passage also specifies that Muslim combatants should not fight for war booty, for fame, or for "showing off." A third example relates to terror. It is one of the few passages in the Hadith that explicitly mentions terror. Verse #1279 says: "Narrated Abu Huraira: Allah's Messenger said, ' I have been sent with the shortest expressions bearing the widest meanings, and I have been made victorious with terror (cast in the hearts of the enemy), and while I was sleeping, the keys of the treasures of the world were brought to me and put in my hand.'" As such, this verse is similar to Qur'anic passages #50-53 that appear earlier in this Chapter in its endorsement of terror against the enemies of Islam. And yet the Hadith's verse also goes somewhat further than the Qur'an's by having Allah's Prophet, Muhammad, admit that he personally used terror against Islam's enemies and that he benefited from it.

While there are obvious similarities between the Qur'an's and the Hadith's verses on some of the topics that involve war, it is also true that the Hadith has much less to say than does the Qur'an about many topics including peace, peace treaties, ways to end wars, conditions that require Muslims fight, strategies and tactics for Muslim warfare, how Muslim combatants should behave before, during, and after battles against non-Muslims, and treatment of enemy prisoners of war.

Probably even more important than these similarities and omissions is the fact that the Hadith's verses rarely if ever contradict or neutralize the Qur'an's verses regarding war. For instance, the Hadith would contradict the Qur'an if it allowed Muslims to call out for peace whenever they are winning in battle against non-Muslims. But the Hadith does not do this. Furthermore, just like the Qur'an, the Hadith does not prohibit Muslims from taking war booty or from destroying non-Muslim communities whose defenders have been vanquished in battle. Neither the Hadith nor the Qur'an prohibits Muslims from entering into honorable treaties with non-Muslims when they are proposed by the non-Muslims.

It also is true that quite a few of the Hadith's verses extend beyond comparable verses of the Qur'an without contradicting the Qur'an. These extensions, elaborations, and extrapolations in the Hadith beyond the Qur'an can be particularly valuable to current government and military leaders who must deal with proponents of both the Qur'an and the Hadith. For this reason, more than a dozen of these extensions will be mentioned next.[28]

BEYOND THE QUR'AN

Here are some of the pronouncements and directives about war in the Hadith that extend beyond the passages about war in the Qur'an. Current and future military and government leaders might be wise to take note of these and to anticipate how these items might be used by their proponents to motivate combatants and to make strategic and tactical decisions.

1. Regarding the timing of attacks by Muslim military forces: Muhammad encouraged his followers to attack in the forenoon and in the afternoon (verses #1208-1209). But sometimes it is also permissible for Muslims to be patient and to wait until after the sun has declined before they launch their attacks (verse #1276).

2. Regarding wounds suffered in battle: When Muhammad suffered a stab wound to one of his fingers during battle, he simply said "You are just a finger that bled, and what you got is in Allah's Cause" (verse #1215). Muhammad also said that "...Whoever is wounded in Allah's Cause.... his wound having the colour of blood but its smell will be the smell of musk [perfume]" (verse #1213).

3. Regarding "martyrs" in military jihad: Chapter 15 of Book 53 of the Hadith has Muhammad extending martyrdom to Muslim combatants who die because of plague, other illnesses, drownings, and accidents while fighting in Allah's Cause.

4. Regarding special status to combatants who are willing to perform reconnaissance before battles: Muhammad gave special commendation to Muslim combatants who were willing to perform reconnaissance of enemy positions in order to provide fresh intelligence to Muhammad before he launched attacks (verse #1233).

5. Regarding the importance of equipment suppliers, water carriers, nurses, night sentries, and rear guards: Muhammad also commended his followers who participated in military jihad by serving as suppliers of equipment, water carriers, nurses, night sentries, and rear guards (verses #1236, 1244-1247).

6. Regarding war booty for the leader's family: Muhammad gave some forms of war booty to his family as "...their yearly expenditure and spend what remained thereof on arms and horses to be used in Allah's Cause" (verse #1254).

7. Regarding war booty for other purposes: Several verses of the Hadith (#1309, 1312, 1313, 1323, 1326) indicate that Muhammad was very concerned about his followers misappropriating war booty. He warned them about confiscating too much war booty for their personal use and about stealing war booty from the Muslim state.

8. Regarding fighting against Jews and Turks: Verses #1261 and 1262 quote Muhammad as explicitly calling for attacks against Jews and Turks, respectively.

9. Regarding killing enemy combatants by fire: Verse #1268 quotes Muhammad ordering the capture and killing of two specific enemy soldiers by their names, but he prohibited his followers from burning them to death because "...as punishment with fire is done by none except Allah...." Verse #1294 reinforces this prohibition against using fire in order to kill enemy combatants.

10. Regarding the chain of command and the fallibility of commands given by imams: Verses #1269, 1270, and 1275 quote Muhammad as indicating that Allah's orders

supercede those of the imams, that imams should only give orders to their followers that the followers are able to accomplish, and that followers must obey their imam's orders "...unless these orders involve one in disobedience [to Allah]; but if an act of disobedience [to Allah] is imposed, one should not listen to or obey it."

11. Regarding Muslims taking copies of the Qur'an into hostile countries: "Allah's Messenger forbade the people to travel to a hostile country carrying [copies of] the Qur'an" (verse #1283).

12. Regarding Muslim attacks that might kill the women and children of the enemy: Verses #1292 and 1293 quote Muhammad saying that he "...disapproved the killing of women and children" and that he was concerned that Muslim attacks at night against enemy communities might inflict this kind of what is currently called "collateral damage."

13. Regarding the burning of the enemy's houses and date palms: Verse #1296 indicates that Muhammad personally ordered one of his followers to have one hundred-fifty Ahmas cavalrymen burn the houses and date palms of an enemy tribe. Once this was accomplished "The Prophet invoked Allah to bless the horses and the men of Ahmas five times."

14. Regarding freeing of captives: Verse #1301 reads as follows: "Narrated by Abu Musa: The Prophet said, Free the captives, feed the hungry and pay a visit to the sick."

15. Regarding the killing of enemy spies: Verse #1304 recounts a time when Muhammad detected that an enemy spy had been traveling with his expedition but had just escaped without being discovered. "The Prophet said (to his companions) 'Chase and kill him.' Salama bin Al-Akwa did just that. Then he reported that "The Prophet then gave me the belongings of the killed spy (in addition to my share of the war booty)."

16. Regarding a naval expedition and an invasion of "Caesar's city:" Muhammad offered Paradise to "the first

batch of followers who will undertake a naval expedition"
and he promised to forgive the sins of "The first army
amongst my followers who will invade Caesar's city...."
(verse #1260).

17. Regarding the future of Muslim warfare: Several fascinating verses in the Hadith (#1345-1347) indicate that
Muhammad predicted that his followers would face much
treachery and suffering at the hands of their enemies as
well as some remarkable successes after his death, including the conquest of Jerusalem.

"...He said, 'Count six signs that indicate the approach of the
Hour: my death, the conquest of Jerusalem, a plague that
will afflict you (and kill you in great numbers) as the plague
that afflicts sheep, the increase of wealth to such an extent
that even if one is given one hundred Dinars, he will not be
satisfied; then an affliction which no Arab house will escape,
and then a truce between you and Bani Al-Asfar (i.e. the
Byzantines) who will betray you and attack you under eighty
flags. Under each flag will be twelve thousand soldiers.'"

18. Regarding non-Muslims on the Arabian Peninsula:
For current and future leaders in government and military
service, possibly the most noteworthy of the Hadith's
thousands of verses is verse #1305. For it is this verse that
quotes Muhammad on his deathbed, barely having the
energy to issue his final three orders. Curiously the witness
who narrated this verse, Sa'id bin Jubair, admits to having
forgotten Muhammad's third order. He remembers that
Muhammad's second order was to "respect and give gifts to
the foreign delegates as you have seen me dealing with
them" And he also remembers the order that Muhammad
issued first as he lay dying: "expel *Al-Mushrikun* (pagans,
idolaters and disbelievers in the Oneness of Allah and in his
Messenger Muhammad) from the Arabian Peninsula...."

Could it be that the first of Muhammad's last three orders — to
expel *Al-Mushrikun* from the Arabian Peninsula — has become the first
commandment in the minds and hearts of many of the Muslims
throughout the world today who fight so violently against non-Muslims?

Could it be that this commandment will never change? Could it be that leaders of government and military forces would be wise to never overlook these possibilities?

LOOKING BACK AND LOOKING AHEAD

The one hundred-fourteen passages of the Qur'an that have been presented in this chapter provide plenty of guidance to Muslim combatants, but they also allow considerable room for ambiguity and differing interpretations regarding how, when, where, and why Muslims should wage war or settle for peace. While there is no reason to believe that the Qur'an was ever assembled by Muhammad's followers to be a guidebook for international peace and war, the one hundred-fourteen passages just presented reveal that the Qur'an provides considerable instruction and guidance to its proponents on these matters. Still, there are many common topics in diplomatic and military affairs regarding peace and war that are not broached in the Qur'an. Among the topics not addressed are: espionage and sabotage, emissaries, protocols, procedures for negotiating differences between and among nations, reparations, and ways to achieve permanent peace. Common topics in military affairs that are not addressed include: recruitment, selection, and training of combatants, logistics, tactics (other than to fight as cohesive units), military organization and ranks, selection and maintenance of weapons, treatment of casualties, repatriation of deserters, and conscription of Muslims other than able-bodied males as combatants. The Qur'an makes little if any reference to naval warfare, guerrilla warfare, night warfare, mountain warfare, jungle warfare, or to any types of warfare other than raids on caravans and rather conventional land warfare, including sieges of towns and cities, by battalion to regiment-sized infantry and cavalry units in xeric environments. Of course, this is the kind of warfare that was characteristic among many tribes that inhabited the Arabian Peninsula during Muhammad's life (to be discussed in next chapter). This is the kind of warfare that he came to know and to command. This is the kind of warfare that ultimately helped to spread Islam far beyond the Arabian Peninsula. Nonetheless, this chapter has shown us that the Qur'an addresses a rather impressive range of topics related to war — if not to peace — between and among nations. This is all the more reason to be familiar with the Qur'an and to strive to understand its proponents.

The next three chapters consider how closely these passages

from the Qur'an are manifested in the military history of Muhammad and of Islam. This is done in order to help military and political leaders anticipate how armed forces comprised of ardent reciters of the Qur'an and admirers of Muslim military history might behave regarding peace, and in warfare, in the years ahead.

---

[1] For easy reference, each of the passages that I have excerpted from Pickthall's translation of the Qur'an is presented in this Chapter with a chronological number, the number of the page on which it appears in Pickthall's translation, the chapter number, and the verse number of the passage in the Qur'an.

[2] Muhammad Abdel Haleem, *Understanding The Qur'an: Themes and Style*. London: I.B. Taurus Publishers, 1999, p. 62. Haleem's interpretation of the Qur'an, while valuable and sincere, is very liberal, defensive, and apologetic. As discussed in later chapters, some of his statements about the Qur'an seem unfounded, if not factually incorrect, to my way of thinking.

[3] For a recent review of the four "Basic Principles of the Law of War" that have been adopted by the Hague and Geneva Conventions see "Basic Principles of the Law of War," The Center for Law and Military Operations, *Marine Corps Gazette*, October, 2002, pp. 36-37.

[4] "Mankind" is a word that is used variably and ambiguously in the Qur'an, or at least in English language translations of the Qur'an, a subject that will be examined further in Chapter 6 regarding literary contexts. At some places in the Qur'an it seems to refer to all human beings; at other times to all believers in monotheism, and at other times, to only those who believe in Allah and practice Islam — true Muslims. Majid Khadduri, for instance, says that the Arabic word "*Umma*," which is so important in Islam, refers to the community of all Muslims and is usually translated into English as "nation" or "brotherhood." (Khadduri, 1955: p. 4). Several Muslim scholars that I spoke with about this passage (#11) differed in how they interpreted the word "mankind." One of them, Najih Lazar, said in personal conversation with me that "mankind" in the Qur'an can refer to three categories of people: all human beings on Earth (*nass*), only the people who are believers (*amanu*), or only the people who are non-believers (*kafeerun*). Lazar felt quite certain that this passage denotes nass — all human beings on Earth, regardless of their religious orientation. In passage #7, however, "mankind" seems to refer only to believers.

[5] *Holy Bible* (King James Version). Gideon's International, 1978. 4:14. pp. iv, 1257.

[6] The meaning of the term "Jinn" in the Qur'an is the subject of considerable disagreement among some scholars. Esposito (1998: 254) says that it refers to what Westerners think of as "genies" — magical creatures that are part human and part angel. On the other hand, Pickthall (1955: 360, 382, 384, 416) says that the term has different meanings at different places in the Qur'an and that it often is used as a derogatory term for "tricky foreigners" including Jewish tribes that oppose Muslim tribes in various ways.

[7] Pickthall, 1955: 32-33. Similar renderings of the origins of war and peace in the Qur'an are presented in Rodinson and Khadduri and are discussed in Chapter 6 regarding differing interpretations of the Qur'an.

[8] I have been unable to find in the Qur'an evidence that supports this contention by some scholars of Islam that Muslims are obliged to offer peaceful resolutions to the conflicts with their oppressors and, if necessary, to consider emigrating to distant lands in order to escape persecution, prior to engaging in warfare.

[9] It is not clear in the Qur'an as to whether religious persecution of Muslims by non-Muslims constitutes war, although it probably does. Certainly the prescribed reactions of Muslims under Allah's command to religious persecution can constitute war.

[10] Of course, it is worth considering that there would be no clear-cut winner in a war in which the proportionality principle was followed precisely and both forces were equivalent in all resources before warfare began.

[11] Dan Van Natta, Jr. and Daniel Johnston, "Attacks Sow Fears of al-Qaida Resurgence," *The New York Times*, October 18, 2002, p. 1.

[12] Passages with the word "terror" in the Qur'an are analyzed in depth in one of my articles, "Terror and Terrorism in the Koran," 2002. This article explains that while the Qur'an has at least nine passages that describe how Muslim armies inflicted terror on enemy forces, their supporters, and their civilian communities, these acts where not primarily acts of terrorism, conducted by terrorists, so much as they were acts of military conquest conducted by Muslim military forces under the command of Muhammad. Also, for easier reading, I have italicized the word "terror" in passages #50-60 of the Qur'an that follow.

[13] Pickthall (pp. 61, 72, 74, 299-300, 393) explains these historical contexts very well. See Chapters 3-5 for descriptions of these and other battles in relation to pronouncements in the Qur'an.

[14] Esposito, 1998: p. 12 (regarding Muslims not qualifying as martyrs and gaining paradise if they intentionally get themselves killed in combat or only fight in order to gain paradise).

[15] Pickthall (1998: 73) says that "witness" and "martyr" are synonyms in the Qur'an.

[16] See Lawrence Wright's description of these events and the collaboration between Zawahiri and bin Laden in his article, "The Man Behind Bin Laden," *The New Yorker*, September 16, 2002.

[17] Pickthall, p. 141. Nothing in the Qur'an instructs believers on how the other four-fifths of the spoils are to be used.

[18] Pickthall (p. 366) inserts a footnote in conjunction with this verse saying that "this prophecy is taken to refer to the war with the Persian or the Byzantine empire." Notice that Pickthall calls it a "war" rather than a battle. Of course, literalists and opportunists may ignore contextual considerations like this — a point that I make throughout this book.

[19] The popularity of "The Elephant" chapter in the Qur'an was explained to me by several knowledgeable Muslims in the U.S. including Najih Lazar, a member of the Rhode Island Islamic Center, Wakefield, Rhode Island, December 6, 2002.

[20] Pickthall, p. 450.

[21] Chapter 17, verses 68-69, for example, mentions landslides, sandstorms, hurricanes as punishments inflicted on enemies by Allah.

[22] Chapter 14, verses 16-17. "Hell is before him, and he is made to drink a festering water. Which he sippeth but can hardly swallow, and death cometh unto him from every side while yet he cannot die, and before him is a harsh doom."

[23] Pickthall, pp. xxiii-xxiv.

[24] Rodinson, p. 254.

[25] Hamid, p. 1.

[26] Fregosi, pp. 48, 64.

[27] In addition to these two translations of the Hadith, I also used Khan's *"The Translation of the Meanings of Summarized Sahih Al-Bukhari."* All quotations from the Hadith that follow are from Khan's two books.

[28] Some readers might wonder about the historical authenticity of some of the passages of the Hadith that extend beyond the Qur'an. For instance, it seems unlikely that Muhammad would have ever called for a naval attack against "Caesar's city." And yet verse #1260 of the Hadith quotes Muhammad as saying exactly this. To the best of my knowledge, Muhammad had no experience with, or interest in, naval warfare. His political and military focus seemed to have been on the Arabian peninsula as far north as Tabuk — not across the Mediterranean Sea to Rome, to Athens, or even to Constantinople. On the other hand, the historical authenticity of specific passages in the Hadith, or in the Qur'an for that matter, might be irrelevant for contemporary proponents of these books who are trying to justify the use of terrorism and warfare against non-Muslims.

CHAPTER THREE

MUHAMMAD AS A MILITARY COMMANDER

"Both during his lifetime and throughout the following centuries,
Muhammad has served as the ideal model for Muslim life, providing the pattern that all believers are to emulate. He is, as some
Muslims say, the 'living Quran' — the witness whose behavior and
words reveal God's will. Thus the practices of the Prophet became
a material source of Islamic law alongside the Quran. Muslims
look to Muhammad's example for guidance in all aspects of life:
how to treat friends as well as enemies, what to eat and drink,
how to make love and war."[1]

This assessment of Muhammad's enduring and pervasive influence on the beliefs, values, and behaviors of Muslims is by one
of the most widely recognized scholars of Islam, John L.
Esposito, who is Professor of Religion, International Affairs, and
Islamic Studies and Director of the Center for Muslim-Christian
Understanding at Georgetown University in Washington, DC. Notice
that Esposito asserts that Muhammad is the "ideal model for Muslim
life" whose own behaviors are to be emulated by all Muslims in "all
aspects of life" including "how to treat friends as well as enemies" and
"how to make love and war." Certainly, this statement implies that
Muslims expect to have *enemies* as well as friends. It also implies that
Muslims expect to make *war* as well as make love. Esposito's statement also asserts that many Muslims consider Muhammad to be the
"living Quran" through which "God's will" is revealed. Both the
Qur'an and Muhammad's "practices" are the basis for Islamic law (a
topic that is discussed in some detail in Chapter 6).

Thus, it is appropriate to consider not just the Qur'an's instructions regarding peace and war (as we did in Chapter 2), but also to
consider Muhammad's practices in peace and war. This is the purpose
of this chapter. We will review some of the political and military
events in Muhammad's life that show us how Muhammad and his followers dealt with some of the principal groups that opposed them, in
light of the Qur'an's passages about peace, conflict, and war. Did
Muhammad and his followers fight according to the instructions in
the Qur'an? Some readers might think that this is a preposterous
question because the Qur'an was not compiled until after Muhammad

95

died (as discussed in Chapter 1). For these readers a more logical question might be: do the instructions in the Qur'an correspond to the way that Muhammad and the Muslims fought? As discussed in Chapter 1, the Qur'an was being revealed to Muhammad on many occasions from the year 610 until his death in 632. Some of these revelations occurred before he had followers. Other revelations occurred before he and his followers started fighting outsiders. Still other revelations occurred in the days immediately after some of his battles, or even *during* his battles. Thus, it is highly likely that the revelations that are presented in the Qur'an had great impact on Muhammad and his followers in peace, conflict, and war even though the revelations were not compiled in written form until after Muhammad's death.

Several caveats should be kept in mind while reading this chapter. This chapter is only a concise review of some of the highlights of Muslim military history while Muhammad was alive. It is not meant to be a full, comprehensive, or new rendering on these topics or on the battles that are briefly summarized and analyzed here. There are dozens of books for these purposes that describe Muhammad's life and battles in painstaking detail (sometimes in contradiction to each other). I focus on the armed conflicts and related negotiations that are often taught in Muslim schools and those that were especially consequential to Muslims and their opponents.[2]

I have tried to select and synthesize knowledge on these topics from a variety of sources that are widely respected, including authors with very different ideological and theoretical orientations about Islam, and from encyclopedias and other compendia.[3] Sometimes they vary from each other or disagree as to dates, spelling, and many other facts, let alone as to their interpretations of these facts. This concern is so important that Chapter 6 describes and discusses these and other interpretations of the Qur'an and of Islam. Consider for a moment the uncertainty of such a basic fact as Muhammad's birth year.

"No one knows exactly when Muhammad, who was to become the Prophet of Allah, was born. It was believed to have been during the reign of Khusro Anosharwan, that is before 579, which seems probable. It was said to have been in the Year of the Elephant — the year, that is, in which the birds of the air routed the army of Abraha before Mecca — but that is certainly untrue. The precise date, arrived at by means of some highly dubious calculations, varies between 567 and 573. The most commonly accepted year is 571."[4]

96

In fact, I found that the author of this passage, Maxime Rodinson, was often the most thorough, credible, and cautious analyst of Muhammad's life and the more than twenty military expeditions that Muhammad personally led during his life.[5] For this reason, much of the factual material in this chapter draws heavily on Rodinson, but by no means exclusively on him.

PEACE, CONFLICT, AND WAR IN AND AROUND ARABIA PRIOR TO MUHAMMAD

There is considerable variation (and sometimes blatant contra-diction) among many scholars regarding the frequency and lethality of warfare among human societies in and around the Arabian Peninsula at the time of Muhammad. It seems prudent to say that peace often was tenuous at best, conflict was common, and yet actual warfare was rather infrequent, brief, sometimes violent, and often inconclusive. This was particularly true of the nomadic Bedouin tribes that roamed the Arabian Peninsula in the years preceding Muhammad's birth. Often the "real" wars (i.e. "social conflict between organizations that possess trained and disciplined combat forces equipped with deadly weapons")[6] occurred on the periphery of Arabia as armies of the Persian, Byzantine, and Abyssinian empires clashed in efforts to preserve or extend their empires. These empires are depicted on Map 3-1.

Nomadic pastoralists, principally Bedouin tribes, constituted a considerable portion of the Arab population of the peninsula. They were pantheistic, worshipped a variety of places, animals, and forces of nature, and housed some of their sacred icons in and around the Ka'ba in Mecca. They often quarreled with each other over access to sacred shrines, oases, grazing lands, palm trees, and livestock. They raided each other's camps and settlements at the oases and along the caravan routes to Gaza, Damascus, and Baghdad. Sometimes power-ful merchants in the settlements bribed Bedouin tribes to protect their own caravans or to raid caravans of competing tribes and settlements, sharing in the booty. Weapons were rather primitive compared to the weapons of the Roman Empire. The xeric environment limited popu-lation and settlement size, density, and growth. Violent encounters usually lasted only a few minutes, or a few hours, at most, although the confrontations could drag on for weeks, even months. Casualties usually were limited, especially fatalities. Most combatants lived to quarrel, feud, and fight another day, for days upon days. This is the world that Muhammad experienced: first as a poor shepherd boy, then as a hostler in his uncle's caravans, and then in much more illustrious and influential statuses.

The settlements were hardly homogenous and peaceful places to live. Conflict was common among the many families, kin groups, sects, and tribes of Arabs, as well as Jews, Christian refugees, and

MAP 3-1

THE MIDDLE EAST
c. 570 A.D.

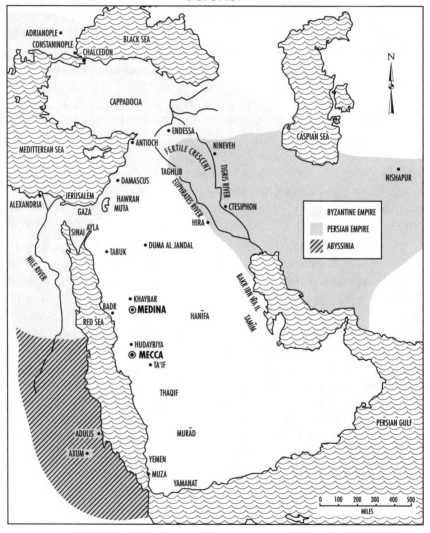

traders, slaves, minions, and people of uncertain ethnicity, orientation, and purpose. The threat of periodic raids by Persians, Byzantines, Abyssinians, and other military forces often aggravated endogenous conflict, fear, and suspicion within the larger cities, such as Mecca, rather than unify its polyglot communities. In Mecca, one clan, the Quraysh (one of many spellings for this clan) generally had the most power and prestige. However, the clan itself was factionalized according to family, wealth and occupation. Its power often was challenged by many other clans and factions within Mecca and from other Arab settlements. Given such a tumultuous and conflictory social stew, it is hardly surprising that the Qur'an so often describes conflicting religious beliefs, social mores, group relationships, threats, insults, fighting, booty, vengeance, and warfare, and far less often describes peace within and between societies.

MUHAMMAD IN PEACE, CONFLICT, AND WAR

For convenience, a capsule summary of commonly accepted dates and major events in Muhammad's life is given in Table 3-1 in order to serve as context for understanding Muhammad's experiences as they relate to the Qur'an on the subjects at hand.

At about the time of Muhammad's birth, Mecca was a growing city of about 40,000 people. It was situated near a caravan route that ran north-south about 45 miles inland and parallel to the eastern shore of the Red Sea, as represented in Map 3-2.

Its residents included unskilled laborers, farm workers, slaves, traders, merchants, scribes, craftsmen, artists, hostlers, and guards. They were members of various Arab families, kin groups, tribes, and sects, as well as Jewish families and clans, Christian refugees, and Africans. Slaves, which were quite common, had been captured in raids or purchased at foreign markets. To the extent that it was governed, it was governed by an oligarchy of the richest trading families, principally from the Quraysh tribe, while the other factions vied for political influence through coalitions, machinations, and intrigue. Quarrels were common about private and public property, privileges, civil rights, religious beliefs and freedom, and commerce. They often led to bitter feuds, shifting allegiances, and ad hoc coalitions.

The Prophet Muhammad was born into the clan that was often at the epicenter of this social turmoil. He was the posthumous son of Abdulla, a merchant from a prominent family of the Quraysh.[7] His

---

TABLE 3-1:
MUHAMMAD AS A MILITARY COMMANDER:
SOME APPROXIMATE DATES AND KEY EVENTS

570-571 Born in Mecca as a member of the Quraysh clan. Father deceased.

576-577 Mother dies. Muhammad is cared for by relatives and a Bedouin nurse.

577-587 Occasionally works as a shepherd boy and as a hostler on caravans.

595 Marries Khadija, a wealthy widow. Becomes a successful merchant.

610 Experiences first revelation while meditating in a cave at Mt. Hira.

619 Khadija dies.

622 *Hegira (Hirii):* Escapes with guards to Medina under pressure from Meccans.

624 Nakhla: Orders a raid on a caravan at Nakhla, which succeeds.

Badr: Leads small army on an ambush that becomes a stunning victory.

625 Uhud: Wounded and almost defeated while leading army in defense of Medina.

627 The Trench: Leads army that withstands Meccan attack outside Medina.

Directs the slaughter and enslaving of Banu Qurayza at Medina.

628 Hudaybiya: Negotiates a truce with Quraysh while trying to return to Mecca.

Khaybar: Poisoned by Zanab after the siege and sacking of Khaybar.

629 *Hajj:* Leads peaceful first pilgrimage into Mecca.

Mu'ta: Orders Muslim army into Palestine against Byzantines. This foray is repulsed.

630 *Al-Fat'h:* Leads 10,000 troops towards Mecca. Negotiates terms of surrender for Mecca. Occupies Mecca and establishes Islamic rule. Leads 20,000 troops to Tabuk, Palestine, to collect tribute.

632 Makes "Pilgrimage of Farewell" to Mecca. Dies in Medina.

---

mother died when he was about six years old. Orphaned, Muhammad became a poor shepherd boy who was nominally cared for by one grandfather and then by one uncle, a caravan merchant. Often Muhammad was left in the care of a Bedouin nurse. Muhammad would sometimes accompany his uncle on caravans to Syria and Yemen. He took care of the camels and livestock and learned the basics of the caravan trade. In time he gained a reputation for honesty that eventually led to his being hired by a wealthy widow, Khadija, to manage her business ventures. Around the year 595 Muhammad married Khadija, who was fifteen years older, and he began what is said to have been a very dedicated and prosperous marriage (until her

MAP 3-2
WESTERN ARABIAN PENINSULA
c. 570 A.D.

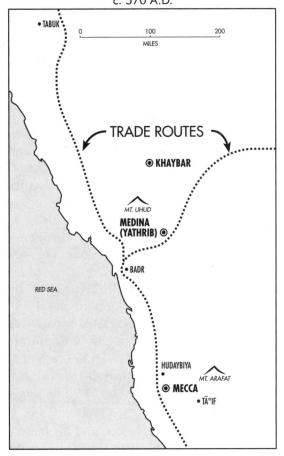

death, about 619). By 610 Muhammad was a middle-aged and successful merchant who was respected in Mecca. During a particularly intense heat wave, he retreated to meditate for several days, as was his custom, in a small cave at Mr. Hira on the outskirts of Mecca. There he experienced the first of his many revelations that he believed to be from Allah through the archangel Gabriel (as recounted in quotations from Pickthall in Chapter 1). Disturbed and uncertain about what to make of this experience, Muhammad confided in his wife and some close relatives, most of whom reassured him and encouraged him to continue. Over the next twelve years Muhammad experienced an increasing number of revelations and began reciting them in public. He witnessed a range of reactions: rapt attention by a growing number of followers, indifference by many others, alarm, mockery, and threats by others (especially by some of the richest merchants from his own clan, the Quraysh). Many critics objected to his increasingly strident condemnations of idol worship, his deviations from the scriptures of the early Jewish and Christian prophets, and his criticisms of slavery, the breaking of contracts and treaties, and sexual immorality.

By 622, Muhammad and his followers were under growing pressure and threats from some of the most powerful antagonists in Mecca. Word of these reactions and of his growing reputation as a preacher of reconciliation attracted interest among some of the leaders of tribes in the agricultural oasis city of Medina (Yathrib), about 240 miles from Mecca. Muhammad received overtures from some Medinans that he would be welcome in Medina as something of an arbiter and conciliator of quarrels among factions in that city. Under increasing threats to his life in Mecca, Muhammad encouraged more and more of his followers to emigrate to Medina in order to establish an enclave that would be protected from religious persecution. Many of them did this, although they initially considered the move to be temporary exile from Mecca, as did Muhammad. In September 622, hearing that he was about to be assassinated by some of the Quraysh, Muhammad fled Mecca at night with a few of his most trusted guards. He spent the first night in a cave outside Mecca and barely avoided being discovered by some of the Quraysh who were pursuing him. Thus began his famous flight *hegira (hirii)* to Medina — the birth of Islam to many of its followers.

By almost all accounts, Muhammad and his band of exiles were accepted quite well in Medina, except that they had some difficulty finding gainful employment and providing for their daily sustenance needs. Medina was a small, farming town situated around an oasis and surrounded by date palms and garden crops, lava fields, wadis, and rocky ridges. It was more self-reliant and much more isolated from trade routes than was Mecca. Intergroup conflicts often were easier to mediate and external threats were less frequent. Muhammad quickly became a mediator of disputes. This allowed him considerable freedom to administer to his growing band of followers and to develop the tenets and structure of a new religious-political system — Islam.

Exactly how and why Muhammad ordered the first armed expedition by his followers is the subject of centuries of rancorous debate. However, as we consider the most famous and consequential of his military operations, it can be useful to keep in mind that intergroup conflict in the forms of threats, feuds, vendettas, and armed attacks, both feigned and very real, were relatively common within many Arab settlements of Muhammad's time. They were spawned by economic competition for trade goods, temporary agricultural surpluses, and access to scarce oases, grazing lands, habitable terrain, smeltable metals, and livestock. These could be acquired more quickly through political coalitions and treaties, and by raids, than by the slower and more labor-intensive means of agricultural labor and commerce. And thus there were many conflicts which escalated into what Rodinson has called "private wars" that were "a matter of custom."[8] Often these private wars occurred when clan or tribal leaders in two different settlements were able to muster 20-200 men, including slaves, mercenaries, and other residents of their settlement, into an ad hoc private "army." They would be provided with whatever spare swords, bows and arrows, javelins, axes, body armor, horses, and camels that could be pressed into service. Thus armed, the impromptu raiding party or "army" would then move across the desert to an ambush site along a caravan route, or to the outskirts of the settlement where the adversary resided. Envoys would then be dispatched to the adversary's compound in the settlement, essentially challenging the adversary to meet certain demands, usually in the form of bribes or tribute, or to "come out and fight."

Whether a fight occurred often depended on how long the aggressor had to wait for a definitive response and whether the adversary was able to raise a private army of his own to meet the challenge. If the defender was able to muster an army that appeared to be at least comparable in size and weapons to the aggressor's army, the aggressor often would withdraw after only a few brief skirmishes. Thus, it was that so called "battles" and "wars" often amounted to little more than patrols, reconnaissances, stand-offs, skirmishes, aborted ambushes, reprisals, and counter-reprisals. When actual battles occurred between opposing armies,[9] more often than not they were brief, inconclusive, and not very profitable or bloody. The infrequent but decisive battles tended to occur when the losers surrendered unconditionally or were soundly beaten after grievously aggravating the victors, the losers became despised captives, they lost plenty of material possessions of great value to the victors (typically metal weapons, jewelry, slaves, women, horses, and camels), and the loser's settlements were conveniently close to the battlefield so that the victors could plunder and pillage for days on end. Again, it is worth remembering that these occasions were as infrequent as they were devastating. "They were not particularly profitable and, as was usual with Arab forays, fighting was avoided when it was clear that the victims were numerous and on their guard. They were careful to refrain from bloodshed as far as was possible, out of fear of becoming entangled in the vicious circle of vendettas with very little to show for it."[10]

Another consideration to keep in mind when reading about Muhammad as a military commander is that by 622, before his first foray into armed conflict, Muhammad had lived a rather unpredictable and occasionally traumatic life. He was at least fifty years old — old by the standards of those times and places. At times he had been a member of the privileged set in his society — a successful merchant who had been born into the Quraysh clan. At other times he was on the margins — an orphan, a poor shepherd boy, a fugitive from Mecca, an annoying mystic to some very powerful people. Is it any surprise, then, to realize that his personality was complex, multi-faceted, unpredictable, and destined to be controversial forever? Rodinson conveys some of the complexity of Muhammad's personality this way:

"We know very little for certain about this man whose ideas and actions have shaken the world, but, as with Jesus, we may get, through the unreliable tales and one-sided traditions, a glimpse of something that is the echo of a remarkable personality which astonished the ordinary men who gathered around it.... The picture is not a simple one. It is neither the satanic monster of some or the 'best of all created things' of others, neither the cold-blooded imposter nor the political theorist, nor the mystic wholly in love with God.... He was fond of his pleasures, yet indulged in bouts of asceticism. He was often compassionate, yet sometimes cruel. He was a believer, consumed with the love and fear of his God, and a politician ready for any expedient. Without any great gift of eloquence in ordinary life, he was able for a short period to produce, from his unconscious, phrases of disturbing poetic quality. He was cool and nervous, brave and timid, a mixture of cunning and frankness, forgiving and at the same time capable of terrible vindictiveness, proud and humble, chaste and sensual, intelligent and, in certain things, oddly stupid. But there was a power in him which, with the help of circumstances, was to make him one of the rare men who have turned the world upside down."[11]

Possibly because of some of the complexities of his personality, combined with pressure that he felt to support his band of exiles from Mecca, lingering animosity against some of the Quraysh in Mecca who had spurned him, and the familiarity that he had with caravan routes across Arabia, Muhammad made a decision that must have startled and perplexed many of his followers. For, within eighteen months of taking up what he considered to be temporary exile in Medina, Muhammad began sending out small raiding parties to plunder caravans returning to Mecca loaded with merchandise. The first of these ambushes on record was the Muslim ambush at Nakhla.[12]

THE MUSLIM AMBUSH AT NAKHLA

The first armed conflict that Muhammad ordered probably was an ambush of a small Meccan caravan at Nakhla, south of Mecca on the route to the trading center of Ta'if, about fifteen months after Muhammad escaped to Medina. Little is know about his motives, but it is speculated that he wanted to capture some of the material goods that were rumored to be on the caravan and that he felt that it would be an easy target because the Meccans were not expecting an ambush, especially an ambush south of Mecca, in the direction opposite from Medina.[13] At any rate, Muhammad sent out a raiding party of seven to ten men under Abdallah without disclosing the exact location of their target, and possibly without specifying the purpose of the mission or how it should be executed. The target was written on a sealed order that Abdallah was not to open until two days into the march. Abdallah's ambush surprised the caravan as it approached Nakhla. The caravan's merchandise was plundered. Two of the four Meccans who were escorting it were captured. One Meccan escaped and the other was killed, possibly by mistake. Apparently none of the Muslim ambushers were killed or wounded, although some accounts differ on this matter and suggest that two of the Muslim attackers disappeared for a short time during or after the ambush and might have been captured by other Meccans at some other location. When the Muslim raiding party returned to Medina with its plunder, the reaction of Muhammad and many residents apparently soon shifted from exhilaration to controversy.

"Plunder and prisoners were borne back to Medina in triumph.
But then a wave of feeling arose because the murder had been
committed in the month of Rajab, one of the holy months during

which, according to pagan Arab conventions, bloodshed was forbidden... had Muhammad deliberately intended to flout this pagan
prohibition, had he relied on the business going off without bloodshed, or had his lieutenant perhaps exceeded his instructions by
taking it on himself to launch the attack before the end of Rajab....
It is impossible to say."[14]

Thus it was that Muhammad's first military venture raised issues
that have confronted so many military leaders through the ages. Were
his orders vague regarding killing of enemy forces? What were the
purposes of the ambush: To acquire booty? Prisoners? To inflict casualties? To avenge Muhammad's persecution by the Quraysh Mecca
and his forced exile? Certainly, it would be understandable if this first
experience with warfare left Muhammad with mixed feelings about
warfare. At very little direct cost he had captured valuable booty and
prisoners. On the other hand, there were negative repercussions,
especially later, when the Quraysh in Mecca learned about the
ambush, how it was conducted, and by whom. The Nakhla ambush
was the beginning of an undeclared war between the Meccans and
Medinans that erupted repeatedly over the next five years. It included
many small raids as well as the famous battles of Badr, Uhud, and "the
Ditch," the surprise "Truce of al-Hudaybiya," and the Muslim sacking
of the Israelite community at the Khaybar oasis. Ultimately this undeclared war against the Quraysh led to Muhammad's claiming of
Mecca, and so much more, for Islam.

The Nakhla ambush was important in forging patterns of Muslim
warfare in other ways as well. Negative public reaction in Medina
kept Muhammad from taking possession of any of the booty from the
ambush until he experienced another revelation from Allah — one
that reassured him that his offense was less serious than the many
offenses that the Meccans had committed against the Muslims when
they resided in Mecca. Rodinson indicates that Muhammad's revelation is conveyed in the following passage in the Qur'an (2:217-218)
that is repeated here from Chapter 2 because of special significance.

"They question thee (O Muhammad) with regard to warfare in the
sacred month. Say: Warfare therein is a great (transgression), but
to turn (men) from the way of Allah, and to disbelieve in Him and
in the Inviolable Place of Worship, and to expel his people thence,
is a greater (offense) with Allah; for persecution is worse than
killing. And they will not cease from fighting against you till they

106

have made you renegades from your religion, if they can. And whoso becometh a renegade and dieth in his disbelief: such are they whose works have fallen both in the world and the Hereafter. Such are rightful owners of the Fire: they will abide herein. Lo! those who believe, and those who emigrate (to escape the persecution) and strive in the way of Allah, these have hope of Allah's mercy. Allah is Forgiving, Merciful."[15]

We are told that Muhammad bowed to public reaction and "refrained from laying a finger on the booty until a timely revelation from God assured him that 'to fight (during the holy months) was certainly serious but that the sins of Meccans were much more so.'" Based on this revelation, Muhammad took one-fifth of the booty from the Nakhla ambush and gave the rest to his companions. This event is considered to have started the practice of one-fifth of the booty of warfare being acquired by the Muslim state for support of needy people in the community. The two Meccan prisoners were ransomed by their families for 1,600 dirhams each, although one of them subsequently joined the Muslims and remained in Medina. The Quraysh in Mecca became infuriated at the news of the Nakhla ambush and vowed severe revenge against Muhammad. This set the stage for the first real battle in Muslim military history — the famous Battle of Badr.

In terms of correspondence with the Qur'an, the Nakhla ambush seems to violate most, but not all, of its most salient pronouncements about war and peace. Muhammad's forces clearly were the aggressors. It was an offensive operation far from Muslim lands — probably in lands considered to belong to the Meccans. There is no record of Muhammad and the Muslims being subjected to religious persecution by the Meccans in the eighteen months after they escaped Mecca and resided in Medina. It was a surprise attack — an ambush, and the Muslims had numerical superiority of about 2:1 or 3:1. One Medina guard was slain, although possibly in error. There is no evidence as to whether the Meccans fought courageously, but it is hard to image that they fought in the "way of Allah" in that it was an unprovoked attack. While the Qur'an certainly allows Muslims to capture prisoners and booty as a consequence of fighting courageously in war, the Nakhla raid would not seem to be an obvious example of war in that the Meccan escorts were not military men armed to fight a military engagement. Furthermore, the Muslim raiders seem to have behaved more like robbers, highwaymen, and brigands, rather than as soldiers. The controversy that erupted back in Medina regarding the timing of the raid and the "murder" of one Meccan escort, among both Muslims and those of other religious orientations, indicates rather clearly that those actions were violations of the revelations that Muhammad had received up until that time, (although they were subsequently revised in the revelation that was just presented a few pages ago). More congruent with the Qur'an was the treatment of the two Meccan prisoners. They were ransomed at a profit, and one of them remained voluntarily in Medina, probably converting to Islam. In any case, the Nakhla raid seems to have emboldened Muhammad and the Muslims, as evidenced by the very audacious attack that they initiated next: the Battle of Badr.

THE STUNNING MUSLIM VICTORY AT BADR

Within two months of the ambush at Nakhla, Muhammad learned that a large Quraysh caravan loaded with merchandise soon would be returning to Mecca from Syria and Gaza along the main route. Muhammad was able to organize an ad hoc raiding party of about 300 Medina residents that included 90 of his original followers who had emigrated with him from Mecca, as well as some Bedouin guides. He led this force to the wells of Badr where the route from Medina intersected with the Gaza-to-Mecca caravan route. There his troops prepared their ambush site. Meanwhile the leader of the approaching Quraysh caravan, Abu Sufyan, anticipated danger ahead. He sent messengers ahead to Mecca by a circuitous route with an urgent request for a large armed force to be dispatched to meet him and escort his caravan safely back to Mecca. In Mecca, some of the Quraysh elders were able to muster an army of about 900 infantry and cavalry, heavily armed, apparently intending to not only protect the caravan but, if possible, to engage and destroy Muhammad's forces if they encountered them. Before they could reach the caravan, however, Abu Sufyan decided to bypass the wells at Badr and pushed his caravan ahead to Mecca by an alternate route. He sent word of this change to the relief force. The leader of that force, Abu Jahl, was able to convince about 700-800 of his troops to press on in an effort to find and destroy Muhammad and the would be Muslim raiders, once and for all. Muhammad reportedly learned in advance of Abu Jahl's approaching army, but he underestimated its size. He deployed his troops in solid ranks around one of the wells at Badr and had the other wells sealed with stones in order to force the Meccans to fight for the water that they would surely need after such a long march. A sudden rainstorm hardened the ground on which the Muslims were deployed, giving them and their mounts good traction for maneuvers. Muhammad organized his archers in close, neat ranks on terrain that would allow them to "rain arrows on the enemy without breaking ranks."[16] When the Quraysh found the Muslim forces deployed at the well they advanced in a haphazard manner in small groups according to the statuses of their families and clans. Drawing closer, some Meccans ran forward as individuals and small groups to insult, taunt, and harass the Muslim ranks, foregoing the chance to engage them in a unified effort. This approach was also hampered by the fact that the Meccans were facing east into the glare of the morning sun. Several of their senior leaders were slain early in the battle. Their large and superior cavalry was not used effectively.

For much of the battle Muhammad remained at the rear of his formations in a hut or a tent that had been erected for him. He was in a highly anxious and agitated state, alternately aggressive, then hesitant (which is not all that surprising considering that this was his first experience in actual battle and he had no training as a combat commander). Suddenly, Muhammad shouted out that he was seeing hundreds of angels arriving from heaven to aid his warriors. He exhorted his troops with an exclamation that was to become the famous battle cry for Muslim armies ever since: "Allah Akbar!" He also offered for the first time on record the promise of eternal paradise for Muslims who died courageously in battle. "By him who holds Muhammad's soul in his hands, no one who fights this day, if he has borne himself with steadfast courage, if he has gone forward and not back, shall meet his death without Allah's bringing him to paradise!"[17] Not surprisingly, many of his troops were immediately inspired to fight even more vigorously. The Meccans were shocked as the stiff resistance from the Medinans turned into an over-powering counter-attack. They were reluctant to wound or kill the Muslims, many of whom were their relatives and former friends from Mecca, in fear of starting more feuds and vendettas among the many families and clans. By midday, scarcely four hours into the battle, panic swept through the ranks of the Meccans. Many of them turned and fled from Badr, leaving 50-70 dead including their leader Abu-Jahl. The Medinans suffered about fifteen dead. Several Medinans severed Abu-Jahl's head from his body and placed it at Muhammad's feet as a trophy, according to at least one account.[18] The Medinans captured 70 Meccans as prisoners and confiscated more than 150 camels and horses, many weapons, and much body armor. Soon heated disputes broke out among Muhammad's men about how the spoils should be divided. One issue was whether the members of the Muslim rear guard should receive any spoils. Frustrated by the bickering, Muhammad eventually resolved the controversy by having all spoils placed in one pile and then divided them equally among the survivors. Flush with emotions from such a surprising victory, many of Muhammad's men wanted to slaughter the prisoners. Muhammad hesitated and then issued a number of very different orders. Two prisoners were released immediately. Most were eventually ransomed for heavy profits. Two were executed on the spot on orders of Muhammad because they had mocked him and Islam. When one of them asked, "But who will take care of my sons, Muhammad?" he answered, "Hell!"[19]

CORRESPONDENCE WITH THE QUR'AN

Treating prisoners in these ways is only partially compatible with the Qur'an, which prescribes discretion by the captor in ransoming prisoners or releasing them as "grace," but does not allow executing them. Execution is far harsher than the other treatments. There are at least three other ways that behaviors of the Muslim forces at Badr seem to be incompatible with the Qur'anic passages that I presented in Chapter 2. As best as we can tell from published accounts, the purpose of Muhammad's expedition to Badr was economic — to capture the caravan that was laden with valuable merchandise. There is no record that indicates that the Meccans were trying to persecute Muslims once they emigrated from Mecca. The Muslims were on the offensive more than 100 miles from their homes in Medina. They waited in ambush at the wells of Badr, which were probably considered public wells at the time, along what amounted to a public caravan route. The beheading of the enemy leader, Abu-Jahl has no precedent in the Qur'an, nor does the presentation of his head to Muhammad as a trophy. Neither of these actions is in keeping with the letter or the spirit of the Qur'an's frequent commands to believers that they must avoid transgressions and fight "in the way of Allah." It is hard to imagine that Allah would fight in these ways or that a beheading would be necessary to achieve Allah's purpose. Also, contrary to the Qur'an, Muhammad made no offer of peace before he had his forces engage the Meccans, nor did he try to escape. Rather, he went out of his way to force the Meccans to engage in battle when he ordered all but one of the wells to be filled with stones and then deployed his forces around the one remaining open well. By doing this Muhammad essentially forced the Meccans (who had marched for several days from Mecca) to either fight his forces in order to have access to the well, or to try to return to Mecca with men and mounts that were suffering from extreme thirst.

At the same time, however, several aspects of the Battle of Badr were compatible with the Qur'an. Muslim forces did fight cohesively, it seems, and in solid ranks. They must have fought steadfastly, courageously, and obediently, given the impressive results that they achieved in only four hours of battle. They killed 50-70 Meccan soldiers including the leader. They took at least 70 Meccan prisoners and captured plenty of booty. After considerable bickering over the spoils, the Medinan soldiers apparently obeyed Muhammad's decision that all of the front line combat troops (but not the troops in the rear guard) should share equally in the spoils after one-fifth was given to Muhammad, ostensibly for Allah's honor and purpose. Overall, the battle of Badr — one of the greatest Muslim "battles" of all time and the first true battle — was only partially compatible with the Qur'an. It seems fair to say that, had more of the Qur'an's instructions about war and peace been followed, the battle of Badr never would have happened.

The effects of the Muslim victory at Badr were profound. Muhammad and his followers gained great prestige and power in Medina and far beyond. Word of the stunning victory quickly traveled the caravan routes throughout the Middle East. Many non-Muslim tribes came to Medina to pay homage to Muhammad and to curry his favor. Muhammad took one-fifth of the spoils from the plunder and began a rudimentary treasury that could distribute benefits to orphans, the poor and itinerant travelers in the community. The characteristics of a state emerged slowly as Muhammad became more confident that he was the vehicle of Allah's will. "He believed Allah had ordained him, He believed Allah had sent legions of angels to help the Muslims while Muhammad himself had been fearful and uncertain." Furthermore, he believed that "It was Allah who had caused the encounter to take place although none of the participants has, strictly speaking, intended it."[20] Both Pickthall and Rodinson mention the following Qur'anic verses (8:43-46) as having been revealed to Muhammad in the month following Badr.

"When Allah showed them unto thee (O Muhammad) in thy
dream as few in number, and if He had shown them to thee as
many, ye (Muslims) would have faltered and would have quarreled over the affair. But Allah saved (you). Lo! He knoweth what
is in the breasts (of men). And when He made you (Muslims),

when ye met (them), see them with your eyes as few, and less-
ened you in their eyes, (it was) that Allah might conclude a thing
that must be done. Unto Allah all things are brought back. Oh ye
who believe! When ye meet an army, hold firm and think of Allah
much, that ye may be successful."[21]

Muhammad also became more assertive in confronting dissension within Medina from pagans, Jews, Christians, and others who
objected to some of his public policies and to the emerging practices
of Islam regarding prayer rituals and standards of behavior in public.
He also sent out another raiding party, of 100 men, that made a surprise attack on a Quraysh caravan on the way to Mesopotamia. It captured all of the merchandise when the caravan's escorts "with the
dreadful memory of Badr fresh in their minds, took to their heels."[22]

Back in Mecca, the Quraysh resolved to eradicate Muhammad's
threat to their trade and supply lines. Under the leadership of Abu
Safyan (who had led the caravan that escaped Muhammad's forces at
Badr) the Quraysh formed coalitions with many other tribes that had
been their archenemies and mobilized for what they promised to be a
decisive attack on Medina.

THE REVERSAL AND WOUNDING AT MT. UHUD (OHOD)

By early March of 625, Abu Sufyan and his council of senior
Quraysh had forged a coalition of tribes including the Ta'if and Aws,
supplemented by some Bedouins, Jews, Christians, and slaves. He
was able to assemble about 3,000 soldiers and cavalry, 700 of whom
had body armor. Hundreds of camels and horses supported this force.
Following a Bedouin custom, the Meccan force also added at least
twelve women including Hind, Sufyan's wife, for the purpose of moti-
vating the Meccans to fight furiously and shaming them if they did not
do so. Among other incentives, "She made a vow neither to wash nor
to sleep with her husband until they had been avenged."[23] Thus motivated, Sufyan's army marched for ten days to reach the farmland
northwest of Medina near Mt. Uhud. Once there, he ordered his units
to set up a series of camps along the barley fields beneath Mt. Uhud
in a rich plain of agricultural land, about ten miles northwest of
Medina. The Meccans looted the gardens and allowed their camels
and horses to graze and trample the crops in the fields. Terrified, the
local farmers retreated into their dwellings and a series of forts and
watchtowers that stretched back to the mud-walled compounds of

Medina. There, a great debate raged within the Muslim council of war. Muhammad favored caution and a staunch defense of the town. Young firebrands and agitators accused him of cowardice and insisted that he should march out to Uhud and attack the Meccans before they were ready to do battle. Reluctantly he agreed.

Following noon prayers, Muhammad assembled a makeshift army of about 1,000 men, one hundred of whom had body armor, and a small number of camels and horses for mounts. Not all clans and tribes of Medina participated equally in this effort. Many of the adult Jewish males of Medina remained there, possibly because it was Friday and the Sabbath would begin at sundown. Along the way to Uhud, Muhammad decided that some of the boys who had joined the march were too young and inexperienced to fight in war. He sent them back to Medina. More damaging was the decision of one of leaders of an allied tribe to abandon the march with his 200-300 followers and return to Medina, reportedly because he envied Muhammad's power and wanted Muhammad to be embarrassed by defeat.

As his shrunken army of 700 approached the Meccan camps and Muhammad realized the size and alignment of Meccan troops, Muhammad decided to disperse his troops into small units and position them in some of the many ridges of basalt rock at the foot of Mt. Uhud, where they would be less vulnerable to attacks by Meccan cavalry. That night Muhammad was able to move his archers into position on one of the slopes of Mt. Uhud from which they could shoot their arrows effectively against Meccan forces who might attack Medinan infantry below them. Muhammad ordered his archers to stay in their positions on the slope until he ordered them down.

The next morning the Meccans tried to move into the breach between Muhammad's forces and the route back to Medina, probably intending to cut supply lines and preclude reinforcements from Medina. As was the custom in Arab warfare, soldiers on both sides taunted each other individually and in small groups with insults and threats. They dashed back-and-forth, jousting, parrying, and throwing spears, rocks, and other objects at each other. The clashes grew more heated, frenzied, and lethal. Confusion mounted as each side struggled for a clear advantage. Muhammad and about fifteen of his guards moved up one of the slopes of Mt. Uhud into some rock outcroppings that afforded considerable protection from Meccan cavalry and the arrows of the archers. Meanwhile, Hind and the other Meccan women screamed encouragements to the Meccans and insults at Muhammad and his soldiers.

As the battle swung in favor of the Meccans, they closed around the Medinan infantry units on the plains. In doing so, they came within the firing range of the Medinan archers. Volleys of arrows soon rained-down upon the clusters of Meccan cavalry and foot soldiers as they closed in, killing some but wounding many more men and their mounts. Some of the Medinan foot soldiers misperceived the extent of the damage done to the Meccans. They stopped fighting and started to collect booty. Seeing this, and believing that the tide of battle had turned, many of the Medinan archers stopped shooting arrows, abandoned their protected positions on the slope, and moved down onto the battlefields in order to get in on the "take" of Meccan booty. It was not long until a few perceptive Meccan leaders realized that they could resume their attack against the distracted Medinans. Walid, one of the Meccan commanders, "took advantage of the situation to drive right through the Muslims left flank with his men and fall upon the mass of combatants from the rear, creating total panic."[24] The Muslims lost their unity of command and, with it, the coherence of their infantry formations dissolved. They broke into small groups and scattered, with many of them seeking whatever protection they could find in some of the rock formations on the small hills and ridges. Muhammad and his personal guards were forced to retreat further up the slope of Mt. Uhud, where they were pursued by Meccan swordsmen. Muhammad's standard bearer was struck down next to him and Muhammad was forced to draw a sword and fight in hand-to-hand combat for the first time in his life. Suddenly he was "knocked backwards into a hole" by a fusillade of stones that smashed into the "cheekpiece of his helmet," split his lip, and broke at least one of his teeth.[25] Rumors quickly passed through the battlefield that Muhammad had been slain. Panic swept through the ranks. But then, several of Muhammad's guards were able to revive him and drag him to a more protected rock outcropping, where they barely survived other attacks during the remainder of the day and through the night. Other Muslim combatants also retreated up the slopes of the mountain, while many others who were not too severely injured abandoned the battlefield and fled back towards Medina.

The Meccans scavenged over the battlefield, finished off the wounded, mutilated some corpses, and grabbed as much plunder as possible. Reportedly, Hind brazenly desecrated the body of Muhammad's uncle, Hamza, who had been javelined by an Abyssinian slave, Wahshi. She cut open Hamza's chest, tore out his liver, chewed it up, and spit it out for all to witness — an ultimate insult to the losers. Loaded with booty and delighted with such a dramatic victory, the Meccans did not press on with the attack against the fortified dwellings and fortifications that led to Medina. More importantly, Abu Sufyan did not press on with the attack against the retreating (or deserting) forces of Muhammad. He did not search-out and slay Muhammad and he did not forge ahead to capture and destroy Medina.

By morning, the Meccan attack had subsided to the point that Muhammad and the survivors were able to leave their hiding places and assess the battlefield.

"Then the company of the survivors, emerging from the various crannies in the rocks where they had been hiding, wounded and bleeding, made their way slowly back to Medina where they were greeted by the shrill cries with which the Arab women used to mourn the death of their kinfolk."[26]

There is no doubt that Abu Sufyan's forces had "won a great victory." Only about 10 of the 3000 Meccan troops had been slain, although many more had been wounded. The Medinans lost at least 70 dead, including ten who had been émigrés with Muhammad from Mecca three years earlier. Many more Medinans had been wounded, including Muhammad. Equally telling, many of Muhammad's men had deserted the battlefield, and Muhammad. Psychologically, this could have been a total disaster — but it did not turn out that way. For Muhammad and his guards had survived the night and stayed at the battle site without retreating. Apparently, Muhammad himself quickly recovered from his brush with death. After his wounds were dressed, he recovered sufficiently that within hours he was able to resume command. He ordered that his dead soldiers be buried in long trenches on the plains beneath Mt. Uhud. Then he organized some of his troops and led them in the trace of the departed Meccan army, at a safe distance. Along the way, he had his troops light bonfires to give the impression that reinforcements had joined the Medinans and that they were in hot pursuit of the Meccans. Probably this was meant to discourage the Meccans from returning in order to press their victory into Medina.

Speculation abounds as to why the Abu Sufyan and the Meccans did not complete their destruction of Muhammad's forces. The Meccans might have been exhausted from the ten-day march from Mecca and the considerable degradation to their own fighting capa-

115

bility during the battle. Many of their horses and camels had been wounded by the Medinan archers' arrows. What is more, probably they were eager to return to Mecca with the good news, the captured booty, and the claim that they had avenged the defeat at Badr. Rodinson states that they also worried that a full scale attack on the fortified dwellings on the way to Medina and a siege of Medina (which was protected by a "labyrinth of forts"), might outrage and then unify many of the clans and tribes in Medina, including the Jews, most of whom had not joined Muhammad's private army for the battle.[27] It is also possible that Abu Sufyan realized that he had lost the opportunity to destroy Muhammad's army once and for all because so many of Muhammad's troops had abandoned the battlefield and retreated to Medina, thus denying him the chance to destroy them in place. As he withdrew from the battlefield on his way back to Mecca, Abu Sufyan reportedly "flung his challenge to the Muslims. 'In one year at Badr!'" This was a reference to a popular, yearly market and fair that was held each year at Badr. It was not far from the wells were his earlier loss to Muhammad's forces had taken place and it attracted many tribes from across the Arabian Peninsula each year.[28]

It would be hard to overstate the enormous impact that the Battle of Uhud had on Muhammad, his followers, and his adversaries. Uhud was the first military defeat of Muhammad and the Muslims. No longer would he be seen as invincible — at least not to his enemies. It was his most obvious military defeat during his lifetime. Still, Uhud was not any where near as decisive as it could have been. Most of the Medinan troops survived to fight another day. Muhammad "bounced back" and resumed the initiative in his war against the Quraysh much quicker than anyone might have expected, and for reasons that will be debated forever.

CONGRUENCE WITH THE QUR'AN

In contrast to the Battle of Badr, where Muhammad had revelations that appeared years later in the written compilation of the Qur'an, revelations did not seem to occur to Muhammad during, immediately before, or after the Battle of Mt. Uhud. Nor did he refer to previous revelations during the battle. There is no record of Muhammad calling out to Allah or trying to rally his forces by referring to Allah. Nothing that occurred before, during, or after Uhud relates to passages in the Qur'an about sustaining peace and using treaties. As the Meccans advanced on Medina and then deployed around Mt. Uhud, Muhammad and his war council in Medina apparently did not try to negotiate a peaceful resolution, offer a treaty, or consider having the Muslims emigrate elsewhere to avoid war — actions that are said to be prescribed in the Qur'an. The Medinans did not invest heavily in defending their far borders in order to preclude their adversaries from occupying their croplands and keep the Meccans far from Medina. Neither side made peace offerings before, during, or after the battle. Every indication is that both the Meccan and the Medinan forces were intent on sustaining the confrontation until one side retreated, conceded defeat, or surrendered. Muhammad's goal at Uhud probably was to keep the Meccans from capturing Medina. This motive was in sharp contrast to his primary motive for the ambushes at Nakhla and Badr — easy booty.

Both sides were aggressors to some extent. Religious persecution had little if anything to do with their aggression, as best as we can tell. The Meccans marched into Medinan territory but stopped some ten miles northwest of Medina. They did not launch an attack on the farmers, their fortified dwellings, or any other target, although they might have intended to do so after taking several days to recover from their ten-day march from Mecca. Abu Sufyan allowed his forces to plunder fruits and vegetables from the gardens of the Medinan farmers. But the Meccans could have been much more aggressive in all of these ways. They did not attack or destroy holy places or interfere with locals worshipping as they pleased. They made no threats against Muhammad or his followers based on religion. Rather, all indications are that Abu-Sufyan and the Quraysh had two motives: to avenge the defeat that they had suffered at Badr and to eliminate further threats to Meccan commerce by Muhammad.

Muhammad's actions were not totally defensive, by any means, even though he originally had been inclined to keep his forces in defensive positions at Medina. He was persuaded to march his troops out of Medina to confront the Meccans around Uhud. He deployed them close enough to the Meccan camps that verbal and physical assaults began without the Meccans having to move far forward from their camps in order to engage at least a few of the Medinan units. It can also be said that the Medinan archers were not fighting defensively when they left their positions on the slope of Mr. Uhud and moved down into the killing fields in order to loot from the dead and wounded Meccans. Nor was Muhammad defensive the next day when he organized a pursuit force that chased after the departing Meccans, albeit at a safe distance. Of course, it can be speculated that this action actually was defensive in that Muhammad's motive probably was to discourage the Meccans from returning to complete their victory by sacking Medina.

The Medinan archers tried to take booty from the dead and wounded Meccans when the brief opportunity to do so occurred. They did so by ignoring Muhammad's direct order to them to remain in position until he told them to move. It is not known if they fought courageously or in "Allah's way." Therefore, it can be said that they were not obviously entitled to the booty, given the qualifications in the passages in the Qur'an about this kind of behavior (as presented in Chapter 2). Many of the Medinans deserted the battlefield without Muhammad's order for them to do so. Probably they were not as steadfast, obedient, and courageous as instructed by the Qur'an. They did not fight for long in solid ranks as a cohesive unit, possibly in part, because Muhammad apparently deployed many of them as small units in the rock outcroppings.

Overall, Muslim behaviors at the Battle of Uhud did not correspond very closely to the instructions in the Qur'an. It was not ostensibly a battle that was inspired by religion, nor was it fought according to religion. Yet, it hardly can be doubted that Uhud had an enormous impact on how Muhammad used his military forces during the rest of his life. After Uhud, Muhammad became more cautious and calculative. He became more inclined to avoid undue risks, more inclined to use diplomacy, delays, threats, and deceptions rather than resort to full-scale warfare, particularly warfare close to his home. All of these techniques he used with telling effects two years later at the "Battle of the Trench" and for much of the rest of his life.

FROM UHUD TO "THE TRENCH:"
TWO YEARS OF TROUBLE, TURMOIL, AND TREACHERY

For Muhammad and his followers in Medina, the two years between their setback at Uhud and their next major military engagement against the Quraysh, the "Battle of the Ditch" (also called the "Battle of the Trench" by some scholars) were filled with troublesome events and political maneuvers. Some of these are reflected in passages of the Qur'an and in enduring Muslim dispositions towards war, conflict, and, to a lesser extent, peace. Recovering from his wounds, losses, and disappointments at Uhud, Muhammad eventually went through an intense period of introspection that crystallized many of his religious and political beliefs and strengthened his resolve to protect himself and his followers by whatever means available to him. His new resolve was manifested in at least three ways. First, Muhammad emphasized to his followers that they all belonged to a distinctive religious and political system that had its own rules for behavior in all circumstances including war and peace. This new system needed its own identity, institutions, and economic resources.

> "It was about this time that the name by which they were most generally known became, once and for all, the 'surrendered' to the will of Allah, in Arabic *muslimun*, more familiar to us in its singular form *muslim*. The corresponding infinitive, *islam*, 'surrender,' was destined for far-reaching influence."[29]

Second, Muhammad became much more assertive in repressing dissent, in confronting antagonists, and in banishing from Medina any people, tribes, or sects that he felt were suspicious, troublesome, hypocritical, or not sufficiently supportive of him, his initiatives, and his followers. The Qaynuqa and Nadir tribes were two of the tribes that experienced his growing political skill and decisiveness.

> "The protests of the Jews and the Doubters were reaching a peak. Some answer had to be made. As we have seen, Muhammad had moved away from the Jews after the brief period in which he had thought he would be able to make converts among them. He adopted different rites and customs. He had forced the Qaynuqa to emigrate and seized their possessions."[30]

Muhammad's method of dealing with another Jewish tribe in Medina, the Nadir, concentrated his power and wealth. It also set the stage for Muhammad sending his army to destroy the famous Jewish settlement at Khaybar, years later, after his victories at The Trench and Hudaybiya, and after he had re-claimed Mecca. Muhammad took his counselors to meet with the council of the Nadir and press for financial and political support.

> "Among those in Medina he approached for contributions was the Jewish tribe of Banu n-Nadir, who lived on the extreme south-east corner of the oasis.... Suddenly Muhammad got to his feet. Allah had warned him, he explained afterwards, that some such conspiracy was being hatched at that very moment. In fact it was a not altogether unlikely assumption and one which, given a minimum of political intuition, anyone less intelligent that the Prophet

might have suspected.... Muslim accounts claimed to know who at the council had proposed dropping a large boulder, a millstone, from the rooftop on to the Prophet's head, who had agreed to do it and who had opposed it. At all events, Muhammad slipped quietly away 'as though answering a call of nature.'"[31]

Soon after this close encounter Muhammad mobilized his followers into a small army and laid siege to the Nadir's neighborhood in Medina.

"Muhammad began felling the Nadir's palm trees. This was an act that went strongly against all Arab principles although, as always, these were frequently subordinated to the demands of war.... All the same this act of total war, coming on top of the desertion of their allies, broke the Nadir's nerve. They registered a solemn protest, and some of the besiegers felt a twinge of conscience. But a revelation came from Allah to assure them that the Prophet's warlike behaviour was perfectly right."[32]

The Nadir surrendered to Muhammad's siege within two weeks. Their lives were spared but they were only allowed to take with them the possessions that they could load upon their camels. For the few doubters of Islam who remained in Medina, this banishment of the Nadir was proof that Muhammad now controlled Medina.

"Muhammad himself was adding to the spoils: fifty coats of mail, fifty helmets and three hundred and forty swords would be very useful. And then there were the Jewish lands, their palm plantations and what was left of their houses. Muhammad explained to the Medinans that so far the Meccan Emigrants had been a burden to them because they were unable to supply their own needs. It was in their own interests that the Emigrants should have these lands, so that they would be able to make a living without begging from their brothers. As a result of this reasoning, the Jewish lands were divided up solely amongst the Muslims of Qurayshite origin."[33]

Third, Muhammad engaged in an increasingly treacherous power struggle against Abu Sufyan and his Quraysh of Mecca by using a growing arsenal of innovative political techniques. Both leaders tried to persuade or bribe Bedouins and other tribes into supplying them with the manpower and weapons that would give them a clear advantage over their adversary. Each leader also tried to seize any opportunity to diminish the fighting capabilities and resource network of the other.

> "Muhammad, for his part, was now the possessor of money and a large, devoted following; he too sent agents, whose business was to counter the efforts of the Qurayshites. This diplomatic tussle was productive of a good deal of plotting. The Bedouin chiefs, predictably in the circumstances, took advantage of the situation to sell to the highest bidder. Rival chiefs contending for leadership of a particular tribe endeavoured to make use of the help proffered by Meccans or Muslims to gain their ends. All this is the familiar and everlasting stuff of politics."[34]

These machinations often involved sending spies, infiltrators, double agents, and assassins into the enemy's camps. For example, when spies informed Muhammad that the tribe of the Banu Lihyan was about to join with the Quraysh in a joint plot against him, Muhammad resorted to a method other than warfare that was extremely effective and bloody.

> "Apparently, Muhammad learned that their chief, Sufyan ibn Khalid (nb. not to be confused for Abu Sufyan, the leader of the Meccans), was gathering men to attack him. He sent one of his followers, Abdallah ibn Unays, to him with permission to say whatever he liked: even to abuse the Prophet if necessary, in order to win the confidence of the Lihyanite shaikh. Everything worked perfectly....Abdallah cut off his head in the night and succeeded in making his escape in spite of the screams of his victim's wives. Travelling only at night, he came to Medina and flung Sufyan's head at Muhammad's feet. The Prophet was well pleased and gave Abdallah ibn Unays a rod. The man took it and thanked him; but he was a killer and not over-intelligent."[35]

In April 626, Muhammad kept his date with destiny and answered Abu Sufyan's challenge by mustering his forces at the yearly fair at Uhud. Apparently both sides backed-off after sizing-up each other. Possibly both sides were becoming increasingly weary of the conflict and the seemingly endless search for a clear advantage over the other.

> "The Muslims duly put in an appearance in April 626 with fifteen hundred men and ten horses to make a show of strength. They did some good business there and their profits amounted to as much

as a hundred percent. The Meccans brought two thousand men and fifty horses to within sight of Badr but did not enter the fair itself. Each side had shown its colours."[36]

After this show of force at the fair, Muhammad became more aggressive with pre-emptive strikes to offset the Quraysh's influence in Arabia. He sent out or led several military expeditions that easily won tribute and booty by intimidating adversaries without much bloodshed. "This was already the fifth year of the hegira (June 626) Muhammad spent a fortnight on an expedition aimed at frightening two tribes that were massing troops for use against him. They fled and the Prophet returned to Medina, having shown his strength and captured a few pretty girls who had been left behind."[37]

> "In December the Prophet set out on another expedition which was to produce one or two especially noteworthy incidents. He scattered the Banu l-Mustaliq, another tribe which was apparently mobilizing for an attack on Medina. Taken by surprise at the well of Muraysi near the shore of the Red Sea, the army was swiftly put to flight. The Muslims lost one man killed; their enemies lost ten. But they took two thousand of their camels, five thousand head of sheep and goats and also two hundred women."[38]

THE BATTLE OF THE TRENCH: A DECISIVE POLITICAL VICTORY WITHOUT MUCH BLOODSHED[39]

By March of 627 Abu Sufyan had formed a coalition between his Quraysh in Mecca, the Ghatafan tribe, many other Bedouin tribes, and the Jews of Khaybar (who were supplemented by many of the Banu n-Nadir Jews that had emigrated to Khaybar when Muhammad expelled them from Medina). This coalition amassed three armies of more than 10,000 troops and hundreds of horses and camels. Once assembled, Abu Sufyan marched this force for ten days towards Medina for what he intended to be a conclusive defeat of Muhammad and his Muslims. Muhammad soon got word of this approaching threat and scurried to raise as many troops as possible from the tribes in Medina and Bedouins that had not already committed to support Abu Sufyan's coalition.

Muhammad could only muster about 3,000 combatants, however, and after considerable debate with his war council, he decided that his forces would be so outnumbered that he could not hope to repeat his earlier victory at Badr. Muhammad also was concerned that members of what remained of the last Jewish tribe in Medina, the Qurayza, might not be trustworthy if he moved his forces outside of Medina. So, for the first time, he decided to fight defensively and to protect Medina and its precious oasis as best he could. Women, children, and other non-combatants were sent into the fortified dwellings and towers throughout the city. Muhammad guessed that Abu Sufyan would attack the city from the north because the irregular terrain of steep basalt ridges and deep gullies around the rest of Medina was unsuitable for approaches and attacks by cavalry and infantry. One story goes that a Persian freedman named Salman convinced Muhammad to have a long trench (*khandaq*) dug across the probable attack route of the Meccans and to position the Medinan forces behind the embankments that could be constructed from the excavated earth.[40] The story also goes that Muhammad rallied all Medinans to help his troops excavate the trench. The project was completed in six days, just before the advance guard of the Meccans arrived to witness the spectacle. Reportedly the Meccans were disgusted by the trench because they considered trenches and digging as being too undignified for Arab warfare. They were also perplexed because they had not brought along ladders or other means to breech the trench.

> "Most of the men had come tamely expecting to take part in a
> general assault in which the cavalry would have played the major
> role. It now became clear that they would have to attack an
> enemy who was well dug in behind the embankment made from
> the earth that had been taken from the ditch. They had to face
> bombardment with stones and arrows. All this promised a great
> many casualties, which Arab warfare in the old style tended to
> avoid wherever possible. The attackers had no ladders or siege
> engines and despised manual labour too much to build any."[41]

A stalemate ensued for the next few weeks as combatants on each side hurled insults, threats, and stones at their adversaries across the trench. Meccan cavalry tried to jump the trench at least once, but with no success. Meccan soldiers who tried to cross the trench were intercepted, often with stones. Eventually three Meccans and five Medinans were killed in these parries, mainly from arrows shot over the trench by both sides.

Meanwhile Muhammad and Abu Sufyan resorted to trickery,

bribes, threats, and rumors to try to weaken the opposition through defections of one tribe or another. Heavy pressure was brought upon the Jews on the Banu Qurayza in their fortified village in the southeast corner of Medina. Each leader cultivated secret sympathizers, spies, and double agents in the camps of the others in an effort to gain strategic advantage. Then, after nearly a month of these deceptions, an unusually severe heat wave swept over Medina. It took a heavy toll on the morale of the Meccans, who lacked access to drinking water and whose horses and camels had little forage because the crops had already been harvested from the fields on the outskirts of Medina. Then another freak turn of nature struck the Meccan camps — a blinding windstorm.

> "The obstacle of the trench was unexpected and seemed formidable; and when a fierce, bitter wind from the sea blew for three days and nights so furiously that they could not keep a shelter up, or light a fire, or boil a pot, Abu Sufian, the leader of the Quraysh, raised the siege disgust. And when Ghatafan one morning found Quraysh had gone, they too departed for their homes."[42]

The sudden withdrawal of the Meccans must have seemed miraculous to the Medinans in their camps across the trench. Militarily, the Meccans certainly had not been defeated or even badly damaged. Withdrawal had been their decision alone. Politically, however, Muhammad was the clear winner. Throughout Arabia he was now regarded as the ascendant political force. He was now the man to be feared and patronized. "For Muhammad, this was a great triumph. It had been proved before the watching eyes of all Arabia that he was not to be defeated by force. What the coalition with its ten thousand men had failed to achieve, no one could. The Muslim state of Medina was a force to be reckoned with."[43]

Rather surprisingly, however, there are few reports of widespread celebration in Medina. Rather, on the day the Meccans departed, Muhammad turned against the remaining Jews of the Banu Qurayza who were residing in their fortified village in the southeast corner of Medina. The Qurayza "dug themselves in, exchanging reproaches and abuse with the attackers," and the siege began. During the next 25 days the Qurayza tried to get other tribes to come to their relief. When that failed, they asked Muhammad to allow them to go into exile as he had done with the Banu n-Nadir. Several Qurayza families quit their tribe and converted to Islam. However,

Muhammad was uncompromising. "This time he meant to have unconditional surrender."[44] Accounts vary as to how the unconditional surrender was achieved, but there is no doubting that the consequences for the Qurayza were devastating. First, Muhammad ordered his men to dig trenches in the public marketplace.

> "The Jews were led out tied together in groups, and beheaded, one by one, on the edge of the trenches and thrown in. According to some, there were six or seven hundred of them, while others say eight or nine hundred. Some individuals were spared at the request of one or other of the Muslims.... After this, the women and children were sold. The money they fetched and the chattels were divided up, two extra shares being given to the horsemen."[45]

CONGRUENCE WITH THE QUR'AN

The Battle of the Trench was the last time Muhammad faced a major military attack in his lifetime. His "massacre of the Qurayza," as Rodinson called it, eliminated internal dissent in Medina and presaged Muhammad's even more destructive massacre of the Jews at Khaybar two years later. All three of these events are referred to in the Qur'an and all three of them correspond with some instructions in the Qur'an regarding war and conflict, while either ignoring or violating other instructions. Certainly, the Qur'an tells Muslims that they should steadfastly defend their communities if they are subjected to sustained religious persecution that becomes intolerable, after peace initiatives fail. However, there is no evidence that Muhammad tried to offer peace or to negotiate with Abu Sufyan before or during the Battle of the Trench. It also seems that the primary motive of the Meccans was to stop Muhammad's raids against caravan trade as well as his growing military and political influence in the Arabian Peninsula, rather than to force Muhammad and his followers to renounce Islam, to destroy their mosques, to destroy or plunder Medina, or to expand the Meccan state by acquiring Medina as a satellite. Nonetheless, Muhammad and the Medians did invest rather heavily with their own sweat and labor in digging the trench. They successfully defended Medina even though the defense was not "at the far borders" of the Medinan territory, as preferred in the Qur'an. It is not known whether Muhammad's forces fought as a cohesive unit, steadfastly, courageously, and in "Allah's way," although they probably did so. It seems fair to say that they were never fully tested by the Meccans, who were unduly disturbed by the very presence of the trench. They grew ever more frustrated at the adverse weather, the shortages of water and food, and the endless squabbles among their factions. Neither side seems to have taken prisoners or gained very much in terms of spoils of war from the battle. This was a disappointment to many of the young Medinan warriors. They complained bitterly to Muhammad and might have pressured him into allowing them to sack Khaybar a few months later. The Medinans did not pursue the departing Meccans or sow panic and terror in all of those who supported the Meccans. Obviously too, the battle produced very few Muslim martyrs (only 5 were killed and there were no reports of pronounced heroism). The Muslim combatants did not seem intent on becoming martyrs by launching suicide attacks against the Meccans.

The subsequent massacre of the Qurayza by the Medinans is not wholly incompatible with the Qur'an. Recall from Chapter 2 that some of the Qur'anic passages admit that Muslim armies had annihilated entire communities of disbelievers so thoroughly that entire generations were extinct. On the other hand, these passages seem to refer to massacres of enemies in communities outside of Muslim communities and homelands — foreigners, if you will — and these other massacres probably followed the massacre of the Qurayza. The Qur'an instructs Muslims to first send orders or warnings into enemy communities. It only allows attacks against enemy settlements if their residents continue to commit "abominations." It is not known whether Muhammad and his Muslims behaved in accordance with these instructions or what the abominations of the Qurayza might have been other than the possibility that some of them were (or seemed to have been) untrustworthy to Muhammad. Of course, the twenty-five day siege of the fortified village of the Qurayza was against what was wholly or mainly a civilian population, rather than a trained army. The surrender provided Muhammad with Qurayza captives, rather than soldiers who became prisoners of war, per se. Yet, Muslim treatment of those Qurayza captives certainly was not compatible with Qur'anic passages regarding treatment of POWs. Those passages prescribe "grace," ransom, conversion of Islam, or voluntary permanent residency in Muslim communities. They seem to prohibit, in letter and spirit, mass executions, beheading, enslaving, and similar treatments by Muslims of enemy prisoners. However, the passages about annihilating entire communities are somewhat ambiguous as to how so many residents can be annihilated so conclusively. Burning their homes, poisoning their water, and starving them might be some of the methods, only scarcely less violent than beheadings.

Allow me to suggest that, had the instructions and prohibitions of the spoken Qur'an been obeyed by the Muslims of Medina, neither the Battle of the Trench nor, even more certainly, the massacre of the Qurayza would have ever occurred. Then again, without the instructions and prohibitions of the spoken Qur'an, Muslim combatants might have behaved even more violently against their enemies. Fueled by their surprisingly easy victories, many Muslims might have disobeyed Muhammad completely and engaged in plundering non-Muslim enclaves in Medina and beyond.

THE TRUCE AT HUDAYBIYA AND THE SACKING OF KHAYBAR

Muhammad's power grew deeper and wider in the year following the Battle of the Trench. While councils comprised of the leaders of each tribe and clan in Medina continued to make some administrative decisions for Medina, very few of these were made without Muhammad's blessing. Additional spiritual revelations convinced him to form councils of his own from his closest Muslim companions. They produced new sets of rules regarding almost every aspect of Muslim life: personal, public, and institutional. Some scholars consider this the time when the first Islamic State emerged. "As we have said, Medina was now a state: a state of a rather special kind, but indubitably a state. It was a theocratic state; that is to say, the supreme power belonged to Allah himself. Allah made his will known through Muhammad and through him alone."[46]

Muhammad exercised even greater control over Medina's external relations. The Quraysh no longer posed much of a threat to Muhammad because so many tribes had defected from the coalition that the Quraysh had forged before the Battle of the Trench. Muhammad was able to turn his attention to possible threats or resistance from other tribes. Prominent among these were the Jews at Khaybar, a wealthy oasis community surrounded by plantations of dates palms and gardens ninety miles north of Medina. He also sent well-armed expeditions to conduct profitable raids against caravans and oasis communities at the far reaches of the Arabian Peninsula.

"He it was who decided peace or war. But there was nothing resembling a standing army. For each expedition it was necessary to summon the chiefs of the Muslim tribes, who then appealed for volunteers from their ranks. The Prophet reviewed them and

ruled out those who were weak or undesirable. He either appointed a leader or took command himself. He seems to have had a gift
for military as he had for political strategy. He was continually
inventing all kinds of stratagems and was especially fond of
pretending to send his forces somewhere other than their real
objective. The saying 'War is cunning' has been attributed to him.
Once the expedition was over, everyone went home with his share
of the booty."[47]

Then, in March of 628, Muhammad seems to have undergone a
rather sudden transformation, possibly the result of a spiritual revelation, that led to a permanent resolution to his longstanding conflict
with the Meccans, with very little bloodshed. It set a pattern for
Muslim practices of peace making for centuries to come, possibly
even to the present day. Muhammad suddenly announced that he
would lead a peaceful pilgrimage to Mecca in order to worship at the
Ka'ba. He assembled as many as 1400 of his followers, instructed
them to dress as pilgrims rather than warriors, and to leave all
weapons behind except for swords, which were to be kept in sheaths.
The Meccans soon learned of the approaching Medinans and debated
how to deal with the threat. Abu Sufyan was away from Mecca at the
time. They decided to send a large military force to intercept
Muhammad along the route of march.

One account says that spies alerted Muhammad of the approaching Meccan force. He diverted his entourage along a circuitous route
through inhospitable terrain until he reached a place called
Hudaybiya, a small hill with a large tree about 10 miles from Mecca.
At this point Muhammad's horse refused to go further. The Prophet
dismounted and ordered his followers to make camp. Soon this camp
was discovered and approached by 200 Meccan soldiers. Young hot-
heads tried to persuade Muhammad to take advantage of their
numerical superiority and attack the Meccans. However, Muhammad
refused to fight. Envoys were dispatched back and forth between the
Meccans and Medinans for days — without resolution. Finally,
Muhammad sent his most trusted disciple, Othman, to Mecca to negotiate directly with the war council. The next day a wild rumor circu-
lated through Muhammad's camp that Othman had been murdered by
the Meccans and that a full scale Meccan attack was imminent. One
hundred of Muhammad's closest supporters then took "the pledge
under the tree at Hudaybiya" that they would fight to the death, if
attacked. Negotiations resumed once it became apparent that Othman

had not been murdered and that the Meccans were reluctant to attack. These negotiations led to a treaty that was far more favorable to anything that Muhammad and the Medinans could have hoped for. The provisions of the treaty allowed that there would be no hostility between the parties for ten years and that Muhammad and his followers would be allowed to return the following year for three days of unrestricted visits to Mecca and the Ka'ba, so long as the Muslims departed after that and returned to the Quraysh their fugitives living in Medina.

The wording and terms of the treaty were worked out through direct negotiations between Muhammad and Suhayl ibn Amr, the ad hoc leader of the Quraysh. It begins, "This is the treaty of peace concluded by Muhammad ibn Abdallah with Suhayl ibn Amr." Then it specified directly the conditions:

"War was to cease for ten years. During this time, all Qurayshites who might go to Muhammad without permission from their legal guardians were to be sent back, but Muslims who might return to Mecca were not to be. The tribes were to be free to make alliances with either side. For this year, Muhammad and his followers were to abandon their proposed entry into Mecca; but the following years the Qurashites would evacuate the city for three days so that the Muslims could come and perform their devotions, armed only with the traveler's weapon of a sheathed sword."[48]

With this non-aggression pact established, Muhammad returned to Medina and assembled a large army to launch a decisive attack against the Jews of Khaybar. Its purposes were to provide an outlet for the belligerence of his many young warriors who lusted after booty and adventure and to destroy remaining elements of the coalition that had opposed him at the Battle of the Trench. Muhammad's army of 1600 laid siege to Khaybar for a month. The Bedouin tribes that had been part of the enemy opposition did not come to the relief of the Jewish tribes. Muhammad had bribed them to abandon the several Jewish tribes at Khaybar who remained disorganized in the face of the Muslim's siege. One by one, the forts of Khaybar surrendered until Muhammad and his followers were able to plunder and then destroy the entire community, taking concubines and slaves, and executing many others. Chapter 2 presents a number of Qur'anic passages that seem to pertain to the annihilation of Jewish settlements such as Khaybar (although not all scholars agree on this matter). Consider, for example, Sura 17: 16-17

("The Children of Israel") of the Qur'an:

> "And when We would destroy a township We send commandment
> to its folk who live at ease, and afterward they commit abomina-
> tion therein, and so the Word (of doom) hath effect for it, and We
> annihilate it with complete annihilation. How many generations
> have we destroyed since Noah! And Allah sufficeth as Knower and
> Beholder of the sins of His slaves."[49]

While the Muslims were dividing the booty and celebrating their
victory at Khaybar, Muhammad was poisoned in an incident that I
described in Chapter 2. Zanab, one of the Jewish women who had
been taken prisoner, poisoned a shoulder of lamb that she had been
ordered to cook for the Prophet's meal. One of Muhammad's soldiers
died as a result. Muhammad survived because he became suspicious
at his first taste of the meat and spat it out. Muhammad spared
Zanab's life when she told him that she believed that if he were the
true prophet, he would know that the meat was poisoned and would
survive it.[50]

In other respects the annihilation of Khaybar was so decisive that
all of the other Jewish settlements in the region soon accepted
Muhammad's terms without a fight. "The other Jewish colonies in the
region, at Fadak, Wadi l-Qura and Tayma, all learned their lesson
from Khaybar. They submitted without argument and were given the
same terms as Khaybar or better. They were allowed to keep their
possessions on payment of a tax. As far as Muhammad was concerned, the Jewish problem was practically solved."[51]

ISLAM EXTENDS INTO MECCA AND BEYOND
THE FIRST PILGRIMAGE TO MECCA *(HAJJ)*

In March 629, one year after the Truce at Hudaybiya, and seven
years after being exiled from Mecca, Muhammad returned to Mecca
with a large group of his followers, worshipped at the Ka'ba for three
days, and departed, as agreed upon in that truce. He took 2000 well-
armed supporters with him but had them store all of their weapons,
except for sheathed swords, on the outskirts of Mecca under the security of a guard detachment. The Quraysh had vacated Mecca according
to the terms of the Truce and many of them watched from the hills on
the outskirts as Muhammad and his pilgrims worshipped at the Ka'Ba
according to established Muslim practice without major confronta-

tions or problems.[52] Certainly, this return to Mecca is noteworthy because it was the second major peaceful encounter between the Muslims and the Meccans (and it was much more peaceful than the first one — the Truce at Hudaybiya). It also provides an example of how the behaviors of the Muslims could be compatible with passages in the Qur'an regarding the purposes of treaties and the obligations that Muslims have to comply with treaties that are made without deception. The event demonstrated that a large Muslim military force could behave obediently and peacefully in a very tense situation that could have turned violent at any moment. Furthermore, neither party was opposed based on religion. In fact, Muslims were allowed to practice their religion to the fullest by making their pilgrimage to Mecca without any interference or harassment from anyone.

MU'TA: A FAILED FORAY INTO THE BYZANTINE EMPIRE

Unfortunately, the unprecedented peacefulness and triumph of the Muslims pilgrimage to Mecca did not suppress Muhammad's inclination to expand his power base and his treasury. Nor did it satisfy many of his younger soldiers and the leaders of some of the other tribes in Medina. They complained that the Truce of Hudaybiya favored the Meccans by forcing Muhammad to return to Mecca all the Meccan fugitives who had converted to Islam, while the Meccans were not required to return to Medina any of their Muslim prisoners. Faced with growing unrest, Muhammad authorized a number of small expeditions to raid caravans and to extract tribute from distant tribes. In September 629, Muhammad sent an army of 3,000 men under his adopted son, Zayd ibn Haritha, in search of easy plunder so far to the north that they penetrated the Byzantine Empire for the first time. At Mu'ta in Transjordan, southeast of the Dead Sea, Haritha's force was intercepted by an army of Christian and Arab auxiliaries led by Theodore the Vicar. The Muslims were soundly defeated in a bloody battle. Haritha and two other senior commanders were killed. Mauled and scattered, the Muslim force was saved only when Walid Khalid, a famed former adversary from Mecca, re-organized the Muslims and kept them together during the long, difficult march back to Medina, 250 miles to the South across some of the most difficult terrain on the Peninsula.

"The fleeing Muslims were rallied by the former Qurayshite commander-in-chief, who had recently become a Muslim and been assigned to a subordinate position in the army. Khalid ibn al-Walid, who came to be called 'the Sword of Allah', succeeded in restoring some degree of order and led the disgruntled survivors back to Medina; there they were met with such furious mockery and abuse that Muhammad was obliged to take them under his lofty protection."[53]

Regarding compatibility with the passages of the Qur'an, it is difficult to find any aspect of the Mu'ta expedition that is compatible with the Qur'an. It was an utterly offensive operation far from Medina whose purpose was to plunder and subjugate distant tribes. The Muslim force did not fight cohesively or steadfastly, as best as we can tell from the very limited accounts of the battle. The Muslims fell back in something of a rout. They were saved only by the courage and example of Walid Khalid.

Back in Medina, Muhammad faced increasing pressure from his own followers to re-negotiate the treaty of Hudaybiya so that Mecca was more accessible to Muslims for worship and trade. Meanwhile in Mecca, many of the wealthy merchants were becoming more favorable towards Muhammad. They were reassured by the fact that he and his Muslim pilgrims had not damaged the Ka'Ba or been disruptive during their pilgrimage the previous year. The merchants realized that Medina had become so powerful and wealthy that their businesses could profit from open trade with Medina and from the protection that Muhammad could provide for their caravans. Even the leader of the Quraysh, Abu Sufyan, had become more amenable to the Muslims. The previous year, 628, his daughter converted to Islam and became one of Muhammad's wives, making Abu the father-in-law of the Prophet.[54] Speculation continues as to who co-opted whom.

THE ACQUISITION OF MECCA (*AL-FAT'H*)

By late December 629 Muhammad began calling in contingent forces from his allied tribes, ostensibly in order to amass an army for a campaign on the northern border against the Byzantines. Instead, on 1 January 630 (10 Ramadan of the Muslim year 8), Muhammad led his army of more than 10,000 troops southwest towards Mecca. "The army encamped two days' march from Mecca and lit ten thousand fires. Panic grew in Mecca."[55] Abu Sufyan, whose disposition towards Muhammad must have been altered by his daughter's marriage to Muhammad, personally represented the Quraysh as the envoy to Muhammad's camp. In yet another stunning bout of diplomacy, Abu Sufyan conferred briefly with Muhammad, announced that he had converted to Islam, and then departed back to Mecca with Muhammad's terms for its surrender.

"The city was in no danger if it welcomed the conqueror peacefully. In the face of his strength all resistance was in vain. The life
and property of all those who did not resist would be safe."[56]

Within a week, the Quraysh agreed to the terms. On 11 January
630, Mecca became part of the new Islamic State and thereby sustained its trajectory towards empire.

"(T)he Muslims made their entry in four columns into the deserted streets of the city. Only a handful of extremists offered some
resistance in one corner of the city. Khalid ibn al-Walid routed
them easily, with the loss of ten or twenty lives as against two or
three on the Muslim side."[57]

Muhammad remained in Mecca only for a short time. He super-
vised the disarming of the Quraysh who refused to disarm otherwise.
He established the laws and institutions of the Islamic State within
Mecca. He invited all of the Quraysh to pay homage to him, to acknowledge him as the Messenger of Allah, and to swear fealty to him. Most of
them did so as they filed passed him in a long procession, bowing.
Muhammad declared amnesty for past offenses by all but ten Meccan
residents, several of whom were summarily executed. Muhammad also
borrowed large amounts of money from some of the wealthiest merchants in order to provide compensation to more than 2,000 of his need-
iest and most demanding soldiers. This was necessary because he had
allowed little or no booty to be taken from the Meccan residents. Then
he departed Mecca on a military expedition to destroy an alliance of
troublesome tribes near Ta'if, sixty miles southeast of Mecca. While the
expedition succeeded after a substantial battle, Muhammad was disap-
pointed at the greediness of many of his soldiers for booty. "The share-
out of the spoils was turned into a riot by the greed of those taking part.
Mohamed himself was pushed up against a tree and had his clothes
torn. Not without some trouble, he succeeded in restoring order and
making himself obeyed."[58] Shaken, he decided to suspend the expedition and return to Medina with his army and heavy booty.

CORRESPONDENCE WITH THE QUR'AN

As mentioned previously, many passages of the Qur'an that are
presented in Chapter 2 are compatible with Muslim behaviors during
their pilgrimage to Mecca in March 629. In many ways the pilgrimage
was a model of peaceful comportment and observance of treaty obliga-

tions. Of course, this is what might be expected from pilgrims on a pilgrimage. Yet, historically, too many "pilgrimages" have turned violent.[59] Fortunately, this was not one of them. The fact that this pilgrimage was so peaceful probably is the strongest evidence that neither the Muslims nor the Meccans engaged in religious persecution of each other.

In contrast to the first pilgrimage, the acquisition of Mecca in January 630, however, seems to violate some of the provisions of the Qur'an regarding observance of treaty provisions. It also goes beyond the Qur'an in that it expanded the Muslim state by threat, force, and intimidation (and by the sheer size and proximity of the 10,000 man army only two miles outside of Mecca) after less than two years since the Truce at Hudaybiya. Some observers might also consider the capture of Mecca to constitute religious persecution by Muslims of non-Muslims. While all Meccan residents were invited to acknowledge Islam and were not forced to join Islam, it is unlikely that the non-believers felt that they had much of an option. Conversion afforded the least risk. It was an expedient and a safeguard. It is often said "there are no atheists in combat." It is not hard to imagine that the same was true for any atheists in Mecca once Muhammad had re-occupied it and claimed it for Islam.

FAR BEYOND MECCA: MUHAMMAD'S LAST TWO YEARS

In March 630, two months after capturing Mecca, Muhammad returned to Medina for what would be the last two years of his life. During this time, he sent several expeditions to the far reaches of the Arabian Peninsula and into the near edges of the declining Byzantine and Persian Empires. The results were mixed: a few victories, a few setbacks, and some draws. Probably the most famous of these was a massive expedition that Muhammad himself led to Tabuk, Palestine.

Only ten months after his capture of Mecca, in October 630, Muhammad wanted to avenge the loss at Mu'ta a year earlier. Yet he faced growing opposition from some of his tribal leaders and many Bedouin who had been his soldiers in previous wars. Now they wanted to remain in the comfort of Medina and share in the burgeoning wealth of the Islamic State. With some difficulty Muhammad was able to assemble a huge if somewhat reluctant army of about 20,000 troops. This expedition marched its way north for weeks until it reached Tabuk, in what is now Palestine, 250 miles north of Medina. Using Tabuk as his base, Muhammad sent out emissaries with battalions of troops to collect tribute and pledges from local rulers and Christian dignitaries.

"During this same stay at Tabuk, Muhammad also sent Khalid with a few hundred men to the oasis of Dumat al-Jandal. Khalid forced the Christian king there to go to Tabuk to meet with Muhammad and agree to pay the tribute."[60]

None of these confrontations led to significant armed opposition that would have allowed the Muslim army to engage in battle and collect a wealth of prisoners and booty. Despite several political successes like this, Muhammad was soon forced to withdraw his army back to Medina because of oppressive heat wave and flagging motivation in many of his troops who were eager to return to the comforts of Mecca. Upon returning to Mecca, Muhammad found that opposition to him had grown in some quarters and that a plot existed to capture him and throw him over a cliff to his death. Loyalists alerted Muhammad in time so that he avoided this threat. He was able to purge the plotters without having to execute them. Later he even forgave many of them. The long, hot expedition to Tabuk and the disappointment of discovering the plot against him took its toll on Muhammad, as did the deaths to aging of several of his longest-serving companions in his war council. Muhammad also encountered wearying daily discord in his large personal household among his many wives, servants, and dependents despite finding that a son, his first (Ibrahim), finally had been born to one of his concubines, Mariya. In his sixties, tired and in failing health, Muhammad decided to lead one last pilgrimage, his "pilgrimage of farewell" to Mecca, in March 632. By all accounts, this was a most memorable event. It was attended by thousands of Muslims from across Arabia. On display was all of Muhammad's complex charisma and the immense power and wealth of the Islamic State.[61] Tired but fulfilled, Muhammad returned to Medina from Mecca as soon as the ceremony concluded. He began planning "another raid on a few small towns in Transjordan" to avenge the death of his adopted son, Zayd, in the Battle of Mu'ta two years earlier. His health grew progressively worse from a number of illnesses and injuries over the years. "Sometimes, also, it is said, he remembered the piece of poisoned meat he had had in his mouth for a moment at Khaybar four years before."[62]

Muhammad The Prophet died in early June 632 in his compound in Medina. He was surrounded by his family and what remained of his closest companions from his many encounters with both war and peace.

MUHAMMAD AS A COMMANDER AND AS THE RECITER OF THE QUR'AN

In reviewing the historical record on Muhammad's experiences as a military commander and of the armed forces that served under him, it seems rather clear that compatibility with instruction in the Qur'an passages is very mixed. Consider the focal points of this chapter: the Muslim raid at Nakhla, the stunning victory at Badr, the nearly disastrous engagement at Uhud, the surprising withdrawal of the Meccans at the Battle of the Trench, the even more surprising concessions won from the Meccans at the Truce of Hudaybiya, the Muslim sacking of the Jewish community at Khaybar, Muhammad's peaceful pilgrimage to Mecca, and his acquisition of Mecca one year later. Consider also the very mixed results that his armies had when Muhammad sent them to the far edges of the Arabian Peninsula and beyond it to Mu'ta and Tabuk. Taken in their entirety, it can be said that most of Muhammad's military campaigns were offensive — not defensive. Most of the battles were waged far away from Medina, Muhammad's adopted center. They were intended to acquire material resources for economic gain — not to end overt and oppressive religious persecution, for very little of that was in evidence. These battles did not always (or even often) require inferior Muslim forces to fight steadfastly, courageously, and obediently against enemy forces that outnumbered them by ratios of 3:1 or even 10:1 (although in the battles at Uhud and the Trench Muslim forces were by as much as 3:1). After these two battles (and at Nakhla and Badr before them), Muslim forces usually had decided numerical superiority over their foes, and it showed. Muslim casualties usually were light — not heavy. Only at Uhud did Muslim battle deaths approach ten percent of the army.

Contrary to the Qur'an, Muslim combatants sometimes retreated or abandoned the battlefield and Muhammad, as was the case at Uhud. Muslim forces never routed the enemy forces so decisively as to spread panic back through an adversary's army and into the units of support personnel, supply caravans, and civilian communities. Then there were the ghastly attacks by Muhammad's forces against the Banu Qurayza and the Jewish community at Khaybar. These seem to have been unprovoked Muslim attacks that turned into mass executions — if not genocide. Even the Qur'an seems to testify that these were "annihilations," that they were intentional, and that they went without apology, guilt, shame, or disgust on the part of Muhammad or anyone else. I feel obliged to suggest that current government and military commanders should hope that all contemporary proponents of the Qur'an disavow or ignore facts like these in the Qur'an and in Muslim military history. Otherwise, contemporary leaders should prepare to safeguard likely targets of annihilation so that history is not repeated in this way.

Returning to the subject at hand, it can be said that Muslim victories certainly produced a great deal of booty and a great deal of conflict about how the booty would be distributed, despite the Qur'an's insistence that one-fifth should be given to Muhammad and the State treasury to support needy Muslims in the community. Often Muslim victories also produced large numbers of prisoners, some of whom were ransomed, some of whom converted to Islam, some of whom were freed. However, some prisoners were also executed under direct orders of Muhammad — actions that certainly are not endorsed in passages of the Qur'an (although torture and mutilation might be allowed, as discussed in Chapter 2). The Qur'an also does not appear to allow Muslim soldiers to behead the enemy's leaders in order to present the detached heads as trophies to Muslim commanders. Yet beheadings happened, without punishments by Muslim leaders.

Treaties and peace negotiations were not used by Muhammad in any of these battles until the Truce at Hudaybiya, which occurred in the last four years of The Prophet's life. Treaties were used mainly with just one of his adversaries, the Quraysh. A truce was not broken in one very important instance — Muhammad's first pilgrimage to Mecca in March 629. Much of that truce was ignored or abrogated one year later by Muhammad's surprising march upon Mecca in January 630, with an army of 10,000 men, and his absorption of Mecca into the Islamic State.

Finally, in the last two years of his life, following his acquisition of Mecca and consolidation of his power through much of Arabia, Muhammad launched offensive expeditions into Transjordan in search of booty, pledges, and obeisance. There is little if any credible historical evidence that Muhammad intended these to be pre-emptive strikes against formidable foes. These expeditions went far beyond Islam's borders and far beyond the instructions in the Qur'an about not starting wars and about defending the Muslim homeland. Of course, over the last 1300 years since these events occurred, many different and often-conflicting interpretations have been published about these events. In Chapter 6 I examine some of these other interpretations. I encourage you to do likewise. But first I describe and interpret in Chapters 4 and 5 some of the highlights of Muslim political and military history since Muhammad's death in the light of the

Qur'an's many directives to its followers.

Did the Qur'an become more or less influential in the centuries since Muhammad's death regarding peace, terror, and war? What influences has it had — is it having now on the battlefields of the world?

---

[1] Esposito, p. 11.

[2] Conversations that I have had with Najih Lazar of Narragansett, Rhode Island, and several other Muslims who were born in Arab societies, support Esposito's point that many Muslim children learn in school and at home about some of the major events in Muhammad's life, including the battles of Badr, Uhud, and possibly a few others. These are the events in Islamic history that are given great value and meaning. For example, Najih Lazar told me that the Battle of Uhud is usually taught to children because it was the battle that brought about something of a "reconciliation" between Muhammad, his followers from Medina, and the members of the Quraysh tribe of Mecca who almost killed him during the battle. Mr. Lazar told me that this battle "teaches moderation." This is somewhat surprising, in that Muhammad was wounded and almost killed there and many of his troops abandoned the battlefield. On the other hand, the Battle of Badr is widely considered to have been Muhammad's first and most stunning battlefield victory.

[3] The main sources of information in this chapter are books by Rodinson (1971), Esposito (1998), Lewis (1966, 1974), Khadduri (1941), and the *Encyclopedia Britannica* on Muslim warfare, Muhammad's life, and related subjects.

[4] Rodinson, p. 38.

[5] Majid Khadduri, p. 87, estimated that Muhammad authorized fifty-five military expeditions during his lifetime and that he personally led twenty-six or twenty-seven of these, which are called *ghazwas* in Arabic, in contrast to *sariyyas*, which are the expeditions that Muhammad entrusted to other leaders among his Muslim followers.

[6] This definition is the one used by Theodore Caplow and Louis Hicks, *Systems of War and Peace*. Lanham, MD: University Press of America, Inc., 1995, p. 3. I believe that a more useful definition of military war and warfare is "sustained, violent, armed, social conflict between significant numbers of members of military organizations of different nations, states, or societies, or within the same nation, state, or society." Caplow and Hicks do not define "battle." However, a war usually consists of more than one battle. In this book I use David Eggenberger's definition of "battle" on page iv of his *An Encyclopedia of Battles*: "A battle is usually defined as a general fight or encounter between hostile military forces." He points-out that battles are somewhat distinct from wars, skirmishes, and raids in terms of duration, scale, intensity, size of the forces involved in the encounter, and decisiveness of the action, among other differentia. Furthermore, a battle usually is a "confrontation between opposing armed forces that resulted in casualties or in a change in the military situation."

[7] Rodinson, pp. 38-59, 110-147. These pages in Rodinson's book, *Muhammad*, are the principal source of the material in this chapter, supplemented by many other sources that are identified in the "Bibliography," especially the section, "Mohammed," in the *Encyclopedia Britannica*, Volume 15, 1973, pp. 639-642.

[8] Rodinson, p. 148.

[9] Please refer to endnote #6 for definitions of "battle" and "war."

[10] Rodinson, p. 162.

[11] Rodinson, p. 313.

[12] I use the term "Muslim" here for convenience even though the name probably was not adopted by Muhammad and his followers until after their defeat at Uhud. Rodinson, p. 188.

[13] Rodinson (p. 193) says that Muhammad was very concerned that his fellow émigrés from Mecca were a burden to their brethren in Medina because they were "unable to supply their own needs." Muhammad was constantly looking for ways to reduce this burden, shore up their confidence, and increase their self-sufficiency and wealth. Ultimately he did this by confiscating land from tribes and clans, often Jewish ones, which he suspected were traitorous or unreliable as allies.

[14] Rodinson, p. 163.

[15] Rodinson, p. 163. This passage is sura 2:217-218 in Pickthall's translation of the Qur'an. It is the same passage as 2:214 in the translation of the Qur'an that Rodinson referred to.

[16] Rodinson, p. 166.

[17] Rodinson, p. 167.

[18] Fregosi, p. 42. Fregosi's accounts often are dubious and sensationalistic and his overall perspective is extremely cynical about Islam as well as Christianity and all religions. However, his research methods are very industrious. It is possible that he is more candid and less concerned about political correctness than are the accounts of many other authors about these battles.

[19] Rodinson, p. 168.

[20] Rodinson, p. 168.

[21] This translation of sura 8, verses 43-46 is from page 139 of Pickthall's book. Rodinson's translation of these verses varies slightly from Pickthall's.

[22] Rodinson, p. 170.

[23] Rodinson, p. 177.

[24] Rodinson, p. 180.

[25] Fregosi, p. 53, wrote that two of Muhammad's front teeth that were knocked-out during this attack are on display at a museum in Istanbul.

[26] Rodinson, p. 182.

[27] Rodinson, p. 180.

[28] Rodinson, p. 195.

[29] Rodinson, p. 188.

[30] Rodinson, p. 185.

[31] Rodinson, pp. 191-192.

[32] Rodinson, p. 193.

[33] Rodinson, p. 193.

[34] Rodinson, p. 188.

[35] Rodinson, p. 189.

[36] Rodinson, p. 195.

[37] Rodinson, p. 196.

[38] Rodinson, p. 196.

[39] My account of this battle and related developments is a synthesis of many sources, especially Rodinson, pp. 208-211, and Pickthall, pp. 299-301, who based his account heavily on those of famed classical Islamic historians, Ibn Khaldun and Ibn Hisham.

[40] Thus the purpose of this trench, which was unusual but not unprecedented in warfare in the Middle East, was to be an impediment against an offense, not cover and concealment for the defense, as was the primary purpose of the trenches in the "trench warfare" of WWI. By the way, I have been told by pilgrims to Medina that some of the trench still exists as a venerated Islamic holy place.

[41] Rodinson, p. 210.

[42] Rodinson, p. 299. This blinding windstorm at Medina might remind us of more recent blinding windstorms that struck U.S. forces in Iraq during the 2003 invasion.

[43] Rodinson, p. 211.

[44] Rodinson, p. 212.

[45] Rodinson, p. 213.

[46] Rodinson, p. 220.

[47] Rodinson, p. 223.

[48] Rodinson, p. 252.

[49] Pickthall, p. 205.

[50] Rodinson, p. 254.

[51] Rodinson, p. 254.

[52] Rodinson, p. 255.

[53] Rodinson, p. 256.

[54] Rodinson, p. 259.

[55] Rodinson, p. 259.

[56] Rodinson, p. 260.

[57] Rodinson, p. 260. Note that Rodinson uses the term "extremists" rather than "loyalists" or some other term that is more neutral. Possibly this reveals some favoritism on his part.

[58] Rodinson, p. 264.

[59] One cannot help but wonder whether the decreased number of lethal weapons among the Muslim pilgrims contributed to their peaceful behavior, or whether the Muslim pilgrims included relatively few young soldiers who had been veterans of battles such as Uhud and might be holding grudges. In other words, Muhammad's pilgrims might not have included many of his soldiers. Unfortunately, the sources in the "Bibliography" that I consulted did not illuminate these matters.

[60] Rodinson, p. 275.

[61] Rodinson, p. 286.

[62] Rodinson, p. 287.

CHAPTER FOUR

THE QUR'AN AND MUSLIM WARS, 632-1984 A.D.

"The grand vizier opened the Koran at random seeking inspiration. His eyes fell upon the verse that said, 'Oh Prophet, fight the hypocrites and unbelievers.' 'These Christian dogs are unbelievers and hypocrites,' he said. 'We fight them.' He opened the Koran a second time. This time he read, 'A large host is often beaten by a weaker one.' 'They are the large host. We are the weak one,' he said. 'We fight them.'"[1]

This quotation refers to one of the events that preceded the Battle of Kosovo in 1389. Murad, the grand vizier of the Ottoman Turks, is said to have consulted his copy of the Qur'an while he was trying to decide whether to attack the much larger army of the Serbian King Lazar. Murad found verses in the Qur'an in which the Prophet Muhammad instructs believers to "fight the hypocrites and unbelievers" in part because the believers will win even if they are outnumbered. Murad believed that these verses presaged victory. He decided to attack (and subsequently won a stunning victory that continues to haunt the collective memories and politics of Serbia and its neighbors even today — as we will see later in this chapter and in Chapter 5). The case of Murad raises a key question to be addressed in the next two chapters: *After Muhammad's death, how congruent were the behaviors of Muslim political and military leaders and combatants with the Qur'an's instructions about peace, conflict and war?*

MUSLIM EMPIRES AFTER MUHAMMAD

John Esposito has indicated that much of Muslim military history after Muhammad's death has been an extension of Muslim military traditions that he established during his life. This is because Muhammad's successors have often attempted to wage war and make peace according to the practices and beliefs that Muhammad established during his lifetime and as they were laid down in the Qur'an and the Hadith.[2] For this reason it should not be surprising to find that most Muslims living today know considerably more about Muhammad's life

141

and a small number of his most famous battles (Badr, Uhud, the Trench, the Truce at Hudaybiya, and the acquisition of Mecca) than about the later history of Islam and of Muslim battles since then.[3]

"Despite the turmoil during the early caliphal years, Muslims regard the period of Muhammad and the first generation of companions or elders as normative for a variety of reasons. First, God sent down His final and complete revelation in the Qur'an and the last of His prophets, Muhammad. Second, the Islamic community-state was created, bonded by a common religious identity and purpose. Third, the sources of Islamic law, the Qur'an and the example of the Prophet, originated at this time. Fourth, this period of the early companions serves as the reference point for all Islamic revival and reform, both traditionalist and modernist. Fifth, the success and power that resulted from the near-miraculous victories and geographic expansion of Islam constitute, in the eyes of believers, historical validation of the message of Islam."[4]

Esposito has a useful scheme for naming and dating major periods in the long and complex history of Muslim empires and military events after Muhammad's death. I will describe these periods briefly, generally following Esposito's presentation of them, but occasionally augmenting it with insights from other scholars including Mohammed Marmaduke Pickthall, Magid Khadduri, and Bernard Lewis. For convenience, these periods are listed in Table 4-0.

TABLE 4-0:
MUSLIM EMPIRES AFTER MUHAMMAD

THE CALIPHATE: 632 - 1258 A.D.
The Rightly Guided Caliphs (Medina): 632 - 661 A.D.
The Umayyed Dynasty (Kafu, Damascus): 661 - 750 A.D.
The Abbasid Empire (Baghdad): 750 - 1258 A.D.

THE SULTANATE-MEDIEVAL PERIOD: 1258 - 1919 A.D.
The Ottoman-Turkish Empire (Istanbul): 1258 - 1919 A.D.
The Persian-Safavid Empire (Isfahan): 1258 - 1736 A.D.
The Mughul Empire (Delhi): 1258 - 1857 A.D.

THE INDEPENDENT MUSLIM NATION-STATES: 1919 - CURRENT

THE CALIPHATE PERIOD

As shown in Table 4-0, a period of about 600 years following Muhammad's death often is referred to as the Caliphate because many of the most distinguished Muslim leaders assumed the status of caliph (derived from the Arabic word *khalifa*, a successor). The Caliphate often is divided into three consecutive periods. The period of "The Rightly Guided Caliphs" (632-661) saw a succession of Muhammad's companions who ruled from Medina: Abu Bakr (632-634), Umar ibn al-Khattab (634-644), Uthman ibn Affan (644-656 — and who was assassinated by mutineers from Egypt), and Ali ibn Abi Talib (656-661 — considered by the Shiite sect as the only true descendant and successor of Muhammad among all of the others). During this period Islam spread rapidly beyond the Arabian Peninsula through the infamous "Wars of Conquest." This was also a period of tribal fratricides, rebellions, and bitter civil wars, including the "Wars of Apostasy," "The Battle of the Camel," and the famous "Battle of Siffin" (Syria) in 657.

Siffin is especially noteworthy in Islamic history because it started the sectoral split between Sunnis and Shiites and because the Qur'an was so prominent and influential. The revered Caliph Ali led his Muslim army from Medina to put-down a rebellion by Muawiyah, the recalcitrant Muslim governor of Damascus. As Esposito recounts the key event, after weeks of bloody but brief skirmishes "faced with defeat, Muawiyah's men raised Qurans on the tips of their spears and called for arbitration according to the Quran, crying out, 'Let God decide.'"[5] Arbitration followed but dragged on for months and was inconclusive. Ali was murdered by Kharijite Separatists within several years. Separatist movements have continued to flourish in Islam since then to the present time.

During this period, major changes occurred in the structure of military conquest. The caliphs appointed veteran military commanders to maintain standing armies of hundreds of veteran combatants that engaged in more or less constant military activities and to occupy the garrison towns that were established near large conquered cities in order to maintain Islamic rule, suppress rebellions, and serve as base camps to extend Islamic rule further into frontier territory.

"In general, the Arabs did not occupy conquered cities but established garrison towns nearby, such as Basra and Kufa in Iraq, Fustat (Cairo) in Egypt, and Qairawan in North Africa. From these towns, conquered territories were governed and expeditions launched. They were centered around a mosque, which served as the religious and public focal point of the towns. Conquered territories were divided into provinces, each of which was administered by a governor who was usually a military commander. The internal civil and religious administration remained in the hands of local officials. An agent of the caliph oversaw the collection of taxes and other administrative activities. Revenue for the state came from the captured lands and taxes."[6]

The murder of Ali by Kharijites in 661 enabled Muawiyah to claim the caliphate and move Islam's capitol from Medina to Damascus. He soon created the foundation of dynastic imperial monarchy, dominated by an Arab military aristocracy and protected by a full-time army of Syrian warriors, that extended Islam's influence into southern Europe and India.

"From this new center, the Umayyads completed the conquest of the entire Persian and half the Roman (Byzantine) empire. When Muawiyah seized power, Islam had already spread to Egypt, Libya, the Fertile Crescent, Syria, Iraq, and Persia across Armenia to the borders of Afghanistan. Under the Umayyads, Muslims captured the Maghreb (North Africa), Spain, and Portugal, marched across Europe until they were halted in the heart of France by Charles Martel at the Battle of Tours in 732, and extended the empire's borders to the Indian subcontinent."[7]

For all of its external expansion, the Umayyad dynasty was fraught with internal dissent because so much power and wealth was concentrated into a small authoritarian and exploitative elite in Damascus. Kharijites seceded from the empire. The Shiite sect permanently split from the Sunnis when Muawiyah's son and successor, Yazid, came to power in 680 and ordered his army to suppress an uprising at Karbala by Husayn, the son of the late Caliph Ali.

"Husayn and his small band of followers were slaughtered by an Umayyad army at Karbala. The memory of this tragedy, the "martyrdom" of Ali's forces, provided the paradigm of suffering and protest that has guided and inspired Shii Islam. For these partisans (Shii) of Ali, the original injustice that had denied Ali his succession to Muhammad had been repeated, thwarting the rightful rule of the Prophet's family. Thus, the Shii developed their own distinctive vision of leadership and of history, centered on the martyred family of the Prophet and based on a belief that leadership of the Muslim community belonged to the descendants of Ali and Husayn."[8]

These events further aggravated the animosities between Sunnis and Shiites that remain to this day and that can be important in dealing with so many of their followers on matters of peace and in war. For example, on February 22, 2003, seven Shiite (Shii) worshippers in a Shiite mosque in Karachi, Pakistan, were shot and killed by a gang of terrorists, believed to be from a Sunni militant group. According to an article by Raymond Bonner in *The New York Times*, this was just the latest incident in a centuries-old sectarian dispute between the Sunni majority and the Shiite minority. "Although no one took responsibility for the attack, suspicions immediately fell on a militant Sunni group, Lashar-e-Jahngi." Bonner also noted that Karachi is a "city plagued by violence," and it is the same city where the late Daniel Pearl, a reporter for *The Wall Street Journal*, was kidnapped and executed. It was also the location where a bus loaded with explosives was detonated at the Sheraton Hotel, killing many European guests.[9]

The Shiite "doctrine of the imamate" holds that leadership of the Muslim community must be vested in a direct descendant of Muhammad and Ali, the first Imam. As such, the Imam is both the religious and political leader of Islam. He governs as "the final authoritative interpreter of God's will as formulated in Islamic law."[10] The Imam is not, however, the military leader, although he appoints and has final authority over military commanders and he uses them to fulfill the religious obligations of the *Umma* in keeping with Allah's instructions in the Qur'an. While not a prophet himself, the Imam is considered by Shiites to be the divine guide of Islam. His decisions are considered to be inspired, final, and infallible. By contrast, in the Sunni doctrine of the Caliphate, power is vested in a caliph who is supposed to be selected or elected by the general leadership of the Muslim community to serve as the political and military leader, but not the religious leader of the Muslim *Umma*. Decisions about religion are supposed to be made according to consensus (*ijma*) of the entire community, the *ulama* (the body of traditional religious scholars), or both.

Of course there are factions within Sunni and Shiite as well as many other sects, factions, and schools in Islam (Karijites, Ismailis, Druze, Sufis — to name but a few). Contemporary leaders in government and military should be aware of these factions within Islam and take them into account as much as possible in planning negotiations and strategies. One way to do this is to determine whether all relevant sects are represented in negotiations. If so, it is important to avoid assuming that members of different sects will react the same way to proposals or will consider each other to be equal and to have an equal voice. Having translators and interpreters from each of the sects represented also can be a wise idea. Esposito's perspective implies that, all other things being equal, representatives of Shiite regimes might be more authoritarian, fundamentalist, and rigid regarding interpretations of the Qur'an on war and peace. They might also be more decisive, conclusive, and easier to predict regarding how, when, and why they fight — and they might be more prone to fight. Sunni regimes might have the opposite characteristics. They might be less decisive, less predictable, and more inclined to persuasion, consensus, and peace negotiations. They might be more democratic in their decision-making and they might be more willing to deal with democratic foreign governments. They also might be more willing and able to control military forces because this is one of their long-standing responsibilities.[11]

In any case, by 747 A.D., factionalism and dissatisfaction with the authoritarian elites of the Ummayad rulers escalated into a *coup d'etat* by Abu Muslim, a former Abbasid slave. Within three years this allowed Abu al-Abbas, a descendant of Muhammad's uncle, al-Abbas, to become caliph and to move the capital of Islam to Baghdad (Arabic for "City of Peace"). Once there, he promptly assumed the nickname Abu Abbas al-Saffah (Abu "the blood shedder"), crushed opposition from the Shiites, claimed absolute power and proceeded to rule by fear and "the executioner." He also paved the way for splendid public works projects and economic prosperity based on trade and commerce throughout the Mediterranean. Industry, science, agriculture, and the fine arts flourished during his regime.

"Persian influence was especially evident in the government and military. Pre-empting critics of the previous regime, the Arab Syrian-dominated military aristocracy was replaced by a salaried army and bureaucracy in which non-Arab Muslims, especially Persians, played a major role. The Abbasids explained this change in terms of Islamic egalitarianism. More often than not, however, it was royal favor and fear, symbolized by the royal executioner who stood by the side of the caliph, that brought him prestige and motivated obedience."[12]

146

To Esposito the early Abbasid period was unparalleled in its splendor, learning, civility, and absence of warfare. Its grandeur was immortalized in "Arabian Nights" (*The Thousand and One Nights*), the story of the exploits of Caliph Harun al-Rashid (786-809). "Unlike the modern period, Muslims controlled the process of assimilation and acculturation. Their autonomy and identity were not seriously threatened by the specter of political and cultural domination. As with the early conquests and expansion of Islam, Muslims then (and now) regarded this brilliant period as a sign of God's favor and a validation of Islam's message and the Muslim community's universal mission."[13]

By 945 A.D., however, the Abassid empire was hopelessly overextended. Political unity deteriorated and the Abbasid rulers had to make major concessions to other Muslim sects, especially to the Buyids (a Shiite sect from Western Persia) and the Seljuks (a Turkish sect that attacked and occupied Baghdad, leaving the Abbasids as titular caliphs). The empire was weakened further by the protracted battles against European armies that struggled to reconquer Spain (1000-1492), Italy and Sicily (1061), and Jerusalem with the Crusades (1095-1453). Still, there were some astounding Muslim battlefield victories from time-to-time including Arp Arslan's victory at Manzikert, Armenia, in 1071 and Salah al-Din's (Saladin's) recapturing of Jerusalem in 1187.

By 1258 A.D., the once proud Abbasid empire "was a sprawling, fragmented, deteriorating commonwealth of semi-autonomous states, sultanates, governed by military commanders."[14] Genghis Khan's Mongol armies continually penetrated and shrank its borders, plundered its cities, decimated its armies. Then in 1258, Hulaga Khan, grandson of Genghis, captured Baghdad, "burned and pillaged the city, slaughtered its Muslim inhabitants, and executed the Caliph and his family."[15] Eventually only Egypt and Syria remained from the Abbasid Empire.

SULTANATE PERIOD: THE "MEDIEVAL" EMPIRES

Within 150 years, by 1400, the Muslim states that had endured in Syria and Egypt had been shifted from governments based on caliphs to those that were based on sultans (literally "one who possesses power"). Three of the most dominant of these sultanates were: the Ottoman Turkish Empire, with its capital in Istanbul and its territory encompassing Eastern Europe, Arab lands, and much of North Africa; the Persian Safavid Empire, centered in Isfahan, Iran, and using Shiite Islam as its state religion; and the Mughal Empire, administered from

Delhi and controlling much of what is now Bangladesh, India, and Pakistan.[16] All three of these were imperial sultanates that achieved great progress in science, learning, arts, architecture, and city building. Esposito says that they expanded more through Muslim traders and missionaries than through military conquest. At the same time, he calls them "the great Muslim gunpowder empires."[17]

Among the most significant military events of the Ottoman Empire were the fall of Constantinople-Istanbul in 1453 to Ottoman Sultan Mehmet II "The Conqueror," which "realized the cherished dreams of Muslim rulers and armies since the seventh century;" the decisive defeat of Muslim naval forces by Christian European navies in 1571 at the Battle of Lepanto; the truce of 1580 that "confirmed the frontier between Christian and Muslim civilizations that has lasted to the present day;" and the collapse of the Ottoman siege of Vienna in 1683. This marked the end of Muslim expansion into central Europe.[18]

Two of the highlights of the Persian Safavid Empire were the conquest of all of Iran under Ismail (1487-1524), who proclaimed himself the first Shah of Iran and instituted Shiite as the state religion and the rule of Shah Abbas (1588-1629). He established an autonomous sultanate state that encompassed all of Iran and was never seriously challenged by non-Muslims or by the other two Muslim empires.

Esposito portrays the emergence of the Mughal Empire as being more a consequence of commercial expansion and religious proselytizing by missionaries and merchants than by military conquest. Emperor Akbar (1565-1605) was able to form this empire by appealing to many Hindus and dozens of tribal sects across the Indian subcontinent with a combination of religious tolerance and incentives from the economic surplus that had been amassed through extensive trade in the Middle East in spices, silk, metals, food supplies, and the fine arts. "The emperor initiated policies to foster greater political centralization and the social integration of his Muslim and Hindu subjects. Religious learning, tolerance, harmony, and syncretism were hallmarks of Akbar's reign. Royal patronage sponsored the building of schools and libraries. A policy of universal tolerance and abolition of the poll tax as well as a tax on Hindu pilgrims fostered loyalty among Hindus, who constituted the majority of his subjects."[19]

Esposito claims that, despite their differences in geography, ethnicity, and some aspects of religious ideology, all three Muslim sultanate empires constituted an "international Islamic order" that superceded state boundaries and virtually all other differences among its participants. This new Islamic order allowed all Muslim citizens to travel freely throughout all three empires. It also constituted the *dar al-Islam* (abode of Islam) in contrast to the non-Islamic world (*dar al-harb*) the "abode of warfare."[20] Esposito laments the gradual demise of these three sultanates, which he portrays almost wistfully as comprising what was probably the most cultivated, tolerant, and learned civilization of all time. Whatever the case, they ruled far and wide until European states emerged in the 1700s. Funded by wealth gained from colonializing the Americas, and armed with the weapons and machines of the Industrial Revolution, European armies were able to push back Muslim armies in the Balkans, the Mediterranean islands, southern Russia, and North Africa. Then they penetrated into the homelands of all three Muslim sultanates. Only the Ottoman Empire survived into the 20th Century. Since then many efforts have been made to create independent Muslim nation-states, but with great variations in terms of stability and success. Esposito generally seems to assume that the Qur'an has continued to influence political and military affairs in many of these nation-states, despite the avowed secular orientation of some of them, such as Turkey. But, as with his accounting of the many Muslim empires that preceded them, he does not provide specific examples of how the Qur'an influenced government and military policy let alone the behavior of Muslim combatants in the wars of these nation-states. It is for this reason that we will now turn to accounts of specific Muslim battles in order to see if they reveal more evidence of the influence of the Qur'an on Muslim warfare through the ages.

A QUESTION OF CONGRUENCE: THE QUR'AN AND 214 BATTLES

How much congruence is there between battles that have involved Muslim armed forces since Muhammad's death and the Qur'an's instructions to its followers regarding peace, conflict, and war? To answer this question I collected, content-analyzed and coded accounts of 214 of the most famous "Muslim" battles, using a variety of sources including Eggenberger's *An Encyclopedia of Battles: Accounts of Over 1,560 Battles from 1479 B.C. to the Present*, Esposito's *Islam: The Straight Path*, Fregosi's *Jihad in the West: Muslim Conquests from the 7th to the 21st Centuries*, MacDonald's *Great Battlefields of the World*, and other sources indicated in the Bibliography. Appendix A provides a list of these battles and some basic information about them. They range from the battle of Ajnadain, near Jerusalem, in 634, only two years after Muhammad's death, to the battle of Beirut, Lebanon, 1982-85. Chapter 5 extends this analysis to nine wars and battles from 1984 through 2003.

Before presenting the results of my analysis, I want to acknowledge that all data sources and research methods have limitations as well as strengths. In the case of the research that I present in this chapter, accounts of these battles by military historians do not always agree as to what constitutes a battle (especially a famous battle), about the appropriate names of battles, or about the exact starting and ending dates of some battles. Occasionally there are also disagreements about the national, ethnic, and religious identities of some of the adversaries, about which adversaries were on the offense more than on the defense, about which adversary won, why, and with what consequences, and about many other features of a particular battle. When faced with ambiguities or contradictions, I usually relied on Eggenberger's accounts on these matters. Despite occasional disagreements, I found essential agreement among different sources more than ninety percent of the time. However, the purpose of this analysis is not to provide a definitive account on matters like these. Rather, the purpose is to determine, if only in a preliminary manner, in what ways a large number of Muslim battles have been congruent with instructions in the Qur'an as to how its followers should behave regarding peace, conflict, and war between and among nations and groups, including different groups of Muslims.

Before I present a quantitative analysis of the 214 battles in the data set, it might be helpful to consider two common stereotypes of Muslim battles and some illustrative cases of specific battles from the data set. Doing this might help readers to understand more fully the nuances in the quantitative analysis.

TWO STEREOTYPES OF MUSLIM BATTLES

MUSLIM-DOMINANT: MUSLIM BATTLES EXPAND RELIGIOUS AND ECONOMIC DOMINION

One stereotype of Muslim warfare is that, at least up until the "fall" of the Ottoman Empire after WWI, Muslim armies were decidedly invasive, aggressive, violent, brutal and uncompromising against their enemies' armed forces, civilians, and communities. Their enemies included other Muslim nations, sects, and groups as well as virtually any and all nations, sects, and groups that encroached on

Muslim communities or interfered with the expansion of Muslim economic and religious empire. Special vengeance was directed at
nations and groups comprised of idolaters, Jews, and Christians that
were believed to have opposed or violated Islamic religious practice.

Characteristically, Muslim armies were comprised of well-armed
young men on horses or camels who were motivated by the Qur'an's
promises of plenteous booty and eternal paradise. Muslim armies
always were in the attack in foreign lands. Almost always they won
decisively, although there were a few exceptions, such as several battles against the Christians during the Crusades, a perplexing loss to
Charles Martel at Tours, France, in 732, and a few frustrated sieges of
Constantinople and Vienna. Countless Muslim victories were attributable to the mobility and skill of Muslim cavalry and the unparalleled
commitment and savagery of Muslim combatants. Invariably their invasions into foreign lands were concluded by quick, bloody battles in
which Muslim troops viciously killed and mutilated the enemies' troops
and civilians who refused to surrender. Those who did surrender were
tortured, sometimes beheaded or executed in other gruesome ways, or
forced to work as slaves for the Muslim conquerors. Others were ransomed for handsome profits or they were sold into slavery. Civilian
males were treated likewise. According to this stereotype, Muslim combatants were glorious victors if they survived or glorious martyrs if they
perished honorably. Rarely if ever did they desert, surrender, or become
prisoners or apostates. Battles and wars, as well as cease-fires, peace
treaties, and foreign relations all should serve the purpose of spreading
Islam throughout the world. Worldwide expansion is allowed to cease
only when "all religion is for Allah." One variation on this stereotype
emphasizes worldwide economic domination rather than religious
domination.

For easy reference, the term "Muslim-Dominant" will be used
hereafter to refer to this stereotype of Muslim warfare. This stereotype
is in direct contrast to a second stereotype, which will be called
"Muslim-Defendent" (the spelling of "defendent" is meant to distinguish this term from the legal term "defendant" so as to emphasize the
military and political aspects of this concept).

Muslim-Defendent: Muslim Battles As Desperate Efforts To Protect Persecuted Communities

A second stereotype is in many ways the direct opposite of the
first. In this stereotype, Muslim battles are almost always the last

resort and are justified only when all other efforts fail to relieve relentless religious persecution against Muslims in Muslim homelands by idolaters, Jews, and Christians. All members of Muslim communities must invest heavily in the costs of defending the far borders of Islam. Muslim combatants must fight steadfastly because they will be vastly outnumbered by the enemy forces. They must also follow the many rules of the Qur'an (as presented in Chapter 2), and the more general principles of righteous intent, proportionality, discrimination, and transgression avoidance. Following these rules and principles will result in stunning Muslim victories against all odds in battles and in eventual withdrawal, surrender, or destruction of the enemy's military forces. Only then will Muslims be fully free to practice Islam in their communities according to the will of Allah. On rare occasions Muslim forces might be compelled to launch pre-emptive strikes outside their homelands in order to discourage non-Muslims from encroaching on Muslim lands ever again. Muslims leaders must be wary of being deceived, weakened, and exploited in peace treaties with non-Muslims. Peace probably will be only a temporary state of affairs until Muslim communities will be persecuted again by non-Muslims.

How closely do these stereotypes diverge from the historical record of Muslim battles? Let us now consider some illustrative cases of some of the 214 battles after Muhammad's death that involved large numbers of Muslim combatants.

KADISIYA, IRAQ, 637:
MUSLIM INVADERS OVERWHELM PERSIANS

In 637, only five years after Muhammad's death, his successor, Caliph Omar I, sent Sa'ad ibn Abi-Waqqas with 30,000 Arab infantry and horse cavalry to conquer parts of the Persian Empire. The Muslim invaders were confronted by about 100,000 troops, some with elephants, under Rustam, the regent-general for Emperor Yazdegerd III.

"The battle began with the usual series of cavalry rushes by the Arabs. But the huge Persian force held its ground and then counterattacked with elephants, which terrified the Arabian horses. Sa'ad was barely able to prevent a rout at the end of the first day's combat. Fighting resumed the second day, and although the slashing Moslem attacks inflicted heavier casualties than were received, no decision was reached. On the third day Sa'ad was reinforced by some veterans of the Syrian campaign who knew how to fight elephants with arrows and javelins. The beasts were wounded and then stampeded back through the Persian lines, opening holes for the Arabian cavalry to charge through. The Moslems pressed home their attacks throughout the day and during the night (called the "Night of the Clangor"). At daybreak a sandstorm began blowing in the faces of the stubborn Persians. Rustam sought personal safety by swimming across a canal running to the Euphrates. He was caught and beheaded. The Persian army then disintegrated, taking terrible losses from the Arabians, who gave no quarter. Moslem losses in the battle totaled 7,500 killed. In the booty captured by the Arabs was the jewel-encrusted sacred banner of Persia."[21]

Emperor Yazdegerd then offered peace and additional land to the Muslims if they called-off the invasion. They rejected the offer, forced him to abandon his capital at Ctesiphon, and then sacked the city. 'The decisive battle of the Arabian Persian War had already been fought at Kadisiya.'"[22]

In relating this battle to the Qur'an's instructions about peace, conflict, and war, consider that Muslim behaviors violated many (but not all) of the prohibitions of the Qur'an. The Muslims invaded lands of the Persians, apparently without provocation, let alone sustained religious persecution. The Muslims also launched the first attack against the Persian force, which had massed in order to defend against further incursion into its lands by the Muslims. Apparently, both sides fought courageously and violently for three days, with the Muslims suffering 7,500 killed out of its 30,000-man army — a remarkably high killed-in-action rate (25%) in the entire history of warfare (and a dubious estimate to my way of thinking). After the battle turned in their favor, the Muslims also pursued aggressively as their adversaries retreated into their homelands. So these are two ways in which the Muslim behaviors were somewhat consistent with the Qur'an (capturing booty is a third way). However, in almost all other ways Muslim behaviors might well have violated the Qur'an. Muslims caught, executed, and even beheaded some of the Persian prisoners, including the regent general, Rustam. They did not accept a peace offering or additional concessions from the Persian emperor. Rather, the Muslims went on to sack the capital city and to conquer the rest of the Persian Empire. There is no claim that they ransomed prisoners, laid down their arms after the victory was theirs, or returned to their own lands in order to live peacefully ever after. It also might be worth noting that this battle has gained fame in the history of Muslim warfare as the "Night of Clangor," and that a sudden sandstorm is believed to have played an important role in completing the Muslim victory. Contemporary proponents of the Qur'an might interpret this fortuitous event as another example of how Muslim armies often have been "saved by Allah" despite being outnumbered by more than 3 to 1.

The Battle of Kadisiya, then, seems to have been a marked departure from the most famous Muslim battles during Muhammad's life in almost all respects, including its decided incongruity with almost all aspects of the Qur'an. Was it an aberration then? Or, because it was such a decisive victory over such a powerful archrival, did it become an ideal standard of sorts for Muslim warfare ever after? Did the heavy toll of Muslim KIAs dampen the willingness of subsequent generations of Muslim combatants to fight as their predecessors did at Kadisiya?

SIFFIN, SYRIA, 657: TWO MUSLIM FACTIONS INVOKE THE QUR'AN

"The first great battle between Muslims" occurred because Islam's fourth caliph, Ali, marched his army into Syria to suppress a rebellion led by his governor there, Muawiyah.[23] Accounts vary somewhat as to how much fighting really occurred. One story goes that their forces clashed periodically but inconclusively for three months, until some of the frustrated combatants impaled their Qur'ans on the points of their lances, held them aloft, and implored the armies to "Let Allah decide."

> "When neither side could gain an advantage, a truce was declared and the quarrel submitted to arbitration in August, 657. But no agreement was reached. The conflict dragged on until January, 661, when Ali was assassinated. Muawiyah then became undisputed ruler and the first in a long line of Ommiad (Omayyad) caliphs. His reign was one of violent conquest in both Arabia and Africa."[24]

Siffin is mentioned again for several reasons. Copies of the Qur'an were present, they were referred to by some of the combatants, and they had at least a symbolic role in moderating the violence of the battle and in restoring some semblance of peace, at least temporarily. Unfortunately, we do not know if specific verses of the Qur'an were recited publicly by the combatants or, if so, what the reactions were to the verses.[25] Siffin also should remind us that the Qur'an allows for Muslims to suppress dissent by other Muslims, at least during times of war. Certainly Muslim armies were engaged in many other wars around the year 657 against non-Muslim forces throughout the Middle East, particularly the Persians, as can be seen in the list of battles in Appendix A. Siffin also indicates that truces were part of Muslim military history in the years immediately after Muhammad's death, as they were during his life, and that the truces were only temporary stopgaps, in some instances, that did not resolve conflict or preclude violent conflicts from erupting into new battles within a few years. Siffin also suggests that some Muslim leaders, including Muawiyah, were much more belligerent than others, possibly because they paid less attention to the Qur'an than did others.

RIO BARBATE, SPAIN, 711:
MUSLIM INVASION AND VICTORY WITH FEW EXCESSES

After sweeping across North Africa in 708-11, the Arab General Musa ibn-Nasayr sent his subordinate, Tarik, with an army of about 12,000 Arab and Berber horsemen across the Strait of Gibraltar in search of plunder, in what is generally considered to have been the first invasion of mainland Europe by a Muslim army. This army eventually was confronted along the Barbate River near Cape Trafalgar by King Rodrigo (Roderick) and his Visigoth army of 15,000 infantry.

> "Roderick's 15,000 defenders proved to be no match for the swift, slashing charges of Tariq's cavalry. They were soundly defeated after an hour of fighting on July 19. Roderick, last of the Gothic kings, was either slain or drowned in the Guadalquivir River trying to escape. The Muslims rode on to take Cordova (the Moor capital-to-be), Toledo (the Visigoth capital), and half of the Iberian Peninsula by the end of the summer."[26]

This battle set the pattern for much of the Muslim conquest of Spain, Portugal, and a fair portion of western France, that culminated in the Battle of Tours. The Muslims were the invaders. They were the attackers. They often were outnumbered by far more than 3:1. They plundered and then occupied important cities such as Bordeaux and

Narbonne; but they did not always engage in wholesale massacres of the defeated armies or the civilian populations that supported those armies. The battles were not always particularly brutal or bloody.[27] Desertions were not uncommon. Sometimes there were rather gruesome mutilations that seemed to be intended primarily for symbolic value and were ordered by the generals, rather than acts of passion by the troops. For example, at Rio Barbate, King Rodrigo apparently survived the battle but died accidentally while escaping from the battlefield.

> "Witiza's sons and Bishop Oppas deserted to the Muslim enemy. Rodrigo fled from the battlefield on his fleetest horse and apparently drowned. His horse, his robes, and his diadem were found on the riverbank — a slipper recognized from its pattern as belonging to him. An unrecognizable corpse was lying nearby, and to satisfy Muslim requirements it was decided that the body was the dead monarch's. Its head was ceremoniously cut off, perfumed, packed in camphor, soaked in brine, and urgently sent off by special messenger to the caliph in Damascus for his contemplation and delectation."[28]

TOURS, FRANCE, 732:
A DECISIVE MUSLIM DEFEAT SURROUNDED BY EXCESSES

The battle of Tours was "the high-water mark of the Moslem invasion of western Europe" and one of the most decisive battles in the history of warfare.[29] Somewhat ironically, it can be understood as violating the Qur'an in many ways by the Muslim forces, and as being rather congruent with the Qur'an in terms of the behaviors of the Frankish forces. In 732 the Arab emir of Spain, Abd-er-Rahman (Abderman) led an army of more than 60,000 Muslim cavalry over the western Pyrenees to expand and enrich his empire.

> "Abderman's army, once over the Pyrenees, headed for Bordeaux (not yet famous for its vintage clarets), killing or enslaving all who opposed them and burning or plundering every church and monastery on the way north. Their reasons were excellent and were not motivated by religious fanaticism. The churches were then the repositories of wealth, money, and jewels; rather like banks today."[30]

Rahman's army easily brushed aside several small Frank armies on the way to the Loire River valley where the basilica of St. Martin of Tours "became a magnet that drew the Saracens on."[31] Charles Martel, a provincial "mayor" who had united a number of Frankish forces in central France, assembled an unknown number of seasoned infantrymen with battle-axes into a blocking position between Poitiers and Tours, directly in the path of Abd-er-Rahman's cavalry.

"The invaders rushed forward, relying on the tactics that had won them so many victories during their century of conquest — slashing attacks, an overwhelming number of horsemen, and a wild fervor that could be stopped only by killing. Despite the ferocity of the assault, the Frankish square stood firm while the foot soldiers chopped down men and horses with their swords and axes. It was one of the rare times in the Middle Ages when infantry held its ground against mounted attack. The Moslems struck again and again — for two days according to Arab sources, seven days by Christian accounts. Finally the fall of Abd-er-Rahman himself took the steam out of the Moslem onslaught. Under cover of night the invaders began to fall back. Not wishing to trust his undisciplined Franks to a pursuit, Charles Martel permitted the Moslems to withdraw unhindered. But a pursuit was unnecessary. The sharp setback, the death of their leader, and frightful casualties combined to mark Tours as the high water mark of the Moslem invasion of Western Europe."[32]

The battle of Tours is remarkable not only for its decisiveness, but also because there is little record of what would be considered "crimes of war" having been committed by either side, during or immediately after the battle. Martel did not pursue the retreating Muslim forces, nor did the retreating Muslim forces lay waste to the land as they retreated back towards the Pyrenees. In many ways the Frank forces seem to have behaved more in accordance with the Qur'an than did the Muslim forces. The Franks defended their lands, churches, and communities, fought vigorously against what probably was a much larger Muslim army, and did not obviously violate the principles said to be inherent in the Qur'an: righteous intention, proportionality, discrimination, and transgression avoidance. There was only one report of an exception. Apparently, Martel allowed his soldiers to take as personal booty many of the possessions that the Muslim soldiers had looted from the churches that they captured on the way to Tours and had discarded as they abandoned the battlefield.

"To make sure of the soldiers' loyalty, and to the great anger of the Church, he distributed among his men the ecclesiastical property he recovered instead of returning it to its former owners."[33]

There is some indication that the Frankish and "Christian" European armies might have become less disciplined in the years immediately after Tours, especially after Charles Martel died in 741 and the Frankish armies began the reconquest of Muslim France, Portugal, and Spain. This shift to excessive violence, plundering, and execution of enemy prisoners by Christian armies shortly after Tours might have carried over into some of the battles of the Crusades and the wars in the Balkans, the Mediterranean islands, and the Crimea. For example, as Charles Martel dispatched his armies to recapture cities from the Muslims, those armies often executed Muslim prisoners and civilian sympathizers, and they sacked, plundered, and pillaged formerly "Christian" cities which had been occupied for decades by the Muslims, as if in retribution.

"In about 737 Charles Martel sent this brother Childebrand to lay siege to Avignon, which he took by storm, putting every one of its Muslim defenders to the sword. Next he attacked the main Saracen bases north of the Pyrenees and, in turn, took Narbonne, Beziers, Montpellier, and Nimes. In 739 he captured Marseilles, at a time when, in other parts of Mediterranean France, the coastal region began to endure the first of those Arab slave raids from the sea which turned the northern Mediterranean shore into a danger zone for Christians for the next thousand years."[34]

One result of this shift in army behaviors was that by 750, less than twenty years after the battle of Tours, there were few if any Muslims and no Muslim armies remaining north of the Pyrenees. By some accounts, the liberating Frankish armies often were more brutal and genocidal than the Muslim armies that they were replacing. "The inhabitants of Narbonne, who were nearly all Christian and Visigoth, also decided to rally to Pepin the Short. They massacred their Saracen neighbors and overlords and suddenly there were no Saracens left north of the Pyrenees."[35]

JERUSALEM VII, 1099:
FIRST CRUSADERS "MASSACRE MUSLIMS AND JEWS"

As mentioned earlier, Jerusalem has the lamentable and tragic distinction of being "the most fought-over place in the world" in terms of major battles by a widely varying cast of adversaries, with at least nine battles occurring before 1985.[36] The first five battles did not include Muslims. These were the Babylonian Conquest (586 B.C.), the Revolt of the Maccabees (168-165 B.C.), the Conquest by Rome (66-63 B.C.), the Jewish Wars of the Roman Empire (70 A.D.) and the Byzantine Persian Wars (615). Muslims first conquered Jerusalem in 637, only five years after Muhammad's death, and after a four-month siege by Caliph Omar I. Under patriarch Sophronius the defenders surrendered the city and apparently were spared major destruction, damage, and indignities.[37] More than 400 years later, in 1099 (by most accounts), the seventh major battle of Jerusalem occurred when the First Crusaders arrived, sacked the city, and ended Muslim rule until the battle of Jerusalem VIII, almost ninety years later.

Christian armies of more than 1,200 knights and 11,000 foot soldiers under Raymond IV of Toulouse reached Jerusalem on June 7, 1099 and promptly encircled the city and constructed three huge siege towers. The Muslim garrison under the Egyptian Caliph Al-Musta'li fired arrows and hurled stones at the attackers. After several days of very heavy fighting a detachment led by Godfrey of Bouillon fought its way across a flying bridge from one of the towers, dropped down inside the walls of the city and threw open the Gate of Saint Stephen.

> "The knights of Godfrey and Tancred poured into the city, launching a wholesale massacre of Moslems and Jews. Tancred seized the Temple in the southeast. Here the defenders, with their rear now exposed, fell back to the Tower of David and surrendered to Raymond. One account reports the death of 70,000 non-Christians by nightfall of July 15."[38]

Accounts of excesses by the Crusaders are based on letters written by some of the Crusaders who participated in the sacking of the city and the slaughter of its defenders and residents. For example, one of the Crusaders described what he did and saw this way, as recorded in *The Gesta Francorum.*

> "Our pilgrims entered the city, and chased the Saracens, killing as they went, as far as the Temple of Solomon. There the enemy

assembled, and fought a furious battle for the whole day, so that their blood flowed all over the Temple. At last the pagans were overcome, and our men captured a good number of men and women in the Temple; they killed whomsoever they wished, and chose to keep others alive.

Soon our army overran the whole city, seizing gold and silver, horses and mules, and houses full of riches of all kinds. All our men came rejoicing and weeping for joy, to worship at the church of the Holy Sepulchre.

In the morning our men climbed up cautiously on to the roof of the Temple and attacked the Saracens, both male and female, and beheaded them with unsheathed swords. The Saracens threw themselves from the Temple....They gave orders that all the dead Saracens should be cast out on account of the terrible stench; because nearly the whole city was crammed with their bodies. The Saracens who were still alive dragged the dead ones out in front of the gates, and made huge piles of them, as big as houses. Such a slaughter of pagans no one has ever seen or heard of; the pyres they made were like pyramids. Raymond of Toulouse had the emir and the others with him brought to him at Ascalon, safe and unharmed."[39]

The same sources contend that the massacre of the Jews and Christians at Jerusalem was not simply a one-time deviancy by Crusaders. Rather, several contingents of the First Crusade had massacred Jews and plundered cities all along the routes of march through Italy, the Balkans, Turkey, and Syria before their depredation in Jerusalem in 1099.

"The People's Crusade left for Jerusalem in the spring of 1096, some months before the departure of the official princely armies. On their route overland to the east, the crusaders encountered the flourishing Jewish communities of the expanding cities of the Rhineland: Speyer, Worms, Mainz, Cologne, and Trier. In all of them except Speyer, where Bishop John was able to avert a catastrophe, there were horrifying scenes of forced baptism, murder and pillage. In many cases the Jews' response to this unprecedented onslaught was mass suicide: on no account were they prepared to fall into the hands of the crusaders."[40]

Saloman bar Simson, a Jewish chronicler, described a massacre this way:

> "Count Emich was the enemy of all the Jews — may his bones be crushed to pieces in millstones of iron. He was known as a man who had no mercy on the old, or on young women, who took no pity on babies or sucklings or the sick, who pulverized God's people like the dust in threshing, who slew their young men with the sword and cut open pregnant women."[41]

The motives and reasons for the massacres by Christian military forces probably had more to do with greed, monetary gain, and some sense of religious vengeance, than with an institutional policy of religious persecution.

> "The massacres did not reflect any official policy of the Church. Forced conversion, for instance, was contrary to canon law, and, although the bishops of the cities involved may have been unwilling to risk their lives for the Jews, this does not mean that any of them favored their persecution. Contemporary western sources almost invariable condemn the crusaders' actions."[42]

Nevertheless, the massacres were not mindless attacks by an uninformed rabble. First, many of the participants in the People's Crusade were knights of some standing. Second, there were specific reasons why the crusaders behaved as they did. Greed was one of their motives. Real need, too, made them desperate for supplies. It is likely that they saw the Jews as a medium through which to obtain money and food by whatever means they found to be most expedient. Certainly, Jews paid bribes to the Crusaders in the hope of being left alone. However, Hebrew chroniclers of the First Crusade emphasize another motive: vengeance for the crucifixion of Christ.[43]

Thus, in many ways, Battle VII for Jerusalem reveals that the Christians — not the Muslims — behaved more as violators of the Qur'an in almost all respects. They were the invaders, the attackers, the pillagers, and the executioners of many (but not all) prisoners despite the surrender of all of the defenders and inhabitants of the city, including both Muslims and Jews. Possibly the many massacres of Jews that they had conducted in their pilgrimage across Europe and Asia Minor desensitized some of the Crusaders and made massacring almost habitual, so that they no longer discriminated among their prisoners as to who would and would not be executed. This, of course, would be a violation of the implicit Qur'anic principle of discrimination, as well as the other principles of proportionality, righteous intention, and transgression avoidance. This battle also is remarkable for so many other reasons. Not only did the Muslims surrender (and suffer horribly for it), but they also were allies with the Jewish inhabitants. Most of the members of both groups perished together at the hands of the Crusaders. Because of this, it would not be surprising if Muslim armies subsequently would avenge the violence that their ancestors suffered in Jerusalem when their successors recaptured Jerusalem in 1187. What is surprising is that they did *not* do so.

JERUSALEM VIII, 1187:
SALADIN SHOWS SOME RESTRAINT

There were many significant changes in the ninety years between the battles Jerusalem VII and VIII. Muslim Turks superceded the Muslim Egyptians as the primary opponents against the disastrous Second Crusade (1147-49). Next came the controversial and confused Third Crusade (1189-1192). The emergence to power of the famous Muslim general Saladin had much to do with this change of fortunes. As he reconquered Palestine, Saladin used masterful tactics and knowledge of open terrain to defeat King Guy, Amalric, Reynald, and several large, Christian armies. At the battle of Tiberias, near Haifa, in 1187, Saladin's army not only dispatched the Christian army quickly, but it then engaged in ransacking the captured garrison and in executing and enslaving Christian prisoners. Yet, when Saladin moved on to Jerusalem to complete his sweep of Palestine, his army apparently performed much more consistently with regards to the Qur'an — although there is no evidence that the Qur'an directly influenced its behaviors. The Muslim forces sieged Jerusalem, but apparently did not use what would have been disproportionate force for that era in the process of capturing it. Saladin's soldiers apparently discriminated in their treatment of enemy soldiers and civilians. They accepted the offer of surrender by the Christian governor, Balian of Ibelin.

"On September 20 Saladin appeared before the city and laid siege
to it. Nine days later his engineers had battered a breach in the
wall. Moslem attempts to penetrate the opening were repulsed by
gallant fighting on the part of the defenders. But the shortage of
fighting men and the absence of any reserve whatsoever doomed

the Holy City. Balian asked for terms and Saladin agreed to ransom captives at the rate of ten dinars for a man, five for a woman, and one for a child. On October 2 the Moslems poured into the city and expelled all the Franks. Those that could pay the ransom became free; the others were sold as slaves. Jerusalem reverted to Moslem control. The Christian castles in the interior fell like tenpins. A year later Saladin dismissed his victorious army, convinced that his countercrusade was ended. But the Frankish hold on Tyre spurred Europe to still another crusade."[44]

At the risk of being too gracious, it seems to me that accounts like these of the eighth battle of Jerusalem suggest to us that Muslim behaviors associated with this battle often were congruent with the Qur'an. Consider that Saladin, the victorious Muslim general, actually accepted peace terms, ransomed prisoners, and then disbanded his army — laid down his arms — in the language of the Qur'an, once he believed that the threat to religious freedom of his Muslims had been restored. Unfortunately, this eighth battle of Jerusalem is in stark contrast to many of the other 213 battles that are under consideration in this chapter.

LAS NAVAS DE TOLOSA, 1212: CHRISTIAN RECONQUEST OF SPAIN

This battle has sometimes been considered more momentous than the Christian victory under Charles Martel at Tours, 480 years earlier, because it massacred so many Muslim combatants that Islam has never fully recovered.[45] Pope Innocent IV ordered a crusade to rid the Iberian Peninsula of Moors once and for all. King Alfonso VIII of Castile assembled a heavily armored army estimated at 100,000 and moved south from Toledo towards Granada, the capital city of the Moors. Muhammad I deployed an army estimated at several hundred thousand into defensive positions on the plain of Tolosa north of Granada. Supposedly, a local shepherd showed Alfonso a secret route through a mountain pass that enabled him to move a large contingent of his cavalry into position for a surprise assault on the Moors. "Violent fighting raged back and forth across the plain" until the Moorish resistance collapsed. "Alfonso's whole army swept forward, turning the battle into a massacre. An estimated 150,000 Moors fell to Christian sword and spear."[46]

Tolosa is noteworthy not just because of its historical importance and the extraordinary number of casualties said to have been suffered by the Moors, but also because there is no evidence that either side engaged in gross excesses against prisoners or the civilian population. Badly damaged, the Moors apparently withdrew back to their fortress at Granada without surrendering. They held on to their last foothold in the peninsula until the famous, even more consequential, (but less bloody) Battle of Granada two hundred-fifty years later.

GRANADA, SPAIN, 1491-92: A PEACEFUL RESOLUTION DESPITE THE OPPORTUNITY FOR A BLOODBATH

The end of Muslim military presence in Spain finally came about when King Ferdinand assembled an army large enough to completely encircle Granada and maintain a vise-like siege for eight months despite very stiff resistance by Mohammed XI (Boabdil). When a Berber relief force from Morocco failed to materialize, Muhammad XI capitulated and negotiated some of the most amenable provisions that Muslim armies would ever know (although King Ferdinand apparently decided later to ignore many of those provisions).

> "Negotiations between Muslim and Christian representatives were secretly conducted at night. They were ratified by the two monarchs at the end of November, 1491. The date of capitulation was fixed for January 2, 1492. The Jihad was now over in Spain, but the Moors of Granada were to be allowed to keep their mosques and their religion, a condition which the Spaniards were later to ignore completely. Boabdil was allotted a small kingdom to govern in the nearby Alpujarras mountains, just to the south, as vassal to Castile.

> The capitulation ceremony was largely religious rather than military, as befitted a war that, to both sides, had probably had a far more enforced, embattled holy character than any other in which they had taken part. A cardinal led the Spanish forces to the ceremony. Ferdinand stood by a mosque, later consecrated to St. Sebastian, a symbol of the Jihad that had failed. The cardinal greeted Boabdil as, glumfaced, he rode out of Granada with his family around him, and escorted him toward the king, who embraced him and accepted the keys to the city from him. 'These keys are thine, O King, since Allah so decrees it,' humbly said the deposed king.... One of the people present at the ceremony was a

Genoese navigator of the name of Christopher Columbus, who was seeking aid from Queen Isabella for a voyage he wished to make west, across the Atlantic to the Indies."[47]

Thus, a strong case can be made to the effect that Columbus's discovery of America would have been delayed, or it might not even have occurred, if Granada had not fallen to Ferdinand and Isabella when it did. More to the point, however, is that there is no evidence that the Qur'an was present at the battle of Granada or that its verses influenced the battle or the negotiations after the battle. Still, Muslim behavior at Granada was congruent with the Qur'an in at least several ways. Boabdil's army was defending Granada, a city that had been a Muslim stronghold for hundreds of years. It had dozens of mosques and thousands of Muslim inhabitants. Boabdil's forces apparently fought steadfastly for eight months and until further resistance was futile. Boabdil accepted a peace offering from Ferdinand, capitulated without surrendering his troops, and negotiated favorable provisions that included access to mosques in the city (although at least one of the mosques was subsequently converted into a church). Few if any of the victors in the other 213 battles that are under consideration in this chapter allowed the Muslim forces that they had vanquished to have such favorable provisions as they received at Granada.

So much attention has been given to battles between European and Muslim forces that it is easy to overlook the fact that Muslim armies have fought many major battles across North Africa, in Central Asia, and even in India and China (some of which are identified in Appendix A). These battles varied considerably in terms of excessive violence, outcomes, and congruence with the instructions of the Qur'an by Muslim forces and by their adversaries. Four of the battles that underscore this variety when they are analyzed and contrasted are Taraori, Talikota, Bamian, and Baghdad I (the first of at least five major battles at this unfortunate city, one of which was raging when I first drafted this paragraph on April 9, 2003).

TARAORI, INDIA, 1192 AND TALIKOTA, INDIA, 1565: MUSLIM CONQUESTS TO THE FAR EAST OF MECCA

Persian Muslim armies were invading Afghanistan, India and western China at about the same time as Muslim forces were being pushed-out of the Iberian Peninsula by the Franks and Turkish Muslim forces were reconquering Palestine. For instance, the Persian

Sultan Muhammad of Ghor captured Sind in 1182, Punjab in 1187 and, after a failed attack against a Hindu army at the Saraswoti River in 1188, destroyed a Hindu army near the same site in 1192. "Near the site of his earlier defeat, at Taraori, 14 miles from Thanesar, Mohammed's mounted archers crushed a Hindu army. The defenders handicapped themselves by a disunited command and caste restrictions that produced clumsy tactics. Mohammed of Ghor plunged on to occupy Delhi and make all northwestern India tributary to him."[48]

Unfortunately, and in contrast to many of the Muslim battles against the Europeans that have already been described, the Muslim battles in central Asia and India from this early period are not described in sufficient detail to tell us what role the Qur'an played, if any, in these battles or if violations of Qur'anic instructions occurred. In the absence of information like this, it seems reasonable to consider that one of the major violations of the Qur'an by the Muslim forces was that Muslims clearly were invading foreign lands, not because of religious persecution against them as Muslims but because of a quest for more wealth and power. Another violation of the Qur'an was that Muslims occupied those foreign lands, suppressed and exploited the civilian populations there for many years, even centuries, after the battles. These inferences are supported by the fact that more than a dozen of the other major battles listed in Appendix A involved Muslim armies fighting in central Asia and the Far East after the Battle of Taraori. One of these battles was Talikota — more than 350 years later and much further south in the Indian Peninsula.

During the reign of Akbar the Great, the Mogul emperor of Afghanistan, Muslim sultans led an army against the Hindu kingdom of Vijayanagar at Talikota in southeastern Bombay province. "The Mohammedans won an overwhelming victory, which destroyed the Hindu kingdom."[49] The paucity of any additional information about these two battles means that the only obvious violations of the Qur'an that are apparent from these battles were that the Muslim forces invaded distant lands, attacked people in those lands, and had not suffered any obvious persecution because of their religion as grounds for retaliation. Some historians claim that the Muslims invaded India in order to expand their empire commercially and to gain revenues through tribute, extortion, and a welter of supposedly protective taxes on the conquered populations.[50]

Bamian, 1221, and Baghdad I, 1258:
Two Mongol Massacres Of Muslim Forces

Between the victories of the Persian armies in India at Taraori and Talikota and a span of more than 350 years were dozens of other major Muslim battles in North Africa, the Balkans, and Asia Minor including remarkably brutal battles against the Mongol armies of Genghis Khan, his grandson Hulagu, and their successors. Two of the first of these battles were also two of the most vicious and annihilative battles in the history of warfare, Bamian and Baghdad I.

Bamian occurred as Genghis Khan overran the Khwarizm Muslim Empire in central Asia with his force in excess of 40,000 Mongol cavalry and pursued the Muslim army of Jalal-ad-Din into Afghanistan. Khan became outraged when his route of march was blocked by Muslim defenders in the city of Bamian, which was situated in a vital mountain pass in the Hindu Kush.

"The Mongols laid siege to the city. During this operation a youthful grandson (son of Ogadai) of the Khan was killed below the city's walls. With cold fury the Mongol chief ordered a relentless assault on Bamian. Despite heavy Mongol casualties, the city was taken. All human life was extinguished and the buildings were burned to the ground. Even the Mongols called Bamian the 'City of Sorrow.'"[51]

If this account can be taken literally, then the Battle of Bamian was perhaps as totally destructive as any of the 214 most famous Muslim battles. In any case, I could find no claims that the Qur'an was present or that it played a crucial role in the course of the battle. It seems reasonable to suggest that the Muslims at Bamian defended their community steadfastly and even courageously. Other than this, it is impossible to find evidence of compliance with the Qur'an by the Muslims, just as it seems fair to suggest that the behaviors of Genghis Khan and his Mongols were incompatible with the Qur'an in so many obvious ways, including the execution of prisoners and civilians.

This assessment also applies to the first major Battle of Baghdad, 1258, less than forty years later. As one of Genghis Khan's grandsons was invading western China, his brother Hulagu swept through Persia and destroyed Muslim forces in his way, "annihilating the Assassin sect, which had spread terror through the region for more than 150 years."[52] Parenthetically we should note and remember the name, "Assassin," of the Muslim sect that Hulagu destroyed. Notice also that

167

the Assassin sect had a reputation for spreading *"terror"* through the region for more than 150 years. This reputation for terror by the Muslim Assassin sect, if widely known by contemporary proponents of the Qur'an, could well serve as a validation for their engaging in various forms of terror include assassinations in public places. Government and military leaders who are responsible for defending against terrorist attacks should keep in mind historical precedents such as this.

In any case, the Mongol General Hulagu brought the full wrath of his army against Baghdad, the longstanding capital of the Abbassid Muslim empire that spanned so much of the Middle East at that time.

> "The Mongols stormed into the city of February 15, 1258, and sacked it ruthlessly. Mutasim, last of the original line of Abbassid caliphs, which had ruled since 750, fell into Mongol hands. He was trampled to death by horses, leaving Mameluke Egypt the last stronghold of Moslem culture. Hulagu pressed on westward into Syria."[53]

It should be noted that the destructiveness and success of the Mongol invaders was not inevitable, however. Only two years later, at the battle of Ain Jalut, on the Sea of Galilee, Hulagu's army summarily was "cut to pieces" by a Mamaluke army led by Bibars (Baybars) — the first Mongol defeat in the West and the end of Hulagu's invasion of Muslim lands in the Middle East.[54]

Regarding the battle of Baghdad I, it can be said that, once again, the Muslim forces were on the defensive and they paid dearly for it. Once again a case can be made that their adversaries violated the provisions of the Qur'an regarding war and peace, more than they did. There also is no evidence of truces, treaties, or other opportunities to secure a lasting peace, possibly because the Muslim forces were so totally destroyed at Baghdad I.

SIX BATTLES BETWEEN EUROPEANS AND OTTOMAN ARMIES ALONG THE "CROSSROADS"

As can been seen in Appendix A, more than forty major battles were fought between European and Ottoman armies, 1300-1920, in and along the crossroads between Europe and the Middle East. In order to provide a sense of the variety of those battles and their congruence with the Qur'an, I will provide brief synopses of seven of them: Kosovo, Mohacs, Vienna I, "The Pyramids," Dardanelles and Gallipoli, and Megiddo.

Kosovo I, 1389: The Brutal Beginning Of Five Centuries Of Ottoman Warfare In The Balkans

From its capital in Adrianople, north of Constantinople, the Ottoman Empire expanded into the Balkans under the leadership of grand vizier Murad I. A black day in Serbian history began when Murad marched northeast towards Belgrade with an estimated 10,000 heavy-mailed cavalry and Janizaries. His march was blocked at Kosovo by Serbian Prince Lazar I and some 25,000 Bosnian, Serb, Albanian, Bulgarian, and Wallachian troops. The armies confronted each other for days as their generals wrestled with strategic considerations. As noted earlier, one account has it that the Qur'an was not only present in the Muslim camp but that its verses were consulted at least several times by Murad in deciding when to attack.

> "The grand vizier opened the Koran at random seeking inspiration. His eyes fell upon the verse that said, 'Oh Prophet, fight the hypocrites and unbelievers.' 'These Christian dogs are unbelievers and hypocrites,' he said. 'We fight them.' He opened the Koran a second time. This time he read, 'A large host is often beaten by a weaker one.' 'They are the large host. We are the weak one,' he said. 'We fight them.'"[55]

Supposedly these consultations with the Qur'an were augmented by what Murad believed to be a favorable omen in the form of two events that involved the weather in the hours just before the battle.

> "During the night, as they slept or prayed or kept vigil, the wind blew over the field of Kosovo, the field of blackbirds as it has come down to us, sweeping a lot of dust with it from the Christian side into the Muslim ranks. Early in the morning, while it was still dark, it began to rain; the rain settled the dust on the ground, and Murad thankfully took this meteorological incident as a sign of Allah's favor."[56]

At daylight a brutal battle began with cavalry rushes into the ranks of each force's infantry.

> "Soon it became clear that the Ottomans were pushing back the Christians. Now was the time for personal sacrifice. From the

Serbian ranks a knight in armor rode out toward the Turkish line, holding his right hand up and shouting words of peace. 'I'm a friend, I'm a friend,' he cried out. The Turks opened their ranks to let him through. The knight, Milosch Kabilovitch, King Lazar's son-in-law, rode to within a few yards from the sultan, was escorted into the presence of the sovereign, knelt as if in homage, bowed, whipped out a hidden knife, and stabbed Murad through the belly. He tried to rush back to his horse but was overtaken by the Janissaries and torn to pieces. So the sultan was murdered and so was his murderer slain. Murad, lying on the ground, began slowly to die from loss of blood, but he remained lucid enough to give the final order that gave the Turks victory. 'Send in the reserves,' the dying sultan ordered."[57]

Bazaret I, Murad's son, immediately replaced him as commander and ordered his reserve forces into a full attack. It quickly shattered the remaining Christian units. King Lazar was captured and executed, as were most of the Christian soldiers who surrendered.

> "After the death of Murad, the silent battlefield of Kosovo turned into a slaughterhouse. Appalled at the Muslim losses, the new sultan decided to avenge his dead by killing all the Christian prisoners. They were tied together in groups of three or four and decapitated by professional executioners who formed part of the royal household. After some hours, their arms aching from the number of decapitations they had carried out, the exhausted executioners asked for permission to cut the throats of the victims with a dagger instead."[58]

The savagery of the victorious Ottoman army of Kosovo I thus can be understood as the source of unrequited animosity between Balkan Christians and Muslims to this day. It often has been mentioned as being the major reason why the regime of now deposed Serb President Slobodan Milosevic (on trial for genocide by the World Court at the Hague in 2003) engaged in genocidal actions against Bosnian Muslims at Srebrenica and elsewhere after the withdrawal of Soviet forces from Yugoslavia in the 1990s (a subject that is analyzed in some detail in Chapter 5). Kosovo I also can be understood as a violation of almost all instructions in the Qur'an to its followers regarding proper conduct in war, with the possible exception that they apparently did not turn their vengeance against the civilian population and communities in the Balkans immediately after the battle.

This is all the more noteworthy because, if the author Paul Fregosi is to be believed, the Qur'an was consulted by Murad before he ordered the bloody attack. Otherwise, however, Eggenberger reports that the Muslim victory at Kosovo I was so conclusive that "Serbia became a vassal state of the Turks."[59]

MOHACS, HUNGARY, 1526:
YET ANOTHER MASSACRE NOT SOON FORGOTTEN

Suleiman I "The Magnificent" followed up his sanguinary sacking of Belgrade in 1521 with raids throughout the Balkans. As he moved towards Budapest with an army of almost 100,000 men and dozens of heavy artillery pieces, his route was blocked at Mohacs along the Danube by an army of about 20,000 Hungarian and Polish troops led by King Louis II of Hungary, hundreds of noblemen and clergy of what has often been called the Holy Roman Empire.

> "Louis unwisely launched a headlong assault on the invading army, despite the poor discipline among his knights and peasants. The Turks, with sound deployment and superior artillery, cut the Christian force to pieces. On the following day an Ottoman counterassault swept the field. Among the 10,000 Western dead lay Louis, seven bishops, and several hundred nobles. The battle of Mohacs broke Hungary's hold on central Europe."[60]

Some of the accounts of Muslim vengeance at Mohacs — and immediately following it — strain credulity.

> "It took Suleiman only two hours to smash the Hungarian army. King Louis, wounded in the head, escorted by his bodyguard, managed to escape from the battlefield, but his horse slipped while crossing a muddy creek, fell back on him and, dragged down by his heavy armor, the king drowned. Seven bishops and archbishops, including Perenyi, were among the slain. Sixteen thousand Hungarians died in the battle, two thousand taken prisoner were all beheaded, and their heads, impaled on pikes, were scattered as decorative pieces around Suleiman's tent that night."[61]

Besides the gruesome slaying and mutilating of prisoners, there is also at least one claim (and a rather exaggerated one, in my opinion) that Suleiman had a staggering number of the Hungarian population enslaved, deported and sold for profit. This same source, Paul

Fregosi, a journalist who reported on the Serb-Bosnian conflict of the 1990s, claims that the taking and sharing of booty was practiced in a way that is congruent with the Qur'an's instructions: one-fifth went to the sultan (although we do not know if it was used to aid the poor and needy, as required by some verses in the Qur'an), and the remainder for the Muslim combatants.

> "Probably three million Hungarians were enslaved and deported all over the Ottoman Empire. A few months after Mohacs, Suleiman marched back to Istanbul with the first batch of 100,000 Hungarians, men, women, and children, to be sold in the slave markets, some in the capital, others in Anatolia, Egypt, Syria, and the Balkans. The ghazis, the soldiers of the Jihad, Janissaries, spahis, and all were richly compensated for their fighting skills. The usual one-fifth of the spoils was allotted to the sultan, now doubly entitled to his share as the caliph of Islam, but the bulk was shared among the soldiers."[62]

VIENNA, 1529:
MUSLIM MASSACRE BEFORE AND AFTER THE FAMOUS FAILED SIEGE

Only three years after his devastating victory over the Hungarians at Mohacs, Suleiman's army of more than 100,000 troops marched up the Danube River valley to Vienna, the seat of the Hapsburg's power, to further his conquest of the Holy Roman Empire.

> "With his Hungarian allies in tow, Suleiman journeyed on to Vienna, taking a few towns on the way, massacring a few garrisons, and torturing, killing and enslaving haphazardly the inhabitants of the villages through which his army passed once they entered Austria. The vanguard of Suleiman's army arrived outside Vienna on September 23 and galloped around the walls of the city on their horses, shouting insults at the defenders and promising them death. Each horseman held his lance aloft, with the head of an Austrian speared at the end of it. The bulk of Suleiman's army reached Vienna a couple of days later and the city settled in for a long siege, in dread and anticipation of defeat, knowing they were outnumbered at least ten to one."[63]

Charles V, the Holy Roman Emperor, sent Spanish and German regiments into Vienna under the command of General Graf Nicholas zu Salm-Reifferscheidt. These forces fought so effectively that the

Ottoman siege lasted only three weeks, despite the decided numerical superiority of the attackers, their record of stunning battlefield successes, and their skilled use of mines, artillery, and explosives.

"The 20,000 man garrison beat off several assaults against the city's walls and in turn hurt the attackers with vigorous sorties through the three gates. In this valiant defense Vienna was aided by foul weather, which prevented the Turks from bringing up their artillery. Finally, after three weeks of failure, Suleiman abandoned the siege on October 16. Hampered by deep snow and harassing cavalry attacks, the Turks lost heavily on the long road back to Adrianople. The repulse at Vienna is often considered the turning point in the Moslem advance against Christian Europe. The Turks, however, refused all offers of a peaceful settlement of the war until 1533. Then Suleiman agreed to terms on Hungary with Ferdinand, but the naval war with Charles V continued."[64]

Reportedly, despite the failure of the siege (or perhaps because of it), Suleiman's forces wrecked havoc on the villages and local villagers as they broke camp and retreated to Adrianople. "Before leaving the Turks burned their camp and massacred all their prisoners, thousands of them, mainly peasants and their families kidnapped from neighboring villages."[65] The atrocities allegedly committed by the retreating Ottoman army became a permanent part of the European history and created an enduring image of the Ottoman Muslim armies as barbarians without equal. This assessment seems exaggerated, however, if we recall the behaviors of some of the Mongol armies at Bamian and Baghdad I, and the behaviors of the Christian armies at Jerusalem I. In terms of congruence with the Qur'an, there is little doubt that the Ottoman army behaved badly at Vienna in 1529. It violated the Qur'an's instructions in almost every way: invading, attacking, executing enemy prisoners and civilians, and pillaging the countryside as it retreated. Suleiman did not accept truces or treaties, at least until four years after the battle. His army probably did not fight particularly steadfastly or as a coherent unit. After all, he lifted the siege after only three weeks and apparently had not suffered particularly heavy casualties before doing so. There is no evidence that the Muslim combatants or their supporters in Adrianople had been persecuted relentlessly because of their religion. By most accounts (admittedly by European authors), their invasions of the northern Balkans were meant to expand their empire and its treasures. Had the Muslim combatants frequently invoked the Qur'an

173

in their confrontations against their Christian adversaries at Vienna and elsewhere in the Balkans, surely this would have been recorded and reviled by their adversaries.

As a postscript, it should be noted that Muslim forces returned to try their hands at Vienna almost 150 years later, in 1683 (as noted in Appendix A). This time the Ottoman forces were almost destroyed when a Christian army relief force attacked it from the rear while it laid siege to Vienna. There is no record of the Muslim forces engaging in executing prisoners and pillaging local villages during or after this battle, in contrast to their behaviors at the Battle of Vienna I. However, their commandant, Grand Vizier Kara Mustafa, reportedly was beheaded because he had failed.

> "Emperor Leopold I and his court fled, leaving the defense to
> Count Ernst Rudiger von Starhemberg. When assaults against the
> city's walls failed, the Turks began mining operations, which
> seemed certain to succeed. But on September 12 John III Sobieski
> of Poland and Charles V, titular duke of Lorraine, arrived with a
> relieving army of 20,000 men. An attack on the Turkish siege lines
> routed the Mohammedans, ending the threat to Vienna. The
> defeated vizier was beheaded for his failure. This second battle of
> Vienna clearly confirmed the declining strength of the Ottoman
> Empire."[66]

PYRAMIDS, 1798:
NAPOLEON STRETCHES HIS EMPIRE AND INVOKES THE QUR'AN

Another campaign to expand an empire, this one into Muslim lands, was Napoleon's. This time the Muslim forces were the defenders. Early in his wars of the French Revolution, Napoleon turned his attention to Egypt, after he drove the Austrian armies out of northern Italy. His goal was to destroy British influence in the Eastern Mediterranean and stretch his empire far to the east, possibly to India. He embarked his expeditionary force of 36,000 soldiers and hundreds of artillery pieces aboard French vessels, seized Malta, then Alexandria, and moved down along the west bank of the Nile towards Cairo. Murad Bey, a Mameluke vizier for the region, decided to use his 40,000 troops and 6,000 cavalry to block Napoleon from Cairo at Embabeh, just north of the pyramids.

"On July 21 Napoleon moved southward on the Egyptian position along the river, while sending a strong flanking column westward to envelop the enemy's left. To avoid being pocketed against the Nile, Murad launched an all-out cavalry assault to this front. The Mameluke horsemen fought fiercely, but they were no matches for French muskets and artillery. When the counterassault failed, the entire Egyptian army collapsed. The French flanking column closed in to take Embbabeh, cutting off large numbers of the disorganized Egyptian infantry. Murad fell back to the south unmolested, while Napoleon, who had suffered only about 300 casualties, crossed the river the next day to occupy Cairo. The invasion of Egypt seemed completely successful. But on August 1 the protecting French fleet was shattered by a British attack at the mouth of the Nile. Cut off from Europe by sea, Napoleon turned eastward to attack the Ottoman Empire in Syria."[67]

After the Battle of the Pyramids, Napoleon used Cairo as his base for military expeditions further down the Nile and into Palestine and Syria. Napoleon's behavior in Cairo is reported to have been rather bizarre and infuriating to many of the Muslim inhabitants — so much so that it caused violent rebellions to which Napoleon often reacted with even more violence.

"In Cairo he would from time to time prance around dressed-up in some sort of Muslim costume, in which he looked absurd, masquerading as a Muslim scholar. He would spout verses from the Koran to his bewildered listeners or learnedly chat about Allah to imams and mullahs who pretended to be impressed but were not. One of his senior commanders, General Menou, tried to win the confidence of the locals by converting to Islam and changing his first name from Jacques to Abdallah. He also married some local bint (Arab word for a young girl) and prayed several times a day, bowing ostentatiously in the direction of Mecca."[68]

Despite these unusual and perplexing behaviors, the presence of the French army in Egypt soon provoked a cycle of violence in which both parties participated.

"The dominant presence in Cairo of the French was foreign and Christian, and therefore intolerable, and when a revolt broke out messengers ran through the street, shouting, 'Let those who believe there is but one God take themselves to the Mosque El Azhar! For today we fight the infidel!' It was the Jihad, in its pure, basic form. Shedding his Islamic pretensions, Bonaparte on this occasion ordered this artillery to start shelling the mosque. 'Exterminate everybody in the mosque!' he shouted to one of his generals. The mob, led by their religious leaders, went on a rampage that lasted until the evening of the next day. They massacred thirty-three French hospital patients caught in a convoy of ambulances and gave the body of a murdered French general to the dogs to eat."[69]

Some of the forms of retaliation by the French forces were no less disgusting than the Muslim behaviors, according to Fregosi.

"Because of the prevalence of syphilis, one of the French generals ordered that all prostitutes caught in the soldiers' barracks should be arrested and executed, which was duly carried out by the Janissaries, who, being disciplined soldiers, were now working for the French. They rounded up and beheaded four hundred women, placed their headless bodies in sacks, and threw them into the Nile."[70]

One account indicates that this accelerating cycle of violence spread far beyond Egypt. "When Bonaparte invaded Syria and laid siege to Acre, the local governor, Djezzar Pasha, a Bosnian from Sarajevo, ordered that all French prisoners have their heads cut off. But the massacring was two-sided. Bonaparte had ordered some two thousand Muslim prisoners captured at Jaffa to be bayoneted to death."[71]

Thus, when reviewing the accounts of combatant behaviors surrounding the Battle of the Pyramids and Napoleon's occupation of Cairo, it seems fair to say that while the Qur'an was present (in Napoleon's camp at least), it apparently had little if any moderating influence on the behaviors of the combatants on either side. Then again, both Murad Bey's army and some portions of the population of Cairo certainly fought steadfastly in opposition to Napoleon's invasion, his presence, and the often brutal orders that he and his generals issued in their efforts to control the local populations and to spread their dominion over the Muslim world.

DARDANELLES AND GALLIPOLI, 1915-16:
THE OTTOMAN-GERMAN COALITION REPULSES ALLIED NAVAL AND GROUND ATTACKS

These two famous battles are especially noteworthy here, not just because they were such decisive failures for the attacking allies, but also because Muslim combatants served on both sides, fought against each other (apparently as steadfastly as they did against their non-Muslim adversaries), and because the Qur'an was present and was not violated by either side to any appreciable extent, so far as we know from published sources. These observations support the argument that national identities were becoming as important as religious identities to many of the combatants in the armies and civilian populations of the nations involved in supporting these battles: Ottoman Turkey, Germany and Austria (the "Coalition" forces) and Britain, France, Russia, and the Australian and New Zealand (Anzac) among the Allies.

Both battles resulted from the decision of the Allies to try to break the deadlock on the Western Front during WWI by opening a new front, against Turkey, that would drain-off German-Austrian resources and open a supply line through the Dardanelles to the Bosporus and the Black Sea. British First Lord of the Admiralty Winston Churchill sent a fleet of minesweepers, cruisers, and battleships under Admirals Carden and Robeck to destroy the coalition fortification along the waterway to the Black Sea. Supposedly the coalition with the Ottomans had many reasons besides simply wanting to deny the Allies a naval supply route to Russia. Ironically similar to Napoleon's motivation for courting Muslim favor in Egypt after the Battle of the Pyramids more than a century earlier (See the preceding section in this chapter), German Monarch Kaiser Wilhelm II believed that the Muslim world could provide Germany with valuable political allies, material resources, and large numbers of military recruits, if he could find ways to undermine the British colonial regime in India and Suez and the French colonial regime in North Africa. "The German emperor, who longed to destroy Britain and its empire, ordered his agents 'to inflame the entire Muslim world against Britain, this hateful, lying, and unscrupulous nation.'"[72] The main target was British-ruled India, with nearly sixty million followers of Allah, the most populous Muslim nation in the world. Earlier, in the first years of the twentieth century, the Kaiser had begun to cultivate assiduously the Islamic world, also spreading the rumor that he had secretly converted to Islam, and incognito, had made the pilgrimage to Mecca. He now called himself "The Prophet of Islam." "The call to war was aimed also at the Muslim North African troops serving in the French army, at the Muslims in the Indian Army, and at the czarist soldiers from the Muslim provinces of Russia. It was a smooth operation that Turks and Germans cunningly hoped would cause chaos in allied ranks."[73]

These efforts to convert Muslim personnel from allegiance to Britain and France to allegiance to the Ottoman-German coalition apparently had limited success, at best.

"It caused a big scare, but that was virtually all. The only troops on which it had the slightest effect were some Indian Muslim troops defending the Suez Canal. Some of the Indian troops, mainly Muslim Baluchis from the Iranian-Indian-Afghan border region, refused to fight their fellow Muslim Turks and deserted to the Turks. A number of Indian troops in faraway Singapore mutinied. Several dozens, not all of them Muslims, were shot. But Muslims in the Allied armies, Jihad notwithstanding, in fact generally fought as bravely against the Muslim Turks in the Dardanelles and Mesopotamian campaigns, as they did against the Germans on the western front."[74]

As far as the battle itself is concerned, the allied naval attack was repeatedly and decisively rebuffed by the German-Turkish defenders.

"Unknown to the Allies, however, German advisor Gen. Otto Liman von Sanders had meanwhile greatly strengthened Turkish defenses on both sides of the waterway. Robeck's attack got underway at 10 A.M. In four hours his warships had closed to The Narrows, but Turkish field guns were taking a heavy toll of the minesweepers. A French battleship, the Bouvet, had been destroyed by an unswept mine. Now another battleship and a cruiser were lost, and a second cruiser damaged by mines. Two other ships were crippled by gunfire. At this point Robeck lost his nerve and withdrew. Never again in the war would the Allies come so close to Constantinople. A purely naval attack was discarded in favor of a land operation against Gallipoli."[75]

Fregosi claims that during the allied naval bombardments the Qur'an was very much in evidence among the Turk defenders and that it inspired them and steeled their resolve and steadfastness:

"The attack had turned into another manifestation of Muslim piety by the devout Turkish defenders who, under the direction of their imams, sang appropriate verses of the Koran as they fired their heavy shells at the allied dreadnoughts, turning the battle into an unscheduled Jihad. Former Private W. Sarrol of the 21st AIF (Australian Imperial Force) Battalion remembers the Turks as par-

178

ticularly 'ferocious soldiers' as, he said, 'they were not only fighting in defense of their homeland, they were also fighting a Jihad, a holy war against the infidel. They were filled with holy zeal. "Allah, Allah, Allah" they shouted as they plunged forward to attack.'"[76]

The Battle of Gallipoli was even more decisive and much more bloody than the Battle of Dardanelles. The Allies decided to land amphibious forces, including 75,000 men under General Sir Ian Hamilton, at the western tip of the Gallipoli Peninsula on the north side of the Dardanelles Strait that would then move east to Constantinople (Istanbul) and the Bosporus, destroying the enemy's fortifications and their resistance along the way. In the meantime, German General von Sanders skillfully redeployed 60,000 of his Turkish forces with heavy artillery above most of the probable landing zones of the attacking amphibious forces.

"Although Turkish resistance was only sporadic, poor coordination among the landing parties held the 35,000 invaders on the beaches the first day. Farther up the west coast, the Anzac Corps of 17,000 men (Sir William Birdwood) landed a mile north of its objective at Ari Burun. Pressing inland, the force was soon checked by a Turkish counterattack lanced by Col. Mustafa Kemal (later Kemal Attaturk). Here too the Allies were still on the beaches at the end of the first day. For almost two weeks neither allied force could push far enough inland to drive the Turks off the heights commanding the beaches. At the same time Liman von Sanders could not drive the invaders into the sea. By May 8 the stalemate was firm, Hamilton having lost almost a third of his army in the total casualties from Cape Helles and Ari Burun, now called Anzac Cove. After considerable controversy (Winston Churchill, who had conceived the operation, was dropped from the cabinet), the British government decided to strengthen the Gallipoli force."[77]

The battle dragged on for more than eight months as the Allies landed more and more waves of reinforcements on the peninsula, repeatedly relieved their generals for delays and blunders, and suffered heavy casualties due to severe weather and epidemics, more than to coalition weaponry.

"Finally, with the consent of London, the operation was called-off. The Suvla Bay and Anzac Cove troops were evacuated by sea on December 20, the Cape Helles force by January 9. Not a single life

179

was lost in the withdrawal. But over all, the mismanaged battle
had cost the British and French some 250,000 casualties out of the
410,000 British and 70,000 French landed at Gallipoli. Turkish
losses were equally high. However, a stout defense had held the
Dardanelles and effectively blocked all aid to Russia by this
route."[78]

In assessing both battles, it is remarkable that violations of the
Qur'an are not more evident, given the large number of combatants,
the heavy weaponry that both sides possessed, the combined duration
of the battles, the long-standing historical antagonisms between and
among the adversaries, and what was at stake, particularly for the
Ottomans. They were, after all, defending their homeland and
beloved capital city of over 400 years (Istanbul). They had the opportunity to reclaim the glory of the Ottoman Empire that had been
declining since the battles of Vienna, hundreds of years earlier.

Although it is admittedly speculative on my part, the absence of
obvious violations of the Qur'an by the Ottoman Turks suggests that
the Qur'an might well have had a moderating influence on their
behaviors, especially in terms of discouraging them from taking prisoners and from mistreating prisoners that they did capture. Then
again, despite its presence, perhaps the Qur'an was no longer as
salient to many of the Ottoman defenders as it had been in earlier battles through the centuries. This observation is compatible with the
fact that Col. Mustafa Kemal was a senior military officer at Gallipoli
and that later, as Kemal Attaturk and as President of the new Republic
of Turkey, he secularized the government by officially separating it
from Islam. Of course it is widely believed that this action ignited bitter controversies and enmities that are raging even to this day in Iran,
Afghanistan, the Sudan, and so many other nations in the Middle East.
The thought also occurs that violations of the Qur'an might be less
common when Muslim armed forces fight in conjunction with non-
Muslim forces — a speculation that is reinforced by the behaviors of
Muslim and non-Muslim forces on both sides of the Battle of Meggido.

MEGIDDO III, PALESTINE, 1918:
SEPARATE MUSLIM FORCES ALLIED WITH BOTH ADVERSARIES FIGHT
WITHOUT OBVIOUS VIOLATIONS OF THE QUR'AN

Repulsed at the battles of Dardanelles and Gallipoli, the British
removed most survivors back to the Western Front in Europe except
for a small detachment of British regulars that were sent into

180

Palestine under General Sir Edmund Allenby (and included Col. T. E. Lawrence "of Arabia") in order to divert and harass German-Ottoman forces and keep them from controlling the Suez Canal. Allenby built his detachment into an army of more than 60,000 with recruits from India and with Muslim recruits from Egypt and Arabia who chaffed at the longstanding oppression by the Ottoman regime in Istanbul. After capturing Jerusalem from the Ottomans in December, 1917, Allenby moved his army deftly in order to destroy a coalition army of 30,000 under the same German general (von Sanders) who had so skillfully defended the Dardanelles and Gallipoli.

"Allenby, who had secretly massed most of his infantry along the coast north of Jaffa, attacked early on September 19 on a 65-mile front. The thinly stretched Turkish line collapsed in three hours. Allenby rushed his cavalry corps through the gap toward Megiddo, then wheeled the horsemen to the right behind the enemy Eighth and Seventh armies. With their route to the north blocked, the Turks fled eastward across the Jordan, leaving 25,000 prisoners in British hands. This retreat caused the Turkish Fourth Army on the eastern flank to withdraw also. As the Turks scrambled northward toward Damascus, they were harassed by British cavalry and air-craft and by raiding Arabs. Liman von Sanders had no opportunity to make a stand. His Asienkorps of German troops joined the retreat. Damascus fell on October 2, and Aleppo, more than 200 miles to the north, on October 28. Two days later the Turkish government asked for and received an armistice. The battle of Megiddo had resulted in the capture of 75,000 prisoners at a cost to the British of 5,600 casualties. In all, the Palestine campaign resulted in more than 550,000 British casualties of which 90 percent were non-battle."[79]

In the absence of contradictory evidence it seems fair to say that Muslim forces on both sides of the Battle of Megiddo and related encounters behaved in ways that were usually congruent with the Qur'an. It is difficult to determine whether either of the Muslim con-tingents in the British-Egyptian or the German-Ottoman armies were invaders. Perhaps both of them were invaders, but to a limited extent, in that the battlefields of Palestine had "belonged" to regimes of their ancestors at various times during the previous 700 years (see Appendix A for identification of some of the earlier battles in Palestine by Egyptian Muslims and by Ottoman Turkish Muslims). Also noteworthy at Megiddo is that the Ottomans asked for and received an armistice.

This is perhaps the only battle among the 214 battles in which a Muslim force (or more correctly the political regime behind a Muslim force) so clearly asked for and received an armistice. Of course, it is worth noting that the armistice concluded the war, rather than the battle of Megiddo, per se, which had been resolved more than one month earlier. Yet it also seems fair to say that the armistice would not have occurred, or occurred so soon, if Megiddo had not been so decisive for the British-Egyptian force. 25,000 Ottoman prisoners were captured. Apparently they were treated reasonably well by their captors. This is compatible with the Qur'an, even if the prisoners were not immediately freed or ransomed. In any case, there is no record of gross violations of the Qur'an at the Battle of Megiddo or in its aftermath by any of the participants. This distinguishes this battle from many of the other battles that have just been highlighted, and from the other dozens of battles that are under consideration here.

SOME NAVAL BATTLES BY AND AGAINST MUSLIM FORCES

Seven of the 214 major battles that involved Muslim forces were naval battles: Lycia, 655 (a resounding Muslim victory over a Byzantine fleet in the first major naval battle by Muslim forces), Lepanto I, 1499 (the Ottoman fleet defeated a Venetian fleet), Preveza, 1538 (a Muslim fleet of Suleiman defeated Andrea Doria and a Holy Roman-Venetian fleet), Lepanto II, 1571 (a Venetian-Austrian fleet smashed an Ottoman fleet and reversed the earlier defeat of Lepanto I in 1499), Cesme, 1770 (a Russian fleet damaged the fleet of Mustafa III), Navarina, 1827 (British, French, Russian, and Greek naval forces destroyed an Ottoman fleet in Navarina harbor) and Sinope, 1853 (a Russian fleet damaged Ottoman forces in the Black Sea). Five of the 214 battles also were partial naval battles in that they involved predominantly naval forces of one adversary engaged against predominantly land forces of the other adversary. Constantinople IV, 717-718, Lisbon, 1147, Rhodes, 1522, Tunis III, 1535, and Dardanelles, 1915, are cases in point.

LEPANTO II, 1571: A BLOODY AND PERMANENT END
TO OTTOMAN DOMINANCE OF THE MEDITERRANEAN

Ottoman naval dominance of the Mediterranean resulted from the first Battle of Lepanto in 1499. In that battle the Ottoman navy under Sultan Bajazet II decisively defeated the navy of the city-republic of Venice, which sued for peace and relinquished some of its trading stations in Greece. Less than a century later Ottoman dominance came to an abrupt halt in what was one of the bloodiest and largest naval battles of all time — Lepanto II — and the last great naval battle by oar-driven ships.

"On May 20, 1571 Pope Pius V and Philip II of Spain formed a Holy League in support of Venice against the Turks. Don John of Austria, 24-year-old half brother of the Spanish ruler, began assembling an allied fleet at Messina. It consisted of 316 ships, including 208 galleys and 6 double-size galleys called galleasses. The ships carried 30,000 veteran troops and 50,000 mariners (each galley carried about 350 men). Before this armada was ready for battle, Cyprus fell on August 3. But Don John sought out the Turkish fleet off Lepanto (Navpaktos), in southwestern Greece, on October 7. The Ottoman navy, commanded by Ali Pasha, consisted of 250 galleys, including some speedy half-size galleys called galiots, all rowed by slaves chained to benches. Some 16,000 Turkish soldiers of an 88,000 man force stood ready to fight from the decks."[80]

It would be easy to understand how the battle, once started, would have degenerated into not just a blood bath, but also into a phantasmagoria of heinous executions, mutilations, and other excesses unmitigated by the Bible, the Qur'an, or any other code of morality, given the extraordinary number of ships, sailors, and soldiers that were massed for this battle in calm seas and close to land, as well as the longstanding hostilities between these forces based on religion and ethnicity. However, the battle apparently did not turn out this way, possibly in part because both sides suffered such heavy casualties that both sides were spent.

"The two hostile forces, both deployed in crescent formations, locked together in a furious fight, dominated by ramming and boarding tactics. During three hours of close combat that resembled a land battle, Don John's troops, aided by heavy arquebus fire, gradually gained the upper hand. Some 130 Turkish galleys were captured and another 80 burned or sunk. Ali Pasha, who fell in the battle, lost 25,000 soldiers and mariners killed and 5,000 taken prisoner. Allied losses amounted to 17 ships and 7,500 killed, but twice this number of Christian galley slaves were freed."[81]

One of the few excesses was the beheading of the Ottoman admiral, Ali Pasha. This occurred after he had died from a mortal shot from an arquebus.

"Ali Pasha, hit by an arquebus shot, fell wounded on the deck. A Spanish soldier, one of the boarding party fighting on the deck of the Turkish flagship, saw him fall, pounced upon him, pulled out his knife and cut Ali Pasha's head off. The Spaniard then rushed over to Don John to present him with the trophy and, hopefully, earn a big reward. But Don John, an aristocrat although conceived on the wrong side of the blanket, had a delicate nature. 'What can I do with that head?' he asked with distaste. 'Throw it into the sea,' he ordered the soldier. Another soldier recovered the head, fixed it to the top of a lance, and the whole of the Turkish fleet soon knew that their admiral was dead."[82]

Possibly the limited number of desecrations like the beheading of Ali Pasha was partly the result of both navies having so many oarsmen who had belonged to the opponent's religious and ethnic groups before they had been enslaved. "Uncounted among the dead must have been eight to ten thousand Christian slaves chained to the oars of the Turkish galleys. However, fifteen thousand [*sic*] of them survived and were freed from the captured Turkish vessels. The Christians lost twelve galleys, which on sinking must have taken close to 1,500 Muslim galley slaves to a watery grave."[83]

Lepanto II certainly was bloody. But it is not apparent that the Ottomans in the battle either violated or complied with the Qur'an to an appreciable extent. They did not attack the navy of the Holy League. Nor were they clearly the invading force in that the Ottoman navy had controlled the Gulf of Patros around Lepanto (and much of the rest of the Mediterranean Sea) since their victory at Lepanto I in 1499. And yet it seems fair to say that the Ottomans, as losers, had less opportunity to commit war crimes in violation of the Qur'an than would have been the case if they had been the victors. Then again, because the Qur'an has no specific provisions about naval warfare, members of Muslim naval forces might have felt less constrained in battles than did their counterparts during land battles. These are speculations, of course. Whatever the reasons, I found little evidence that Muslim combatants at the Battles of Lepanto I and II obviously and extensively violated the Qur'an.

TRIPOLI II, 1804: THE U.S. NAVY DUELS WITH THE BARBARY PIRATES

Accounts of military historians vary considerably about what some of them refer to as the "U.S. war with Tripoli" and others have called the war with the "Barbary pirates." Eggenberger's account is one of the more concise and objective ones. He says that the pirates of the Barbary States (Algiers, Morocco, Tripoli, and Tunis) "declared open warfare on U.S. shipping in 1801." President Jefferson sent warships to protect U.S. shipping in the Mediterranean Sea. Over the next four years dozens of skirmishes occurred between the adversaries, most of which were inconclusive, and none of which seem to have been directly influenced by the Qur'an or by Islamic beliefs that the pirates may or may not have ascribed to.

"On October 31, 1803, the 36 gun frigate USS *Philadelphia* (Capt. William Bainbridge) ran aground in the harbor of Tripoli and was captured. The pirates then turned the ship's guns against the American blockading fleet of Capt. Edward Preble. To eliminate this added enemy firepower, Lt. Stephen Decatur slipped into the harbor with 74 men on the night of February 16, 1804. Boarding the *Philadelphia*, Decatur's party set fire to the ship. Assured of its destruction, the Americans escaped under the fire of shore batteries, suffering only one casualty. The continuing blockade forced Tripoli to sue for peace the following year."[84]

Actually, a fuller account, by E. B. Potter, of the events leading up to this battle make it clear that the U.S. naval force, under the command of Captain Bainbridge, was the invading force and instigated the events that led up to this battle. Potter reports that Bainbridge was blockading Tripoli harbor when he decided to try to chase and capture an enemy corsair that was trying to slip past the blockade into the harbor.

"But the corsair hugged the shallows where the frigate could not follow and made her way to safety. Turning back toward open water, the *Philadelphia* drove hard onto an uncharted reef at such an angle of heel that neither of her broadsides could be brought to bear on the Tripolitan gunboats that soon swarmed around her.... Luckily for them, the Tripolitans restricted their fire mainly to the frigate's masts and rigging — to prevent her escape, to capture the Americans alive to hold for ransom, and to secure the frigate undamaged for their fleet."[85]

Bainbridge, his crew, and his ship were captured, but they were not mistreated. "That evening, he and his crew were led triumphantly into the city to begin a long imprisonment. Two days later, high water during a gale enabled the Tripolitans to free the *Philadelphia* from her reef. They also fished up and remounted all her guns."[86]

It took months for the commander of the U.S. forces in the area, Commodore Preble, to decide that his best course of action would be to have the *Philadelphia* destroyed in the harbor to deny her to the enemy. Lt. Stephen Decatur volunteered to lead a secret boarding party into the harbor under cover of darkness to do the job.

"'Board!' shouted Decatur, and 60 Americans swarmed onto the *Philadelphia*. There were too few guards on board the frigate to put up a fight. Decatur and his men, using sabers and battle-axes, killed four or five and drove the rest overboard. Meanwhile, demolition parties were bringing combustibles from the *Intrepid*. These they distributed about the *Philadelphia* and ignited. The frigate, sunbaked in Tripoli harbor, caught fire and burned like tinder. Some of the demolition teams deep in the hold barely made it back up the ladders, but all boarders at length regained the *Intrepid*. Decatur himself, last to get off the blazing ship, leaped into the rigging of the ketch as she pulled away."[87]

There were many other skirmishes on land and sea in the four years before this "war" ended in 1805. U.S. military historians such as Potter depict the U.S. forces as having been more victorious, less belligerent and invasive than the pirates. The war ended almost as ambiguously as it had begun.

"The pasha, trembling for his throne, had at last capitulated. In return for American withdrawal of support for Hamet (the elder brother of the pasha), he agreed to abandon his pretensions to tribute, and released Bainbridge and his crew for a mere $60,000 ransom. When Eaton (Prebel's senior in command) protested, it was pointed out to him that no nation had ever obtained more favorable terms from a Barbary power, and that the pasha, if forced to relinquish his crown, would doubtless exact advance vengeance by massacring his American prisoners."[88]

Overall then, the Barbary forces usually were on the defensive in the Battle of Tripoli II that involved the burning of the *Philadelphia* by the U.S. Navy, and probably in the rest of the war as well. They were under attack by the U.S. Navy. They did not win or lose so much as they sometimes lost an engagement. There is no evidence that the Qur'an, its verses, or Islam influenced the behaviors of the pirates one way or the other, although they might have done so. Certainly the acts of piracy, stealing, and plundering of U.S. warships would seem to be incompatible with the Qur'an, except perhaps, that the ships were in waters that were considered to belong to one or more Muslim entities. Yet there were no claims of religious persecution by the U.S. forces against the Barbary States. Religion was not an issue. Still, there were some ways in which the behaviors of the pirates and the pasha were congruent with the Qur'an. They vigorously defended their ports and property. They captured prisoners and treated them reasonably well, it seems, holding them for ransom and without torturing or enslaving them or forcing them to convert to Islam. They also engaged in treaties, capitulations, and other mechanisms of international diplomacy. They abided by their treaties reasonably well. Thus, in the most famous (and perhaps the only) military war of note between U.S. forces and presumably "Muslim" forces prior to the modern era, the Muslim forces behaved in ways that were sometimes compatible with the Qur'an and in ways that were sometimes less so. The Barbary pirates hardly seem to have had much in common with the Muslim combatants in most of the other 213 battles that are analyzed quantitatively in the next section of this chapter.

214 BATTLES:
PRESENCE AND DIRECT INFLUENCE OF THE QUR'AN

There is little evidence that specific verses of the Qur'an have directly influenced strategy, tactics, or behaviors of Muslim combatants in the 214 major Muslim battles. From many accounts we do learn that the Qur'an was present and had a direct influence on the Battle of Siffin in 657 A.D. (see Appendix A and the description of Siffin and some other battles in the previous section of this chapter). There it was held aloft by some of the combatants as a way of calling upon Allah to settle a long stalemate between warring factions within Islam. Eventually a contentious truce materialized that stopped the battle but not the disagreements between the factions.

Unfortunately, there is little evidence that the Qur'an played such a moderating role as this in any of the other Muslim battles. Fregosi claims that the Qur'an was present at the Battle of Dardanelles in 1915 and that Muslim soldiers sang verses from it before the battle. He also says that it was present and frequently recited by Ottoman soldiers at the Battle of Gallipoli in 1915.[89] At the Battle of Kosovo I in 1389, Ottoman Vizier Murad supposedly recited verses from the Qur'an that he believed encouraged him to attack the Serbian army of King Lazar despite its numerical superiority.[90] Supposedly something like this also happened at the Battle of Las Navas de Tolosa in 1212. Sultan Muhammad I of Granada recited verses from the Qur'an before the battle. His forces fought steadfastly in a pitched battle against Alfonso's Spaniards and Franks before they were "massacred."[91] Ironically, at the Battle of Pyramids (also described in an earlier section of this chapter) the Qur'an is portrayed as being recited by Napoleon and some of his general officers, possibly as a means to recruit local Muslims into military service, rather than by the French adversaries: Murad, Ibrahim, and their Egyptian soldiers.[92] At the Battle of Simancas, Spain, in 934, the Moorish vizier Almanzor reportedly recited frequently from the Qur'an before his army was routed by the army of King Ramiro II.[93] These are the only seven battles for which I found explicit allegations about the presence of the Qur'an and of its influence on the battles. Of the seven battles, the Qur'an only mitigated the conflict once — at Siffin. In the other six instances the battles still occurred after the recitations of the Qur'an — and they were bloody battles. Muslim forces won two of them and were defeated in the other four battles. With so little direct evidence of the influence of the Qur'an in these battles it is necessary to consider whether there is indirect evidence of the Qur'an's influence.

Indirect influence of the Qur'an might be implied by reports of behaviors of Muslim military forces in battle that would seem to comply with or violate the Qur'an's passages concerning peace, conflict, and war. These behaviors could include invasions of foreign lands (especially without provocation in the form of religious persecution of Muslims), attacks by Muslims against non-Muslims (particularly attacks that are unprovoked), as well as withdrawing, deserting, and surrendering by Muslim forces rather than their fighting until they are victorious or they are exterminated. Other violations of the Qur'an by Muslim combatants might include failure to accept surrendering, truces, treaties, and other peace-oriented gestures by adversaries, mistreating and executing enemy leaders, POWs, and civilians, and needlessly destroying the property, dwellings, and towns of the enemy (rather than just acquiring property as booty, which is allowed by the Qur'an in many instances). Evidence of these behaviors by Muslim forces in the 214 battles is summarized in Tables 4-1 to 4-6.

214 BATTLES: EXPLANATION OF THE TABLES

214 of the Muslim battles that I analyzed for evidence of relevance to the Qur'an are listed in chronological order in Appendix A along with information about the identities of the attacking forces, the forces that were attacked, which force was the winner (or a "draw," if the outcome was inconclusive or mixed), and comments about whether the forces violated or complied with the Qur'an's passages on peace, conflict and war either explicitly or implicitly.[94]

For example, in the Battle of Tripoli II, in 1804 (that was just featured as an illustrative case in the previous section), a landing party of U.S. navy personnel attacked the sailors of the Tripolitan Navy (or "pirates"). These pirates were on board to guard the U.S. Navy ship *Philadelphia* that they had captured after it ran aground in Tripoli Bay while pursuing an enemy corsair. Since the attack took place in the harbor of Tripoli (contemporary Libya), the U.S. Navy was considered the invading force. Both Eggenberger and Potter (see the quotations in the previous section of this chapter) describe the U.S. Navy as having been the essential winner in this battle. U.S. personnel succeeded in boarding the ship and destroying it. This was their mission. Then they withdrew. The Tripolitan defenders on board were heavily outnumbered. Yet they did defend the ship somewhat steadfastly (as the Qur'an requires) at least until they were overwhelmed by the boarding party and several of them were slain. Then some of them more or less withdrew (by jumping overboard) while others were killed while defending the ship. The blockade of Tripoli harbor resumed after this battle until Tripoli sued for peace one year later. The data in Appendix A and the following tables were produced by an analysis such as this on the other 213 Muslim battles.

SOME GENERAL STATISTICS ON 214 MUSLIM BATTLES

As shown in Table 4-1, 198 (92%) of the 214 major Muslim battles involved adversaries who were predominantly Muslim versus adversaries who were predominantly non-Muslim. About 15 of these 198 battles had a small percentage of Muslims supporting the adversary who, in conjunction with a more dominant non-Muslim force, fought against a predominantly or exclusively Muslim force. For example, in the Battle of Acre IV in 1840, British naval and army forces combined with some Ottoman army units to quell a revolt by Egyptian Muslims in Acre. The other 16 (8%) of the 214 battles summarized in Table

4-1 were predominantly or exclusively battles between Muslim forces. These include "civil wars" such as Siffin in 657 and Jidda in 1925 as well as "intra-Muslim" battles between Muslims of different societies, regions, or states such as the battles of Herat II in 1837 and Shatt-al-Arab in 1980 (the first major battle of the Iraq-Iran War of 1980-88).

TABLE 4-1:
214 MAJOR BATTLES THAT INVOLVED MUSLIM FORCES, 632-1984 A.D.

1. Number of battles in which Muslim forces are
   one or more of the major adversaries   214   (100%)
2. Number of battles in which the adversaries are
   predominantly Muslims versus non-Muslims   198   (92%)
3. Number of battles in which the adversaries are
   predominantly Muslims versus Muslims   16   (8%)

While the numbers in Table 4-1 do not provide any direct evidence of the Qur'an's influence on Muslim battle, it might be worth considering that these 214 Muslim battles represent only 13.4% of the 1,560 battles, 1479 B.C. to 1984 A.D., that Eggenberger has determined to be "the major battles in recorded history" of the World — not just the Middle East or the West versus the East.[95] Eggenberger also includes four other Muslim battles: Badr, Uhud, The Trench (Medina), and Mecca (which I described in Chapter 3). Including these four battles raises the total to 218 Muslim battles and increases the percentage of major battles that are Muslim from 13.4% to 13.9% — hardly a significant difference.) 13.4% is a significant but modest percentage, especially when these Muslim battles did not begin until 632 A.D., more than 2,000 years after the first major battle (1479 B.C.) in the data set of 1,560. 217 of the battles in the data set predated 624 A.D. Excluding these 217 earlier battles means that 1,343 of the 1,560 battles in the data set correspond to the post-Muhammad period of 632-1984 A.D. Muslim battles constitute 16% of these 1,343 battles. It seems fair to say that Muslim battles comprise a small but significant percentage of the major battles that have occurred in the World since Muhammad's death.

As to Muslim versus Muslim battles, the fact that only 16 (8%) of the Muslim battles were between Muslim forces indicates that Muslim armed forces have not been as warlike towards each other as suggested by some claims about Muslim warfare. We should keep in mind that the Qur'an does not explicitly prohibit Muslim forces from waging war against other Muslim forces, especially if that adversary consists of dissenters, apostates, or disloyal factions in Islam.

Finally, if we consider that the Muslim battles span a period of 1,352 years (from 632 to 1984 A.D.) the average number of years between the 214 Muslim battles is 6.3 years; and between Muslim versus Muslim battles it is 84.5 years. These estimates suggest that major Muslim battles have occurred very frequently since Muhammad's death in 632, but that Muslim versus Muslim battles have been much less frequent. From these estimates it seems fair to say that the Qur'an certainly has not stopped Muslims from engaging in major battles since his death. On the other hand, it is possible that major Muslim battles would have been much more frequent without the Qur'an's restrictions regarding war and its advocacy, however limited, for peace between Muslims and non-Muslims.

Next, we will consider how often Muslim forces and their adversaries were invaders and attackers.

INVADERS AND ATTACKERS IN MUSLIM VERSUS NON-MUSLIM BATTLES

Consider a historical case in which an invading force also was the attacking force in a battle. For example, at the Battle of Ajnadain (outside of Jerusalem) in 634, only two years after Muhammad's death, 45,000 Muslims from Medina and Mecca under Walid Abu Bakr invaded Arab territory that had been conquered hundreds of years earlier by the Byzantines. There they attacked and decisively defeated the much larger army of Theodorus-Heraclius. While there is no evidence that the Qur'an played a direct role in this battle, the fact that the Muslims were the invaders as well as the attackers implicitly violates the Qur'an's prohibitions against these actions.

An invading force does not necessarily become the attacking force. For example, in the Battle of Acre II in 1291, Franks invaded Palestine and occupied the town of Acre. Muslim Turks then laid siege to the town, ultimately forced most of the Franks to surrender, and sold many of them into slavery.[96] Of course, it is not always possible to know from the historical record which forces were invading and which forces were attacking. This is particularly true in naval battles and in land warfare before the emergence of modern nation-states that were able to establish their land and sea borders with consider-

191

able precision — not that this has eliminated controversies over these matters, by any means.

Verses in the Qur'an that were examined in Chapter 2 prohibit both forms of aggression (invading and attacking) by its followers, unless, perhaps, these actions are pre-emptive, or are decidedly retaliatory, or they are necessary in order to stop adversaries from committing abominations against Muslim communities. This would be the case with severe and sustained religious persecution. If the Muslim-Dominant stereotype of Muslim battle and warfare is correct, we would find that Muslim forces were the invaders and attackers in the vast majority of the 198 major battles. On the other hand, if the Muslim-Defendent stereotype is correct we would find the opposite pattern.

Table 4-2 reveals that neither stereotype is totally correct nor totally incorrect. Muslim forces invaded and attacked their non-Muslim adversaries slightly less often than their non-Muslim adversaries invaded and attacked them. In 50 (25%) of the battles, Muslim forces invaded and attacked their non-Muslim adversaries. However, in 59 (30%) of the battles their non-Muslim adversaries invaded and attacked them (contrast rows 2a and 2b in Table 4-2). The same pattern holds true for battles in which one adversary only attacked or invaded the other adversary. Muslim forces only attacked in 34 (16%) of the battles, whereas non-Muslim forces only attacked in 54 (27%) of the battles (contrast rows 3a and 3b). Similarly, Muslim forces only invaded in 6 (3%) of the battles, while non-Muslim forces only invaded in 11 (5%) of the battles (contrast rows 4a and 4b). So we see that the non-Muslim adversaries of Muslim forces have been somewhat more invasive and offensive than Muslim forces since 632 A.D. Muslim forces certainly have been invasive and offensive in almost one-half of all of their major battles against non-Muslims. The Qur'an's verses prohibiting Muslims from invading and attacking could have been much more and also much less influential. Muslim armed forces since Muhammad's death could have been much more, as well as much less, concordant with the Qur'an. Of course it is impossible to reject out of hand the assertion that, without the Qur'an, Muslim forces would have been much more (or even less) aggressive. What we can say, however, is that Muslim forces have not been so aggressive as some of their critics have claimed (the proponents of the Muslim-Dominant stereotype); nor have they been as defensive as some of their most ardent apologists have claimed (the proponents of the Muslim-Defendent stereotype). These observations raise questions about the identities of the adversaries of Muslim armies. Who

TABLE 4-2:
MUSLIM VERSUS NON-MUSLIM FORCES AS INVADERS AND ATTACKERS

1. Number of battles between Muslim and non-Muslim forces	198	(100%)
2a. Number of battles in which Muslim forces both invade and attack their non-Muslim adversaries	50	(25%)
2b. Number of battles in which non-Muslim forces both invade and attack their Muslim adversaries	59	(30%)
3a. Number of battles in which Muslim forces only attack (not invade) non-Muslims forces	34	(16%)
3b. Number of battles in which non-Muslim forces only attack (not invade) non-Muslim forces	54	(27%)
4a. Number of battles in which Muslim forces only invade (not attack) the territory of non-Muslim forces	6	(3%)
4b. Number of battles in which non-Muslim forces only invade (not attack) the territory of Muslim forces	11	(5%)
Total determinations	*214	**106%

* Total determinations exceed the number of battles because some battles have multiple determinations, as is the case when one military force invades a country but is attacked by the military force of that country.
**Rounding-up decimal percentages produces a sum greater that 100%.

were their adversaries? Is it possible that Muslims were extremely defensive except in the cases of one or two adversaries, such as the Persians, Jews, or Spaniards? If this were the case, then Muslim forces would rarely if ever be the invaders and attackers.

Table 4-3 identifies various categories of adversaries of Muslim forces in the 198 battles between Muslim forces and non-Muslim forces. Starting with battles with Byzantines (row 1), notice that Byzantines were the attackers (cell B1) or both invaders and attackers (cell C1) in 11 battles, whereas Muslims were the attackers (cell E1) or attackers and invaders (cell F1) in 16 battles. Clearly then, Muslims often (27 times) fought major battles against Byzantines, and in 60% of those battles Muslims were the aggressors (16/27 = 60%). Notice also that Muslims invaded and attacked Byzantine territories (N=12) much more frequently than Byzantines invaded and attacked Muslim lands (N=3). Byzantines did "only attacks" against Muslims (N=8) more frequently than Muslims only attacked Byzantines (N=4).[97]

TABLE 4-3:
THE ADVERSARIES AGAINST MUSLIM ARMED FORCES

ADVERSARIES	ADVERSARIES WHO:			ADVERSARIES WHO WERE:			G
	A	B	C	D	E	F	G
	only invaded	only attacked	both invaded & attacked	only invaded	only attacked	both invaded & attacked	Total
1. Byzantines	0	8	3	0	4	12	27
2. Crusaders	4	0	15	0	9	0	28
3. Spanish & Portuguese	0	18	3	0	2	2	25
4. Other European Christians Until 1750	0	9	3	4	4	21	41
5. European, Russian And British After 1750	6	17	22	0	14	1	60
6. Hindu, Sikh, And Punjab	0	0	0	0	0	6	6
7. Mongols	1	0	9	0	1	0	11
8. Jews & Israelis	0	0	3	0	0	2	*6
9. Other Non-Muslims At The Time	0	2	1	2	0	6	11
10. Column Totals	11	54	59	6	34	50	**215

* A determination could not be made about which adversary was the attacker in the Battle of Jerusalem (#93) between Israelis and various Muslim forces and the Battle of Jidda (#94), between Muslim forces.
**Some battles have double entries in this Table because invaders and attackers sometimes differed in a particular battle, such as Abukir, Egypt, in 1799. Napoleon invaded the land but the Ottomans attacked first.

Data in Row 2 of Table 4-3 reveal that the Muslim-Dominant pattern does not apply to the relationship between Crusaders and Muslims as adversaries. Crusaders invaded and attacked Muslims in 15 major battles (cell C2). While Muslims never invaded and attacked

Crusader's lands (cell F2), Muslims did however attack Crusaders nine times (cell E2) without first invading Crusader lands. Overall, Crusaders were the aggressors in 19 (68%) of the 28 battles; Muslims, in only the remaining nine (32%) of the battles. The data support the popular image (especially in some groups in the Middle East, at least) that the Crusaders were more invasive and offensive than were the Muslims. Of course, this is what one might expect if the purpose of the Crusaders was to "liberate the Holy Lands" from what some people considered to be Muslim domination.

Row 3 reveals that the Spanish and Portuguese also were more aggressive than their Muslim adversaries in the 25 major battles between them. Essentially this pattern is a consequence of the fact that Muslim forces were extremely successful during their first invasion of the Iberian peninsular and their first major battles such as Rio Barbate in 711 A.D. Spanish and Portuguese forces then launched many major attacks (N=18) against the Muslims (Moors and Berbers) in their garrison strongholds over the next 781 years (as in the battles of Las Navas de Tolosa in 1212 and Cordoba in 1236) in order to expel them from the Iberian Peninsula. This is not considered to have occurred until the decisive Battle of Granada, 1491-92 (as described earlier in this chapter). The Spanish and Portuguese then crossed the Straits of Gibraltar on numerous occasions to invade and attack the Muslim strongholds in North Africa (cell C3), as was the case in the Battle of Oran I in 1509 and Alacazarquivir in 1578.

Row 4 deals with battles between Muslim forces and adversaries like the members of the Holy Roman Empire principalities prior to 1750 in France, Italy, German, Austria, and the Balkans. These battles usually involved Muslim forces from the emergent Ottoman Empire invading the Balkans and attacking large Christian coalition armies and cities there. This was the case at Adrianople VI in 1365, Kosovo I in 1389, Belgrade II in 1521, Mohacs I in 1526, and the two battles of Vienna in 1529 and 1683 (that ended the Muslim expansion into central Europe) and so many of the other 21 (51%) of the 41 battles between European Christians and Muslims that are represented in row 4. In fact, these other European Christian forces before 1750 were the second most frequent adversaries (N=41) of Muslims in major battles — second only to European, Russian, and British adversaries after 1750 (row 5) which engaged Muslim forces in 60 major battles (30% of the 198 major battles). Those battles (row 5) reveal what might be called a European-Dominant pattern. The European adversaries were the aggressors in 45 (cells A5, B5, and C5) of the 60 battles (cell G5),

195

and they were the invaders in most of those battles. There is evidence that the Muslim forces invaded and attacked only one time (cell F5) in contrast to the Europeans, who invaded and attacked what were then Muslim territories, such as Macedonia, a total of 22 times. Let me suggest that this decidedly European-Dominant pattern in row 5 not only contrasts with the Muslim-Dominant pattern seen in row 4, but that it also reverses it historically. Historically, the Ottoman (Muslim) forces usually invaded Eastern and central Europe and attacked armies there from 1300 until the 1700s. After that, the pattern reversed as European, Russian, British, and other forces fought to expel Muslim forces from these European lands, principally the Balkans, and then launched their own invasions into traditional Muslim homelands. Napoleon's invasion of Egypt and the Battle of the Pyramids in 1798 are cases in point, as are the battles of Sinope in 1853, Plovdin in 1878, and Adrianople VII in 1913.

Row 6 calls attention to the fact that Muslim forces only fought six major battles (cell G6) against Hindu, Sikh, and Punjab forces in the Indian subcontinent and that the Muslims were the aggressors in all six instances (cell F6). This Muslim-Dominant pattern is reversed in the case of Mongol adversaries (row 7). In keeping with the general reputation of Genghis Khan and his successors, Mongol forces were the aggressors in ten of the eleven major battles against Muslims. Mongols did all of the invading (cells A7 and C7) and all but one of the battles attacking (cell E7 — the only Muslim attack).

The data in row 8 might surprise some observers because they suggest that neither Jewish-Israeli forces nor Muslim forces were decidedly more aggressive than the other in terms of the major battles between 632-1984 A.D. Jewish forces invaded and attacked in three (cell C8) of the six battles (cell G8), all of which were after WWII, while Muslim forces invaded and attacked in two of the six battles (cell F8). Regarding the sixth battle, Jerusalem in 1948, the historical record is too ambiguous to determine which adversary invaded (if either one did) and which one attacked first. It might be said that this kind of indeterminacy continues to this day to be characteristic of conflict between Israelis and Muslims in the Middle East. Permit me to also suggest that the relatively low number (N=6) of major battles between Jews and Muslims might certainly reflect the minority status of Jews in Palestine until after WWII. Perhaps Jews were so outnumbered in Palestine until 1948 that they rarely were able to fight overtly as military units with Muslims. And yet, is it possible that the Qur'an's verses about war, conflict, and peace and the frequent mention of Jews as "people of the Scripture" in the Qur'an served to actually moderate warfare between Jews and Christians for much of their common history and until, alas, the last sixty years? This is a counter-intuitive observation, perhaps, but it might be worth pondering.[98]

Finally, consider the data in row 9, a residual category, in that it presents estimates for battles between Muslim forces and all adversaries not accounted for in rows 1-8. It includes tabulations for the battles against other non-Muslim adversaries such as non-Muslim Chinese, Afghans, Persians, and Syrians, and even the U.S. Navy (the Battle of Tripoli II in 1804) against the Barbary pirates. There were only eleven of these battles (cell G9) and Muslim forces were the aggressors in eight of them, including six battles (cell F6) in which Muslim forces invaded and attacked adversaries. Examples include the battle of Hira in 633 A.D. (just one year after Muhammad's death) in which the great Muslim General Walid led a Medina-Mecca army on a raid into Persia and defeated a non-Muslim Persian force under King Rustam; a similar invasion and attack in Persia by Muslim General Waqqas at Jalula in 637 A.D.; and the battles of Kabul I in 709 and Kadisiya, Iraq in 637.

Thus, in summarizing the patterns in Table 4-3, it can be said that in battles against other non-Muslim forces at the time (row 10), Muslim forces were dominant just as they were against Byzantines (row 1), some European Christians until 1750 (row 4), and Hindu, Sikh, and Punjabis in the Indian subcontinent (row 6). On the other hand, Muslim forces were relatively defendent (i.e. less aggressive) in the major battles against Crusaders (row 2), Spanish-Portuguese (row 3), Mongols (row 7), and especially against European, Russian, and British forces after 1750 (row 5). Against Jewish-Israeli forces (row 8) there have been too few major battles, historically, since 632 A.D., to render a clear determination. Muslim forces quickly dominated towns that had Jewish residents during the rapid expansion of Islam in the centuries immediately after Muhammad's death (such as the Battle of Jerusalem in 637). But, Muslim forces have been much more defendent since the end of WWII (the Israeli-Arab war of 1967, Sinai Peninsula in 1956, Beirut, Lebanon, in 1982-83) and in battles since 1984 (as discussed in Chapter 5), with the exception of the Yom Kippur War, 1973, in which Egyptian, Syrian, Iraqi, an Jordanian forces launched coordinated surprise attacks across many borders into Israel. There is also one major battle, Jerusalem VII in 1099, (that was highlighted earlier in this chapter) in which Jews and Muslims fought together against, and were massacred by, a common adversary — Christian armies in the First Crusade under Frank and Italian princes.

> "The knights of Godfrey and Tancred poured into the city, launch-
> ing a wholesale massacre of Moslems and Jews. Tancred seized
> the Temple in the southeast. Here the defenders, with their rear
> now exposed, fell back to the Tower of David and surrendered to
> Raymond. One account reports the death of 70,000 non-Christians
> by nightfall of July 15. The objective of the crusade had been
> achieved. Jerusalem and all its holy places were in Christian
> hands. But the fighting was not over, for a large Egyptian army
> was already on the march into Palestine."[99]

This battle is mentioned again here in order to call attention to the fact that Jews and Muslims have not always been each other's primary adversaries, at least not in terms of major battles in the recorded history of warfare. Surely, the data in Table 4-3 encourage us to understand that there have been many different adversaries in many different major battles (1,560 of them) in recorded history and since Muhammad's death (1,343 major battles). Muslim forces have been involved in less than 20% of them. Muslims were the aggressors in less than one-half of the major battles that they fought, and were usually the defendents in battles against Crusaders, Spanish and Portuguese, Mongols, and Europeans after 1750. Rather than simply concede to their adversaries or retreat from them, Muslims might have fought in many of these battles because many verses of the Qur'an instruct them to defend their far borders, to be steadfast, and to not retreat, among other orders.

Next we will consider in more detail Muslim forces as defenders. What places did they defend? How often? From the verses in the Qur'an we might expect that in the more than 1,300 years since Muhammad's death, Muslim forces would have been forced to fight often in the Arabian Peninsula in order to defend Mecca and Medina as the birthplaces of Islam. They would also have fought frequently and steadfastly to defend Islam's borders and the other capital cities of Islam: Baghdad, Jerusalem, Isfahan, Cairo, Adrianople, and Istanbul. Table 4-4 presents data relevant to these matters.

The table shows that Muslim forces were defending places such as a town, harbor, fortress, garrison, or borders in 113 (57%) of the 198 battles. However, this does not mean that these places defended were

TABLE 4-4:
MUSLIM FORCES AS DEFENDERS OF PLACES, 632-1984 A.D.

1. Number of battles that involved Muslim forces:	198	(100%)
2. Battles where Muslim forces were defending a place:	113	(57%)
3. Battles where Muslim forces were defending capital cities:	16	(8%)

a. Mecca or Medina:	0
b. Other places in Saudi Arabia:	0
c. Damascus, Syria	2
d. Baghdad, Iraq	3
e. Istavan, Persia	0
f. Cairo, Egypt	4
g. Adrianople	1
h. Istanbul	2
i. Jerusalem	4

4. Battles where Muslim forces were defending other places in lands that are currently predominantly Muslim:	62	(31%)
5. Battles where Muslim forces were defending other places outside of lands that are currently predominantly Muslim:	35	(18%)

in traditional Muslim homelands, such as Arabia. In 35 (18%) of these battles the places they were defending often were places that they had captured, occupied, and converted to Islam in lands as far away as India, Spain, and North Africa. At Peiwar Pass in 1878, for example, Afghan Muslims under Shere Ali steadfastly defended a crucial mountain pass on the Afghan-Indian border until they were overwhelmed and routed by more than 3,000 British and Indian infantry and artillerymen, who then marched into Afghanistan and captured Kabul. At the Battle of Alcacer do Sol in Portugal, in 1217, Moors steadfastly defended the fortress that they had occupied for 300 years before they were routed by King Alfonso "the Fat" and his Portuguese forces.

In 62 (31%) of the battles, Muslim forces were defending places in current Muslim homelands other than the capital cities named in Table 4-4. For example, in the Battle of Atbara, Sudan, in 1898, Muslim Mahdists steadfastly defended their stockade there until they

199

were routed by Lord Kitchner and his British-Egyptian forces (before Kitchner went on to victory at the famous Battle of Omdurman, Sudan, that same year). In only 16 (8%) of the major battles (rows 3a-i) were Muslim forces defending what were for a time their capital cities. In fact, since the death of Muhammad in 632 A.D., Muslim forces have never had to fight a major battle against non-Muslim military forces in or around Mecca or Medina — their holiest cities, the birthplace of Islam, and the birth and death places of Muhammad, respectively.[100] To me this is a fact of singular importance because it seriously undermines the argument that Islam has always been under attack by non-Muslims. The only major battle in Saudi Arabia was at Jidda in 1925, and this was a civil war between two Islamic factions that eventually resulted in the supremacy of the House of Saud and the Wahhabi sect and to the emergence of the nation state of Saudi Arabia.[101]

The capital cities most often defended have been Cairo (4 times), Jerusalem (4), and Baghdad (3).[102] It can be argued that all of these capital cities outside Saudi Arabia had once been invaded and captured by Muslim armies, in keeping with the Muslim-Dominant stereotype. The Muslim-Defendent stereotype, then, is a later counterpoint to an earlier historical pattern. Certainly we should not overlook the fact that all of the capital cities, except Jerusalem, named in Table 4-4 are still predominantly Muslim in terms of the religious orientations of the majority of their residents, if not in terms of the nature and policies of their governments. These observations support the argument that Muslim armed forces often (in 57% of their major battles) have defended places that were important to them, such as their far borders, their towns and cities, even though a significant percentage of these places (at least 18%) were places that Muslim armies had invaded and captured in foreign lands, such as Spain and India. Often these places were many hundreds of miles from the birthplaces of Islam — Mecca and Medina.

How much evidence is there that Muslim military forces violated the Qur'an in other ways besides invading and attacking non-Muslim forces? Table 4-5 presents estimations of what might be considered to be various types of violations of the Qur'an by Muslim forces. For comparative purposes, Table 4-5 also estimates violations by their non-Muslim adversaries. We realize, of course, that their adversaries cannot be held to the same standards of behavior in warfare as the Muslim forces. This comparison is being made only in order to provide us with some idea as to whether Muslim forces deviated from the Qur'anic norms more or less frequently than did their adversaries. It is also important to understand that these estimates are only preliminary and suggestive because the historical records are woefully incomplete and they are often biased somewhat by the religious and philosophical ideologies of their producers on many of these matters. With these caveats in mind, notice that Table 4-5 reveals that I found evidence of apparent violations of the Qur'an by Muslim forces in 86 (43%) of the 198 major battles and by non-Muslim forces in 51 (26%) of those battles.

These estimates obviously suggest that Muslim forces violated the Qur'an in a little less than one-half of these battles and that they violated the Qur'an somewhat more frequently than did their non-Muslim adversaries (who violated the Qur'an in a little more than one-quarter of the battles). However, since both Muslims and non-Muslims violated the Qur'an in 16 of the same battles, the total number of battles in which the Qur'an was violated is only 121 — not 137. For example, at the Battle of El Mansura near Cairo, Egypt, in 1250, the 7th Crusaders under King Louis IX of France invaded Egypt and attacked a series of towns and fortifications (apparent violations of the Qur'an's prohibitions about initiating offensive actions). Eventually these invaders were intercepted and defeated by Egyptian Muslim forces under Vizier Bibars and Sultan Turashah. The Muslims then took booty and ransomed some of the Crusader POWs (as allowed in the Qur'an), but also executed many of the POWs, especially POWs who were too sick or injured to march or to be ransomed (in violation of the Qur'an).

Row 3 of Table 4-5 shows that I found evidence of 172 apparent violations of the Qur'an in the 86 battles where Muslims violated the Qur'an and of 82 apparent violations in the 51 battles where non-Muslims violated the Qur'an. These estimates suggest that Muslims committed more violations of the Qur'an in each of these battles than did their non-Muslim adversaries, but I do not believe that the data are reliable or complete enough to allow us to assert any more than this.

As to the frequencies and types of violations, notice that there is some evidence that Muslim forces committed more of every type of violation than did their non-Muslim adversaries. For example, Muslim forces invaded decidedly foreign lands to wage war in at least 58 battles; non-Muslims did so in at least 43 battles (compare cells 4aA and 4aB). Muslim forces violated enemy forces in at least 66 of the battles; non-Muslim forces did so in at least 19 of the battles — a significant difference (compare cells 4eA and 4eB). Muslim forces violated enemy civilians in at least 48 of the battles; non-Muslim forces did so in at least 20 of the battles (compare cells 4fA and 4fB).

Let me call attention to several of the other types of violations that seem to be especially noteworthy. Muslim forces certainly seem to have done more executing, mutilating, and enslaving of enemy prisoners than did their adversaries. Muslim forces also were described

---

TABLE 4-5:

BATTLES IN WHICH APPARENT VIOLATIONS OF THE QUR'AN WERE COMMITTED BY MUSLIM FORCES AND/OR NON MUSLIM FORCES*

1. Number of battles in which violations occurred: 121

	A Muslims	B Non-Muslims
Violator:		
2. Number of battles in which the Qur'an was violated:	86 (43%)	51 (26%)
3. Total # of apparent violations during 198 battles:	172	82
4. Types and numbers of violations:		
a. Invasion of foreign lands:	58	43
b. Surrender to enemy forces:	9	6
c. Reject peace offering:	4	?
d. Desertion:	2	?
e. Total violations against enemy prisoners:	66	19
(1) Execute enemy prisoners:	32	15
(2) Mutilate/behead enemy prisoners:	15	1
(3) Enslave without ransom enemy prisoners:	9	0
(4) Humiliate enemy prisoners in other ways:	10	3
f. Total violations against enemy civilians:	48	20
(1) "Terrorize" civilian population:	3	0
(2) Execute some civilians:	14	10
(3) Rape/abuse/degrade civilians:	3	0
(4) Enslave some civilians without ransom:	8	0
(5) "Sack/pillage/plunder" civilian community:	17	10
(6) Force religious conversions of civilians:	1	0

* Conceptually at least, in a given battle almost all of the types of violations identified above can be committed by both Muslim and non-Muslim forces.

? Unknown, not able to be determined.

202

by military historians as "terrorizing" civilian populations in three of the battles. This number is far smaller than we might expect from the Muslim-Dominant stereotype, considering the gross number of battles that are under consideration here and that many of them occurred in or near towns and cities with considerable numbers of civilians.[103]

Finally, notice in row 4f(6) that there is only one battle for which evidence indicated that Muslim victors forced the religious conversion of the civilians that they captured (and no instances of this for their non-Muslim adversaries). This finding certainly calls into question some aspects of the Muslim-Dominant stereotype, namely that Muslim forces often were used to impose forced conversion to Islam.

In sum, for every type of violation of the Qur'an listed in Table 4-5 there is some evidence, however incomplete and controversial it might be, that Muslim forces were somewhat more active and deviant than were their non-Muslim adversaries. Admittedly, it is possible that these estimates reflect biases in the original sources of information about the battles and by the military historians who produced the accounts of these battles. This issue, an extremely important one, is beyond the scope of this book.

The Qur'an generally holds that Muslim forces ultimately will defeat their adversaries in battles so long as they are steadfast, do not transgress, and they fight "in the way of Allah." The Qur'an also instructs its followers not to desert the battlefield, surrender, or offer peace to the enemy before victory has been achieved. At the same time, however, the Qur'an encourages Muslim forces to be willing to accept peace offerings from their adversaries, before total victory has been achieved, so long as the peace gestures are credible and will allow Muslims to honorably conclude the conflict (implying an end to religious persecution and domination by their enemies). Cells 4cA and 4dA in Table 4-5 reveal that Muslim forces violated the Qur'an regarding not rejecting peace offerings in at least four battles and the prohibition against desertion in at least two battles. Table 4-6 provides some additional estimates related to these matters.

	A MUSLIM FORCES	B UN-KNOWN	C NON-MUSLIM FORCES	D TOTALS
TABLE 4-6: CEASING THE 198 BATTLES: DISPOSITIONS OF ADVERSARIES*				
1. Offered Peace	1		1	2
2. Truce		4		4
3. Escaped	2			2
4. Ceased Fire		2		2
5. Surrendered	9		21	30
6. Damaged / "Routed"	35		30	65
7. Destroyed	16		24	40
8. Withdraws From Battlefield	31		17	48
9. "Capitulates"	12		2	14
10. Unknown / Contradictory Accounts		17		17
11. Totals	106	23	95	224

* These numbers are incomplete and suggestive, at best. These ways of ending a battle are not mutually exclusive. Military historians occasionally specified more than one way that a battle ended for one or both of the adversaries. Some units of an army could surrender while other units escaped and still other units were destroyed. I tried to list only the most decisive way that the battle ended whenever it was possible to make this determination.

Table 4-6 shows that 224 determinations about the final disposition of the adversaries could be made for the 198 major battles. Keep in mind that, with 198 battles and at least two adversaries per battle, it is possible to have at least 396 determinations as to final dispositions. In fact, while it rarely happened in the accounts of the battles under consideration here, it is possible to have even more than 396 determinations because there can be multiple determinations for each adversary, as when one adversary offers peace, then surrenders, but then withdraws from the battlefield before the surrender is implemented.[104]

Of the 224 determinations shown in Table 4-6, notice that peace was rarely offered by either adversary (row 1). Truces were only arranged four times (cell 2B) but it was not clear from the records as to which adversary arranged the truces. Only two battles ended when one adversary "escaped" (and in both battles it was the Muslim force that escaped). Cease-fires ended two battles (cell 4B) but it was impossible to determine which adversary arranged the cease-fire. Much more frequent means of ceasing battles were surrenders (row 5), for which non-Muslim forces were said to have "surrendered" (as distinct from "capitulated," as shown in row 9) more than twice as frequently as Muslim forces.[105] One adversary being "damaged" or "routed" by the other adversary was the most frequent description of why battles ended, with Muslim forces having suffered this fate often, but only slightly more often than non-Muslim forces (row 6). On the other hand, non-Muslim forces were said to have been destroyed in 24 battles (cell 7C) in contrast to 16 battles for Muslim forces (cell 7A). Rather remarkable is the difference between Muslim and non-Muslim forces regarding withdrawing from the battlefield (row 8), with Muslim forces being described by military historians as withdrawing much more frequently (31 times) than non-Muslims (17 times). This action would seem to violate the Qur'an's instructions about being steadfast, as would surrendering (row 5) and capitulating (row 9).

Taken collectively, and acknowledging that the data are very incomplete and less than definitive on the topic of how the 198 battles ceased, there is some indication that Muslim forces often (in more than one-half of their battles) did not end their battles in ways that are congruent with the Qur'an. In at least 31 battles, Muslim forces withdrew from the battlefield without achieving victory. In nine battles they surrendered. In twelve battles they capitulated. In 16 battles Muslim forces were described as having been destroyed. In 35 battles they were damaged or routed. Of course, it is also true that their non-Muslim adversaries often suffered similar fates: surrendering at least 21 times, capitulating twice, withdrawing 17 times, being damaged or routed 30 times, and being destroyed 24 times (considerably more often than their Muslim adversaries).

In conclusion, let me suggest that the data in Table 4-6 join with the data in the other tables in this section to inform us that, after Muhammad's death, Muslim armed forces often fought major battles in ways that were somewhat different than, but not radically different than, their adversaries. At times, especially in the centuries immediately after Muhammad's death, Muslim forces tended to be more invasive and offensive than their adversaries. This was also true of the Ottoman Muslims during their first 500 years of warfare, roughly

1300-1800. On the other hand, Muslim forces were considerably more defensive and conciliatory in other historical eras and against some adversaries, such as the Mongols and the Europeans, British, and Russians after 1750. And yet we should not overlook the simple fact that Muslim forces have never had to fight major battles to defend Mecca and Medina, their holiest cities. Nor can we overlook the fact that, in more than the last 1,300 years, Muslim forces have only fought 16 major battles in or around other cities that were and still are centers of Islam, and that at least seven of those 16 battles originally were battles of Muslim conquest. These facts are very strong evidence indeed that Muslims have not often fought in defense of their most sacred communities in order to stop religious persecution — at least not up until 1984 (the endpoint of the data set that has been the subject of this chapter). Obviously it is time to consider, if only briefly, how Muslim battles since 1984 relate to the Qur'an. This is the purpose of Chapter 5.

---

[1] Fregosi, p. 225. This quotation concerns the decision of the ruler of the Ottoman Turks, Murad, to launch his army against the Serbian King Lazar at Kosovo, 1389. Fregosi is essentially claiming that Murad's reading of the Qur'an convinced him to attack the larger army of King Lazar, in part because it was an army of unbelievers and hypocrites.

[2] Esposito, pp. 32-35.

[3] My interviews and conversation with Muslims living in the U.S., including Najih Lazar of Narragansett, Rhode Island, usually reveal that they are more familiar with a few of Muhammad's battles, especially the Battles of Badr, the Trench, and Hudaybiya, than with the 214 Muslim battles that are analyzed in this chapter.

[4] Esposito, p. 38.

[5] Esposito, p. 36.

[6] Esposito, p. 39.

[7] Esposito, p. 40.

[8] Esposito, p. 43.

[9] Raymond Bonner, "Gunmen Kill Seven Shiite Worshippers in Pakistan." *The New York Times International Sunday Edition*. February 23, 2003, p. 10.

[10] Esposito, p. 43.

[11] As of May 2004, it is not yet clear whether these speculations regarding the differing dispositions of Shiites and Sunnis towards war and peace are being (and will be) contradicted by the behaviors of members of these sects towards U.S. military forces that are occupying Iraq and Afghanistan.

[12] Esposito, p. 51.

[13] Esposito, p. 55.

[14] Esposito, p. 60.

[15] Esposito, p. 60.

[16] Esposito, p. 60.

[17] Esposito, p. 66.

[18] Esposito, p. 61.

[19] Esposito, p. 64. It was Akbar's grandson, Shah Jahan, who had the Taj Mahal built in Agra as a memorial to his beloved wife.

[20] Esposito, p. 66.

[21] Eggenberger, pp. 214-215.

[22] Eggenberger, p. 215.

[23] Rodinson, p. 234.

[24] Eggenberger, p. 401.

[25] Some scholars claim that Muslims are prohibited from carrying Qur'ans with them into battles against non-Muslims for fear that the Qur'ans would be captured and defiled by the non-Muslims. However, I found that Fregosi made reference to Qur'ans being present in at least five famous battles between Muslims and non-Muslims.

[26] Eggenberger, p. 361.

[27] I have not found any casualty estimates for Rio Barbate or for many of the other battles.

[28] Fregosi, p. 96.

[29] Eggenberger, p. 442.

[30] Fregosi, p. 117.

[31] Fregosi, p. 118.

[32] Eggenberger, pp. 441-442.

[33] Fregosi, p. 119.

[34] Fregosi, p. 120. Readers are encouraged to regard with discretion some of Fregosi's descriptions. While I have not found other scholars to contradict Fregosi regarding basic historical facts, Fregosi's choice of adjectives, his depiction of the internal thought processes of historical figures, and his disdain for established religions, including Christianity as well as Islam, should be taken into account.

[35] Fregosi, p. 121.

[36] Eggenberger, p. iv.

[37] Eggenberger, p. 211.

[38] Eggenberger, p. 211.

[39] *The Gesta Francorum.* Anonymous. Edited by R. Hill, London. 1962 (as reported in *Chronicles of the Crusades: Eyewitness Accounts of the Wars Between Christianity and Islam,*" edited by Elizabeth Hallam, NY: Welcome Rain, 2000. p. 93.

[40] *Chronicles of the Crusades,* p. 69.

[41] *Chronicles of the Crusades,* p. 69.

[42] *Chronicles of the Crusades*, p. 70.

[43] *Chronicles of the Crusades*, p. 68.

[44] Eggenberger, p. 211.

[45] Fregosi, p. 193.

[46] Eggenberger, p. 232. As a former infantry officer in Marine Corps battalions in Viet Nam, I must admit that I have doubts about the accuracy of claims by military historians who assert that hundreds of thousands of combatants have been engaged in the same battle, on one battlefield, on the same day. Therefore, I doubt that as many as "150,000 Moors fell at Toloso" during the battle.

[47] Fregosi, p. 273.

[48] Eggenberger, p. 429.

[49] Eggenberger, p. 427.

[50] Eggenberger, p. 427.

[51] Eggenberger, p. 43.

[52] Eggenberger, p. 40.

[53] Eggenberger, p. 40.

[54] Eggenberger, p. 8.

[55] Fregosi, p. 225.

[56] Fregosi, p. 227.

[57] Fregosi, p. 227.

[58] Fregosi, p. 229. Again, I caution readers to use discretion in reading some of Fregosi's descriptions. He is prone to "poetic license" and hyperbole. At times his documentation of original sources leaves much to be desired.

[59] Eggenberger, p. 222.

[60] Eggenberger, p. 279.

[61] Fregosi, p. 283.

[62] Fregosi, p. 283.

[63] Fregosi, p. 286.

[64] Eggenberger, p. 462.

[65] Fregosi, p. 281.

[66] Eggenberger, p. 463.

[67] Eggenberger, p. 350.

[68] Fregosi, p. 372.

[69] Fregosi, p. 372.

[70] Fregosi, p. 372.

[71] Fregosi, p. 372.

[72] Fregosi, p. 402.

[73] Fregosi, p. 402.

[74] Fregosi, p. 402.

[75] Eggenberger, p. 118.

[76] Fregosi, p. 403.

[77] Eggenberger, p. 163.

[78] Eggenberger, pp. 163-164.

[79] Eggenberger, p. 272.

[80] Eggenberger, p. 237.

[81] Eggenberger, p. 237.

[82] Fregosi, p. 327. I feel compelled to caution readers again about taking Fregosi's accounts too literally. For example, I seriously doubt that any combatant can so easily behead another with just a knife, given the thickness of the human spine. I also doubt that holding a human head aloft on a pike would be seen by more than several hundred combatants, at most, in the heat of battle, let alone by more than 50,000 Ottoman combatants fighting on the decks of more than 200 ships.

[83] Fregosi, p. 328. Fregosi is quoted here despite the discrepancies in his estimates in order to underscore the likelihood that both the Christian and Ottoman navies made use of large numbers of slaves as oarsmen and that many or most of these oarsmen ostensibly were from their adversary's religion. In one of his more remarkable (but undocumented) anecdotes, on page 324 Fregosi claims that he found evidence that Cervantes was one of the thousands of soldiers on Don John's galleys who survived the battle — the same Cervantes who went on to write *Don Quixote*.

[84] Eggenberger, p. 445.

[85] Potter, p. 91.

[86] Potter, p. 91.

[87] Potter, p. 92.

[88] Potter, p. 93.

[89] Fregosi, p. 403.

[90] Fregosi, p. 225.

[91] Fregosi, p. 195.

[92] Fregosi, p. 371.

[93] Fregosi, p. 150.

[94] I also collected information on other aspects of these battles, including whether the Muslim forces were invading foreign lands (an action which would violate some of the passages in the Qur'an that were presented in Chapter 2) and on how the battles ended. But much of this other information is too detailed to be presented in tabular form.

[95] Eggenberger, p. iii.

[96] Eggenberger, p. xxx.

[97] Many of these "attack only" determinations are the result of both adversaries claiming authority over a territory or they confront each other in contested or "neutral" lands outside of either of their homelands.

[98] Jews fought a greater number of major battles (N=8) against Romans than against Muslims.

[99] Eggenberger, p. 211.

[100] This finding only pertains to the absence of major battles with non-Muslim military forces.

[101] Eggenberger, p. 212.

[102] Of course the count for Baghdad increases to four times if we include the U.S. invasion of Iraq in 2003.

[103] In all three of these battles military historians used the term "terrorize" in describing Muslim behavior at or immediately following each battle, in contrast to no such description for their non-Muslim adversaries. For Mongol invasions and attacks that were successful, historians usually said that the Mongols annihilated, ravaged, or destroyed the civilian population — rather than terrorize it (i.e. inflict fear and panic upon it).

[104] The terms in Table 4-6, such as "truce," "destroyed", etc. are the terms that military historians such as David Eggenberger used to describe how these battles ended.

[105] Capitulating usually is considered to be a formalized yielding under pressure to the enemy that concedes less to the enemy than does surrendering.

CHAPTER FIVE

SOME RECENT AND CURRENT "MUSLIM" WARS

THE QUR'AN'S INFLUENCE ON SOME BATTLES AND WARS SINCE 1984

How much evidence is there that the Qur'an's verses on peace, conflict, and war have influenced some of the major wars and battles that have involved considerable numbers of Muslim combatants since 1984, including the U.S. led invasion of Iraq in March 2003? Because so little time has elapsed since some of these engagements, this question can only be answered in a preliminary manner based primarily on journalistic accounts rather than on extensive academic research based on government documents, biographies, memoirs, and other "inside" information by the political leaders who shaped these wars and the military leaders and personnel who fought in them. Theoretically, we might expect to find that, despite dozens of other factors that influence the nature of particular wars and battles, the Qur'an's influence would be most obvious in wars and battles where one or both sides are strong proponents of the Qur'an and they have plenty of incentives and opportunities to behave according to the Qur'an. However, given the historical patterns that we reported earlier in Chapters 3 and 4 regarding the history of Muslim warfare (namely that Muslim armed forces usually have been fighting defensively and against heavy odds close to their homelands in the past 250 years) it is not obvious that Muslim forces would actually fight according to the Qur'an. This might be particularly true when they face adversaries whose methods and materials for waging war and peace are so radically different from those of their predecessors.

Let me emphasize that this chapter is not intended to be an in-depth description, analysis, or evaluation of these battles and wars as events in military history. I assume that readers are familiar with the general facts about these wars, especially the three most recent wars in which the United States military was or still is a major participant. Rather, this chapter is meant only to report on my efforts to find direct evidence and indirect indicators of how the Qur'an's passages on peace, terror, and war might have or have not influenced government and military leaders as well as ordinary combatants in any of these wars.[1]

Let us now consider three wars that began before 1984 and continued for years after that, as well as six wars that began after 1984, including the current U.S. led campaigns in Afghanistan and Iraq.

THE USSR WAR IN AFGHANISTAN, 1979-1989

> "In a country like Afghanistan, where the concept of the nation
> has developed but recently, where the state is seen as external to
> society and where people's allegiance is directed primarily
> towards the local community, the only thing which all Afghans
> have in common is Islam."[2]

This long, brutal and singularly decisive war of poorly equipped Afghan tribesmen versus the vaunted army of the Soviet Union at the peak of its superpower status probably did more than any other event in the 1970s to inspire Muslim militants throughout the world to resort to violence against Western nations.[3] The Soviets were the invaders and were usually the attackers, especially early in the war. Their adversaries were members of many Muslim factions, tribes, and sects, as well as non-Muslim financiers and suppliers of military hardware, including the U.S. and Britain. Muslim forces frequently fought courageously against Soviet armor, artillery, and helicopter-borne forces. Often they were portrayed by journalists as being instructed by the Qur'an and motivated primarily to rid their communities of Soviet armed forces.

> "...the seven Mujahidin parties supported by Pakistan, the USA
> and Saudi Arabia were composed of two primary elements: the
> Islamist parties, led by intellectuals, who had borrowed Western
> political concepts in order to create a new political ideology based
> on a reinterpretation of the Qur'an and the Hadith, and the so-
> called traditionalists, who drew their support from the Ulema, the
> mullahs, and tribal and other leaders. They based their interpreta-
> tion of Islam on a long history of scholastic commentary on the
> Qur'an and also drew on other traditions, including those relating
> to the behavior of women."[4]

212

The Afghan tribes did not often fight aggressively on their far borders against the Soviets or rout and overwhelm the enemy and the support forces behind the enemy lines. Nor did they fight in solid ranks as conventional combat units so much as they fought as guerrilla forces with surprise raids and night attacks against isolated Soviet outposts. It was a war of frustrated, slow attrition in which both sides engaged in executions and torture of POWs. Both sides attacked civilian communities when they were suspected of harboring enemy forces. Some Muslim tribesmen occasionally abused and executed other Muslim militia of other tribes as well as unarmed Afghani villagers, particularly if they were from tribes of traditional enemies or if they were suspected of not opposing the Soviets aggressively enough. The guerrillas were especially brutal against captured Soviet personnel, often torturing and executing them, then mutilating their bodies. As the Soviets were gradually withdrawn, Muslim forces did not pursue them or carry the fight across borders into Soviet lands or try to inflict proportionate damage on Soviet communities. The U.S. mediated peace agreement was observed by the Soviets reasonably well (although they tried to install puppet communist regimes in the country). Many of the Afghan rebels rejected it, vowed to fight against any and all foreign influence, and launched a civil war that eventually led to Taliban rule of more than 90% of the country by August 1998.

In general, then, there is indirect evidence that Muslim forces often fought against the Soviets in ways that were congruent with the Qur'an in some aspects (fighting steadfastly until the disbelievers withdrew and Islam flourished in Afghanistan), but less so in other ways (defending the far borders, treating POWs according to the Qur'an without torturing or executing them). Yet, on balance, this war seems considerably more concordant with the Qur'an than were many of the Muslim battles of earlier centuries that were summarized in Chapters 3 and 4. That it was so successful in forcing such a conclusive withdrawal by the powerful and widely feared Soviet Army is all the more reason to expect that it would become the inspiration for warfare by Muslim forces for decades to come. It was a war in which proponents of the Qur'an, both literalists and opportunists, had plenty of incentives and opportunities to fight according to the Qur'an against a non-Muslim invader and aggressor that probably was hostile towards Islam and had historically fought (as Russia) many major battles against Muslim forces during the previous 400 years (note that at least six of the 214 major battles that are listed in Appendix A were between Muslim and Russian military forces). Ironically, these opportunities and incentives for Muslim forces in Afghanistan were enhanced by financial and material support from non-Muslim allies that included the U.S., Britain, and other Cold War opponents of the Soviet Bloc. These allies did not often pressure the Muslim forces to fight according to the Qur'an or to the Geneva Conventions. Their goal was to help the Afghans expel Soviet combatants and repel Soviet influence — not wage a moral war. Ultimately the Soviet Army was withdrawn from Afghanistan not because it had been defeated there but because of internal dissent in Moscow about the cost of the war as the Soviet economy was collapsing and the Cold War was winding-down.[5] Whatever the reasons, the Afghanis could easily claim that they had done far more than anyone else would have imagined to generate so much dissent and suffering in the land of their hated enemy to the north.

THE IRAQ-IRAN WAR, 1980-1988

"On 22 September 1980, the Iraqi army swept across the border into Iran in what was supposed to have been a blitzkrieg operation which would capture Khuzestan province with the help of its Arabic-speaking people and, by cutting off Tehran from its main refinery port, force the mullahs to acknowledge the regional domination of Baghdad, trim their plans to export Ayatollah Khomeini's uncompromising brand of Islam, and accept the terms for peace which President Saddam Hussein would dictate, including a realignment of the border in Iraq's favour. It was not to be."[6]

In many ways this war could have been a near perfect opportunity for both combatants to wage war and make peace according to the Qur'an. And yet, there is little evidence that the Qur'an directly influenced the combat behaviors of most participants, even though copies of the Qur'an in print and audiotape probably were more commonplace on the front lines than in any previous war.

Recall that in 1979 Iran was a new, arch-fundamentalist Muslim state under Ayatollah Khomeini. He quickly and vehemently announced that Iran would export Shiite style Islamic fundamentalism throughout the World. The secular regime of the Baath Party and Saddam Hussein in Iraq would be the first target, both because of its secular state and for persecuting the Shiite majority (60% of the population) in favor of Saddam's own Sunni minority (30% of the population, with the remaining 10% of the population primarily being Kurds).

Religious and ethnic differences and inequalities were major sources of social and political conflict in Iraq. Iran, on the other hand, was much larger, wealthier, Persian rather than Arab, and homogenous, with more than 95% of the population Shiite Muslim and a very small Kurdish minority.[7]

"Khomeini espoused a militant religious doctrine rejecting not only the Middle Eastern political order, but also the contemporary international system since both perpetuated an unjust order imposed on the 'oppressed' Muslims by the 'oppressive' great powers. It was bound to be replaced by an Islamic world order in which the territorial nation-state would be transcended by the broader entity of the 'umma' (or the universal Muslim community); and since Iran was the only country where the 'Government of God' had been established, it had the sacred obligation to serve as the core of the umma and a springboard for the worldwide dissemination of Islam's holy message. As he put it: 'We will export our revolution throughout the world...until the calls "there is no god but God and Muhammad is the messenger of God" are echoed all over the world.'"[8]

By the way, we might recall from Chapter 1 that this last embedded quotation is the opening verse in the Qur'an, that it is mandatory recitation five times a day by all believers, and it is repeated throughout the Qur'an many times.

The first target for Khomeini's exported revolution was Iraq. He made no secret of this. In fact, he made it a major point in his frequent and most threatening public pronouncements. "Yet the main thrust of the subversive effort was directed against Iraq.... In the words of the influential member of the Iranian leadership, Hujjat al-Islam Sadeq Khalhali: 'We have taken the path of true Islam and our aim in defeating Saddam Hussein lies in the fact that we consider him the main obstacle to the advance of Islam in the region.'"[9] Khomeini's government did not so much claim that it was being persecuted by Saddam's regime as it claimed that Saddam's regime needed to be eliminated or converted in order for true Islam to begin to spread throughout the World.

Iraq was a secular state, nominally a republic, although Saddam Hussein built huge mosques, quoted the Qur'an, and claimed Islamic allegiance whenever these efforts suited his political purposes. His objectives in launching the invasion into Iran were not primarily to persecute Shiites for their religious practices so much as to discour-

215

age Khomeini from further threats to his regime, to strike a blow against the Iranian military which Khomeini had purged of many of its best officers, and possibly to acquire the Shatt-al-Arab waterway. He assumed that the Khomeini revolution had gravely damaged the fighting effectiveness of the Iranian army. As the war dragged on into seemingly endless attacks and retreats (not unlike the pattern of warfare in Muhammad's days — as described in Chapter 3) and atrocities became routine, many other nations became suppliers of arms, escorts, and finances. U.S., British, and French shored up the Iraqi forces and the Baath regime with naval escorts, munitions, and other support. The Soviets, Syrians, and Kurds often supported the Iranians. Over the course of the eight-year war many nations including Israel, Spain, China, North Korea, and Portugal supplied arms to one of both adversaries, depending on the vagaries of political and economic competition.

The eight-year war that resulted is generally regarded to have been one of the most brutal, inhumane, misdirected and futile wars of the 20th century. By the time that it was over, Iraq's military had suffered an estimated 200,000 dead, 400,000 wounded, and 70,000 taken prisoner. The war wiped out its foreign exchange reserve of $35 billion and strapped it with an accumulated foreign debt of at least $80 billion — a deficit that soon led Saddam into conflict with Kuwait over oil export prices, and then into another devastating war.[10] Estimates of Iran's losses vary widely but are thought to be at least as high as Iraq's in dead and wounded military. Iran also lost 40,000 prisoners and hundreds of thousands of civilians, many of them "poorly armed Iranian schoolchildren who were deployed against Iraqi tanks and artillery, and sent to sweep mines with their bare feet."[11]

"(It was) one of the longest, bloodiest and costliest Third World armed conflicts in the 20th century. After eight years of bitter fighting, untold casualties, and immeasurable suffering and dislocation, the two combatants were forced, out of sheer exhaustion and debilitation, to settle for the status quo ante existing in September, 1980. Yet there was little doubt that neither of them viewed the cease-fire as the end of the conflict."[12]

Sometimes, especially when they were closely monitored and were defending their borders, both the Iraqi and Iranian army forces fought rather steadfastly and as cohesive units (in keeping with the Qur'an's instructions). As the war dragged on, however, desertion became rampant on both sides and Iraq's Republican Guard troops supposedly hunted down and killed Iraqi deserters. Other violations of the Qur'an abounded on both sides in the later stages of the war. This was true as well of separatist Kurdish forces in the northeast provinces of Iraq. They often fought violently against Iraq troops — at times executing and torturing prisoners.[13] And yet it was the Iraqi forces who most often invaded enemy lands, executed, tortured, and abused prisoners (and held them in deplorable conditions for years — some as recently as 2003). They attacked civilian populations and communities and used women and children as human shields against hostile enemy fire and to clear minefields. Of course, this war became especially infamous for the use of poison gas, particularly by the Iraqis, not only against Iranian Army units in pitched battles along their borders but also against Kurdish and Iranian military and civilian personnel in villages and cities. An Iraqi Air Force bombing attack (really a counter-attack, it seems) on the "Kurdish" city of Halabja, in northern Iraq in 1988 was particularly well publicized.

"The battle for Halabja began on March 15, 1988, when Kurdish rebels and Iranian Revolutionary Guards, equipped with chemical warfare suits, moved into the town, driving our Iraqi units in heavy fighting. Townspeople were then stopped from fleeing Halabja and forced by the invaders to return to their homes. This tactic was to cost thousands of lives. The chemical attack began a day later at 6:20 P.M. and continued sporadically over three days. Wave after wave of bombers — seven to eight in each wing — attacked Halabja, a town of eighty thousand, and all roads leading to the surrounding mountains. They dropped a cocktail of poison gases: mustard gas, the nerve agents sarin, tabun, and, according to a well-informed Iraqi military source, VX, the most lethal of all, which Iraq had just begun to manufacture. Clouds of gas hung over the town and the surrounding hills, blotting out the sky and contaminating the fertile plains nearby. The townspeople had no protection and the chemicals soaked into their clothes, skin, eyes, and lungs. At least five thousand, and probably many more, died within hours. Many were poisoned in the cellars where they had sought refuge — trapped by gases that were heavier than air. It was the largest chemical attack ever launched against a civilian population."[14]

By way of comment, notice that this journalist has written that Halabja, a city in northern Iraq, was invaded by Iranian and Kurdish forces in chemical suits. Apparently these forces prohibited the towns-

217

people from abandoning the city and, from the context of the article, these forces remained in the town. If so, the bombing of the town by the Iraqi Air Force might have been intended to destroy the opposition armed forces in the town who were, in effect, using the townspeople as human shields — a clear violation of the Geneva Conventions. Also, it is worth noting that Kurdish militia, particularly thousands of Peshmerga troops, constantly battled more than 30,000 Iraqi troops during the eight years.[15] Iraqi ground forces also committed massacres of civilians and systematic destruction of mosques and residences in a number of other Kurdish towns, including Koreme. Here, hundreds of villagers who were trying to escape into Turkey reportedly were forced back into Koreme. Thirty-three of the men and teenage boys were surrounded by Iraqi troops. "Meanwhile, a dozen soldiers took up positions opposite the group. Some of them, too, were reassuring the men that they had no reason to worry....The soldiers opened fire with their Kalashnikov AK-47 rifles on the 33 men squatting some few yards ahead of them. Some villagers were killed immediately, while others were wounded and a few were missed altogether."[16]

Apparently Iranian troops committed fewer atrocities of this nature, under orders from the highest officials in the government.

"Certainly Iran had the capacity to produce chemical weapons, and did actually build up a stockpile, but, on the direct orders of Khomeini, gas was never used: in a rare display of Islamic principle, the Ayatollah resisted pressure from more worldly Iranian leaders to retaliate against the Iraqis as a way of stopping the dreadful carnage caused by the Iraqi gas attacks. Iran was engaged in a holy struggle, he decreed, and must set an example to other Muslim nations.[17]

As stated in Chapter 2 of this book when we examined verses of the Qur'an, offenses such as poison gas attacks, using civilian populations as shields, and attacks against civilian populations and communities of the adversary are not explicitly permitted or prohibited in the Qur'an. However, the context and general philosophy of the Qur'an would seem to discourage all of these, and other "war crimes," unless, perhaps, they are "proportionate" and in retaliation for the same offenses committed by military forces of the adversary. And yet, there have been more than a few incidents in well-known Muslim military history that took the form of attacks with toxic substances (as pointed out and described several times in Chapter 2 of this book). Nonetheless, poison attacks and many of these other actions certainly seem to violate the Qur'anic principles of discrimination, righteous intention, and transgression avoidance, as well as various articles in the Geneva Conventions that prohibit these actions.

"Finally, the Iran-Iraq War undermined several crucial thresholds and 'red lines' in inter-state wars. It was the first armed conflict since the First World War to witness the extensive use of poison gas; it involved the most intensive campaign against non-belligerent shipping since the Second World War, and, also, perhaps, the harshest attacks on population centers and economic targets. These escalations entailed far-reaching adverse implications for Middle Eastern stability. With the breaking of so many taboos, and the exceptionally cavalier international response to Iraq's massive use of poison gas, every regional army facing the possibility of war must now be aware that the international accords barring the use of chemical weapons and other non-conventional weapons are apparently of little binding value, as are the international norms pertaining to military attacks on civilian targets."[18]

Thus, it seems fair to say that the Iran-Iraq war and most of its battles constitute rather blatant examples of how the Qur'an can be violated in spirit, if not in word, by the Muslim forces that participated in it. This is sadly disappointing because the Iranian forces were supposed to be fighting as Muslims for a new and better Muslim religious state, for the cause of Jihad and "in the way of Allah." On the other hand, there is evidence that Ayatollah Khomeini did prohibit his Iranian forces from retaliating with poison gas against the Iraqis and that the Iranian forces violated the Qur'an less often than did the Iraqis. Still, the war was sufficiently devastating to bring Khomeini to finally accept in July 1988 what he vowed he would never accept — a cease-fire without total victory. Both Iran and Iraq unconditionally accepted U.N. Resolution 598. Peace talks began in Geneva within one month. Since then the peace has held reasonably well despite occasional border infractions and saber rattling by both regimes, at least until Saddam was ousted by U.S. forces in April 2003.

THE ISRAELI INVASION AND OCCUPATION OF LEBANON, 1982-1993

The Israelis invaded Lebanon in 1982 in order to reduce Syrian influence, to destroy terrorist camps in the Bekka valley east of Beirut, and to stop the PLO, Hezbollah, and other pro-Palestinian militia from using Lebanon as a base for raids and rocket attacks on Israeli settlements across the border.

"Israel's invasion of Lebanon, according to Israeli government spokesmen, was caused or provoked by Palestinian "terrorism" against Israeli targets from southern Lebanon. In fact, during the years between July 1981 and June 1982, when the invasion was launched, there had been practically no terrorist attacks from Lebanon against Israel. But between 1969 and 1981, southern Lebanon had served as a base for Palestine Liberation Organization (PLO) attacks against Israeli targets, the most famous of which was the Coast Road Raid of March, 1978, when seaborne Palestinian terrorists from Lebanon commandeered an Israeli bus on the road between Tel Aviv and Haifa and killed more than thirty of its passengers."[19]

Of course, the cycle of violence between Arab and Israeli forces and governments went back through several previous wars and countless skirmishes and bloody incidents to the 1948 Israeli war of statehood (See various entries in Appendix A). While interpretations of this war remain controversial, as with the others that preceded it in this region, it seems rather clear that Israeli army forces invaded and attacked numerous targets as they pushed north to surround Beirut.[20] Battles occurred in and around Tyre, Sidon, and Beirut that destroyed some quarters of these cities. Lebanese Christian militia soon initiated their own attacks on suspected PLO strongholds and sometimes wrecked havoc on neighborhoods with Palestinian refugees. U.S. and U.N. peacekeeping forces were at first welcomed by most residents of Beirut. Soon they became the targets of mounting hostilities. The infamous "suicide bombings" of a multi-story building that served as a barracks to U.S. Marines, killing more than two hundred, was the turning point in the willingness of the U.S. government to keep regular military units in country as peacekeepers. Then came more abductions, tortures, and executions of U.N. peacekeepers, including the abduction and execution of the head of the mission, USMC Lt. Col. Richard Higgins. These are behaviors that ostensibly violate both the Geneva Conventions and the spirit of the Qur'an, if not specific passages in it. "In 1988, terrorist bombings became a way of life in Beirut as some 50 people were killed in an explosion at the U.S. Embassy, April 18. 241 U.S. servicemen and 58 French soldiers died in separate Muslim suicide attacks, October 23. Kidnapping of foreign nationals by Islamic militants became common in the 1980s. U.S., British, French, and Soviet citizens were victims."[21]

There is considerable evidence that many combatants who were presumably Muslims fought steadfastly to expel non-Muslim forces from Beirut, if not in defense of the far borders of Lebanon. In May 1991, after years of haggling, several of the Muslim factions accepted a treaty between Lebanon and Syria that recognized Lebanon as a separate state for the first time since the countries gained independence in 1943 and that pressured Syria to remove its main forces from Lebanon. However, hostilities between Israel and most of the Muslim factions in Lebanon have continued in the form of periodic raids and artillery shellings across the borders.

The Hezbollah controlled much of Lebanon when Israel withdrew most of its troops in May 2000. Thus, as with so many of the other wars against other adversaries that we have considered so far, the Israeli invasion of Lebanon was responded to by Muslim forces in ways that were only partially and indirectly congruent with the Qur'an. And yet a strong case can be made that since the 1948 war, Muslim forces were fighting at least in part to end what they believed to be religious persecution against them in the form of restricted access to Muslim holy places in Jerusalem. Many young Muslim militants have continued to fight courageously, if sporadically, at the expense of their lives. Suicidal attacks might be inspired by the Qur'an, but they are not explicitly consistent with the Qur'an because jihadists must not intentionally take their own lives, even in battle, according to some Qur'an scholars.[22] Martyrdom is recognized as such only when the combatant's death in battle is an inadvertent and unplanned outcome. Additionally, in the Qur'an, martyrs are combatants who perished in Allah's way while fighting as an integral part of a large, cohesive regular military force.

Thus it is that some aspects (such as steadfastly defending Muslim communities despite being heavily outnumbered and outgunned) of Muslim fighting against the Israelis in Lebanon were very consistent with the Qur'an, while other aspects (such as suicide bombings and the torture and execution of prisoners) were rather obvious violations of passages of the Qur'an, especially because their adversaries and the peacekeeping forces apparently did none of these things. Surely, Muslim militants had many opportunities and incentives to fight and to make peace according to the Qur'an in the more than ten years of fighting that took place in Lebanon. While it can be

221

said that they eventually succeeded in having the Israelis withdraw from Lebanon, it cannot be said that they achieved this goal in ways that were very compatible with many of the Qur'an's directives.

BATTLES BETWEEN SERBIAN FORCES AND MUSLIM SEPARATISTS IN THE FORMER YUGOSLAVIA, 1991-1995

"Bosnia and Herzegovina declared sovereignty October 15, 1991. A referendum for independence was passed February 29, 1992. Bosnic Serbs' opposition to the referendum spurred violent clashes and bombings. The U.S. and European Union recognized the republic April 7. Fierce three-way fighting continued between Bosnia's Serbs, Muslims, and Croats. Serb forces massacred thousands of Bosnian Muslims and engaged in "ethnic cleansing" (the expulsion of Muslims and other non-Serbs from areas under Bosnian Serb control). The capital, Sarajevo, was surrounded and besieged by Bosnian Serb forces. Muslims and Croats in Bosnia reached a cease-fire February 23, 1994, and signed an accord March 18 to create a Muslim-Croat confederation in Bosnia. However, by mid-1994, Bosnian Serbs controlled over 70% of the country."[23]

A widely accepted view of the battles between Serbia forces and Muslim Separatists in the former Yugoslavia, 1991-95, is that the battles occurred because of a policy of ethnic cleansing by the Serbia government. Serbian forces were ordered to expel non-Serbs, especially Muslims, from lands that were believed to have been stolen from Serbs through the Ottoman conquests since the 14th Century. Non-Serb militia often opposed the forced expulsions. Serb forces had such overwhelming superiority in numbers and technology that Muslim opposition usually could only fight as guerrilla forces, blocking mountain passes and occasionally attacking Serbian advance guards and outposts. Muslim units were unable to defend their far borders, let alone villages and key cities including Sarajevo and Srebrenica where Muslims constituted an appreciable percentage of the population. Often the Muslim militias were unable to fight steadfastly and as cohesive units. While there were reports of some executions of Serb POWs by Muslim forces, these seem to have been infrequent, compared to atrocities that were systematically and repeatedly committed by Serb forces under orders from the highest offices of Serbia government, namely President Slobodan Milosevic (for which he has been standing trial at the Hague for many months, as of this writing).

"On July 6, 1995, Mladic's forces began shelling Srebrenica, allegedly in retaliation for forays into Serb territory by Bosnian Muslim forces based in the enclave. Three days later, the Serbs took thirty Dutch peacekeepers hostage. On July 10, they took the town, and the rest of the Dutch soldiers, about 370 people, became hostages. The next day Mladic entered Srebrenica and announced that he was 'presenting this city to the Serbian people as a gift.' He added, 'Finally, after the rebellion of the Dahijas, the time has come to take revenge on the Turks in this region' — a reference to a Serb rebellion against the Ottomans that was brutally crushed in 1804. Mladic's identification of modern-day Bosnian Muslims with the Turks of 191 years earlier was revealing of his dangerously warped mind-set."[24]

There also were instances where Serb forces seemed intent on destroying symbols of Islam and on terrorizing Muslims because of their religion — religious persecution.

"The mosque was on death row. An execution date had not been pronounced, of course, but the Ferhad Pasha mosque was living on borrowed time when I walked through its front gate in the summer of 1992. Nationalist Serbs controlled Banja Luka and were well on their way to destroying all symbols of Muslim culture, and none was so historic or important as Ferhad Pasha, built in 1583 during the Ottoman empire....

A few months later, on May 7, 1993, people who lived near the mosque were woken from their sleep by an explosion that made the earth tremble under their homes. Anti-tank mines were detonated under the ancient building's foundations, turning it to rubble, which was carted away to a secret dump. All that was left behind was a blackened patch of ground. The 'ethnic cleansers' hoped that destroying the spiritual heart of their community would ensure Muslims would leave their homes and never return. Across Bosnia this was done, as one mosque after another was turned to pebbles and dust. With each explosion, a war crime was committed."[25]

It is widely acknowledged that this conflict ended only because of sustained U.N. military intervention that included aerial bombings of

Serb forces and deployment of thousands of peacekeeping forces that remain today in the contested areas. So far, armed conflict has been contained reasonably well, thanks to astute, lengthy, and fortuitous diplomatic negotiations that led to the Dayton Peace Accords of 1995. These were signed by all the major adversaries in Paris. Also crucial were the arrests and trials of some of the principal architects of the violence including the former president, Slobodan Milosevic.

Looking back over the many convoluted aspects of this war, it seems fair to say that this was not really a "war" between organized regular Muslim military forces and the Serb army. Rather, it was a sustained attack by some Serbian armed forces against Muslim populations and communities. Occasionally Muslim paramilitary units made brave but ineffective efforts to protect Muslim communities and people and give them time to flee to safer areas. Most of the Qur'an's proponents had few opportunities to obey it or to violate it regarding defense of their neighborhoods, in part because they were so heavily outgunned, and also because the neighborhoods and villages were not predominantly or clearly Muslim ones. The "lines" did not exist unambiguously. With only a few exceptions the Muslim defenders were unable to comply with the Qur'an except in terms of trying to flee, protect their mosques and property as best they could, and to suffer as displaced persons and victims. There are almost no indications that Muslim forces violated the Qur'an. Surely they embraced the peace negotiations rather fully. By many accounts, they have continued to abide by their agreements to date.

IRAQ INVADES KUWAIT, 1990
(THE BATTLE OF KUWAIT CITY)

As one might expect, there is very little if any evidence that the Qur'an directly influenced the political and military leaders or the ordinary combatants of either Iraq or Kuwait in the events that led up to the Iraqi invasion on August 2, 1990, or in the twelve hours of battle for Kuwait City. While Muslims constituted more than 85% of the populations of both nations and their armed forces, neither government was particularly Islamic in its policies. Iraq's president at the time, Saddam Hussein, occasionally quoted Qur'anic passages and invoked the names of Allah and Islam in order to justify his policies, but neither he nor his Baath Party governed based on the Qur'an.[26] Kuwait was a very liberal constitutional monarchy under Emir Sheikh as-Sabah, the latest member of the Sabah dynasty that had ruled the land at least nominally since

1759, with periodic protectorates under various European colonializers. With a booming economy based almost exclusively on exporting its oil, it was governed as a modern nation state with fully developed social welfare system and a labor force heavily staffed by guest workers from throughout the Middle East.

It is widely accepted that religion was not a factor in leading to the war. Despite the fact that Kuwait had supported Iraq in its war against Iran, 1980-88, Saddam's goal was to reduce the growing economic competition with Kuwait over oil exports in order to generate more revenue with which to rearm and rebuild Iraq after the long and destructive war with Iran. "By this time Saddam's frustration with Kuwait was intense. He was now determined to extract substantial grants plus a complete moratorium on war loans on top of adherence to OPEC quotas. The Kuwaiti indifference to his desperate needs amounted to 'stabbing Iraq in the back with a poisoned dagger.' He had gone our of his way to plead the Iraqi case and further begging would only cause him (and, by extension, Iraq) an unendurable public humiliation."[27]

Iraq's invasion was quick and overwhelming. It had little congruence with any relevant passages of the Qur'an save for the acquisition of a large amount of booty that was pilfered from the Kuwaitis, including the oil fields. The Iraqi forces clearly were the invaders and the attackers. They had technological and numerical superiority far beyond any of the Muslim battles during Muhammad's life and more than in many of the 214 most famous battles in Muslim military history (as described in Chapter 4 and listed in Appendix A).

"The attack began at 01.00 exactly on 2 August 1990. It eventually involved some 140,000 Iraqi troops and 1,800 tanks but was initially spearheaded by two Republican Guard armoured divisions — the Hammurabi and the Medina. They moved rapidly south towards Kuwait City, while a Special Forces commando division attacked the city itself. Simultaneously, heliborne Iraqi units seized selected strategic sites throughout Kuwait, including the coveted islands of Bubiyan and Warba at the northern tip of the Persian Gulf. It was followed the next day by a mechanized division of the Republican Guard — the Tawakalna — with the task of securing the border with Saudi Arabia."

For their part, the Kuwaiti armed forces were unable to offer significant resistance to the Iraqi invaders during the invasion itself.

"The 16,000-strong Kuwaiti Army was not fully mobilized, in line
with the Government's attempt not to provoke the Iraqis. It was no
match for the overwhelmingly superior invading forces and was
crushed within hours, though intermittent armed resistance continued for several days. The fiercest resistance was reported
around the Emir's palace in Kuwait City, which was taken after
only two hours of tough fighting involving heavy machine-gun fire
and air strikes. The Kuwaiti Air Force managed to keep flying and
attacking armoured columns until their base was overrun the next
day. But this was the exception that proved the rule: within twelve
hours of the invasion Kuwait was under Iraq control."[28]

There is little evidence that either the Iraqis or Kuwaitis fought
steadfastly or for any of the many incentives offered in the Qur'an. It is
more likely that the Iraqi forces fought because they were modern military units ordered to do so under strict and punitive controls, and possibly also out of a sense of patriotic duty. Casualties on both sides apparently did not exceed several thousand combatants. The Kuwaiti emir
and royal family escaped into exile and called for armed resistance by
Kuwaitis against the occupying forces. Apparently, this was not in vain.

"Notwithstanding the immediate collapse of the Kuwaiti military,
armed resistance continued throughout the principality, and clan-
destine radio broadcasts urged the Kuwaitis to resist. From a
purely military point of view, this was no match for the formidable
Iraqi contingent. Yet its political consequences were far-reaching:
an unmistakable signal was sent to Saddam that his puppet
regime stood no chance of survival unless propped up by Iraqi
bayonets. Over the following months the resistance tied down an
estimated two divisions of Iraqi troops as well as providing intelligence to the coalition and harassing and sabotaging the occupation. The Kuwaiti government later estimated that some 1,000
civilians were murdered during the occupation, with many more
forcibly deported to Iraq."[29]

Many of the Kuwaiti POWs, both military and civilian, were
removed to Iraq and treated badly. Allegedly some of them had not
been repatriated to Kuwait even ten years later, for whatever reasons.
On the other hand, there are few reports of sustained abuses of
Kuwaiti civilians by the Iraqi forces. An international crisis deepened
when Saddam formally announced the annexation of Kuwait as Iraq's
19th province. The U.N. imposed a ban on all trade with Iraq. The U.S.

quickly declared that Iraq must withdraw or face war — a war that occurred in less that five months.

In sum, the Qur'an does not appear to have been a factor, directly or indirectly, in the Battle for Kuwait City. Most of the Qur'an's provisions were not extensively violated except, of course, that the Iraqis invaded, attacked, and seized another country of predominantly Muslim people. They did this without religious persecution, threats, or any other types of infractions that are identified in the Qur'an as justifications for war. These are hardly minor exceptions to be overlooked, of course. These actions were such obvious violations of Geneva Conventions and other standards of modern warfare, *jus bello*, that more than thirty nations were willing to join a U.S. led coalition in preparing to expel Iraqi forces from Kuwait.

THE COALITION EXPELS IRAQI FORCES FROM KUWAIT, 1991

This is not the place to recount the many efforts that were made by the U.N., the U.S., and the governments of many other nations to coax the Iraqi's out of Kuwait with economic embargoes and diplomatic devices between August 1990 and January 16, 2001, when the coalition's air strikes began against Iraqi forces. Saddam Hussein's refusal to negotiate or withdraw apparently was based on his belief that the longer he held out the greater the likelihood that the coalition would dissolve or that the U.S. would make political or military errors that would aggravate some Arab states into joining him as allies. There is no direct evidence that Saddam based his policies or strategies on specific verses of the Qur'an. However, Saddam often made public pronouncements in Qur'an-like phrases and referred to Islam and Allah as validations for his policies in statements such as this: "When the battle becomes a comprehensive one with all types of weapons, the deaths on the allied side will be increased with God's help. When the deaths and dead mount on them, the infidels will leave and the flag of Allahu Akbar will fly over the mother of all battles."[30]

After five months of trying to find a diplomatic resolution to the impasse, coalition forces began "the first electronics war" — a massive air bombardment with "smart bombs" and submarine-launched cruise missiles on Iraqi naval and land forces, command centers and air defenses throughout Iraq and Kuwait. Scud missile sites within range of Saudi Arabia and Israel were prime targets.[31] Iraq's military response was primarily in the form of more than eighty Scud missile attacks on those countries, apparently without distinguishing military from civilian targets. Surprisingly they did not use biological or chemical warheads in these attacks or in any other combat throughout the war against the coalition forces, for reasons that have not yet been determined. Of course, months after the war, Iraqi forces used chemical weapons against Kurdish militia and civilians in villages in the northeast provinces — and with devastating effects.

"The only offensive action taken by Iraq was the launching of Scud missiles against Israel and Saudi Arabia. On January the first modified al-Hussein Scud missiles were fired against the two countries. Alarm was then heightened by reports of eleven trucks leaving the Samarra chemical weapons storage facility. In the event, no chemical warheads were used, but during the war forty missiles were fired at Israeli civilian targets, first and foremost Tel Aviv, while forty-six were fired at Saudi Arabia. They were largely inaccurate and those, which were not intercepted, caused few fatalities. The total toll in Saudi Arabia was about thirty-one dead and 400 injured, of which twenty-eight dead and ninety injured came in one of the last strikes which hit US personnel in barracks in Dhahran.... In Israel approximately 4,000 buildings were damaged at a cost of millions of dollars, with severe disruption to normal life and considerable psychological stress, especially as there were constant fears that chemical warheads might be used."[32]

For the next month, until the coalition ground force attack began on February 24, the coalition moved more than six infantry and armor divisions into position along the southeast Saudi border with Kuwait and Iraq, backed by many batteries and squadrons of support arms based in Saudi Arabia and other Arab states and on four aircraft carriers in the Persian Gulf. Iraq countered with more than 20 divisions of infantry, armor and artillery in a defense-in-depth all along the Kuwaiti border and much of the western Iraq border with Saudi Arabia. More divisions occupied Kuwait City and were poised behind the beaches of the Persian Gulf in anticipation of a large amphibious landing by U.S. Marines.[33] The Iraqis had other divisions in reinforcing positions throughout Iraq and in defense of Baghdad and other large cities, as well as in holding position on the borders with Turkey, the Kurd autonomous province in the northeast Iraq, and along some sections of the border with Iran. While the total number of Iraqi ground combat forces exceeded those of the coalition, the total number of coalition forces (795,000, of which 541,000 were U.S. forces) actually outnumbered Iraqi forces by at least 3:1 (a situation which coincided with the Qur'an's warning to its believers that they usually would be heavily outnumbered when going into battle) in that so many coalition forces served in naval and air supporting arms, logistics, and communications.[34] It is worth noting that throughout the air bombardment that preceded the assault by coalition ground forces, other than with the Scud missile attacks on Israel and Saudi Arabia, Iraq's military forces were deployed in many ways that were congruent with the Qur'an. They defended their far borders, including the far border of their newly acquired "19th province" (Kuwait) despite devastating air and naval attacks by coalition forces. These attacks destroyed large percentages of Iraqi weapons and equipment, killed and wounded thousands of Iraqi military and also killed more than 2,000 Iraqi civilians and wounded more than 5,000 others.[35]

"On 9 February Brigadier General Neal reported the confirmed destruction of over 750 tanks, 650 artillery pieces and over 600 APCs. Five days later this was up to 1,300 tanks, 800 APCs and 1,100 artillery. This was approaching a third of Iraq's opening inventory. In fact the relevant attrition rate of 50 percent for front-line forces was reached on 23 February. By this time the second-level Iraqi forces were estimated to have suffered some 50 to 75 percent attrition, although the Republican Guard and some other units were still in reasonable shape."[36]

Apparently, this destruction quickly became so great that Saddam revised his strategy. He decided to try to draw and trap under-prepared coalition ground forces into such an intense and bloody battle that the U.S. public would turn against the war. This was in keeping with Saddam's belief that something similar to this had forced the U.S. to withdraw from the war in Vietnam.

"To salvage his strategy Saddam needed to draw the coalition into a premature ground offensive in Kuwait to bring the war to a quick end. This might cost many Iraqi lives but the key political effects would result from the lost Western lives. His hope was that heavy casualties would drive a disillusioned Western public opinion to demand an early cease-fire. He stated this objective at the start of hostilities: 'Not a few drops of blood, but rivers of blood would be shed. And then Bush will have been deceiving America, American public opinion, the American people, the American constitutional institutions.'"[37]

229

The Battle of Khafji, "the first significant ground encounter of the war," was one of the results of this change in strategy.[38] It constituted a pre-emptive surprise night attack by Iraqi naval and land forces (the kind of attack that would seem to be prohibited by some of the passages of the Qur'an that were presented in Chapter 2 of this book). A series of spirited, hotly contested clashes ensued over the next few days between Iraqi forces and coalition forces that included U.S. Marines, Saudi and Qatari unites, British and U.S. helicopters and fixed-wing aircraft. "Saddam also apparently thought that the capture of many coalition prisoners would damage Western morale. If he had picked his spot better, attacked at greater strength and executed the attack more effectively, serious disruption could have been caused to coalition plans." The planned Iraqi attack on Khafji lost the element of surprise when Coalition surveillance aircraft detected the movement of Iraqi forces moving toward Khafji several days before the attack was to begin.

"On 22 January, an E-8A JSTARS detected an armoured division's assemble area and a seventy-one vehicle convoy moving towards Kuwait. Aircraft were called in and fifty-eight of the vehicles were destroyed. On the night of 29-30 January there was another attempt, and this time no early detection. An Iraqi force, comprising two armoured and one mechanized battalion from one of the better Iraqi army divisions, the 5th Mechanized, crossed the Kuwaiti border in the south-eastern front and headed in the direction of Khafji. At the same time an armada of seventeen fast patrol boats carrying landing parties, began to move down the Kuwaiti coast. Behind them three mechanized divisions with some 240 tanks and 60,000 soldiers were massing near Wafra to follow through."[39]

The Iraqi force seized Khafji and held on for two days despite furious bombing by U.S. aircraft, artillery and helicopters. A coalition counterattack by Pakistani, Saudi and Qatari ground forces met stiff opposition from the Iraqis but prevailed after a few days of staunch resistance. "It took another two days to clear up all the remnants of the Iraqi units. The Iraqi losses in men and equipment were high, amounting to dozens dead and hundreds of prisoners. The coalition Arabs lost nineteen killed and thirty-six wounded."[40]

From evidence like this it seems likely that early in the war Iraqi forces were disposed to fight aggressively on and beyond their far borders despite facing extraordinary odds against much larger and far better-equipped coalition forces, including air forces, of many other

230

nations — not just one or two adversaries as was so often the case in the history of Muslim warfare. It might even been fair to suggest that few if any Muslim forces in the 214 most famous battles already analyzed had ever faced such poor prospects of victory. And yet the Iraqi forces fought aggressively, even when it was only for a matter of several hours or a few days. It hardly seems surprising, then, that following their defeat at Khafji, and as the air war intensified during February, at least 30,000 Iraqi soldiers deserted and the Iraqi leaders resorted to drastic and futile measures like burning more than eight hundred oil wells.[41]

The coalition's land war assault, what has been called the "100 hour war,"[42] apparently succeeded so quickly because it surprised many of the Iraqi units in their in-depth defense in the Kuwaiti desert. The U.S. Army's VII Corps circled north, outflanked, and then enveloped several Iraqi divisions. At the same time, two Marine Corps divisions drove directly into Kuwait City from the Saudi border along the Persian Gulf, supported by air and naval gunfire. This left many Iraqi divisions exposed on their western flank as they waited in vain along the beaches east of Kuwait City to defend against an amphibious assault from the Persian Gulf — an amphibious assault that proved to be unnecessary and a ruse. "The land campaign involved two distinct pushes: one, led by the Marines, across the Kuwaiti-Saudi border directly towards Kuwait City; the other involving the relatively light XVIII Corps well to the west and the relatively heavy VII Corps, which constituted the 'left hook' designed to envelop Iraqi forces and destroy their most substantial elements."[43]

Contrary to many reports in the U.S. mass media, some of the Iraqi units, the Tawakalna, Medina, and Hammurabi Divisions among them, and some of the mechanized units, fought staunchly at least for a few hours until they were overwhelmed by helicopter, artillery and tank attacks or until they were overrun by mechanized infantry or simply bypassed. Within two days more than 30,000 Iraqi troops had been taken prisoner. Another 28,000 were captured by the time the cease-fire was put into effect on March 3.[44] "Within less then forty-eight hours of fighting, the backbone of the Iraqi Army had been broken. The apparently formidable line of defence in Kuwait, the so-called 'Saddam line,' collapsed as allied forces pushed through the Iraqi lines and stormed into Kuwait. Iraqi troops were surrendering *en masse*."[45]

"At the same time allied forces were moving rapidly inside Iraq, in a determine thrust to reach the Baghdad-Basra highway and thus encircle the Republican Guard, deployed on Iraqi territory just north of the Kuwaiti border. More than 370 Iraqi tanks had been destroyed and American intelligence sources reported that at least seven Iraqi divisions — up to 100,000 men — were telling their supreme headquarters that they could no longer fight. By sunset on 26 February 30,000 prisoners had been taken and twenty-six Iraqi divisions had been destroyed or rendered ineffective. The rest of the Iraqi Army was largely in retreat with its command system destroyed. The coalition forces, however, had not yet cut off the Iraqi line of retreat."[46]

The final blow, the "turkey shoot at Mutla Pass" along the Kuwait City to Basra highway, took place after the Kuwaiti and Marine Corps forces pushed into Kuwait City and the VII Corps pushed across north of the city, dislodging Iraqi combat and support units in front of them. As a convoy of more than 1,000 Iraqi tanks and support vehicles made a mad dash north for the Iraqi border it was intercepted and destroyed by squadrons of coalition aircraft.

"Waves of aircraft attacked the hopelessly vulnerable convoy — what had been presented as an orderly retreat was now a disorderly rabble. The convoy included senior officers. It was an attempt to escape with arms and weapons intact, as well as plunder, instead of surrendering. On the other hand, once the attack began they were given no opportunity to surrender. Instead, American aircraft queued in the skies to mount their attacks."[47]

Despite the carnage, Saddam resisted a cease-fire for days by trying to portray the withdrawal of the Saudi forces from Kuwait as a voluntary act. On March 3, however, his generals agreed to accept the U.N. mandate, as specified in Security Council Resolution 686.

"The main priorities were the immediate release of the 200 or so allied prisoners, return of goods taken from Kuwait and abducted Kuwaiti citizens, and help with the clearance of mines and booby traps. Most of the time the Iraqis listened in silence as General Schwarzkopf described the terms. They had yet to appreciate the extent of their defeat. Al-Jabber appeared stunned when told that the allies had taken 58,000 prisoners and were still counting, and stunned again when he realized that the US advance was well behind his lines."[48]

The casualty statistics underscore just how devastating this war was for the Iraqis. The U.S. and coalition forces lost 240 KIA, 776 WIA, and about 200 POWs in battle, most of whom were soon repatriated. Another 138 were killed and 2,978 were wounded outside of battle. Estimates of Iraqi losses vary somewhat but 35,000 KIA and 100,000 WIA often are quoted, with more than 58,000 POWs.[49]

Of special interest is the way that Iraqis treated their captives, given that the Qur'an has many specific provisions about Muslim treatment of POWs (as presented in Chapter 2). Twenty-three of the 200 coalition prisoners were U.S. military personnel.[50] One of these cases remains unresolved and very controversial. Navy Lt. Commander Michael Scott Speicher, an F-18 pilot, was shot down in the Iraqi desert on January 17, 1991, and was classified as KIA — the first U.S. serviceman to be killed in the war. His body never was recovered. In October 2001 the U.S. Navy reclassified his case as "missing/captured," based on circumstantial evidence that included his initials carved into a wall of a Baghdad prison. A second exceptional case involved flight surgeon Major Rhoda Cornum, who was shot down and injured while on a rescue mission in a Blackhawk helicopter. She reported that she had been interrogated and sexually assaulted by an Iraqi guard during her eight days in captivity. Her courage under fire and in captivity led to her testifying before Congress about the combat worthiness of women. Many combat posts were opened to women as a result.[51]

Other than these two cases, most evidence indicates that U.S., British, and Anzac POWs were treated roughly immediately after capture but that they were protected reasonably well by most Iraqi troops. Sometimes they were deprived of food, water, medical care, and exercise for several days. This was particularly true of those POWs who were enlisted, rather than officers who piloted downed aircraft, those who had fought back (especially those who had injured or killed Iraqi soldiers during the pursuit), and those who were troublesome and uncompromising. Kuwaiti, Saudi and other Arab POWs reportedly were treated much worse, particularly if they were sick or unstable.[52] Most POWs were interrogated about their units, weapons, troops deployments, and their roles in combat. Most were threatened, physically abused and, in some cases, tortured by Iraqi interrogators. Iraqi guards often treated POWs more leniently, particularly as the war's outcome became apparent to them. For example, U.S. Air Force Colonel David Eberly, the highest-ranking U.S. POW of the war, was shot down and captured while flying an F-15 on a bombing run.

"I was beyond exhaustion. This had to be a day in Hell; machine gunned on the Syrian border, a couple of hours sleep while chained to a cot, interrogated by the area commanders in Al Qaira, attacked by the mob in the village, the never-ending car trip to Baghdad; all the stops, all the same questions and now, stashed here in this kennel."[53]

Eberly was held prisoner for 43 days, until March 10, about one week after the cease-fire. Then he was released with twenty-one other coalition POWs in exchange for 300 Iraqi prisoners. Eberly reported that he was slapped-around, interrogated often, and deprived of food and water. Interrogations could be very trying.

"'We need help,' I started, slowly and cautiously, I continued, 'We aren't getting enough food, no water…we need blankets…it's very cold…we were better in the other prison. These guards aren't taking care of us. I know we have some who need a doctor. Please, help.' My pleas were again met with threats and the normal whacks to the head. I guess I was too pitiful to pursue because I was soon jerked back to my cell."[54]

Eberly reported that POWs were most in danger during U.S. air strikes and that they were treated most harshly after these strikes. He admits that he befriended some of the guards. He often asked questions. He asked for food for himself and his fellow POWs with whom he could communicate occasionally in the hallways and when being transported to other prisons. His main complaint was that the Iraqis never reported information about the POWs to the coalition governments as required by the Geneva Conventions. He also reported that the information that he had received from former Vietnam War POW pilots years ago was very helpful to him in adjusting to prison life and to his interrogators.

It seems likely that Eberly would have reported the influence of the Qur'an and Muslim practices in the prison because he was and is a very religious man. He does not mention any Iraqis praying, using the Qur'an, or mentioning Allah. He wrote that most Iraqis that he encountered — villagers, soldiers, prison guards, and interrogators — seemed to be rather indifferent about ideology and that they were concerned mainly about getting killed in air and ground attacks by coalition forces. They did not hold deep animosities towards ordinary Americans so much as against Jews, Israel, and the fact that the U.S. government ordered the bombing of Iraq villages and cities even though Iraq had never attacked targets in the U.S.

Another coalition combatant who became a POW and recounted his experiences is former British Special Forces Sergeant Andy McNab. According to his memoir, *Bravo Two Zero*, he was captured by Iraqi soldiers in January 1991 while on an eight-man patrol behind enemy lines eighty-five miles southeast of the Syrian border. Their mission was to locate and destroy Scud missile batteries. His captivity was much more precarious and worrisome than David Eberly's, probably because McNab and his buddies had shot at and possibly killed some Iraqi soldiers while he was evading captivity. Also, he was heavily armed and obstreperous when captured. He was an enlisted man, rather than an officer, and he was sometimes antagonistic towards his captors. He tried to escape several times.

> "We had been stripped of all clothing for several days now and left exposed to the damp and bitter cold. We were getting beaten regularly in the cells and tortured to the point of unconsciousness during the interrogations. We were put in stress positions in the cells, blindfolded and handcuffed, and we had to stay that way. They'd come in and beat us when we toppled over. The combined effects were taking more and more of a toll."[55]

Like Eberly, McNab makes no mention of the Qur'an or Muslim rituals influencing the daily lives of the Iraqis soldiers, guards and interrogators. He portrays the Iraqi people and troops as being angry about being bombed by coalition forces, but not being particularly religious, political, or ideological in their daily lives. Most of the guards were lazy and bored. Some guards, those who knew some English, were friendlier towards the prisoners than others. Interrogators varied in their hostility. Some were brutal and sadistic in their pursuit of information about coalition plans, targets, and troop deployments. They often deprived POWs of food, water, and medicine, and they used a variety of psychological measures, from false promises and feigned friendship, to fear tactics, in order to elicit intelligence information from POWs. One of these tricks involved the promise of dental care to repair McNab's broken teeth.

> "'Open wide again, Andy please,' he said in perfect English. 'Oh, dear, that is bad, but I'll soon sort it out for you.' I had my suspicions, but there was nothing I could do. I opened as wide as I could for him, and the cunt gripped the first stump of tooth with

the pliers and twisted hard. I screamed and blood gushed from my mouth.... 'Do you really think we're going to help you?' The Voice laughed. 'Do you really think we're going to help you, you despicable heap of shit? We could just leave you to die, you know — you're so irrelevant to us.... You're going through this for nothing. You're stupid, a stupid, misguided fool, and your teeth are going to come out one by one.'

I couldn't answer. I was screaming. I knew that I was going to die. And I knew now that it wouldn't be clean and quick."[56]

McNab claims that he and his buddies survived the prison experience because they eventually learned to ignore the hard-line, ascetic, strict Geneva Convention Code for POWs that had been taught to them in British Special Forces survival school. McNab also criticized advice offered by a former U.S. Marine who lectured to them about what supposedly was an effective U.S. POW tactic in Vietnam.

"I remembered a lecture we'd had from an American POW at the time.... His Marine training had been that the harder you are and the more aggressive you are if you're captured, the sooner your captors will leave you alone. He stood there in front of us hardened cynics at Hereford, crying his eyes out as he told us about the five years he had been a prisoner of the Viet Cong. 'What a load of shit,' he said. 'The unbelievable nightmares and pain I went through because I really believed what I'd been taught.'"[57]

Nonetheless, McNab reports that he and his fellow POWs witnessed violations of almost all Geneva Conventions regarding treatment of POWs short of sexual molestation, forced labor, forced conversions to Islam, political indoctrination, mutilations and executions — certainly some very considerable exceptions. Guards and interrogators used electric shock, beatings, and deprivation of food, water, and medicine in order to gain compliance and to try to extract information with some intelligence value (e.g. "Why were your packs loaded with high explosives?"). No effort was made to convert them to Islam or to indoctrinate them politically or in any other way. They were not pressured to sign confessions, to denounce the U.S., or to commit actions that would make it easy for their captors to dispose of them. Also similar to what happened to POW David Eberly, a week after the cease-fire, McNab and his fellow prisoners were suddenly fed a full breakfast, clothed in old uniforms, and driven to a hotel in

Baghdad where the Red Cross administered an exchange for Iraqi POWs. He remembered that "this was the first time that the Red Cross had had any news about any of us from the Iraqis. Even then, the lists being handed over were corrupt. It was a breach of the Geneva Conventions, but a rather minor one compared with the rest of our experiences as POWs."[58]

In his "Epilogue" penned in 1993, two years after his POW experience and after he mustered out of the military, McNab concluded that his experience was really not so bad after all:

"As my stress-test score showed, I'm not emotionally affected by what happened. I certainly don't have nightmares. We are big boys and we know the rules that we play by. We've all been close to death before. You accept it. You don't want it to happen, of course, but sometimes, there you go — occupational hazard. In a strange way I'm almost glad I had my Iraqi experience. I wouldn't like to repeat it, but I'm glad that it happened.... Our big joke in prison used to be, 'Well, at least it can't make us pregnant,' and I have learnt that nothing is ever as bad as it seems.... As to the rights and wrongs of the war — well, that's never been a worry to me. I was a soldier; that's what I was paid for. It was very exciting: I got high doing it. And as for the people who interrogated me, if I met any of them in the street tomorrow and thought I could get away with it, I'd slot them."[59]

By way of conclusions about the U.S. led war for the liberation of Kuwait from the Iraqis, it seems fair to say that there is little or no evidence that the Qur'an had direct influence on Iraqi political and military strategy or any combat behaviors. Some Iraqi decisions and behaviors certainly were indirectly congruent with the Qur'an, such as the staunch, massive defenses on the far borders and the stiff, if short-lived, resistance to coalition air and ground attacks. There also was an unwillingness of Iraqi commanders to surrender their units (in contrast to individual and small group surrenders by low-ranking frontline personnel) even after Iraqi forces had suffered more than five weeks of brutal attacks. Some units certainly seemed inclined to plunder, possibly because the Qur'an allows, even encourages, taking booty from POWs. Iraqi troops also abducted Kuwaiti civilians. Possibly this is the modern day equivalent of impressed slavery from Muhammad's days — but probably not. Soldiers have plundered in all armies regardless of religious orientations. The abductions probably were ordered by higher command for possible intelligence value or to retaliate for past offenses, real or imagined.

It might even be possible that the Qur'an and Islamic religious beliefs discouraged the Iraqis from taking some actions, such as the use of biological and chemical weapons against coalition forces, based on the principle of proportionality (i.e. Iraqi forces would not use toxic weapons unless coalition forces used them first). On the other hand, in the later stages of the war Iraqi forces, at the individual, small group, and unit levels, occasionally violated Qur'anic passages about not deserting or being taken prisoner. The many Scud missile attacks that landed in Israel and Saudi Arabia on non-military targets would seem to be inconsistent with the Qur'an. By-and-large, the treatments of POWs were not consistent with the Qur'an, with torture and abuse being commonplace, except that, ultimately, most or all of the non-Arab POWs were repatriated and few if any were executed. No effort was made to convert POWs to Islam. Finally, there is little evidence of the applicability of the many incentives that are offered by the Qur'an to its believers for bravery in combat. Few Iraqi combatants seemed to be fighting for a military Jihad, in the way of Allah, or with righteous intention in mind. Then again, it might well have been very difficult if not impossible for many Iraqi fighters to have violated many of the Qur'an's instructions about waging war, or the principles of discrimination and proportionality, because Iraqi forces were so obviously on the defensive and they were in locations away from major population centers of their adversaries. Said another way, most of the Iraqi troops were "stuck out in the middle of the desert" where it would have been difficult (or perhaps irrelevant) to violate the Qur'an's guidelines about waging war. They rarely got close enough to their adversaries to put many of the Qur'an's instructions to the test. This is particularly true if we contrast this war to many of the other wars since 1984 that have involved Muslim forces, such as the Israeli invasion and occupation of Lebanon, 1982-93, the Iraq-Iran War of 1980-88, and Iraq's invasion of Kuwait.

THE BATTLE OF THE BLACK SEA, SOMALIA, OCTOBER 3-4, 1993

The Battle of the Black Sea, Mogadishu, Somalia, occurred at the end of a frustrating and eventually aborted U.N. peacekeeping and relief mission to reduce starvation and civil war.[60] About 100 U.S. soldiers, supported by a variety of combined arms units, were flown by Black Hawk helicopters into a market and residential area in central

Mogadishu on a "snatch and grab" mission to abduct two lieutenants of Somali warlord, Mohamed Farrah Aidid, leader of the powerful Habr Gidr clan. The two Somalis were quickly abducted; but in the process two helicopters were shot down, some occupants died and others were injured and captured by a mob. Relief forces got lost and ambushed on their way to the downed choppers. The battle that followed was shockingly intense, bloody, and still controversial.

"The mission was supposed to take about an hour. Instead, a large portion of the assault force was stranded through a long night in a hostile city, surrounded and fighting for their lives. Two of their high-tech MH-60 Black Hawk helicopters went down in the city, and two more crash-landed back at the base. When the force was extricated the following morning by a huge multinational rescue convoy, eighteen Americans were dead and dozens more were badly injured. One of them, Black Hawk pilot Michael Durant, had been carried off by an angry Somali mob and would be held captive for eleven days. News of the casualties and images of gleeful Somalis abusing American corpses prompted revulsion and outrage at home, embarrassment at the White House, and such vehement objections in Congress that the mission against Aidid was immediately called off."[61]

The Somali mobs and paramilitary units of the warlord Aidid that attacked the U.S. forces during the next eighteen hours lost an estimated 500 dead and more than 1,000 wounded. Yet, Aidid was able to claim that he had repulsed and defeated the World's dominant armed force and nation when U.S. forces withdrew from Somalia months later and the U.N. aborted its efforts to establish a coalition government in the country.

Evidence of the influence of the Qur'an on this battle and on the combatants in the relief effort in Somalia is indirect at best. And yet the topic is worth considering if we assume that most of the Somali fighters were Muslim by birth or orientation, even if the warlords were not Muslim clerics, their cause was not Islamic *per se*, and the civil war was not being fought over religious persecution. This battle was one of the few times that U.S. forces faced Muslim combatants since the Battle of Tripoli, Libya, against the Barbary pirates in 1804 (described in Chapter 4) and it was a battle that was decidedly unlike any of the battles in the Qur'an and in Muslim military history in its mission, asymmetric technological superiority, and so many other features.

The U.S. force clearly was the invader and attacker — into the very heart of the capital city of the country. Religious persecution was not a motive of any of the adversaries. Still, it would be easy to understand how common Somali citizens were encouraged to fight by opportunists in the warring clans. Ordinary citizens as well as opportunists could easily believe that the very presence of heavily-armed non-Muslim combatants constituted a threat to Islam and a blatant violation of the Qur'an's promise of religious freedom. There is no doubt that some of the Somali militia and street people fought brazenly, even bravely, if not steadfastly. Often they seemed to fight more as enraged individual warriors than as members of cohesive military units using conventional tactics for urban warfare. Their motivations seemed to include obligations to Islam, their friends, and their neighborhoods, as well as revenge for what they believed to be the indiscriminate killing of Somali women and children by the U.S. helicopter forces.

> "Sheik Ali was part of a large number of irregular militia moving in the crowds that had begun to form a wide perimeter in the neighborhood around the crashed helicopter.... When he got to the perimeter around the crash site there were crowds, fighters like himself but mostly people who just came to see, women and children. The Americans were firing down the streets at everyone. Sheik Ali saw women and children fall.... He relished the fight. There was no quarter given on either side. The black vests who came with the Rangers were especially ruthless killers. When they had come to Bakara Market they had come into his home uninvited and they would have to accept his punishment. Sheik Ali believed the radio broadcasts and flyers printed up by the Aidid's SNA. The Americans wanted to force all Somalis to be Christians, to give up Islam. They wanted to turn Somalis into slaves."[62]

Many other Somalis got caught up in the frenzy and paid a terrible price for it. All the while Aidid kept sending in small groups of reinforcements, apparently hoping to capture or kill all of the U.S. soldiers who were pinned-down, hiding in confiscated dwellings along the streets, and hoping to survive the night.

> "From overhead, the commanders watched the contested neighborhood through infrared and heat sensitive cameras that sketched the blocks in monochrome. They could see crowds of Somalis moving around the perimeter in groups of a dozen or more, and kept hitting at them with helicopters. Aidid's militia

was trucking in fighters from other parts of the city. The Little
Birds made wall-rattling gun runs throughout the night."[63]

As shown in Chapter 2, the Qur'an repeatedly instructs its believers to bravely defend their communities against incursions by non-
believers. The Somalis forced the withdrawal of the U.S. forces from
the marketplace in less than one day. The entire mission ended less
than one month later when the Clinton administration decided to withdraw all U.S. forces. Less in keeping with the Qur'an is the fact that
some of the Somalis abused the corpse of at least one dead U.S. soldier
— a fact that was recorded by film crews and broadcasted around the
World. This incident seems to have been a spontaneous behavior on
the part of a few Somali street people rather than a planned or staged
event by Aidid's militiamen. It might have been in retaliation, based on
their belief that the dead U.S. soldier had indiscriminately fired-upon
and killed Somalis in the marketplace, including many women and
children. While this reaction (the mutilating and public desecration of
a body) would hardly seem to be congruent with the Qur'anic principle of proportionality in that U.S. forces had not committed the same
offense, the reaction might have been elicited out of a sense by some
of the Somalis that the U.S. forces had violated the Qur'anic principle
of discrimination when they fired upon and killed non-combatants in
a public setting — the marketplace. Admittedly, this is speculation on
my part. Even so, military leaders might keep it in mind regarding
future operations similar to the Battle of Mogadishu.

Chief warrant Officer Mike Durant (the pilot and only survivor of
the crash of helicopter Black Hawk Super Six Four that was shot down
at the marketplace) was held prisoner by the Habr Gidr clan for two
weeks. He was treated reasonably well by his captors, who saved him
from irate mobs that might have executed him. Durant received rudimentary care for his numerous injuries. He was fed well and even got
to share in a portion of the favorite drug, *khat*, of his captors.

"Durant's fear of being executed or tortured eased after several
days in captivity. After being at the center of that enraged mob on
the day he crashed, he mostly feared being discovered by the
Somali public. It was a fear shared by Firimbi. The propaganda
minister had grown fond of him. It was something Durant worked
at, part of his survival training. He had made an effort to be polite.
He learned the Somali words for 'please,' *pils les an*, and 'thank
you,' *ma hat san-e*. The two men were together day and night for a

241

week. They shared what appeared to be a small apartment. There was a small balcony out the front door, which reminded Durant of an American motel."[64]

Durant also was allowed to receive gifts from the Red Cross. He was encouraged but not pressured into converting to Islam. Firimbi watched the pilot studying and making notes in his Bible and assumed Durant was a very religious man. "If you convert to Islam, you will be freed," the captor said. "You pray to your God, and I'll pray to mine, and maybe we'll both be released," Durant joked. On the radio they played selections of music that Durant liked.[65]

After the battle, the Habr Gidr were reasonably responsive and responsible in negotiations with U.S. representatives about exchanging their prisoners. There were no major follow-up battles and few enduring animosities. CWO Durant was returned to U.S. forces and the Somali prisoners were released within several months. U.S. forces departed Somalia, thus ending the saga of what is widely claimed to have been "the longest sustained firefight involving U.S. troops since the Vietnam War."[66]

Mark Bowden, author of the acclaimed recounting of the battle, *Black Hawk Down*, provided a chilling and prescient prediction about the battle's influence on Muslim opinion. "The lesson our retreat taught the world's terrorists and despots is that killing a few American soldiers, even at a cost of more than five hundred of your own fighters, is enough to spook Uncle Sam."[67]

WAR AGAINST THE TALIBAN AND AL-QAEDA IN AFGHANISTAN, 2001–

More than with all the other wars since 1984, we might expect that the Qur'an would have had (and still is having) the greatest influence on the Muslim combatants in Afghanistan and Pakistan. The government that the Taliban imposed on Afghanistan in 1997 was intended to be an arch-fundamentalist Islamic state in which the Qur'an would become the primary law of the land, if not the constitution, as it is in Saudi Arabia.[68] Mullah Mohammed Omar had become the *de facto* head of state. As described in Chapter 1, Omar had been an ordinary peasant who was raised as a devout and strict Muslim. While still a boy, he lost an eye while fighting as a foot soldier for a tribal warlord against the Soviets. He then started his own religious school (*madrassa*) and gradually gained power as an enforcer of strict Islamic codes. He indoc-

242

trinated hundreds of recruits into his Taliban movement (including Naji — another case that is described in Chapter 1). Omar had met with Osama bin Laden, who recognized him as the supreme mullah of Afghanistan and became a major financier for the Taliban, in exchange for their harboring his al-Qaeda operatives and allowing his training camps inside Afghanistan. Omar came to see himself as "the rightful successor to the prophet." The Islamic state that he created in 1997-2001 was utterly tribal, autocratic, closed, and belligerent towards the West. Omar was supremely confident that his Taliban could repel or defeat any invaders because they had subjugated the warlords who had forced the powerful Soviet army to withdraw from Afghanistan after many years of brutal fighting in a guerrilla-style war. The Taliban had acquired many of the weapons that the Soviets had left behind.

The Qur'an played a vital role in Omar's thinking, in his government, and in the daily lives of the Taliban soldiers. Case materials presented in Chapter 1 on former Taliban soldier Naji and former al-Qaeda fighter Aukai Collins make it clear that the Qur'an was an integral part of their lives even before they joined the training camps that prepared them to fight. It was an integral part of daily life and training in those camps as well. In Naji's case, eventually he defected from the Taliban to the Northern Alliance forces because he believed that the Taliban too often violated the Qur'an's prohibitions against harming innocent civilians in their attacks. Ironically, it was U.S. air attacks on the Taliban in November 2001 that enabled Naji to escape to the Northern Alliance where, based on what has been published so far, he should have found fewer violations such as this.

The Qur'an also had a major influence on the U.S. born Aukai Collins. Collins converted to Islam and decided to become a jihadist because of his readings of the Qur'an while in a detention center in California. He went on to serve in that capacity in Afghanistan, Pakistan, and Chechneya. In the training camps in Pakistan, the Qur'an was essential to the training of the mujahideen.

"When the *azan* sounded over the loudspeakers, the seemingly deserted camp came to life. Mujahideen streamed out of the tents and mud shacks all over the camp to create a sort of rush-hour traffic headed toward the mosque. Some walked and chatted in little groups, while others made their way alone. Once inside, the mosque looked like any other mosque in the world, with one important exception. Muslims usually empty their pockets when they pray, and before prayer you'll usually see a little pile of car keys or a cell phone next to each person. Here, however, it was an AK-47 or perhaps an old Russian SKS rifle. Some men sat quietly and recited the Qur'an while others said optional prayers before the *Salaatul Fajr*. Fifteen minutes or so after the call to prayer the Imam would get up and everyone would perform *Salaatul Fajr*. The camp would be quiet for at least an hour or so afterward. Many of the mujahideen sat in groups of three or four to recite verses from the Qur'an."[69]

Collins remained committed to the Qur'an and to Islam even after eight years of fighting for Islam and losing his leg from tripping a land-mine while attacking an enemy outpost. He decided to leave his life as a combatant because the terrorist behaviors of his comrades too often deviated from the standards set in the Qur'an. Still he remained com-mitted to the goals of stopping religious persecution and violence against Muslims in Muslim communities in the Middle East.

Reports like these from former Taliban and al-Qaeda fighters cor-respond with plenty of indirect evidence that their successors often fought the U.S. and allied forces in Afghanistan in ways that are con-sistent with the Qur'an. Following the airliner attacks of September 11, 2001 on the World Trade Center and Pentagon, Mullah Omar and his government repeatedly refused to negotiate, to turn over Osama bin Laden, and to expel the al-Qaeda in compliance with U.S. and U.N. demands.[70]

The Qur'an instructs its believers to invest heavily in the defens-es of their country and to defend the far borders staunchly against the infidels who would persecute them because of their religion. Despite the poverty of the country and the treasury, Mullah Omar's govern-ment invested heavily in its military forces and in preparing for the invasion by the U.S. forces. Although it was too poor to be able to acquire the most advanced weapons from the global market, Omar's government distributed to its 10-20,000 Taliban militia large quanti-ties of small arms, anti-aircraft weapons, rockets, and some old Soviet tanks that had been captured from or abandoned by the Soviet army when it withdrew in the early 1990s. Taliban also acquired thousands of small pick-up trucks and installed machine guns and rocket launchers on the cargo beds. Perhaps they intended these to serve as modern versions of the camel and horse cavalry of Muhammad's armies long ago. The Taliban did not defend heavily the far borders of Afghanistan, probably because they realized that the allied forces would fly over the borders in order to capture airfields close to the largest cities of Kabul, Herat, Kandahar, Kanduz, Khost, and Muzar-i-Sharif. The Taliban generally deployed their forces in company size units throughout country that they expected to be the landing areas for the allied troops and the transportation choke points along rivers and in mountain passes. Thousands of Taliban soldiers also were deployed in the northeast border against the rebellious Northern Alliance forces under Hamad Karzai that had been locked in battle with them there for several years.

The invasion strategy for allied forces had several concurrent objectives under the command of U.S. Army General Tommy Franks. One was to try to locate and destroy by aerial bombardment the senior members of the Taliban government, including Mullah Omar, and al-Qaeda, including Osama bin Laden. Another was to destroy communications centers and to secure airfields near Kabul and a few other cities in order to free those cities from Taliban control, preferably by destroying Taliban forces in and around those cities and forcing what was left of the Taliban government and military forces to surrender. However, during the first three weeks of the invasion, October-November 2001, it soon became apparent that many members of the Taliban government and military had fled from the cities into the mountains after they weathered the aerial bombardments and their first encounters with allied ground forces. Nonetheless, at times resistance was surprisingly formidable. U.S. military commanders tried to have the Northern Alliance do the bulk of the fighting on the ground for them, but these forces often were reluctant to close with and destroy the Taliban. It took three weeks of experimentation until Allied commanders discovered that the Taliban were most vulnerable when units of 100-200 Northern Alliance militia, often on horseback, were augmented with a squad of U.S. Special Forces and one or more members of Special Tactics "Air Commando" units of the Air Force. These commandos served as sophisticated forward observers who could direct air, artillery, and other supporting arms fire on even the smallest and most remote targets in the mountain hiding places of the Taliban and al-Qaeda. They were equipped with the very latest electronic devices: a global positioning system, scope, battery backs, three different radios for communicating with a satellite, aircraft on station overhead, and members of their protective units, a control pad for air to ground target acquisition and bomb control, a protective head system with night vision goggles, a headset antenna and boom mike for communicating simultaneously through all three radios, an M-4 rifle with laser pointer, and enough food, water and medicine to allow them to operate under battle conditions for more than five days without resupply.[71] This equipment permitted the Air Commandos to locate individual enemy soldiers and bunkers several miles away, quickly fix their coordinates with a global positioning system and lasers, call in air strikes from the aircraft circling on station overhead, and then direct the falling "smart" bombs directly into their assigned targets using lasers — and all with devastating effects.

One of these new age, cyber-warriors was "Matt," an Air Commando Staff Sergeant who was instrumental in the destruction of hundreds of Taliban personnel, attack vehicles and bunkers in the critical battle of Dar-I-Suf Canyon, a crucial terrain feature, that led to the Taliban stronghold city of Mazar-I-Sharif in north central Afghanistan, October 31, 2001.

> "He carried an M-4 rifle, but his radio was his weapon. With it, he controlled a flight of F-14s and F/A-18s armed with 20mm cannon and laser-guided bombs. With it, he controlled B-2's and B-52's armed with thousand-pound MK-83 dumb bombs and two-thousand-pound JDAM satellite-guided bombs. With it, he controlled a battalion's worth of firepower in all. A Commando with a radio was the most dangerous man on the battlefield.... With his scope, he spotted another enemy bunker where some of the men were reconvening, and he calculated new coordinates and waited for the planes again. Finally, one came. He heard the crackle on his radio and spoke to the pilot... and soon a streak of bomb came pouring through at five hundred miles per hour, following the energy through the opening of the bunker, bursting into a massive flash, booming echoes across the valley and sending billows of black smoke and burned dirt into the sky.... Fragments of blackened timber poked up from the crater, and enemy soldiers poured in from the hillsides to dig out their wounded from it. He reached for his radio again. He was becoming a warrior fast. He called for a second strike on the same location. He watched the new explosion atomize the men digging for their friends."[72]

Apparently this kind of interception of Taliban assaults by Air Commandos was repeated time and time again during the next few weeks until the Taliban broke down into small teams and retreated into the mountains on the border with Pakistan. One of the most decisive battles was at Tarin Kot.

"At a decisive battle south of Tarin Kot on November 18, 2001, 100-300 pick-up trucks carrying hundreds of Taliban raced north from Kandahar in column in an apparent frontal assault on Northern Alliance forces under Hamid Karzai (currently the appointed President of Afghanistan) that had captured Tarin Kot weeks earlier without firing a shot. It was the hometown of many Taliban elders. However, the truck column was intercepted by squadrons of U.S. Air Force and Navy fighter aircraft, directed by U.S. Air Commandos, that destroyed approximately 30 trucks and their occupants in the initial engagement."[73]

Of course there were more conventional battles than this, some of which posed significant threats to the allied forces. They revealed that the Taliban and al-Qaeda often fought steadfastly, and that they could inflict considerable damage on U.S. forces at close range if they were not destroyed quickly.

The Battle at Shah-I-Kot valley, near Gardez, March 2-3, 2002, has been called "the bloodiest battle since Somalia a decade ago."[74] As part of Operation "Anaconda" infantry companies A, B, and C of the U.S. Army 10th Mountain Division were inserted by helicopters into blocking positions to keep hundreds of al-Qaeda (suspected of escorting Osama bin Laden at the time) from escaping the valley into the mountains to the east as other U.S. Army units swept down the valley from Gardez to the north. Unfortunately the three companies were flown into "hot" landing zones that had been zeroed-in for mortar fire and surrounded by al-Qaeda combatants. In the battle that followed, the al-Qaeda were able to put enough deadly mortar, rocket, and gunfire on the positions of Company C that, according to veteran war correspondent John Sack, the Company "would not have survived without Eddie Rivera of Ellenville, New York."[75] Rivera was the company corpsman, by the way. As C Company's casualties mounted, the al-Qaeda kept pouring so much gunfire on the landing zones that the med-evac choppers could not land to evacuate the wounded soldiers.

"The LZ's too hot! The landing zone's inaccessible. Then *boooooom*! The soldiers cringe, the bombers conclude, the Qaedas, unchastened, undismayed, come from their caves, their rifles, launchers, and mortars coming, too, and 'Incoming!' the soldiers shout. To shield him, Rivera lies on top of McGovern, the boy with wounded feet, legs, arms, the boy benumbed by Nubain, he puts his head on McGovern's and hears him say, 'Please please

please.' Then *boom*, a mortar round hits First Lieutenant Maroyka. Then *ffft*, a bullet hits Specialist Almay, a boy who played basketball with Rivera.... Then *boom*, a mortar round hits Major Byrne, the doctor far from a MASH and, with Rivera, the last practitioner here.... It's mid-afternoon and its still going on. How many soldiers in two platoons of Company C of the 1st Battalion of the 87th Regiment of the 10th Mountain Division of the American Army were hit? Restrict yourself, the Army adjures me, to "Casualties were 'light,' 'were moderate,' 'were heavy.' Casualties were heavy."[76]

Clearly, these reports portray al-Qaeda units fighting cohesively and steadfastly in defense of their terrain against far more numerous foreign forces few of whom were likely to be Muslims. And yet there is no direct evidence that al-Qaeda fighters like these fought so stead-fastly because of their knowledge of or adherence to passages in the Qur'an. However, as U.S. forces combed through the possession that were left behind by al-Qaeda combatants in other places, they fre-quently found evidence that the Qur'an was an integral part of the training and daily lives of the Al-Qaeda. For convenience, some of the evidence that was presented in Chapter 1 is repeated here.

Evidence was captured by U.S. Special Forces troops in al-Qaeda safe houses in Kabul, in March 2002 that indicates that the Qur'an was used extensively in the military training of thirty-nine recruits. All of the recruits were unmarried. Most of them came from impoverished, peas-ant families in Afghanistan, Pakistan, and several other countries where, as children, they had memorized a few passages from the Qur'an in their native languages. Several had studied the Qur'an exten-sively in *madrassas* before joining the al-Qaeda, and several had sup-posedly memorized all of it. Several of the recruits had been associated with fundamentalist groups in their native countries. The evidence indicated that these recruits had been trained for months in a camp in Rishkan, about twenty miles south of Kabul. The "walls are still paint-ed with Koranic verses and slogans involving the jihad. 'All the Christians, Jews and infidels have joined hands against Afghanistan,' one poster claimed." Training documents advocated an "Islamic fervor" in the camp. Training materials and pamphlets were printed in Arabic, and in many other languages, and emphasized passages of the Qur'an about the necessity of waging jihad against foreign enemies throughout the world. One pamphlet depicted an anti-American scene and urged readers to "Fight until there is no discord and all of religion is for God."

Military instruction drew heavily from religious doctrine. Abandoned notes of a student in a class on ambush tactics read, "Without a sign from the leader you should not retreat, because the Koran says 'Do not retreat; in time of war there is no death. My only power is the power of Allah.'"[77]

This is not the place to try to describe and analyze the many other widely published events of the war in Afghanistan since October 2001. It seems fair to say, however, that many of the events that have been reported so far suggest that the Taliban and al-Qaeda have been very formidable opponents who often have fought in ways that are congruent with the Qur'an. For example, the Taliban and al-Qaeda obviously fought staunchly before, during, and after their holdout and attempted escape from Kandahar Prison. It was there that they killed CIA officer Johnny "Mike" Spann (and where the "American Taliban," John Walker Lindh, was captured by U.S. forces). Casualty figures continue to climb, but we know that dozens of Allied forces (including at least 15 U.S. soldiers) have been KIA, hundreds WIA, and considerably more troops than that have been killed and injured in non-combat incidents, mainly in aircraft crashes.[78] Taliban and al-Qaeda KIAs and WIAs are believed to be in the thousands. The allied forces apparently have been extremely fortunate in avoiding capture. While one or a few U.S. soldiers who were shot down in October 2001 may have been captured and executed by their captors, a final determination has not been announced on this matter since their bodies were recovered only days after they were shot down. Fortunately the Taliban and al-Qaeda have not had many opportunities to violate or comply with the Qur'an in this regard. More than 3,000 Taliban and al-Qaeda militia have been captured since October 2001, and hundreds of them have been held under increasingly controversial terms at the U.S. prison in Guantanamo Bay, Cuba. Newspaper reports indicate some of them are repatriated back to their native country, from time-to-time.

As of the time of this writing, there are many indications that the Taliban and al-Qaeda have reorganized in Pakistan and that they are re-emerging as hit-and-run guerrilla forces and terrorists in Afghanistan and in neighboring nations. The simple fact that the war continues and that they never surrendered (or negotiated) certainly testifies to the fact that they have been steadfast and brave despite overwhelming inferiority in numbers, equipment and so many other resources. There have been relatively few reports of Taliban and Al-Qaeda in Afghanistan misusing civilians, of using toxic weapons, or of fighting in ways that obviously violate the Qur'an's principles of proportionality, discrimination, righteous intention, and transgression avoidance. This is all the more noteworthy because allied forces clearly were the invaders and the attackers in the vast majority of incidents in Afghanistan after October 2001. This also was true of the Soviet invasion a decade ago. However, the Taliban and al-Qaeda seem to be less deviant towards allied forces now than they were towards the Soviets (as described earlier in this chapter). It might also be said that while allied forces occupy Afghanistan, apparently with few or no encroachments or restrictions on the religious freedoms of the Afghan population, the Taliban and al-Qaeda in effect do not have easy access to mosques and other Muslim holy places and to their families and communities because of allied presence in their country. I will leave it to others to decide whether this constitutes religious persecution, but I could understand how it would constitute religious persecution to members of the Taliban and al-Qaeda.

In sum then, in the ongoing war in Afghanistan there is considerable indirect evidence that the Qur'an has been an influence on the Taliban and al-Qaeda, both organizationally and individually. There are many ways in which they have fought consistent with the Qur'an (except, perhaps, for considerable surrendering in the first few months of the invasion) and relatively few instances of their violating the Qur'an blatantly and repeatedly. This war clearly is a war in progress (as ironic as this phrase might be, in one sense). The Qur'an could be a very significant factor on its future course — hopefully in the course of a sustained and just peace.

THE U.S. LED INVASION AND OCCUPATION OF IRAQ, 2003-

"2 Soldiers Killed, 4 Injured in Convoy Ambushes in Iraq."

"Three other U.S. soldiers are killed in separate incidents, all believed to be accidents."

"Baghdad, Iraq (May 27, 2003) — Attacks against the U.S. occupying force in Iraq escalated yesterday. Two soldiers were killed and four were wounded in two separate ambushes on military convoys, in one of the most violent ways since the end of the war."[79]

As of this writing, more than 160,000 U.S. and allied military personnel occupy Iraq following the declared "end" to organized resistance by Iraqi military forces on April 15, 2003.[80] Another 150,000 plus

"Coalition" forces are supporting this occupation from bases throughout the Middle East and from aircraft carrier strike forces in the Persian Gulf. This occupation follows on the heels of a U.S. led invasion on March 19, 2003, of about 120,000 combat and support troops that was preceded by three days of intensive bombing by air and naval forces of Iraqi government and military targets in and around Baghdad and Basra. While the ground war was declared "essentially over" on April 15th, sporadic gun battles erupt and incidents of sabotage and terrorism are reported on a daily basis that sometimes result in deaths and injuries to Coalition forces. As yet, there has been no formal cease-fire or surrender of either the Baath Party, Saddam Hussein (if he is still alive) or large units of the Iraqi Army.

The general consensus of published news and analysis articles in the national news media portray the U.S. led invasion as the consequence of President George W. Bush's decision to invade Iraq with ground forces rather than wait any longer for Saddam Hussein to prove full compliance with U.N. Resolution 686 of 1991 and U.N. Resolution 17 of 2002 regarding disarmament of biological, chemical, and nuclear weapons. This was one of the promises made by Iraq as a condition for ending the Gulf war of 1991 when allied forces expelled Iraqi forces from Kuwait (as discussed in an earlier section of this chapter). The Bush administration also claimed that Saddam's regime harbored al-Qaeda and other terrorist organizations that were responsible for the World Trade Center and Pentagon attacks of 9-11-2001 and committed many other offenses against world order that necessitated "regime change." For six months before the invasion, the Iraqi government took the position that an invasion of Iraq would be illegal and immoral. It argued that Iraq had not threatened, damaged, or attacked the U.S. or any other nation since the war with Kuwait. Supposedly Iraq was complying with the U.N. resolutions reasonably well and it was allowing U.N. weapons inspectors to search the country for evidence of non-compliance — inspections that were not finding significant violations. Saddam's regime also claimed that U.S. threats were motivated by a desire to control Iraq's oil fields and by complicity with Zionist/Israeli efforts to persecute Muslims throughout the Middle East.

The ground war primarily took the form of about 30,000 U.S. army forces, heavily mechanized, pushing north across the Kuwait border along Highway #1 and the Euphrates River towards Najaf and Baghdad while, to the east (on their right flank), another force of about 20,000 U.S. Marines also pushed north towards Kut and

251

Baghdad.[81] Meanwhile, in the southeast corner of Iraq, about 10,000 British troops surrounded Basra and seized oil fields and ports on the Persian Gulf. All of these forces were supported heavily by tanks, artillery, and dozens of squadrons of bombers, fighters and helicopters as well as cruise missiles that were fired from naval forces in the Persian Gulf. On paper, Iraqi military forces numbered about 400,000 personnel and more than twenty-three combat arms divisions. However, many of these personnel were poorly trained and poorly equipped men who had been recently pressed into service. The armed forces were only about one-third their size during the 1991 Gulf War and they had far fewer tanks, artillery, and Scud missiles than during the Gulf war. Most of the regular army divisions were positioned around cities and key terrain features in the south and north of the country. The best-equipped and best-trained forces were six Republican Guard Divisions (two infantry divisions, three armored divisions, and one mechanized division). They were positioned within fifty miles of the outskirts of Baghdad in order to block enemy approaches to the capital and, if necessary, to provide Baghdad with a "Stalingrad defense" of urban warfare and house-to-house fighting. Several regular army divisions were located in northern Iraq to protect Saddam's hometown of Tikrit and other cities as well as the oil-fields in that region. They were also supposed to control Kurdish separatist forces in the hills and mountains on the northeast border with Iran. Augmenting these Iraqi army units were an estimated 20,000 paramilitary fighters called "Fedayeen Saddam." Often they were deployed in small units in villages along major highways where they could harass enemy troop convoys, interdict supply lines, and launch surprise attacks behind enemy lines.

Of primary concern to U.S. government and military leaders was whether Iraqi forces would make extensive and effective use of biological, chemical, or nuclear weapons; whether the Iraqis would use Scud missiles against civilian targets in Israel, Kuwait, and neighboring countries as they had in the 1991 war; and how much resistance the Iraqi army units and civilian population would pose against the U.S. and British forces, particularly in and around Baghdad. Reportedly, Saddam's goal was to have his defensive forces inflict heavy enough casualties on the U.S. ground forces, and capture enough prisoners, that U.S. public opinion would quickly shift to oppose the invasion. Conceivably this would force the Bush administration to negotiate the end of the war before Baghdad was captured and Saddam would be forced out of power.

As the war began, resistance by Iraqi units varied considerably. There were instances of spirited, albeit brief, defenses and even a few attacks by small Iraqi units against U.S. and British ground forces in southern Iraq during the first few days of the invasion, particularly around Basra, Nasiriya, and Najaf. Meanwhile U.S. air attacks around Baghdad heavily damaged the communications system of the government and the military, the air defenses, and the Scud missile batteries, although a few Scud missiles did land in Kuwait but inflicted minimal damage. During the first week the U.S. and British suffered dozens of KIAs and hundreds of WIAs, lost more than a dozen troops to Iraqi captivity, and lost some aircraft, tanks and APCs to Iraqi attacks. Iraqi losses have been estimated to be much larger, with at least hundreds KIA, thousands WIA, and hundreds, possibly thousands taken POW. However, it soon became apparent that many Iraqi soldiers would not surrender when faced with sustained combat if they could escape the battlefields, strip-off their uniforms, don civilian clothing, and blend into the civilian populations of the villages and cities. Dressed as civilians, some of these soldiers continued to engage U.S. ground forces, at times sniping, throwing grenades and exhorting other Iraqis to do the same. Several instances were reported of "suicide bombers" who attacked U.S. military checkpoints and troop carriers.

Some analysts report that the war can be understood to have occurred in six phases.[82] March 19-25 was Phase I — "First Strike and a Dash into the Desert." Aerial bombardment and cruise missile attacks were directed at Saddam Hussein and his senior leaders, at government buildings and communications centers in Baghdad, and at anti-aircraft installations. This so-called "shock and awe" bombardment was supposed to break the will of the Iraqi government, military, and population to resist the invasion. U.S. and British ground forces encountered varying amounts of opposition from Iraqi forces; but at times the fighting was intense. Phase II was March 26-31, a time of "Sandstorms, Supply Lines and Fierce Iraqi Resistance." Convoys of U.S. supply trucks were ambushed around Nasiriya, Najaf, and Basra. Phase III, April 1-2, "Breaking Through Karbala Gap, and a Rush to the East," probably was the decisive ground phase of the war. The U.S. Third Infantry Division was able to feign, isolate, and bypass Republican Guard divisions around Karbala, then rush through the Karbala Gap and move to within fifty miles of Baghdad. Meanwhile Marine Corps regiments turned east, crossed the Tigris River, neutralized Kut, and rushed north to the outskirts of Baghdad. Phase IV,

April 3-5, was "Seizing an Airport and a Foray into Baghdad." At times the fighting was intense, prolonged, and precarious for both the Iraqi and U.S. forces — as was the case in the Battle for Diyala Bridge.

THE BATTLE OF DIYALA BRIDGE

This battle, like dozens of others that took place during the three-week war, is evidence that some Iraqi military and paramilitary forces often fought steadfastly for several days against far larger and better-armed U.S. forces at key transportation points on the way to Baghdad. The U.S. infantry battalion involved in this battle was the 3rd Battalion of the 4th Marine Regiment. Its 1,500 infantry troops were supported by thirty Abrams tanks, sixty armored assault vehicles, 155 mm. howitzers, squadrons of Cobra helicopter gunships and fighter jets. On its assault north from Kuwait towards Baghdad the battalion had taken part in seizing Basra airport. Then it by-passed Nasiriya and "fought fierce but limited battles" in Afaq and Diwaniya.[83] At Al Kut it was engaged in a brief but ferocious battle against Iraqi infantry troops that inflicted its first KIA, Corporal Evnin.

> "Colonel McCoy was just a few feet from where Corporal Evnin was mortally wounded. 'I saw him go down,' he said afterward. 'That fight lasted about nine seconds. We had about 15 human-wave guys attack the tanks. They were mowed down. They drew first blood. They got one of us, but we got all of them.'"[84]

Two days later one of the tanks supporting the battalion was blown-up by a suicide bomber.

> "The day before they arrived at Diyala bridge, a Marine tank was blown up by an explosives-laden truck that drove alongside it and was detonated by its driver. It was the realization of one of the marines' worst fears; suicide bombers.... But the deaths of their comrades deeply affected the grunts, and when the battalion got to Diyala bridge, every man was primed to kill. 'There's an unspoken change in attitude,' McCoy told me a few days before we reached the bridge. 'Their blood is up.'"[85]

The next day the battalion approached Diyala bridge on the outskirts of Baghdad, hardly expecting that it would take two days of intense fighting to secure it.

"The Battle of Diyala Bridge lasted for two days. One of the bridge's main pylons had been badly damaged, and armored vehicles could not move over it. So after the first day of fighting on April 6, the battalion dug itself into the southern side for the night, giving itself time to plan an infantry assault over the span the next morning. In the morning the battalion released another round of heavy artillery barrages to soften up the opposition on the northern side of the river. In the fighting, two more marines were killed when an artillery shell hit their armored vehicle on the southern side of the bridge. Eventually, the battalion killed most of the Republican Guard fighters, or at least pushed them back from their dug-in positions on the northern side, and McCoy decided that it was time to try a crossing.... When the marines crossed to the northern side, they found themselves in a semi-urban neighborhood of one-story shops and two-story houses, a few dozen palm trees and lots of dust. A narrow highway led away from the bridge, towards Baghdad. Immediately, they were met with incoming fire — occasional bullets and the odd rocket-propelled grenade, fired mostly from a palm grove on the eastern side of the road to Baghdad.... The situation was further complicated on the north side of the Diyala bridge, because what was left of the Iraqi resistance had resorted to guerrilla tactics. The Iraqis still firing on the marines were not wearing uniforms. They would fire a few shots from a window, drop their weapons, run away as though they were civilians, then go to another location where they had hidden other weapons and fire those."[86]

Eventually the Iraqis who survived fled back into Baghdad and the "Sunni Triangle" to the north. But it is obvious that many of them and their dead comrades had fought steadfastly enough to stall the advance of 1500 marines for more than two days. It was later discovered that the marines also had mistakenly killed and wounded more than a dozen Iraqi civilians who were trying to flee from this encounter. There were no reports of war crimes by the Iraqi military forces against civilians, or the use of toxic substances. There were no reports of them surrendering. Of course, there was the one incident that involved the suicide bomber who blew-up the tank and killed a Marine.

The last two phases generally had less prolonged and bloody battles than did Phase IV and the Battle for Diyala Bridge. Phase V, April 6-9, was "Convergence on a Falling Statue" (the statue of Saddam Hussein in downtown Baghdad). U.S. Army and Marine Corps forces occupied critical terrain and facilities in Baghdad, mopped-up pockets of Iraqi soldiers who fought back, securing the airbases, and tried to stop looting, crimes and civil unrest. Phase VI, April 10-15, involved capturing the northern cities of Tirit, Kirkuk and Mosul, securing the oil fields in that region, controlling Kurd militia and civilians in that region, and trying to block the escape of Iraqi military and government personnel into Jordan, Syria, Turkey, and Iran.

Did the Qur'an have appreciable influence on this war? There is even less evidence that the Qur'an influenced this war directly than the war of 1991, despite frequent radio and television appeals from Saddam and other leaders for the Iraqi people to engage in holy war against the invading infidels from the West.

> "We say to all sons of Jihad and supporters, to our nation, our
> people, wherever they are, that whoever is able to march and
> reach Iraq, Baghdad, Najaf, and blow himself up in this American
> invasion.... This is the climax of Jihad and climax of martyrdom."[87]

However, no evidence has surfaced as of yet that clearly shows that specific passages of the Qur'an directly influenced Iraqi government decisions or the behaviors of Iraqi troops in battle. And yet this war was in many ways more congruent with the Qur'an than was the Gulf War of 1991. The Iraqis were the defenders — not the invaders here. They were rarely the attackers. Probably in less than ten percent of the firefights were the Iraqis the attackers. In most of these instances probably they were counter-attacking or reacting to attacks by the allies. Sometimes Iraqi forces were intercepted while they were moving into attack positions or while they were moving to reinforce a position that had been attacked by U.S. forces. Certainly, Saddam intended to defend steadfastly his country, as did many of his senior officials in the Baath Party and his senior military officers. For example, on March 31 Iraqi Vice President Taha Yassin Ramadan said Saturday's attack in Najaf was "just the beginning" and even raised the specter of terrorism on U.S. on British soil. "We will use any means to kill our enemy in our land and we will follow the enemy into its land."[88] Surely there were many instances when Iraqi forces fought rather steadfastly, even fiercely — at least until they were damaged so badly by U.S. supporting fires that they had little ability to continue the fight as regular military units. Then, rather than surrender or quit, they escaped and attempted to blend into the civilian population.

Estimated casualties probably understate the ferocity and destructiveness of the war. When the war was unofficially declared "over" on April 15, U.S. forces suffered an estimated 140 KIA, 900 WIA; British about 30 KIA and 200 WIA. Estimates for Iraqi casualties are more than 1,000 KIA, 10,000 WIA, and more than those figures in civilian killed and wounded. Iraqi army deserters (or "escapers") probably number in the tens of thousands. Partly because escaping was so frequent, the number of Iraqi POWs (probably 5-10,000) is much lower than during the 1991 Gulf War. It might be suggested that the behavior of many Iraqi military personnel during this war resembled Muhammad's soldiers at the battle of Uhud (as described in Chapter 3). They escaped the battlefield at Uhud and fled back into Medina. Of course, in that battle the Meccan army failed to pursue them into Medina; whereas in this war of 2003 the U.S. forces certainly pursued escaping Iraqi troops into the cities. So far, however, it appears that many of the Iraqi soldiers have escaped nonetheless.

Recall that the Qur'an encourages but does not compel Muslim soldiers to die as martyrs or to fight to the death. Muhammad himself several times did not fight to the death, but rather lived to fight another day. In the war of 2003 it might be true that many Iraqi combatants fled the battlefields because they had easy opportunities to do so. Many of them were close to large Iraqi cities, possibly even to their homes. Many of them also might have believed U.S. propaganda in leaflets and broadcasts to the effect that Iraqi soldiers would not be harmed unless they fought back, especially if they fought back with toxic weapons "of mass destruction." Propaganda emphasized that the real targets of the U.S. invasion were Saddam, his operatives, and the Baath Party. Perhaps these are also the reasons why Iraqi forces did not engage in many obvious violations of the Qur'an such as attacks on civilian populations, religious minorities, or outgroups within Iraq such as the Kurds, or against their neighbors. There were some reports that Iraqi soldiers in the Basra area tried to hide in columns of refugees or tried to use refugees as cover from which to launch attacks on U.S. forces. There also have been reports that several hundreds or thousands of Muslim militants from Syria, Iran, and other countries joined Iraqi forces in fighting around Baghdad. If so, then these are the only fighters who seemed to be motivated primarily or exclusively by the Qur'an's promises and incentives to jihadists — to fight religious persecution wherever it is, or to fight against the nonbelievers. It appears that most of the Iraqi soldiers fought because they were ordered to do so and, perhaps, they would be shot if they refused to do so. In other words, they fought for non-religious reasons, because of a system of social controls that are commonplace in modern military organizations, and also for national defense. There were a few reported instances of Iraqis committing terrorist actions such as suicide bombings because Saddam had publicly offered incentives of the equivalent of $30,000 to the families of successful suicide bombers. If so, this incentive seems to have failed badly. As to Iraqi violations against POWs, there have been few confirmed reports so far of mutilations, executions, or torture.

Apparently all of the U.S. and British POWs captured by the Iraqis have been repatriated and returned to their home countries. They seem to have been treated rather crudely but less abrasively than were their predecessors in the Gulf War of 1991. For example, two Apache helicopter gunship pilots, David Williams and Ronald Young, were shot down over Karbala in the first few days of the invasion. Both of them were captured and eventually abandoned in Baghdad several days after the regime disintegrated. Both appeared in an interview on CBS's *60 Minutes II* on May 13 as happy, healthy and un-injured.[89] They reported that the Iraqi air defenses were very well organized and that anti-aircraft fire was intense. After they were shot down they were pursued and quickly captured by Iraqi soldiers. They were kicked, beaten and shackled. Their uniforms and equipment were confiscated. Iraqi civilians shouted at them and struck them as they were being taken to jail cells. They were interrogated several times by Iraqi officers about their intended targets and the location of their units. One of these interrogations was videotaped and broadcasted throughout the Middle East on al-Jezeera TV out of Qatar (and later broadcasted in the U.S.). Williams and Young were moved frequently from one jail to the next until they arrived at a large prison in Baghdad that also held U.S. POWs. They said that their eleven days of captivity in Baghdad were especially "terrifying" because of U.S. air bombardments that came close to hitting their cells. They were fed rice and water but were not afforded other rights of POWs according to the Geneva Conventions. As the outcome of the war became obvious, guards abandoned the POWs in Baghdad. Iraqi military and civilians were reluctant to take custody of them.

Probably the most famous case of an American POW in this war is the case of Army Pvt. Jessica Lynch. Newspaper reports indicate that she was seriously injured in the early days of the war when an army truck convoy ran into an Iraqi ambush in Nasiriiyah. Pfc. Lynch was one of several soldiers captured. Contrary to first reports, she apparently received considerable medical care from Iraqi physicians in a local hospital and she was not abused or threatened by Iraqi soldiers. "Despite her pain and fear, Jessica Lynch sipped juice and ate biscuits under the watchful eye of Iraqi doctors and nurses who shielded her from thugs during her eight days of captivity in an Iraqi hospital in March."[90] Lynch was rescued by a Special Forces patrol on April 1 that had been informed of her location by an Iraqi lawyer who had visited her in the hospital (he was subsequently "given asylum in the United States, a book contract and a job offer in Washington"). Her experience, combined with those of pilots Williams, Young, and others, indicates that many if not all POWs were treated somewhat better by their captors in this war than were their predecessors in the Gulf War of 1991 (as described in an earlier section of this chapter). Of course, it is possible that the POWs would have been treated much more severely, even executed, had the war dragged-on or turned particularly vicious. Nonetheless, while the Iraqi military did not ransom or release its POWs, as the Qur'an dictates, the POWs were not treated in ways that clearly violate the spirit or the text of the Qur'an.

In sum, based on what has been published by credible sources so far, Iraqi government and military leaders were not directly influenced by the Qur'an in this war. And yet many of the presumed Muslims in the Iraqi military units and government offices behaved in ways that are congruent with the Qur'an. The most obvious exception is that many soldiers stopped fighting rather quickly as cohesive military units, even if they were not influenced by the Qur'an in behaving this way. This is somewhat surprising, given the great emphasis that the Qur'an places on Muslims fighting steadfastly to defend their homeland and to expel non-believers from their communities. Nor did Iraqis use toxic weapons or engage in "war crimes" to an appreciable extent. It also seems fair to say that neither the Iraqi government, the military commanders, nor the combat soldiers violated the Qur'anic principles of proportionality, discrimination, righteous intention and transgression avoidance in any systematic way.

So, among the many questions yet to be answered about the invasion of Iraq in 2003 is the question of why, with Saddam Hussein at the helm, the government and military forces of Iraq did not behave more badly. However, there are many passages in the Qur'an (that are in Chapter 1 of this book) that could convince the Qur'an's believers to continue to fight in Iraq until "All religion is for Allah."

259

SUMMING UP THE WARS SINCE 1984

In this chapter I have argued that there is little direct evidence that the Qur'an directly influenced the recent "Muslim" wars since 1984, except possibly for the behaviors of the Taliban and al-Qaeda in Afghanistan during the ongoing war there with the U.S. and some allies. Interestingly, this is also a war that, along with the U.S. led invasion of Iraq in 2003, seems to have been fought in many ways that are concordant with the Qur'an, at least indirectly. Violations of the Qur'an have been much less common in this war than in some of the other recent wars, such as the Iraq-Iran war of 1980-88. This finding is all the more noteworthy because, in that war, both adversaries were overwhelmingly Muslim in the religious orientations of their common soldiers, and one adversary (Iran) was one of the very few Muslim nation states in the modern world. Furthermore, its revolutionary leader, the late Ayatollah Khomeini, vowed to spread Islamic fundamentalism throughout the World — starting with Iraq. Of course, that this outcome was not achieved by that war does not mean that it will not be achieved by other means in the future. The ongoing war in Afghanistan, 2003, between U.S. led forces and remnants of the Taliban and al-Qaeda, might be evidence of this. In these two wars, and in the other seven wars since 1984 that have been discussed in this chapter, many of the Muslim military and para-military forces often have fought rather steadfastly in their own lands, despite overwhelming odds against them. Certainly this is in accordance with one of the most prominent instructions in the Qur'an, even if there is no direct influence that the Qur'an is the source of their steadfastness and their continuing violent opposition to foreign armies.

---

[1] My method was to use Internet search engines as well as more traditional library research procedures in order to find and read books, newspaper articles, academic journals and military journals and magazines at the Naval War College, Newport, RI, about these wars. I searched for references to the Qur'an in these materials (and found few such references). I looked for ways in which the Qur'an may have influenced the goals and methods of war, strategy, tactics, when, how, and why Muslim combatants fought, how they treated POWs and civilians, and their willingness to negotiate and to respond to offers of cease-fire and peace.

[2] Peter Marsden, *The Taliban: War, Religion and the New Order in Afghanistan* (London: Oxford University Press (Zed Books), 1998), p. 8. Marsden attributes this quote to Oliver Roy in Roy's book, *Islam and Resistance in Afghanistan* (Cambridge: Cambridge University Press, 1986) , p. 30.

[3] After 1984 this war continued until 1989, with Afghan guerrillas becoming more

aggressive, until Soviet troops were withdrawn according to a U.N.-mediated agreement. Principal sources of information are Dan Smith, *The State of War and Peace Atlas, New Edition,* (Oslo, 1997), p. 38; Mark Urban, *War in Afghanistan, 2nd Edition,* (New York: St. Martin's Press, 1999); Paul Overby, *Holy Blood: An Inside View of the Afghan War,* (Westport, Conn.: Praeger, 1995); Jeri Laber and Barnett R. Rubin. *A Nation Dying: Afghanistan Under the Soviets, 1979-87.* (Evanston, IL: Northwestern University Press, 1993).

[4] Marsden, p. 82.

[5] Marsden, p. 26.

[6] John Bullock and Harvey Morris. *The Gulf War: Its Origins, History, and Consequences.* (London: Methuen, 1989), pp. xv-xvi.

[7] Efriam Karsh, *The Iran-Iraq War, 1980-88.* (Oxford, England: Osprey Publishing, 2002), pp. 13, 88.

[8] Karsh, p. 12.

[9] Karsh, p. 13.

[10] Karsh, p. 91.

[11] Bulloch and Morris, p. 243.

[12] Karsh, p. 83.

[13] Bullock and Morris, p. 268.

[14] Gwynne Roberts, "Poisonous Weapons," pp. 279-281 in Roy Gutman and David Rieff (editors). *Crimes of War: What the Public Should Know,* (New York: W.W. Norton & Company. 1999), p.279.

[15] Bulloch and Morris, p. 263. I offer this speculation not in defense of the actions of either adversary, but only in the pursuit of an honest understanding of what transpired, why, and how it might relate to the Qur'an.

[16] Karsh, p. 77.

[17] Bulloch and Morris, p. 262.

[18] Karsh, p. 85. The welcome absence of toxic weapons in the U.S. led wars against the Taliban and al-Qaeda in Afghanistan and against Saddam Hussein's regime in Iraq might suggest that Karsh was being unduly pessimistic in his prediction here.

[19] Gutman and Rieff, p. 34.

[20] *The State of War and Peace Atlas,* pp. 42-43.

[21] *The World Almanac and Book of Facts, 2003.* New York. World Almanac Books, p. 804.

[22] Haleem, p. x.

[23] *The World Almanac and Fact Book, 2003,* p. 765. See also, *The State of War and Peace Atlas,* pp. 32-35.

[24] Richard Holbrooke. *To End a War, Revised Edition.* New York. The Modern Library. 1999, p. 69.

[25] Peter Maass. "Cultural Property and Historical Monuments," p. 111 (in Gutman and Rieff, pp. 110-112).

[26] Lawrence Freedman and Efriam Karsh, *The Gulf Conflict 1990-1991: Diplomacy and*

War in the New World Order, (Princeton, NJ: Princeton University Press. 1993), chap. 3.

[27] Freedman and Karsh, p. 47.

[28] Freedman and Karsh, p. 67.

[29] Freedman and Karsh, p. 68.

[30] Freedman and Karsh, p. 363.

[31] Freedman and Karsh, pp. 299, 437.

[32] Freedman and Karsh, p. 307.

[33] Tom Clancy and General Fred Franks, Jr. *Into the Storm*. NY: Berkley Books, pp. 4-6.

[34] Freedman and Karsh, pp. 390, 409.

[35] Freedman and Karsh, p. 329.

[36] Freedman and Karsh, p. 372.

[37] Freedman and Karsh, p. 363.

[38] Freedman and Karsh, p. 369.

[39] Freedman and Karsh, p. 364.

[40] Freedman and Karsh, p. 365. Let me suggest that these causality estimates actually seem rather low, given the numbers of troops involved on both sides, the heavy use of supporting arms, and the duration of the battle. The battle might have been much more focused and constrained than the analysts believe to have been the case.

[41] Freedman and Karsh, pp. 384, 390.

[42] Freedman and Karsh, p. 105.

[43] Freedman and Karsh, p. 393.

[44] Freedman and Karsh, pp. 398, 407.

[45] Freedman and Karsh, p. 398.

[46] Freedman and Karsh, p. 398.

[47] Freedman and Karsh, p. 403.

[48] Freedman and Karsh, p. 407.

[49] Freedman and Karsh, p. 408.

[50] Key sources of information on how Iraqi forces treated POWs are Freedman and Karsh, 1993; Joellen Perry, "Rhonda Cornum: The Iraqi Army couldn't quash her fighting spirit," in *U.S. News and World Report*, "Heroes," August 20/August 27, 2001, pp. 30-33; Andy McNab, *Bravo Two Zero*. New York: Dell. 1993; and David Eberly, *Faith Beyond Belief: A Journey to Freedom*. Richmond, VA: Brandylane Publishers, Inc. 2002.

[51] *U.S. News and World Report*, August 20, 2001, p. 32.

[52] Eberly, p. 136.

[53] Eberly, p. 52.

[54] Eberly, p. 91.

[55] McNab, p. 325.

[56] McNab, pp. 328-329.

[57] MacNab, p. 234. I concur with McNab in doubting the wisdom of this "survival" tactic of hard-line, closed-mouth opposition, especially when facing captors who are as determined and well-trained as were many of the Chinese Communist, North Korean, and North Vietnamese interrogators in the Korean and Vietnam wars. For more reinforcement on this position see Stuart I. Rochester and Frederick Kiley, *Honor Bound: The History of American Prisoners of War in Southeast Asia, 1961-1973*, pp. 268,269, 592 and passim. Washington, DC: Office of the Secretary of Defense. 1998. Also see Winston Groom and Duncan Spencer. *Conversations with the Enemy: The Story of Pfc. Robert Garwood.* New York. G.P. Putnam's Sons. 1983, pp. 366-367.

[58] McNab, p. 377.

[59] McNab, pp. 411-412.

[60] Mark Bowden, *Black Hawk Down,* (New York: Signet: New American Library, 1999), especially pp. 399-430.

[61] Bowden, p. 408.

[62] Bowden, pp. 216-217.

[63] Bowden, p. 309.

[64] Bowden, p. 390.

[65] Bowden, p. 399.

[66] Bowden, p. 428.

[67] Bowden, p. 428.

[68] Ahmed Rashid, *Taliban: Militant Islam, Oil, and Fundamentalism in Central Asia.* (New Haven: Yale University Press, 2000), pp. 22-27. Also see "Religion, War are All Omar Knows," *The New York Times.* December 7, 2001, p. 4.

[69] Aukai Collins, *My Jihad* (Guilford, CT: The Lyons Press (an imprint of The Globe Pequot Press). 2002), p. 24.

[70] Primary sources are Eric Schmitt, "Surprise. War Works After All," *The New York Times Sunday Week in Review*, November 18, 2001, pp. 1, 4; John H. Cushman, Jr. et al, "War in Afghanistan Evolves Into a Race to Impose Law and Order," *The New York Times,* December 9, 2001, p. B3; "Shifting Missions Come with Rising Risks," *The New York Times,* December 9, 2001, p. B2.

[71] Wil S. Hylton, "Mazar-I-Sharif," *Esquire*, August 2002, pp. 108-109.

[72] Hylton, pp. 111-112. Readers are encouraged to discount some of the probable exaggerations here by Hylton regarding how much control any one person has on aircraft fighter pilots and on the course of a battle.

[73] Karl Vick, "Rout in the Desert Marked Turning Point of War," *The Washington Post,* December 31, 2001, pp. 1, A13.

[74] John Sack, "Anaconda," *Esquire,* August 2002, pp. 18-36.

[75] Sack, p. 116.

[76] Sack, p. 122.

[77] "A Nation Challenged: Life in bin Laden's Army." *The New York Times*, Sunday, March 17, 2002, pp. 18-20. The Qur'an is mentioned six times in this article.

[78] Helen O'Neill, Associated Press, "Killed in Action," *The Providence Sunday Journal,* May 26, 2002, pp. 1, A22.

[79] "Restoring Iraq," *The Providence Journal*, Tuesday, May 27, 2003, p. A9 (quoting the *Los Angeles Times*).

[80] James Lehrer, "A Summary of the News," PBS, Channel 2, May 28, 2003.

[81] Primary sources on the order of battle and the progress of the war are "A Nation at War," *The New York Times*, March 30,2003, pp. B1-B16 and April 13, 2003, pp. B1-B11, and Murray and Scales, *The Iraq War*, 2004.

[82] "A Nation at War," *The New York Times*, Sunday, April 13, 2003, pp. B10, B11.

[83] Peter Maass, "Good Kills," *The New York Times Magazine*, April 20, 2003, p. 33. All quotes about this battle are from this same source, pp. 32-37.

[84] Maass, p. 35.

[85] Maass, p. 35.

[86] Maass, p. 36.

[87] "Iraq Rewards Family of Suicide Attacker." *The Providence Journal*, March 31, 2003, p. A5 (from the Associated Press).

[88] "Iraq Rewards Family of Suicide Attacker," p. 14.

[89] Both pilots were interviewed by news analyst Dan Rather on CBS's *60 Minutes II*, on May 13, 2003.

[90] Hugh Dellios and E.A. Torriero. "Questions Raised over POW's Rescue," *The Providence Journal*, May 28, 2003, p. A9 (attributed to *The Chicago Tribune*).

INTERPRETATIONS OF THE QUR'AN AND OF MUSLIM WARFARE

"When a Muslim ruler fought a secular war — in which the religious purpose was not apparent — no sin was necessarily to be incurred if he suffered defeat by another ruler, be he a believer or an unbeliever."[1]

"In the sphere of war and peace, there is nothing in the Qur'an or Hadith which should cause Muslims to feel unable to sign and act according to the modern international conventions, and there is much in the Qur'an and Hadith from which modern international law can benefit."[2]

The first quotation, from Majid Khadduri, a respected scholar of Islamic law, suggests several insights about Muslim warfare that are not apparent in the Qur'an. It admits that Muslim rulers have fought secular wars — "in which religious purpose was not apparent." It also contends that Islamic law recognized secular wars and was tolerant of defeat by either a Muslim or a non-Muslim ruler. This is rather remarkable if we consider that none of the passages from the Qur'an that I presented in Chapter 2 conveyed the possibilities of Muslims engaging in secular wars, of Muslim forces suffering defeat at the hands of non-Muslim forces, or of Muslim forces engaging each other in warfare. These are some of the insights that can be gained by considering, if only briefly, how the Qur'an has been interpreted by Islamic jurists and by scholars of Islam over the years.

The second quotation, by contemporary Islamic scholar Muhammad Abdel Haleem, is very hopeful in that it asserts that the Qur'an and Hadith essentially are compatible with contemporary international laws regarding war and peace among nations. Surely, his interpretations on these matters might be worth considering.

Countless books have been published over the ages, many of

them in English, that interpret the Qur'an as a religious, political, philosophical, and legal document.[3] When these books discuss the Qur'an's treatment of the topics of peace, conflict, and war, they do so in a more or less incidental way. The interpretations run the gamut from tolerant to condemnatory, from presenting the Qur'an as being an unparalleled document of peace to others that present it as being a promoter of violent conflict including war. Fortunately there are also some interpretations in the middle ground that are more measured, objective, and balanced. We have already been exposed to two of these rather moderate interpretations: Pickthall in Chapters 1, 2, and 3, and Rodinson in Chapter 3, although neither of these analysts focuses on peace, conflict, and war. Pickthall presents the Qur'an as being a religious document in which war and conflict are addressed mainly as unfortunate occurrences that the Qur'an and Islam can reduce, if not eliminate, if only more people will "believe," and if "believers" obey the Qur'an. Rodinson's topic is Muhammad rather than the Qur'an. In presenting his detailed history of Muhammad's life, he sometimes portrays passages of the Qur'an about war as being the product of Muhammad's imagination and dreams that were provoked by his experiences on the battlefield. Rodinson often mentions that the Qur'an's verses tend to justify how Muhammad and his followers behaved during battles. The verses also specify certain principles for battle (as identified in Chapter 2) and instruct Muslims on how they should behave in future conflicts, wars, and negotiations.

In this chapter I present some of the interpretations that four other scholars have given to the Qur'an regarding war and peace: Majid Khadduri, John Esposito, Maulawi Sher Ali, and Muhammad Abdel Haleem. Most attention will be given to Khadduri (quoted in the epigraph at the head of this chapter) because his work is more focused and objective on these topics than are some of the others.

KHADDURI'S INTERPRETATIONS

Majid Khadduri was a respected legal scholar and theorist who was able to read in Arabic many of the editions of the Qur'an and of Islamic legal codes going back to the origins of Islam. He conducted his original research on these topics at the University of Chicago while studying under Quincy Wright and Leo Strauss, highly regarded experts on the history of warfare and the history of Islam, respectively. His subject is broader than the title of his book: *War and Peace in the Law of Islam.* His book carefully examines the Qur'an's principles about relations between Muslim and non-Muslim nations and explains how these principles have changed since Muhammad's time in conjunction with major events in the history of Islam. Like other mainstream scholars, Khadduri contends that Muhammad and his followers were often, but not always, just as conflict-oriented, combative, brutal, and expansionist as many of the other Arab tribes of their time. Many of Muhammad's successors in the several centuries after his death were even more combative and expansionist than was Muhammad. After that, the belligerence of Islamic regimes varied greatly, often depending on the personality of the ruling caliph or imam and the ease with which empire could be expanded through commercial rather than military means.

> "Islam, emerging in the seventh century as a conquering nation with world domination as its ultimate aim, refused to recognize legal systems other than its own. It was willing to enter into temporary treaty relations with other states, pending consummation of its world mission. The "temporary" period endured for several centuries."[4]

THE ORIGINS OF CONFLICT

Khadduri follows in the tradition of Ibn Khaldun, Bukhari, and other classical interpreters of the Qur'an regarding the origins of conflict between Muslims and non-Muslims.

> "In the Islamic conception the world was at first created to be inhabited not by one, but by a variety of people, each endowed with its own divine order. To each people Allah sent a prophet who communicated the divine law. It was a pluralistic world before Muhammad arrived, but 'these peoples' one after the other broke the covenants and distorted the teaching of the prophets. Allah therefore decided to send one, last prophet, Muhammad (referred to the Qur'an as the 'seal of the Prophets') in order to repair and reconstruct the world into a monistic order. Muhammad was to call all peoples into the 'final and definitive religion for all people.'"[5]

The divine law was revealed to Muhammad by Allah in the form of the verses that Muhammad recited and that were then compiled in the Qur'an after his death. People who accept the Qur'an and practice the five pillars of Islam become part of the Muslim entity, *umma*, (variously translated into English as "community," "nation," and "broth-

267

erhood") that distinguishes them from all other people and helps them to live moral lives, thereby avoiding conflict with other Muslims. People who refuse to do these things (disbelievers) will live immorally, misbehave, and fight continually among themselves and against believers. The Muslim community subordinates the wills of its individual members, makes all members equal, except for differences among them in terms of piety, distinguishes them from all other people in the world, and protects them from external threats to the community.

> "In this tradition, Muhammad is reported to have conceived of the Muslim community as 'a single hand, like a compact wall whose bricks support each other,' and in the Qur'an it is often referred to as a distinct 'nation' (umma) of a 'brotherhood,' bound by common obligations to a superior divine authority."[6]

Again, the Muslim community makes Muslims different from all other people in the world in that they have voluntarily accepted Islam, the straight path, as their way of life. As such, Allah has granted his mercy to them.

> "In his compact with the people of Madina, Muhammad defined his Muslim community as 'an *umma* in distinction from the rest of the people,' in which all loyalties, tribal or otherwise, were superseded by the Muslim brotherhood. 'The protection of Allah' stated Muhammad in another provision of the treaty, 'is one (and is equally) extended to the humblest of the believers.' No social distinction was imposed upon the members of the brotherhood; for, although Allah 'created you of male and female, and made you races and tribes,' He recognized no differences among them save on the basis of 'piety' and 'godfearing'"[7]

This point is emphasized here, just as it was in Chapter 1, because it establishes that, in the Muslim worldview, there are at least two fundamental differences between Muslims and non-Muslims that emerged after the creation of human beings by Allah. These differences make it difficult for Muslims to accept and relate to non-Muslims if they have not accepted Islam and they are not part of the Muslim community. Non-believers are destined to misbehave because all human beings misbehave unless or until they become members of the Muslim brotherhood either by birth or by conversion. Thus, in Islamic law the terms "humanity" and "equality" usually pertain only to Muslims who participate in the *umma*. The *umma* provides Muslims with protection and the authority that they need in order to lead orderly lives. It also provides their humanity and their equality among themselves. Acceptance of Allah and Islam, combined with life in the Muslim community protects Muslims from each other — but not necessarily from non-Muslims. Members of the *umma* must always be prepared to defend the *umma* and Islam by defending the borders of their community or by extending their borders until Islam encompasses all societies — the world.

Contrary to many scholars, Khadduri contends that Islam is a "nomocracy" rather than a theocracy. That is, it is a state that is governed by "the rule of law in a community" based on the Qur'an, rather than by Allah directly. He says that this is also true of Christianity and Judaism. In all three religions there is a widely-held belief that their members are governed by laws given to them by their god, but that they are not directly governed by their god.[8] This distinction between a nomocracy and theocracy could be useful when government and military leaders are negotiating with adversaries who contend that they are governed directly by their god rather than by a body of laws. It might be easier to convince adversaries to alter or re-interpret their laws rather than alter their god or their concept of god.

ISLAMIC LAWS OF WAR

Khadduri says that after Muhammad's death and the compiling of the Qur'an into writing an entire body of Islamic law quickly emerged that, among other things, created a new set of concepts, principles and practices regarding how and why the Islamic state could engage in warfare against non-Muslim entities. Debates will rage forever among scholars about how closely these codes and practices comply with passages in the Qur'an. Khadduri finds that there were many ebbs and flows over the centuries in the spirit and content of Islamic law, back and forth between extremes of conservatism and liberalism. Yet there has been a gradual shift away from the very conservative and absolutist interpretations in the decades following Muhammad's death and during the early expansion of Islam across North Africa and east into the Indus. As expansion slowed and then was reversed in Europe and against the Mongols, Islamic law tended to become more liberal, pragmatic, and tolerant of concessions that Muslim military leaders made on the battlefields in order to avoid annihilation.

As Khadduri tells it, most of Muhammad's early successors

269

believed that the new Islamic state was to put into practice throughout the world Allah's laws as given in the Qur'an. They refused to
accept co-existence with non-Muslim entities except as subordinates.
They believed that non-Muslim states would continually be at war
against each other and against the Islamic State, unless Islam subjugated them. While this could occasionally be accomplished for short
periods in peaceful ways, the most certain way to accomplish this was
by transforming Muslim warfare into holy war. Holy war is to be
waged against all entities on the borders of Islam that have not converted to Islam. In Muslim law the world was divided into two categories: the territory of Islam and the territory of war, where holy war
is to be waged ceaselessly.

"The world accordingly was divided in Muslim law into the *dar al-
Islamm* (abode or territory of Islam) and the *dar al-harb* (abode or
territory of war). These terms may be rendered in less poetic words
as the 'world of Islam' and the 'world of War.' The first correspond-
ed to the territory under Muslim rule. Its inhabitants were Muslims,
by birth or conversion, and the communities of the tolerated religions (the *dhimmis*) who preferred to hold fast to their own culture,
at the price of paying the *jizya* (poll tax).... The *dar al-harb* consisted of all the states and communities outside the world of Islam. Its
inhabitants were often called infidels, or, better, unbelievers."[9]

Before considering the doctrine of jihad in some detail, it is worth
noting that Khadduri admits that Islamic law has not been uniform and
invariant. Just like so many systems of law related to other religions and
ideologies, there have been, and are, significant differences between
schools and varieties of Islamic law. After the Muslim expansion into
Europe was stopped at the Battle of Tours in 732, Islamic laws sometimes became more liberal, pragmatic, concessionary, and accommo-
dating to the exigencies of the times. Laws emerged that allowed
Muslim caliphs and imams to end battles and wars without achieving
clear-cut victories. Imams also were allowed to wage "secular wars"
rather than holy war by military forces (military jihad).[10] Khadduri suggests that this shift probably was partially due to the many connotations
that are attached to Arabic words for conflict, struggle, battle, war,
truce, and peace. He also points-out that the Hadith often is more
lenient than the Qur'an about Muslims being forgiven for retreating,
being defeated, accepting unfavorable treaties, and engaging in secular
wars rather than strictly battles of military jihad.[11]

THE DOCTRINE AND PRACTICE OF JIHAD

Khadduri says that the word "jihad" is derived from the Arabic verb *jahada* (abstract noun, *juhd*), which means "exerted," among other meanings.[12] The Qur'an compels believers to exert themselves to spread the belief in Allah over the entire world. In Muslim law, believers can fulfill their obligation to jihad in four ways, only one of which is through armed violence in warfare.

> "The jurists, however, have distinguished four different ways in which the believers may fulfill his jihad obligation: by his heart, his tongue, his hands, and by the sword. The first is concerned with combating the devil, and in the eyes of the Prophet this was the most important type of Jihad. The second and third are mainly fulfilled in supporting the right and correcting the wrong. The fourth is precisely equivalent to the meaning of war, and is concerned with fighting the unbelievers and the enemies of the faith. The believers are under the obligation of sacrificing their 'wealth and their lives.'"[13]

What is especially important here (and is a point that is emphasized throughout this book) is that, while all Muslims are obligated to engage in *some* form of jihad until the entire world has converted to Islam, they can engage in three other types of jihad besides what is called "military jihad." The other forms of jihad are prescribed for all Muslims because they involve prayer, persuasion, and being good examples to others by behaving morally and chastising those who behave immorally. These are obligations every Muslim must fulfill individually. By contrast, in all but one situation military jihad must be approved and declared by the highest authorities in the Muslim state before individual Muslims can participate in it. Even then, only those individual Muslims who are selected by the imam or his delegates are allowed to participate in military jihad, except in the case of one type of dire emergency. If the "Muslim community is subjected to a sudden attack," then all Muslims are obligated to fight as part of military jihad. Otherwise military jihad is a collective obligation of the Muslim community (*umma*), but an individual obligation or right.

> "In the technical language, the five pillars — the basic articles of the faith — are regarded as individual duties (*fard'ayn*), like prayer or fasting.... The jihad, on the other hand — unless the Muslim community is subjected to a sudden attack and therefore

all believers, including women and children, are under the obligation to fight — is regarded by all jurists, with almost no exception, as a collective obligation of the whole Muslim community.... If the duty is fulfilled by a part of the community it ceases to be obligatory on others; the whole community, however, falls into error if the duty is not performed at all."[14]

Military jihad usually exempts women, children, the elderly, and the infirm, except in dire emergencies that constitute an imminent threat of destruction to the entire Muslim community. It is for this reason that government and military leaders should be prepared for the likelihood that all of these kinds of people might try to participate in military jihad if they are convinced by their leaders that Islamic law requires them to do so.

Khadduri stresses that paradise is promised to all believers who perform the five pillars of Islam, but that performing *any* of the four forms of jihad — not necessarily military jihad — is an even more certain way to attain paradise.[15] Military and government leaders would be wise to keep this in mind and to find discreet ways to remind proponents of the Qur'an that military jihad is not necessary in order to attain paradise.

In addition to these constraints about individual participation in military jihad, Khadduri finds that Islamic law prohibits "all forms of war except the jihad that is the war in Allah's path."[16] Military jihad must be waged for "justifiable reasons," according to the laws established for this purpose. It also must be pious. This means that it must be performed with reverence for the commandments of Allah as given in the Qur'an. Khadduri indicates that these concepts in Islamic law are similar to, and possibly even derived from, the concepts of *bellum justum* and *pium* in Roman law.[17] Leaders might be prepared to mention these similarities in concepts and practices at opportune times in diplomatic negotiations with adversaries who espouse the Qur'an and traditional Islamic law.

Not widely known is the fact that Islamic law established that military jihad means *constant struggle* until Islam is universal, but that it does not necessarily mean *constant fighting*.

"Although the jihad was regarded as the permanent basis of Islam's relations with its neighbors, it did not at all mean continuous fighting. Not only could the obligation be performed by nonviolent means, but also relations with the enemy did not necessarily

272

mean an endless or constant violent conflict with him. The jihad, accordingly, may be stated as a doctrine of a permanent state of war, not of continuous fighting."[18]

While there are differences between various schools of Islamic law, such as Shii and Khariji, regarding military jihad, the concept of military jihad has taken many forms besides Muslims defending their mosques and settlements against invaders who are non-Muslims that are engaged in religious persecution. Military jihad often has been invoked in order to justify offensive operations in distant lands, to suppress and punish dissent, secession, and rebellion. The state, however, must be prepared militarily not only to repel a sudden attack on Islam, but also to use its military forces for offensive purposes when the caliph deems it is necessary to do so.

"Islam, it will be recalled, abolished all kinds of warfare except the jihad. Only a war which has an ultimate religious purpose, that is to enforce God's law or to check transgression against it, is a just war.... Throughout the history of Islam, however, fighting between Muslim rulers and contending parties was as continuous as between Islam and its external enemies."[19]

In Islamic law the principle of military jihad also was extended to include various contingencies in the relations between the Islamic state and its adversaries: temporary truces, unfavorable peace treaties, strategic retreats and capitulations, and allegiances with non-Muslim entities that would achieve numerical superiority over a common enemy (despite prohibitions against this in one of the passages of the Qur'an that was presented in Chapter 2).

"If the imam finds it necessary to come to terms with the enemy, he may do so; he may even deem it necessary to seek the support of non-Muslims (including polytheists) in order to avoid risking defeat by the enemy. Under no circumstances, however, should the imam risk a jihad if he considers the enemy too powerful for him to win a victory, namely, if the enemy is at least twice as powerful as the Muslims."[20]

Khadduri goes on to indicate that by the 14th century military jihad was so broadly defined in Islam, and bloody conflict had become so rampant between Muslims and non-Muslim states, that Ibn Khaldun and other Islamic scholars and jurists re-specified the principles of military jihad. Like Hobbes, they contended that war (*harb*) is the normal state of human societies, but that the Islamic state must avoid all wars except holy war (in the form of military jihad) conducted according to strict principles derived from Allah's revelations in the Qur'an.[21] To these writers the only lawful purpose of military jihad must be universalizing the Islamic faith, not acquisition of material goods, fame, revenge, or prestige. Tribal warfare, feuds, and raids were prohibited. Military jihad could be waged legally against four types of people, defined according to how closely their religious beliefs and practices approximate those in the Qur'an: polytheists, apostates, scripturaries ("people of the Book"), and dissenters-rebels. However, this must be done according to what they believed to be a very strict code for military jihad. Among the features alleged to be extrapolated from the Qur'an are the following criteria for military jihadists.

1. "Must be a believer"

2. "Must be a mature and sound-minded person"

3. "Must be a male, women are, in principle, non-jihadists"

4. "Must be an able-bodied person"

5. "Must be independent economically" (slaves have no jihadist obligation unless the entire Muslim community is under attack and is facing impending destruction)

6. "Jihadist must proceed to action with good intentions"

7. "Jihadist must fulfill certain duties while he is on active service. These include obedience and loyalty to the commander of the army in accordance with the Qur'anic rules. The jihadist must never 'entertain the idea of desertion unless the enemy is very powerful — at least twice the number of Muslims — and no retreat is permitted unless he is overpowered by the enemy and threatened with extermination.' The jihadist must be 'honest and straightforward and avoid treacherous acts. For instance, if he gave an oath, he must abide by it; and if he has killed, he must not mutilate.'"[22]

INITIATION OF BATTLE

Only the commander of the Muslim army, usually a caliph, sultan, or imam, depending on the sect, can give the order to start fighting, except in the case of sudden invasions of Muslim territory. If this happens, the commanders of the Muslim forces that are assigned to safeguard the frontiers (*ribat*) may immediately authorize fighting in order to repel the invaders.

"The *ribat* is the safeguarding of the frontiers of the *dar al-Islam* by stationing forces in the harbors and frontier townes for defense purposes. This type of jihad, although based on a Quranic injunction, developed at a time when the Islamic State was on the defensive."[23]

"The commanders of the frontier forces (*ribat*) were under permanent orders to call for fighting when they were attacked; indeed, if the enemy overruns the frontiers, the jihad at once becomes an individual obligation and all the believers have to rise-up in arms without a call to expel the enemy from the land."[24]

In all other cases, before attacking enemy forces or targets the commander of the Muslim army must send emissaries or envoys to enemy commanders and invite them to negotiate, redress grievances, join Islam, pay the poll tax, or make other concessions in order to avoid an attack. Enemy commanders were to be given three days to reach a peaceful settlement or face attack, although situations often were so volatile and hostile that armed conflict erupted beforehand. Once the three days elapsed without the enemy accepting any of the peace initiatives "the jihadists were allowed in principle to kill any one of them, combatants or noncombatants, provided they were not killed treacherously and with mutilation."[25]

MILITARY ORGANIZATION AND STRATEGY

Islamic law is predicated upon and endorses the traditional form of Muslim warfare that had emerged by the time of Muhammad's death and that was so successful in the decades after his death as Islam expanded west and east more than a thousand miles.

The laws have relatively little to say about how Muslim army commanders should conduct their battles in terms of strategy and tactics, but they have quite a bit to say about conditions for ceasing a war and re-establishing peace. They also have many provisions about how individual Muslim combatants should behave in battle regarding desertion, taking enemy prisoners and booty.[26]

After Muhammad's death, Muslim armies often numbered 4,000-12,000 men. Often the enemy forces outnumbered them by at least 3:1, sometimes reportedly 10:1.[27] Muslim military commanders would first attempt to discourage, intimidate, and scare-off their adversaries with a deceptive or brash show of force. If that failed they might send envoys into the enemy camp in order to try to arrange favorable resolutions to the confrontation short of actual battle. If battle seemed unavoidable, they would prepare by dividing their army into five units, often along tribal lines: center, two wings, vanguard, and the rear guard. The wings usually were the decisive elements in battle because, compared to the other units, they had the most cavalry and were the most maneuverable, as well as better armed, better trained, and better motivated. Lances, pikes, bows and arrows, and shields and swords were the main weapons, supplemented by burning objects, stones, and dead or diseased animals that were thrown by hand or catapults. Before the fighting began Muslim leaders would incite their troops with fiery exhortations, recitations of the Qur'an, and chivalrous poetry. Appeals would be made to their piety, courage, and honor. Troops would be reminded of the Qur'an's promises of eternal paradise if they were steadfast and proved themselves in battle, even if they perished as a result. "Verses of the Qur'an and chivalrous poetry were recited even during the fighting."[28]

Upon order of the military commander, actual combat often started with a flurry of insults, taunts, threats hurled back and forth between small groups of adversaries in the vanguards. Personal parries, duels, escalated into clashes between small units of infantry, and then into full scale attacks and counter-attacks by the infantry centers, while one or both wings would try to envelope or attack the enemy from the flanks. Often this led to the syndrome of *karr* and *farr* — attack, retreat, and counter-attack until one side gained clear advantage over the other, or, as was often the case, until one side grew weary, frustrated, or befuddled. While many theories abound as to why Muslim armies were often so successful, especially in the first few decades after Muhammad's death, the factors that are cited very often are that the Muslim forces usually had more unified command (less fragmentation of authority along tribal lines than did their adversaries), higher morale due to their common religion, and proportionately more and better trained cavalry than did their adversaries. Combined, these factors gave the Muslims forces more staying power and more maneuverability than their adversaries.[29]

SIEGE WARFARE AND COLLATERAL DAMAGE

Much of the expansion of the Muslim Empire in the 500 years after Muhammad's death occurred not as a result of classic land battles on open terrain between a Muslim army and an army of non-Muslims, such as the battle of Badr. The expansion was due to the more or less voluntary acceptance of protection from a Muslim state by non-Muslim tribes, settlements, cities, and principalities. Typically, Muslim envoys were escorted by a military detachment into an adversary's camp or city. Bribes, truces, treaties, or alliances against other common enemies would be offered. If these failed to resolve the differences, military jihad often took the form of siege warfare, a type of warfare that made many Muslim armies famous in Islamic history and decidedly infamous in European history. The success of many of these sieges led to a proliferation of Islamic laws regarding appropriation and destruction of the adversary's settlements, lands, resources, and populations.

In reviewing these laws, Khadduri reports that they are not uniform nor are they very restrictive. Muslim military commanders were allowed to do whatever was necessary to defeat the enemy forces and to satisfy the caliphs or imams who authorized the campaign so long as their purpose was to universalize the Islamic faith in Allah's way. According to Khadduri (but not according to some of the other interpreters such as Ali and Haleem whose work is reviewed later in this chapter) some Islamic laws allowed Muslim commanders to destroy the enemy's crops, fields, trees, roads, bridges, walls, infrastructure, dwellings, and storehouses. "They are also permitted to cut water canals and destroy water supplies to prevent the *harbis* (enemy) from using them. Poison, blood, or any material that may spoil the drinking water may be thrown into the water supplies or canals in order to force the enemy to capitulate."[30] If necessary to achieve victory, Muslim combatants also were allowed to kill not only members of the enemy's civilian population but any other residents in enemy communities that get in the way, including other Muslims who reside in the enemy settlements as captives, although this should be avoided insofar as possible. Khadduri found that Islamic law generally prohibits "treacherous killing and mutilation" of adversaries, but it is less severe in punishing infractions by Muslims if this is done in retaliation for equally treacherous killing and mutilation. The precedent for this was Muhammad's own dispensation to some of his troops who killed Muslim residents when they captured the settlement of Makka.[31] In addition to this, foreign spies have not always been protected in Islamic law, particularly in cases where an imam has decided that a foreign spy should be tortured, crucified, or killed in order to discourage others from spying. Scriptuary spies (Jews and

277

Christians) generally are given exile, prison, and "tortuous punishment" until they repent.[32]

SPOILS OF WAR

As Khadduri presents it, much of Islamic law about spoils of war and treatment of prisoners is consistent with the Qur'an, but it is more specific and elaborate than the Qur'an, as we might expect. One of the clearest and most concise statements of definitions and principles is this:

> "The term spoil (*ghanima*) is applied specifically to property acquired by force from non-Muslims. It includes, however, not only property (moveable and immovable) but also persons, whether in the capacity of *asra* (POWs) or *sabi* (women and children). The element of force and the imam's permission are essential prerequisites since property taken without force would be regarded as *fay*."[33]

Generally, in keeping with the Qur'an passages presented in Chapter 2, Khadduri says that Islamic law reinforces the Qur'an prescription that one-fifth of the spoils should become the property of the Muslim state and that "four-fifths was usually divided among the mature male jihadists who were in the field."[34] Prisoners of war often were considered part of the spoils and were treated very cruelly in many Arab Eastern societies of Muhammad's time. Muhammad is reported to have had considerable success restricting if not eliminating mistreatment of prisoners, starting with the Battle of Badr, except for those prisoners who had insulted Islam or offended their captors.[35] Furthermore, Islamic laws after Muhammad's death often changed according to political circumstances to accommodate caliphs or imams who had acquired overwhelming power. Jurists often allowed them to choose among four alternatives:[36]

1. He may order the immediate execution of some or all of the captives.

2. He may release captives in exchange for ransom as provided in the Qur'an, or set them free without compensation.

3. He may exchange them for Muslim POWs.

4. He may condemn them to be slaves.

Regarding Muslim combatants who become prisoners of the enemy, Islamic law offers several instructions (at least one of which is rather liberal) and few sanctions against those who violate these instructions. It was also ruled that Muslim prisoners must observe faithfully their parole and must not escape from the enemy if they had pledged not to escape.

"Muslim prisoners, captured by the enemy, were under no obligation to submit or obey the orders of the enemy. They should try to escape or destroy enemy property. Must not give valuable information to the enemy, must refuse to take part in war against Islam, and to refuse to abandon the faith unless forced to do so."[37]

Overall, Islamic law allows a wide range of behaviors by victorious Muslim combatants towards the land, property, army and civilian population of the vanquished enemy forces, short of self-serving violence. Islamic law does not make as explicit as does the Qur'an (as shown in several passages in Chapter 2) that Muslims should self-indulge and enjoy fully the spoils that they won honorably in battle. However, neither Islamic law nor the Qur'an prohibit self-gratification in this situation — one of the few times that self-gratification seems to be allowed in Muslim warfare.

MARITIME WARFARE

Khadduri finds that Islamic law has relatively little to say about maritime warfare. He suggests that this is because Arab culture before, during, and for centuries after Muhammad was almost exclusively a xeric culture that generally ignored, disregarded, or avoided expeditions across large bodies of water, especially salt water (although he never goes so far as to mention hydrophobia).[38] Therefore it is not surprising that it was not until the 10th Century that Muslim states became a formidable naval force in the Mediterranean. By-and-large Islamic law allows at least as much latitude to Muslim naval officers in naval warfare as to their counterparts in land warfare regarding taking spoils, initiating and ceasing battles, and fighting steadfastly against numerically superior enemy forces. In some ways it allows Muslim naval forces more discretion to use extreme violence in order to force enemy naval forces to submit to the will of Allah. About this, Khadduri says "so were the sea jihadists permitted to attack and destroy enemy vessels by fire or by sinking until their crews were brought to their knees and capitulated.[39] Islamic maritime laws allowed Muslims to use catapults of Greek fire (phosphorous), poisons, and dead animals to "create panic and help a direct assault on their vessels."

279

"Thus the Muslims often hurled on enemy vessels not only stones and fire bundles, but also snakes and scorpions and harmful powders in order to injure as well as to scare the enemy and create confusion and panic among all on board their vessels."[40]

Muslim seamen in battle were allowed to drown prisoners, if necessary. They were also allowed to use booty captured in naval battles as they wanted. This could include throwing into the sea the weapons, supplies, enemy prisoners, and women and children who were passengers on enemy vessels. If enemy forces used captive Muslims on deck to shield their ships from attack, Muslims could attack and kill all of them regardless of religion. If Muslim boats were shipwrecked and about to be captured, Muslims were allowed to remain on board, to sink the boats, or to throw themselves into the sea and drown.[41] This raises questions about the allegation that Islam prohibits all suicide in all forms and circumstances. Of course, in cases like these the Muslims who commit suicide are doing so in order to escape capture and they are not killing their adversaries in the process, in contrast to "suicide bombers" of contemporary times. Yet, given latitude like this in Muslim maritime laws and in Muslim naval history, is it so difficult to understand how some contemporary violence-oriented Muslim opportunists could plan and execute attacks on U.S. naval vessels such as the attack on the *U.S.S. Cole* in Yemen in 2002?

TERMINATION OF FIGHTING

As presented by Khadduri, Islamic law regarding termination of fighting is not very extensive or elaborate. It allows Muslim military commanders much more latitude than what is allowed in the Qur'an. Relevant Qur'anic passages that were presented in Chapter 2 basically establish that Muslim armies must not retreat and that they must fight steadfastly until the battle and war is won, the enemy forces and their supporters have been routed, all religion is for Allah, and none of the enemy continues to do wrong or to "commit abomination." Khadduri says that since Muhammad's experience at the Battle of Uhud, where many of his soldiers retreated or deserted without him, Muslim law has allowed leaders to retreat or make compromises in order to save their troops so that they can live to fight more successfully on another day. At the same time, however, it should be considered that there is no record of Muhammad having punished his troops who retreated without him at Uhud or any other battle. Khadduri repeatedly mentions that Islamic law encourages and allows Muslim imams "to have continuous patience" regarding the time it might take and the reversals and disappointments that might accumulate until they finally achieve victory.[42] Islamic law portrays defeat as "an anomaly which could be tolerated only under *force majeur*, thus the imam is advised either to abstain from going to war if his forces are insufficient to attain victory or, if he should suffer defeat, to withdraw and save the lives of surviving believers."[43] Islamic laws also discouraged imams from engaging enemy forces more than twice their size, thus preferring one part of a Qur'anic passage (Qur'an 8:66-67, see Chapter 2) which allows a 2:1 ratio over another part of the same Qur'anic passage that assures Muslims warriors who are steadfast in battle that they can defeat adversaries that outnumber them by 10:1.

Despite these assurances, many jurists after 1200 A.D. were tolerant of imams who broke from battle and withdrew their forces not just when they were outnumbered but also when their forces were too thirsty, hungry, or tired to continue the battle, so long as the intent was to conserve the army so as to be able to resume the fight another day. Khadduri mentions that a possible basis for this tolerance is not a Qur'anic passage but rather a passage in the Hadith which admits that, when Muhammad was informed that some of his soldiers had been defeated in battle, he replied that "they were not deserters, but '*akkarun*,' i.e. that they will resume later this fight to victory."[44]

Islamic law became more tolerant of stalemates, unfavorable treaties, retreats and defeats by Muslim forces as secular wars became more commonplace among imams, particularly after 1350 A.D., and the Christian Crusades had run their course. Islamic law regarded the outcomes of secular wars to be a consequence of the imam's war strategy, battlefield tactics, and morale of the army, rather than whether the war had been fought for a just cause or whether it was fought "in the way of Allah."

"When a Muslim ruler fought a secular war — in which the religious purpose was not apparent — no sin was necessarily to be incurred if he suffered defeat by another ruler, be he a believer or an unbeliever."[45]

Insights such as this from Khadduri can be useful to contemporary government and military leaders. They can refer to these distinctions, establish the case that adversaries are engaging in secular wars, rather than military jihad, and mention that, as such, <u>compromises, treaties,</u>

capitulations, or withdrawals of Muslim forces are *not* prohibited in the tradition of Islamic law and military history.

ISLAMIC LAW OF PEACE

Khadduri demonstrates that the concept of peace in Islamic law has been variable and that it is not extensively developed. Only one short chapter in his book of twenty-two chapters addresses the topic of peace. He finds that in Islamic legal theory "the ultimate objective of Islam was not war per se but the ultimate establishment of peace."[46] As such, military jihad is an instrument that can lead to peace once Islam is universalized as a political-religious system. He speculates that this is another reason why jihad is not the sixth pillar of Islam. In contrast to the five pillars, which each Muslim must practice each day, forever, jihad will no longer be necessary once Islam is universal. In effect, there will no longer be a need to defend borders against non-believers and infidels because there will no longer be borders, non-believers, or infidels.

Khadduri says that an important variation to the Islamic dichotomization of the world into *dar al-Islam* (world of Islam) and *dar al-harb* (world of war) occurred under the Shafi'is. They devised a third category, *dar al-Sulh* (world of peace) or *dar al-ahd* (world of covenant) that gives "qualified recognition to a non-Muslim state if it entered into treaty relations with Islam either before hostilities began or after offering stiff resistance, on condition that the non-Muslim state should either pay an annual tribute, a poll tax *(jizya)* or ceded a portion of its territory."[47] Thus in some Islamic law, a formal condition of peace is a temporary way station between Muslim states and non-Muslim states, without military battle or conflict, while the Muslim states arrange to extend *dar al-Islam* throughout the world. Following in the tradition of Muhammad who, as a military commander, dictated and signed many treaties during his life, Islamic law allows frequent use of treaties that will serve the ultimate goal of Islam.

TREATIES

Muhammad made a number of treaties in accordance with his changing political objectives and his perception of external threats to Islam. These treaties became models for his successors. His most famous one was the treaty of Hudaybiya (which was discussed at some length in Chapter 3).

"In the name of Allah, the Compassionate, the Merciful: This is a document from Muhammad, the Apostle of Allah to the believers and Muslims of Quraysh and Yathrib, and to all who followed them and fought (*jahada*) with them. They constitute one *umma* (nation) in distinction from the rest of the people: The émigrés of Quraysh unite together and pay ransom graciously for acquiring their relative-prisoners...."[48]

In Islamic law, treaties were meant to be temporary expedients, for no more than ten years (the term of the treaty at Hudaybiya) that will enable Muslim states the time to recover from a setback or avoid disadvantageous warfare until they become more formidable *vis a vis* their adversaries.

"Thus on the basis of the Qur'an and Hadith, the jurists are agreed that a peace treaty with the enemy, if it serves Muslim interests, is a valid instrument, the provisions of which must be binding upon all Muslims.... Although the normal relationship between Islam and non-Muslim communities is a state of hostility, it is not considered inconsistent with Islam's ultimate objective if a peace treaty is concluded with the enemy, whether for purposes of expediency or because Islam suffered a setback."[49]

Treaties are to be honored by Muslim leaders unless they become untenable or the enemy becomes deceitful. Muhammad and his successors often delegated treaty-making authority to their military field commanders, but reserved the right to repudiate treaties or arrangements that they felt were dishonorable to Islam. Muslim treaties usually were "brief and general" and included exchanges of hostages between the adversaries to help assure that the treaties were not broken.

MUSLIM DIPLOMACY

Like treaties, Muslim diplomacy with non-Muslim entities usually has been used to delay armed conflict long enough to enable Muslim states to achieve the goal of Islamic expansion, to universalize the religion, and to do so without armed conflict. In Muhammad's time and in the rapid expansion of Islam in the decades immediately after that, "diplomacy was resorted to as an auxiliary to or as a substitute for war: it served either as a herald to deliver the message of Islam before fighting began or as a means to exchange prisoners after the termination of fighting."[50] Muslim diplomacy became somewhat more moderate and flexible in later centuries although its overall purpose has remained that of avoiding extreme risks until conditions are more propitious for expanding the Muslim state. Other purposes of diplomacy, such as to facilitate intercourse among nations, have never been given much weight in Islamic law.[51] Formally, Islamic law does not recognize the status of neutrality in other nations although Ethiopia and Nubia in effect became historical exceptions in that they were never absorbed fully into Muslim states.

KHADDURI'S VIEW OF THE FUTURE

Khadduri wrote that Muslim states would need to modernize Islamic law and make it more compatible with Western law as they moved towards fuller participation in international affairs, modernized their economies, and contemplated whether to join international organizations including the United Nations. He was impressed by the fact that Islamic law regarding war and peace became less influential under the Ottomans and that Attaturk repealed Islam as the state religion in Turkey. Khadduri did not predict the re-emergence of Islamic fundamentalism and he believed that the appearance of Whahhabism in Saudi Arabia in the 1920s was an isolated case that would eventually subside.

In sum, Khadduri shows that Islamic law has supported many of the Qur'an's passages on peace, conflict, and war that were presented in Chapters 2. However, it also has tolerated and legitimized a wider range of behaviors by Muslim leaders than in the Qur'an, based on exigencies and contingencies that arise occasionally, so long as the ultimate goal of Muslim leaders is to universalize Islam.

JOHN ESPOSITO: A POPULAR AND SYMPATHETIC INTERPRETER OF ISLAM'S ORIGINS, HISTORY, AND CURRENT STATUS

"Muslims look to Muhammad's example for guidance in all aspects of life and how to treat friends as well as enemies, what to eat and drink, how to make love and war."[52]

There is high regard among scholars in the Middle East and in the U.S. for *Islam: The Straight Path*, and its author, John Esposito, Professor of Religion, Islamic Studies and International Affairs, and Director of the Center for Muslim-Christian Understanding at Georgetown University. This is one reason why I have already quoted

from his work throughout this book. Nonetheless, at times his interpretations of Muhammad's life, of the Qur'an, and of Muslim military
and political history vary significantly from the interpretations of
some of the other scholars that I have relied upon throughout this
book, Pickthall and Rodinson in particular. I will focus upon some of
these differences in covering some of Esposito's interpretations.

Esposito presents a sympathetic, moderate, and integrated view
on the antecedents, history, and current status of Islam, primarily as a
world religion, but also as a political force in modern world affairs that
include peace and war. He contends that modern Muslims continue to
admire Muhammad. Many of them are familiar with some of the facts
of his life, including his most famous battles and negotiations. Many
Muslims try to apply to their own lives the guidance that the Qur'an
provides about Muhammad's experiences, insofar as possible.

Esposito persuasively argues that Muhammad and his followers
behaved in ways that were similar to many other tribal people in the
Middle East. "Muhammad's use of warfare in general was alien neither to Arab custom nor to that of the Hebrew prophets. Both believed
that God had sanctioned battle with the enemies of the Lord."[53] Islam
was not an isolated, unique new monotheistic religion. It had its roots
in Semitic and Persian belief systems. It was influenced by cultural
contacts that had occurred during previous centuries via commercial
and military expeditions from the Roman, Greek, Egyptian, Persian,
and Abyssinian empires as well as by the influx of Christians, Jews,
and African tribal people into Arab societies. While he was growing-
up Muhammad was exposed to sects, to feuds, and to raids, both in
Mecca and in his distant travels on trade caravans.

Esposito takes it as a matter of course that "Muhammad initiated
a series of raids against Meccan caravans" as his influence grew in
Medina, following his forced emigration from Mecca.[54] He also agrees
that the Battle of Badr was "the first and most decisive victory for the
forces of monotheism over those of polytheism" and that this was the
most stunning military victory Muhammad accomplished in his lifetime in that his other victories were primarily political. Esposito contends that while Muhammad was a "shrewd military strategist," the
primary reason for his success was that he was a "reformer" who was
"righteous, trustworthy, pious, compassionate, and honest" and that
he used military force as a last resort, preferring instead to befuddle,
surprise, and outsmart his adversaries rather than have to out-
maneuver them militarily. As a reformer, Muhammad first convinced

his small band of followers in Mecca that they were faced with unreasonable persecution simply because of the religious beliefs that had been revealed to them by Allah. "They had two choices: emigration (*hijra*) or armed resistance (jihad)."[55] If emigration fails to free Muslims from persecution, then they are compelled by Allah to engage in armed resistance even if they must sacrifice their lives in doing so. As proof of this Esposito quotes the Qur'an, 4:74, "So let them fight in the way of God who sell the present life for the world to come, and whosoever fights in the way of God and is slain, or conquers, We shall bring him a mighty wage."[56]

Esposito says that Muhammad convinced his followers that those who wage war are holy warriors. They fight for the highest possible purpose, obedience to Allah, and, as such, cannot lose. This is because they gain eternal life as martyrs if they are slain and, if they are not slain, they will experience glorious victory, a fair share of the spoils of war, and esteem within the Muslim community. In Esposito's words: "These holy warriors (*mujahidin*) will be rewarded in this life with victory and the spoils of war. Those who fall in battle will be rewarded with eternal life as martyrs (*shahid*, or witness) for the faith."[57]

Esposito agrees with Pickthall and Rodinson that Muhammad barely survived the Battle of Uhud, was very lucky to have survived at the Battle of the Trench (when the Meccans became frustrated and quit the battlefield without a decisive battle), and used long drawn-out negotiations to achieve favorable results with the Truce at Hudaybiya. However, Esposito contends that Muhammad accused the Quraysh of breaking the treaty of Hudaybiya within two years — not that Muhammad himself actually broke the treaty. He then led his army of 10,000 against the Meccans, who had little choice but to surrender Mecca to him. Esposito does not mention that some bloodshed, plundering, and enslavement occurred during the occupation of Mecca. Rather, he says that "Muhammad eschewed vengeance and plunder, granted amnesty," and that the Meccans converted to Islam, accepted Muhammad's leadership and were incorporated into the *umma*.[58] While Esposito admits that Muhammad occasionally used military force to defeat the few Bedouin tribes that resisted his rule, and that not all of them converted to Islam, he emphasizes that Islam spread more through the influence of Muslim missionaries, merchants and mystics than through military force. Yet, when negotiation and other means failed, Muhammad continued to resort to military means to achieve what he could not achieve in other ways. For example, Esposito acknowledges that Muhammad occasionally ordered the

286

destruction of certain tribes and settlements. "After the Battle of the Ditch in 627, the Jews of the Banu Qurayza were denounced as traitors who had consorted with the Meccans. As was common in Arab (and, indeed Semitic) practice, the men were massacred, the women and children were spared but enslaved."[59] Esposito contends that there were mitigating circumstances and the Muhammad's actions were "political" rather than "racial or theological."

"However, it is important to note that the motivation for such actions was political rather than racial or theological. Although the Banu Qurayza had remained neutral, they had also negotiated with the Quraysh. Moreover, the exiled Jewish clans had actively supported the Meccans. Muhammad moved decisively to crush the Jews who remained in Medina, viewing them as a continued political threat to the consolidation of Muslim dominance and rule in Arabia."[60]

Following Muhammad's death his successors launched "the Wars of Conquest (*fath*)" far beyond the Arabian Peninsula. These conquests bore stunning results within a decade. Yet Esposito claims that this expansion occurred more through acquisition of surpluses and settlements and the superimposition of Islamic institutions on its acquisitions than through dramatic battles and the destruction of opposing forces.

"Within a decade, Arab forces overran the Byzantine and Persian armies, exhausted by years of warfare, and conquered Iraq, Syria, Palestine, Persian, and Egypt. The momentum of these early victories was extended to a series of brilliant battles under great generals like Khalid ibn al-Walid and Amr ibn al-As, which extended the boundaries of the Muslim empire to Morocco and Spain in the west and across Central Asia to India in the east. Driven by the economic rewards from conquest of richer, more developed areas, united and inspired by their new faith, Muslim armies proved to be formidable conquerors and effective rulers, builders rather than destroyers. They replaced the indigenous rulers and armies of the conquered countries, but preserved much of their government, bureaucracy and culture."[61]

Esposito insists that most of these conquests were rather benign, even progressive, and that they were often welcomed by the civilian populations, if not the rulers of the enemy citadels. "The conquests destroyed little, what they did suppress were imperial rivalries and sectarian bloodletting among the newly subjected population."[62] He says that this was the case because the purpose of early conquests was to spread Muslim rule — not to spread the faith through forced conversion to Islam. Many of the early Muslim conquerors regarded Islam as an Arab religion that was unsuitable for their newly acquired subjects. They did not want to increase the size of the Muslim community because doing so would reduce their share of the spoils of conquest by dividing the spoils among more believers, including the recent converts. Muslim conquerors preferred that their new subjects accept Muslim rule as protected people and pay the required taxes each year rather than convert to Islam with full rights and duties. In later centuries, as the Muslim empires amassed wealth, power, and prestige, they spread into the Indian subcontinent and Southeast Asia through the efforts of Muslim traders and Sufi missionaries "who won converts by their example and their preaching" rather than by the swords, arrows, guns and maneuvers of Muslim armies and navies.[63]

As presented already in Chapter 4 of this book, Esposito agrees that Islamic expansion took many different forms and suffered many setbacks as well as victories after Muhammad's death. Its expansion through 1258 can be understood in terms of the three periods of The Caliphate: the "Rightly Guided Caliphs" (632-661), the Umayyad empire (661-750), and the Abbasid empire (750-1258) during which time Islam's capital shifted from Medina to Kufa, Damascus, and Baghdad. He indicates that for most Muslims alive today, Muslim military history after the death of Muhammad and his immediate successors is much less important than the military events that happened during those earliest times in Islamic history. Probably this is because there were so many military battles after 650 A.D. between Muslim armies, such as the famous Battle of Siffin (657 A.D.), and between Muslim and non-Muslim forces. Another reason for Muslims dwelling on the classical period is that so many rather embarrassing impasses, reversals, and defeats occurred after the first decades of success, especially after the defeat at Tours, France in 732. Yet another reason for the overriding importance of the early years of Muslim warfare to contemporary Muslims is that those early victories can be apparent to them every day as they read references to Muhammad's battles in the Qur'an. Esposito's position is worth repeating from earlier chapters in this book.

"Muslims regard the period of Muhammad and the first generation of companions or elders as normative for a variety of reasons. First, God sent down His final and complete revelation in the Qur'an and

288

the last of His prophets, Muhammad. Second, the Islamic community-state was created, bonded by a common religious identity and
purpose. Third, the sources of Islamic law, the Quran and the
example of the Prophet, originated at this time. Fourth, this period
of the early companions serves as the reference point for all-Islamic
revival and reform, both traditionalist and modernist. Fifth, the success and power that resulted from the near-miraculous victories
and geographic expansion of Islam constitute, in the eyes of believers, historical validation of the message of Islam."[64]

Esposito generally has a favorable view of most of Muslim military events from the Caliphate period and up to the current time.
Although he admits that Muslim armies overran the Eastern Roman
Empire, Spain, and the Mediterranean from Sicily to Anatolia, he contends that this was because Islam as a world religion was continually
threatened by Christianity, which portrayed Muhammad as an "infidel
driven by a lust for power and women."[65] The Crusades were motivated more by the commercial, political, and military ambitions of
Christian rulers, knights, and merchants than by Muslim persecution
of Christian pilgrims on their way to Jerusalem. The Crusaders were
much more destructive and bloodthirsty than were the Muslim
defenders, in Esposito's view.

"In 1099, the Crusaders stormed Jerusalem and established
Christian sovereignty over the Holy Land. They left no Muslim
survivors; women and children were massacred. The Noble
Sanctuary, the Haram al-Sharif, was desecrated as the Dome of
the Rock was converted into a church and the al-Aqsa mosque,
renamed the Temple of Solomon, became a residence for the king.
Latin principalities were established in Antioch, Edessa, Tripoli,
and Tyre. The Latin Kingdom of Jerusalem lasted less than a century. In 1187, Salah al-Din (Saladin), having reestablished Abbasid
rule over Fatimid Egypt, led his army in a fierce battle and recaptured Jerusalem."[66]

According to Esposito, Muslim military forces were repeatedly
less destructive and genocidal than were Christian military forces as
the famed cities of the Middle East changed hands, flags, allegiances,
and religions so often as to boggle the memories of even the most
steadfast historians.

289

"The Muslim army was as magnanimous in victory as it had been tenacious in battle. Civilians were spared, churches and shrines were generally left untouched. The striking differences in military conduct were epitomized by the two dominant figures of the Crusades: Saladin and Richard the Lion-Hearted. The chivalrous Saladin was faithful to his word and compassionate toward non-combatants. Richard accepted the surrender of Acre and then proceeded to massacre all its inhabitants, including women and children, despite promises to the contrary."[67]

Regarding the more current status of Muslim societies and their relationship to Western societies, Esposito portrays Muslim-initiated conflict, violence, and war as being relatively infrequent, misguided, and unfortunate consequences of misunderstandings between nations or as the work of a small number of extremist elements in non-Muslim as well as Muslim societies. He admits that some extreme factions in some Muslim societies have committed assassinations and suicide bombings from time to time, and that some of these have been inspired by violent Islamic sects from the early periods, such as the Kharijites. "Despite the fact that jihad is not supposed to include aggressive warfare, this has occurred, as exemplified by early extremists like the Kharijites and contemporary groups like Egypt's Jihad Organization (which assassinated Anwar Sadat) as well as Jihad organizations in Lebanon, the Gulf States and Indonesia."[68] Esposito mentions terrorism rarely and he tends to dismiss it as being the work of a very small number of people (that he does not identify as being Muslims). He agrees that an "Islamic Revolution" is underway, but he sees it as being essentially a constructive, non-violent social movement that is bringing about much needed changes in the Middle East and beyond.

"There is indeed an Islamic revolution occurring in many parts of the Muslim world. However, the most significant and pervasive revolution is not that of bombs and hostages, but of clinics and schools. It is dominated by social activists (teachers, doctors, lawyers, dentists) and preachers rather than warriors. The battle is often one of the pen, tongue, and heart rather than the sword. Radicalism and terrorism, though capturing the headlines, are a very small though at times deadly part of a phenomenon characterized more by a broad-based religiosocial revolution in Muslim societies."[69]

Esposito provides only a short, three-page interpretation of "Radical Activists." He sees them as a small minority that advocate violence almost for the sake of violence while "the moderate majority seek reform through the gradual transformation of Muslim society."

"...radicals believe that Islam is in danger, locked in a defensive war against repressive anti-Islamic or un-Islamic rulers and states. They regard themselves as the true defenders of Islam, in whose name they have assassinated opponents like Egypt's Anwar Sadat, kidnapped and murdered, and attacked government installations and foreign embassies."[70]

He does not link radical activists to neo-traditionalists, neo-fundamentalists, or to any other faction that gives great weight to the Qur'an. He portrays Islamic neo-fundamentalists as being concerned mainly with re-instituting strict controls over amoral personal behaviors such as drinking alcohol, dressing immodestly, and engaging in public displays of affection and sexuality.

In sum, John Esposito provides interpretations of the Qur'an and of Islam that are very descriptive and acceptant. He emphasizes how constructive they both have been in giving daily direction and meaning to millions of Muslims throughout the world. For Esposito the gains far outweigh the costs, both to Muslims and to the rest of the world. This is reflected in his conclusion. He ends his book by quoting from the Qur'an and by portraying the history and the contemporary status of Islam in a most favorable light.

"As the history of Islam has shown, belief in one God, one revelation, and one final Prophet has been the basis for a strong, vibrant monotheistic faith. However, monotheistic has not meant monolithic. The unity of Islam from its early formation to contemporary developments, has encompassed a diversity of interpretations and expressions of faith. So too today, one-fifth of the world's population testifies to the dynamism of Islam and the continued commitment of Muslims to follow 'the straight path, the way of God, to whom belongs all that is in the heavens and all that is on earth.' (42:52-53)."[71]

ALI'S INTERPRETATIONS: A FORGIVING PACIFIST

Maulawi Sher Ali's 1955 translation and commentary on the Qur'an, *The Holy Qur'an*, provides both the Arabic text and his English translation of it, side-by-side. His interpretation is compassionate, forgiving, and pacifistic. His English translation is almost identical to Pickthall's translation regarding the nouns and verbs in the Qur'an's instructive passages about making war and sustaining peace (as shown in Chapter 2 where I compare Pickthall's and Ali's translations). Ali was a respected scholar in the Ahmadiyya Movement of Islam in Pakistan. Some scholars consider this movement to be a heretical branch of Islam because some of its members believe that some Indian prophets are the rightful heirs to Muhammad. I did not find any distortions in Ali's interpretations that verify this criticism. However I did find that some of his interpretations of specific passages of the Qur'an are somewhat discursive and puzzling, given the content of the passages.

Ali contends that the Qur'an espouses democratic government, minimal social stratification by wealth or lineage, especially inherited wealth, and peaceful cooperation among all people, both Muslim and non-Muslim. He says that the Qur'an "dissuades people from entering into conflicts and going to war with each other and prohibits aggression." He emphasizes that the Qur'an places many restrictions on the conduct of war and on the treatment of prisoners, and that it requires strict obedience to many rules of personal behavior.

"The Qur'an enjoins constant alertness upon a believer. It exhorts Muslims to be diligent and condemns cowardice, bullying and fanaticism. It encourages the exercise of reason and reflection. It prohibits suicide and all acts or conduct that may result in self-destruction. It enjoins upon Governments the obligation of safeguarding their frontiers. It prohibits aggression but enjoins unyielding resistance to it. In a war it prohibits surprise night attacks. It insists upon the rigid observance of treaties and enjoins that no opportunity of making peace should be missed."[72]

Ali claims that the Qur'an is especially specific and extensive in its instructions regarding prisoners and slavery.[73] He says that the Qur'an prohibits "enslavement of one's countrymen or foreigners." Prisoners can be captured only temporarily. "Every prisoner is entitled to his freedom on payment of ransom (47:5)." He also says that all prisoners must be released as soon as they pay a fair ransom and that prisoners who cannot pay a ransom must be allowed to "earn his freedom by means of labour." If unable to do this, then "the Qur'an exhorts Muslims to help him and to find a means for procuring his liberty (24: 34)." Prisoners who prefer to remain to live in Muslim communities must be given the same kind of food, clothing and other material goods as his "master." Ali also insists that the Qur'an "stresses the equality of all mankind" and that all "mankind is one community," regardless of differences in countries, tribes, nations. These exist only "for the purpose of identification." He also says that the Qur'an dismisses all distinctions based on race and economic status, but he does not mention religious status as grounds for equality or for inequality.

I have found that while Ali certainly is compassionate and sincere in his interpretations of the Qur'an, some of his interpretations deny, if not contradict, his own translations of the Qur'an. For example, his translation of sura 8 ("The Spoils") verses 13-16 (that were also presented in Chapter 2 of this book) mention terror, violence, fire, and possibly mutilation. They certainly do not suggest restraint, proportionality, or transgression avoidance. They specify behaviors that would hardly seem to be "in the way of Allah." Here is Ali's translation of Sura 8:13-16:

"When thy Lord revealed to the angels, saying, 'I am with you; so give firmness to those who believe. I will cast terror into the hearts of those who disbelieve. Smite, then, the upper parts of their necks, and smite off all fingertips.'

That is because they have opposed Allah and His Messenger. And who opposes Allah and His Messenger, then Allah is surely severe in retribution.

That is your punishment, taste it then; and know that for disbelievers there is the punishment of the Fire.

O ye who believe! when you meet those who disbelieve, advancing in force, turn not your backs to them."[74]

Readers might recall from Chapter 2 that passages like this are neither frequent nor rare in the Qur'an. Yet Ali generally writes that the Qur'an prohibits believers from using undue force and violence against their enemies. He also portrays the Qur'an as discouraging conflict and emphasizing education and intellectual development.

"The Qur'an stresses the need of education and intellectual development. It prescribes reflection and contemplation as religious
obligations. It dissuades people from entering into conflicts and
going to war with each other and prohibits aggression. It lays
down detailed rules for the regulation of relations between the
followers of different religions. It prohibits Muslims from saying
anything derogatory to the Founders of other religions."[75]

Ali also states that the Qur'an insists that all human beings are
equal — not just Muslims among themselves.

"The Qur'an stresses the equality of all mankind. It is the first
Scripture that teaches that mankind is one community. It recog-
nizes the division into countries, nations and tribes but explains
that this is only for the purpose of identification and that with
regard to rights all mankind are equal. It deprecates all distinctions based on racial, economic or other fancied superiority."[76]

Yet, Ali's translations of relevant verses from the Qur'an (which
are highly consistent with Pickthall's, as shown in Chapter 2) indicate
that equality, peace, and brotherhood surely are benefits that are
bestowed upon "believers" (i.e. Muslims). Whether they are bestowed
upon non-believers is much less explicit, given Ali's translations of
passages from the Qur'an such as sura 49, verses 10 and 11.

"And if two parties of believers fight against each other, make
peace between them; then if after that one of them transgresses
against the other, fight the party that transgresses until it returns
to the command of Allah. Then if it returns, make peace between
them with equity, and act justly. Verily, Allah loves the just.

Surely all believers are brothers. So make peace between brothers, and fear Allah that mercy may be shown to you."[77]

In sum, Maulawi Sher Ali's interpretations of the Qur'an
undoubtedly are sincere and well intended. They also might be unduly idealistic. And yet, familiarity with interpretations like those of Ali
can help government and military leaders appreciate the fact that the
Qur'an is *not* a sourcebook of violence, terror, war, and genocide to all
Muslims. Quite the contrary. Ali's interpretations can help us to
understand how pacifistic the Qur'an can be when it is taken in its
totality by its most reverent and forgiving proponents.

HALEEM'S INTERPRETATIONS:
CONTEXTUALIZING THE WAY TO FORGIVENESS

Muhammad Abdel Haleem provides a very current, forgiving, and defensive interpretation of the Qur'an in his 1999 book, *Understanding the Qur'an: Themes and Style*. Haleem is considered by some other scholars to be a reliable and informed student of the Qur'an. He is a professor of Islamic studies at a university in London and he is editor of a journal of Qur'anic studies. At times he seems to present the Qur'an as something of a guidebook to tranquil international relations as well as to individual spiritual fulfillment. He has a tendency to explain away, based on rhetorical and historical context, almost any verse in the Qur'an that might sound bellicose. Haleem agrees with many scholars that the Qur'an and the Hadith (which he does not capitalize) are the only two fundamental and binding sources of Islamic law regarding war and peace. They are complete and sufficient for guiding Muslims in all situations.

THE CONDITIONS ALLOWING MUSLIMS TO WAGE WAR

According to Haleem the Qur'an (49:13) established peace as the proper relationship among both individuals and nations.[78] He cites sura 2:216 as indicating that all war is hateful in Islam and that it can only be waged under very limited conditions and for one purpose. Waging war in order to convert people to Islam is not allowed. To Haleem the Qur'an (2:251) allows Muslims to engage in war "only to stop evil from triumphing in a way that would corrupt the earth." Among the conditions that allow war are self defense, to pre-empt an imminent attack by adversaries, to win back religious freedom, and to defend oppressed people: men, women, and children who "cry for help." He cites the Qur'an 4:75 as his source.

Haleem contends that all Muslim battles during Muhammad's life were preceded by great restraint, patience, and fortitude on the part of Muslims under Muhammad and that the battles were waged only in self-defense or to pre-empt an attack that was imminent. The Qur'an and the Prophet guided each battle accordingly.

> "All the battles that took place during the Prophet's lifetime, under guidance of the Qur'an and the Prophet, have been surveyed and shown to have been waged only in self-defence or to pre-empt an imminent attack. For more than ten years in Mecca, Muslims were persecuted, but before permission was given to fight they

were instructed to restrain themselves (4:77) and endure with patience and fortitude."[79]

Haleem often mentions that the adversaries were "polytheists" who continually persecuted Muslims for their religious beliefs and practices. He does not address the possibility that Muslims might have been threatened by non-polytheists (e.g. other Muslims, atheists, or other monotheists) or that they might have opposed Muslims for non-religious reasons such as border disputes and economic competition. Haleem contends that Muhammad and his followers only fought for three reasons that are allowed in the Qur'an, all of which involved intolerable actions by adversaries. "They continuously broke their agreements and aided others against the Muslims. They started hostilities against the Muslims and barred others from becoming Muslims. And they expelled Muslims from the Holy Mosque and even from their own homes."[80] He says that the Qur'an is even more restrictive because, even under one or more of these conditions, Muslims must be careful not to wage war against any adversaries with whom Muslims have treaties. For Haleem, the Qur'an prohibits Muslims from fighting against adversaries who do not "break their agreements," those who "keep the peace with the Muslims," and those who seek "safe conduct" out of contested areas. These adversaries should be protected and delivered to places of safety.

THE CONDUCT OF WAR

As mentioned several times previously in this book, Haleem says that the Qur'an closely and carefully delimits how Muslims can wage war in keeping with three or four principles: "righteous intention," "discrimination," "proportionality," and what might be considered either as a part of proportionality or as a fourth principle that can be called "transgression avoidance." Righteous intention means that the fighting must only be done "in the way of God," to serve God's purpose of religious freedom for Muslims, and only as God himself would fight. This excludes fighting for booty, for self-aggrandizement, or "to be seen as a hero."[81]. The word of God must always remain uppermost while one is fighting. Haleem contends that the principle of righteous intention dictates how and when jihad might be pursued by Muslims. "When there is a just cause for jihad, which must have a righteous intention, it then becomes an obligation. It becomes an obligation for defending religious freedom (22:39-41), for self-defence (2:190) and defending those who are oppressed: men, women and children who cry for help (4:75)."[82] In contrast to so many commentators about current usage of the term "jihad," Haleem says that jihad does not means "holy war," that the word jihad is not in the Qur'an, and that jihad can be pursued in several ways beside warfare. These other ways are more important and challenging in Islam than is warfare.

> "Another term which is misunderstood and misrepresented is *jihad*. This does not mean 'Holy War.' 'Holy War' does not exist as a term in Arabic, and its translation into Arabic sounds quite alien. The term which is specifically used in the Qur'an for fighting is *qital*. Jihad can be by argumentation (25:52), financial help or actual fighting. Jihad is always described in the Qur'an as *fi sabil illah*. On returning from a military campaign, the Prophet said to his followers: 'We have returned from the minor jihad to the major jihad — the struggle of the individual with his own self.'"[83]

Given these intricacies and controversies about the term "jihad," I encourage government and military leaders to be very informed about this matter so as to be able to respond to any proponents of the Qur'an, or their antagonists, who might claim that the Qur'an explicitly requires all Muslims to engage in military warfare as a prerequisite for being true Muslims or for gaining paradise.

Haleem explains that the principle of "discrimination" has nothing to do with race relations. It means that the Qur'an restricts Muslims to only fighting against actual combatants of the adversary — not non-combatants of their communities. Proportionality means that damage inflicted by Muslims must not exceed the damage that was inflicted upon them.

> "Only the combatants are to be fought, and no more harm should be caused to them than they have caused (2:194). Thus wars and weapons of destruction that destroy civilians and their towns are ruled out by the Qur'an and the word and deed of the Prophet, these being the only binding authority in Islamic law."[84]

Military and government leaders would do well to give special attention to this claim by Haleem. It essentially says that the Qur'an and the Hadith prohibit Muslims from attacking an adversary's civilians and towns and cities. Drawing an implication from Haleem on this matter, the Qur'an would therefore prohibit and denounce the attacks on the World Trade Center in 1993 and 2001 — but *not necessarily* the attacks on the Pentagon. At least it is not so obvious that the attacks on the Pentagon would be prohibited by the Qur'an, unless, perhaps, the attackers knew that "innocent" civilians would also be present in the Pentagon, along with U.S. military personnel.

Haleem emphasizes that the Qur'an repeatedly instructs Muslims not to transgress in matters related to war. Haleem says that the specific types of transgressions to be avoided are spelled-out by "exegetes" of the Qur'an rather than in the Qur'an itself.

"Transgression has been interpreted by Qur'anic exegetes as meaning initiation of fighting, fighting those with whom a treaty has been concluded, surprising the enemy without first inviting them to make peace, destroying crops or killing those who should be protected."[85]

Haleem is particularly incensed about non-Muslims who ignore historical and literary context and thereby misinterpret what he calls the Qur'an's "sword verse" (9:5): "Then, when the sacred months have passed, slay the idolators wherever you find them, take them and besiege them and prepare for then every ambush." As I wrote in Chapter 2 when I dealt with this famous verse, it is mitigated and qualified by other passages adjacent to it in the Qur'an. Haleem is correct in pointing-out this feature. He says, "Consistent with restrictions on war elsewhere in the Qur'an, the immediate context of this 'sword verse' exempts such polytheists as do not break their agreements and who keep the peace with the Muslims (9:7)."[86] Haleem then mentions several other restrictions on the applicability of this "sword verse." However, he seems to be oblivious to several of the basic premises that I have mentioned several times in this book, namely, that some violence-prone proponents of the Qur'an and opportunists can readily ignore or disregard contextual considerations in selecting and employing certain passages of the Qur'an to satisfy their political and military purposes. Even with all of the qualifications mentioned by Haleem, the sword verse can be applied violently to a variety of adversaries, such as to those who have broken treaties or those who have not been peaceful enough towards Muslims.

PRISONERS OF WAR

Haleem claims that the Qur'an is very humane regarding taking and treating prisoners of war and that it is congruent with "present international humanitarian conventions."[87] Like other interpreters including Khadduri and Pickthall, Haleem finds that the Qur'an instructs Muslims to treat prisoners first with "grace," then "ransom," and that they must be treated humanely, regardless of how they behaved towards their captors. If they so chose, prisoners are allowed to remain in Muslim lands, with guaranteed protections for their lives, property, and religious freedom. In exchange for these benefits they must pay various taxes that are appropriate to their status. They are allowed to convert to Islam and they are also to be afforded safe passage if they prefer to return to their homelands.

CEASING WAR AND FINDING PEACE

Haleem states that the Qur'an obligates Muslims to accept peace whenever it is offered by adversaries. He does not mention that this implies the resumption of religious freedom and the withdrawal of all adversaries from the Muslim homelands that they occupied, but this might be implied by him or it might be obvious to him. He says that a Muslim state can have only one of four types of relationships with a "neighboring warring enemy." These are: defensive war as prescribed in the Qur'an, a "peace treaty for a limited or unlimited period," a "state of truce," or a situation in which an enemy envoy can come to a "Muslim land for special purposes under safe conduct." He says that these last-named situations constitute *dar al-sulh* (world of treaty), the third category besides *dar al-Islam* (world of Islam) and *dar al-harb* (world of war).[88] This is in keeping with Khadduri's interpretation of the three categories of nations according to the Islamic cosmology that was mentioned earlier in this chapter.

Treaties are to be fully honored, Haleem says, and breaking them is despised. Haleem does not mention the passages from the Qur'an that I presented in Chapter 2 that allow Muslims to break treaties under various conditions. International cooperation, treaties, conventions, and humanitarian aid and intervention are also completely compatible with the Qur'an, according to Haleem, based on Qur'anic passages such as 60:8: "God does not forbid you from being kind and equitable to those who have neither made war on you on account of your religion nor driven you from your homes. God loves those who are equitable." From passages like this Haleem infers that "In the sphere of war and peace, there is nothing in the Qur'an or Hadith which should cause Muslims to feel unable to sign and act according to the modern international conventions, and there is much in the Qur'an and Hadith from which modern international law can benefit."[89]

Let us hope that Haleem is right about the Qur'an and the Hadith being very compatible with international law and international peace making. Certainly current military and government leaders should consider quoting him at appropriate times on matters such as this.

In sum, Haleem believes that the Qur'an only allows Muslims to engage in very limited, highly qualified defensive wars after they suffer repeated injustices because of their religion. He stresses (as do I) the considerable number of constraints that the Qur'an places on Muslims before they can engage in war and, once engaged, during the conduct of war. Haleem does not mention the possibility of Muslims offering peace first, engaging in offensive warfare (he denies that it ever happened while Muhammad was alive), fighting outside their homelands (he denies this), and fighting adversaries other than "polytheists." He does not mention distinctions in Muslim warfare regarding the religious orientations of different adversaries, including Christians and Jews. He does not extend the Qur'an to modern day warfare by nations that involves air, sea, and motorized forces, biological, chemical, and nuclear weapons, psychological warfare, or wars that involve multiple allies and adversaries, some of which might be predominantly Muslim on both sides. So, while Haleem's interpretations often seem somewhat naive and wishful regarding the amount of war, conflict, and violence in the Qur'an and in the history of Islam, his work should be appreciated for providing a hopeful reading of the Qur'an as a document of peace, not only in the distant past, but also for resolving international conflicts in the modern world.

SOME CONCLUDING THOUGHTS ABOUT INTERPRETATIONS

This chapter has recounted some of the interpretations of Majid Khadduri, John Esposito, Maulawi Sher Ali, and Muhammad Abdel Haleem regarding peace, conflict, and war in the Qur'an and in Islam. In doing so, we have found that except for Khadduri, these scholars focus on a much smaller number of the relevant verses in the Qur'an than were presented in Chapter 2 of this book. These scholars seem to be less aware of the more ambiguous and even contradictory Qur'anic verses such as the verses that admit that Muslim armies annihilated entire enemy communities, conducted surprise attacks while the enemy was sleeping, and at times tortured and mutilated prisoners, at least in a few instances. Ali and Haleem do not report significant discrepancies between the Qur'an's instructions about the conduct of war and the military and political history of some Muslim regimes in the distant past as well as the modern age. Esposito reports only a few inconsistencies and he regards these as being the consequence of radical activists who believe that violence is necessary to bring about significant changes in the international status quo. Khadduri's interpretations are especially useful because they reveal the many instances and ways in which Islamic laws have changed since Muhammad's days so as to accommodate both the Qur'an's instructions and the actual behaviors of Muslim military commanders and their armies and navies in the thick of battle and in the many defeats and victories that followed.

In all fairness to these interpreters, it should be acknowledged that none of them are military historians and their subject matter was not primarily war, terror, and peace in Islam. Only Khadduri, a legal scholar, gave considerable attention to legal codes about war and peace. Nonetheless, it seems that all of their perspectives fall short of comprehending the rather stupendous quantity and perplexing qualities of Muslim warfare that started with Muhammad. They also fail to recognize that few if any world religions besides Islam were founded by a person who led his armies in more than twenty-five battles (only two of which were in defense of Medina, the Muslim capital at the time) and ordered his armies to fight more than thirty additional battles during his lifetime. Unfortunately they also fail to acknowledge, let alone explain, the considerable discrepancy between Muslim military and political history and the guidance given to proponents of the Qur'an in its many and more enlightened, restrained, and compassionate verses. Hopefully this book is helping to reduce these omissions. The next chapter is intended to make this all the more apparent by showing how the Qur'an can be used to restrain the conduct of wars and enhance peace and understanding in the future.

---

[1] Khadduri, p. 137.

[2] Haleem, p. 69.

[3] To the best of my knowledge, no book until now has interpreted the Qur'an primarily as a military document. This is one of the purposes of the book that you are now reading.

[4] Khadduri, p. vii.

[5] Khadduri, p. 7-8.

[6] Khadduri, p. 3.

[7] Khadduri, p. 4.

[8] Khadduri, pp. 8-10.

[9] Khadduri, p. 52.

[10] Khadduri, p. 137.

[11] Khadduri, p. 137.

[12] Khadduri, p. 55.

[13] Khadduri, p. 56. Khadduri mentions that this phrase is from chapter 61, verse 11 of the Qur'an.

[14] Khadduri, pp. 60-61. One implication of this mandate is that government and military leaders should not authorize massive, surprise attacks that might be perceived by Muslim as compelling all members of their communities to fight, including women, children, the elderly, and the infirm. This is one of the more important insights in this book, to my way of thinking. It is an insight that will be repeated several times.

[15] Khadduri, p. 62.

[16] Khadduri, p. 62.

[17] Khadduri, p. 57.

[18] Khadduri, p. 64.

[19] Khadduri, pp. 65-66.

[20] Khadduri, p. 67.

[21] Khadduri, p. 72.

[22] Khadduri, p. 86.

[23] Khadduri, p. 81.

[24] Khadduri, p. 95.

[25] Khadduri, p. 106.

[26] Not surprisingly, Islamic law parallels the Qur'an in terms of these areas of interest — as evidenced in the Qur'anic passages that I presented in Chapter 2.

[27] Khadduri, p. 89.

[28] Khadduri, p. 92.

[29] Khadduri, p. 92. Khadduri relies heavily on the assessments of Philip K. Hitti's work in his *History of the Arabs* to explain the many battlefield successes of the Muslim armies in the first few centuries after Muhammad.

[30] Khadduri, pp. 104-106.

[31] Khadduri, p. 107.

[32] Khadduri, p. 107.

[33] Khadduri, p. 119. According to Khadduri the concepts of property, prisoner, captive and slave were not clearly distinguished in Arab societies during Muhammad's lifetime. Probably this was because a great deal of warfare was for economic purposes that involved raids and sieges against walled settlements. Often it was difficult for Muslim victors to determine which captives had participated as combatants in defending the settlements (and had committed offenses against the Muslims in the process) and which captives were simply residents of the settlements. Also, it is understandable that victorious Muslim soldiers would be more inclined to acquire young, attractive female captives from the settlement as their slaves or concubines, than to acquire injured, hostile, male enemy soldiers in this way.

[34] Khadduri, p. 123.

[35] Khadduri, p. 132. After 622 Muhammad himself practiced slavery and concubinage at times, although with increasing reluctance, especially after he had enslaved several thousands of the Hawazin tribe, only to encounter so much squabbling and trouble protecting these slaves that he later freed most of them. After that, Muhammad strongly encouraged that slaves should be ransomed or set free by their captors/owners, for "worldly or heavenly compensation."

[36] Khadduri, p. 127.

[37] Khadduri, p. 129.

[38] Khadduri, p. 109.

[39] Khadduri, p. 113.

[40] Khadduri, p. 114. Notice that Khadduri uses the term "panic" here, and recall that in Chapter 2 I reported that the terms "panic," "terror," and "fear" often are used synonymously in different translations of the Qur'an into English. These features should be of special interest to government and military leaders who are committed to defending naval forces against terrorist attacks.

[41] Khadduri, p. 115. Supposedly this happened at the Battle of Tripoli, Libya, in 1804, against U.S. naval forces, as reported in Chapter 4.

[42] Khadduri, p. 133.

[43] Khadduri, p. 17.

[44] Khadduri, p. 136.

[45] Khadduri, p. 137. This quotation is so insightful, for reasons that were explained on the first page of this chapter, that it is repeated here. Contemporary government and military leaders can use this insight to rebuff claims by opportunists, agitators, and ideologues that all wars by Muslims have been or are "holy wars," that Islam prohibits Muslims from accepting defeat in battle, and that Muslim armies have never been defeated.

[46] Khadduri, p. 18.

[47] Khadduri, p. 143.

[48] Khadduri, p. 206.

[49] Khadduri, pp. 402, 403.

[50] Khadduri, p. 239.

[51] Khadduri, p. 239.

[52] Esposito, p. 11.

[53] Esposito, p. 15.

[54] Esposito, p. 9.

[55] Esposito, p. 13. Note that in this situation Esposito chooses the term "armed resistance" as the translation of the Arabic term "jihad." At other places, including the same page (13), Esposito translates jihad to mean "wage war." In his "Glossary" and on page 34 he translates jihad as "strive, effort, struggle to follow Islam; can include defense of the faith, armed struggle, holy war."

[56] Esposito, p. 13.

[57] Esposito, p. 14.

[58] Esposito, p. 10.

[59] Esposito, p. 15.

[60] Esposito, p. 15.

[61] Esposito, p. 33.

[62] Esposito, p. 34.

[63] Esposito, p. 35.

[64] Esposito, p. 38. All capitalization and grammar in this quotation is Esposito's.

[65] Esposito, p. 58.

[66] Esposito, p. 59.

[67] Esposito, p. 59. Esposito does not identify the sources of this information regarding the totally different reactions of Muslim and Christian conquerors. Even if he is unintentionally exaggerating the differences, however, current military and government leaders should anticipate the likelihood that many contemporary Muslims continue to hold animosities about the Crusades.

[68] Esposito, p. 93.

[69] Esposito, p. 251. This is the only reference to terrorism that I found in Esposito's book. Possibly this is because it is the 3rd edition and was published in 1998, several years before the attacks of 9-11-2001 made the subject of terrorism so commonplace in the United States.

[70] Esposito, p. 169.

[71] Esposito, p. 252.

[72] Ali, p. 141.

[73] Ali, p. 142. The quotations from Ali are from pages 140-149 of his book unless noted otherwise. The numbers in parentheses, such as (47:5), are references to chapter and verse in the Qur'an as Ali presents them in his book.

[74] Ali, p. 165. All spelling and grammar is presented here as it appeared in Ali's book, regardless of idiosyncrasies.

[75] Ali, p. 140.

[76] Ali, p. 142.

[77] Ali, p. 518.

[78] Haleem, p. 60. All quotations from Haleem are from pages 59-69 of his book.

[79] Haleem, p. 61. I find that assertions like these by Haleem are questionable in the light of the interpretations that Pickthall and Rodinson offered on these topics, as presented in Chapters 2 and 3. For example, the raid at Nakhla, the Battle of Badr, the raid at Mutah, and the massacre at Khaybar, among other events such as the raids into the Transjordan area, were not obviously in self-defense and they were not obviously pre-emptive.

[80] Haleem, p. 65.

[81] Haleem, p. 62.

[82] Haleem, p. 63.

[83] Haleem, p. 62. Haleem's observation regarding the Qur'an not having the word "Jihad" in it, and the other observations in this quotation, are supported by several Muslims with whom I have spoken. For example, on March 1, 2003, I had a phone conversation with Mr. Najih Lazar in which I read Haleem's quotation to him and asked him to respond. Mr. Lazar thought for a moment and then said, "Yes, that is correct. I agree 100% with his statements about the Qur'an and the word 'jihad.'"

[84] Haleem, p. 63.

[85] Haleem, pp. 63-64.

[86] Haleem, p. 65.

[87] Haleem, p. 67.

[88] Haleem, p. 66.

[89] Haleem, p. 69.

Egyptian President Anwar Sadat, left, U.S. President Jimmy Carter, center, and Israeli Prime Minister Menachem Begin clasp hands on the north lawn of the White House after signing the peace treaty between Egypt and Israel on March 26, 1979. Sadat and Begin were awarded the Nobel Peace Prize for accomplishing peace negotiations in 1978. (AP Photo/ Bob Daugherty)

CHAPTER SEVEN

INSIGHTS: HOW THE QUR'AN CAN HELP
IN PEACE AND IN WAR WITH ITS PROPONENTS

"If I see an American soldier in Jordan on his way to Iraq, I'll kill him."[1]

"If they come to fight, maybe a big war will happen," said Abden Mohammed, a 22-year-old Islamic teacher. "As Muslims, we are all soldiers. You can call us *moujehedeen*. We must defend our place. Our religion obligates us to fight."[2]

"Speaking in Arabic in what sounded like bin Laden's usual level voice, his comments interspersed with pious expressions, the man said recent attacks were 'merely a reciprocal reaction to what Bush, the modern-day pharaoh, did by murdering our children in Iraq and what Israel, the ally of America, did in bombing houses of the elderly, women and children in Palestine, using American planes.' The use of the word pharaoh is a heavily freighted term drawn from Quranic texts, where the lesson of the fall of the pharaoh is deemed an example of the fate of arrogant leaders who think their own power equals God's."[3]

RELIGIOUS PERSECUTION AND OTHER MOTIVES
FOR VIOLENCE

One story that emerged out of the many conflicts over Arab oil in the 1970s could be well worth remembering now and in the years ahead regarding religious persecution as a motive for war. A veteran U.S. war correspondent was trying to arrange an interview with an Arab sheik who was threatening to use his personal army and anti-tank rockets to attack oil tankers that would try to move through the Suez Canal while the Israelis and Arab states were at war. The correspondent's Arab guides drove him to the sheik's base camp far out in the Saudi desert. There they found the sheik and his followers absorbed in reciting the Qur'an at evening prayers. Afterwards, the correspondent was ushered into the sheik's tent, where he found the sheik to be a very proud, informed, and hospitable fellow who spoke English. He invited the correspondent to share with him a sumptuous meal of barbecued lamb and dates. As the meal concluded late at night, the correspondent mustered the courage to ask the sheik what he thought of Americans. The sheik grew pensive, stroked his beard, and then replied. "I tell you. They are not so bad. The Americans — they only want our oil. They are not like the infidel Greeks and Romans. Not like the Christians who crusade against us to destroy our mosques. Those who would deny us Islam."

Government and military leaders who face adversaries who espouse the Qur'an might draw at least two implications from this story. One is to keep in mind that religious persecution, real or imagined, probably is the most enduring motivation and rationalization for many Muslims to engage in violence and war against non-Muslims. Certainly, alleged religious persecution was a primary reason why Naji, Mullah Omar, and Aukai Collins engaged in combat against non-Muslims (as I described their cases in Chapter 1). Another implication is that, just like the sheik, many educated Muslims realize that there are other motives and reasons for war in the modern age. Given the opportunity, they can discriminate among different adversaries and their various motives. These other motives, such as the quest for reliable supplies of cheap oil, usually have elicited less public outrage and opposition on the part of many Muslims than has the belief that Muslims are being persecuted solely because of their religion. This might be changing, however. In one of the epigraphs at the head of this chapter, the quotation attributed to Osama bin Laden implies that arrogance and the bombing of non-combatants in Palestine and Iraq were the reasons mentioned publicly for retaliation—not religious persecution *per se.*

DEALING WITH PROPONENTS OF THE QUR'AN WHO USE VIOLENCE

Far more than at any other time in the history of the United States, leaders are now facing many foreign adversaries who insist that their threats and their violence are because of religion — their religion. They contend that their violence is in response to non-Muslims persecuting them because of their religion or because of wanton attacks on Muslim people and communities. They avow that others insult and violate their most sacred religious beliefs, practices, and holy places. Furthermore, they claim that their threats and their violence against non-Muslims are legitimized and obligated by commandments from their god, Allah, in their holy book, the Qur'an. Of course, these claims might be erroneous. The claims-makers might know that they are erroneous. And yet, rather than dismiss these claims outright as being transparent, self-serving rationalizations, it would be wiser for leaders to be familiar enough with the Qur'an so that they can know how to anticipate them and invalidate them. Doing this can reduce threats now and for as long as violence-oriented people try to use the Qur'an for their own purposes. Leaders run the risk of just facing one crisis after another if they react only to the proximate causes of international conflict that are time and place specific, rather than to the underlying and enduring causes of international conflict. Instead of reacting only to a specific hostile action such as a border incursion, a terrorist act, a hostage-taking, or a build-up of biological, chemical, and nuclear weapons, leaders should try to reduce misunderstandings about core religious beliefs as well as abuses of religious sensitivities, no matter how inadvertent these might be.

If war does occur with proponents of the Qur'an, nations might sustain higher casualties and costs than necessary because leaders have neglected their religious sensitivities and have failed to prepare adequately for their behaviors in combat that they derive from the Qur'an. The purpose of this chapter is to summarize and expand upon the insights that I have suggested in the preceding chapters so that leaders can avoid errors in the future. It is obvious that the U.S. led forces had great successes in the wars against Saddam Hussein's Iraqi regime in 1991 and 2003 and that there has been considerable success so far against the Taliban and al-Qaeda forces in and around Afghanistan (as described in Chapter 5). And yet it is also obvious that despite the successes in these endeavors (and quite possibly because of them), religion-based hostility against the U.S. and the West has increased dramatically in many areas of the Muslim world and within some sub-cultures in the nations of the West, including the United States. For instance, two weeks after Saddam's regime was displaced in Iraq in April 2003, the Pew Research Center conducted a survey of 16,000 people across twenty countries and the Palestinian Authority. It found that negative attitudes towards the U.S. increased dramatically in most Arab countries except Lebanon and Kuwait since the invasion and occupation of Iraq in 2003. It also found that Muslims have far more positive attitudes towards Osama bin Laden than towards President George W. Bush.

"Bush Slips, Bin Laden Gains In Poll"

"The United States is losing a propaganda war for the hearts and minds of millions of Arabs spurred by the Sept. 11 attacks, according to a 21 nation survey released yesterday.... 'We have gone from bad to worse over the past year,' said Andrew Kohut, director of the Pew Research Center, noting that hostility toward America had increased as a result of war in Iraq. 'We have been unable to make the case against bin Laden with Muslims because they see the United States as a threat.'"[4]

THE QUR'AN AS AN ALLY: HOW THE QUR'AN CAN HELP IN PEACE AND IN WAR

How can the passages on peace and war in the Qur'an help us, especially officers in the Department of Defense, the State Department, Department of Homeland Security, and other agencies of the governments of the U.S. and its allies? How can these passages help sustain peace and, if necessary, wage war against enemy forces, from their senior commanders to their lowest-ranking combatants?

I believe that there are at least six ways that awareness of the Qur'an can help government and military leaders. It can help leaders:

1. Understand some of their opponents' most deeply ingrained beliefs and expectations about war and peace.

2. Anticipate how some of their adversaries might behave, diplomatically and militarily, regarding war and peace.

3. Develop informed plans, policies, and training procedures for their personnel in the military, foreign service, and homeland security.

4. Sustain peaceful relations with Qur'an-oriented governments and people as long and as far as possible.

5. Conduct combat operations as effectively and justly as possible, if and when war is deemed to be necessary.

6. Conclude hostilities in ways that will be auspicious for re-establishing constructive international relations and enduring peace with former adversaries, particularly regarding disposition of prisoners of war and settling claims regarding reparations.

These, then, are six ways in which familiarity with the Qur'an can help leaders in the years ahead. Essentially what I am proposing is a thesis that might seem to be heresy when you first encounter it: *the Qur'an can become an ally in peace and in war.*

The Qur'an can be an ally by helping leaders:

1. Hold their adversaries to the most humane and tolerant provisions in the Qur'an and to its constraints against violence that are favorable to leaders.

2. Emphasize that the four overarching principles of Muslim warfare (righteous intention, discrimination, proportionality, and transgression avoidance) often are compatible with the Geneva Convention's four principles of ethical warfare: military necessity, humanity, proportionality, and distinction (as described in Chapter 2).

3. Avoid situations that might tempt adversaries to use the most strident and violent passages of the Qur'an.

4. Continually reassure the nation's troops, civilian population, and allies that the most sacred canons of the Qur'an are not being disrespected. Transmit the same reassurances throughout the world, especially to the civilian populations of adversaries and to Muslim nations that are not yet engaged.

Said another way, the Qur'an can help leaders hold their adversaries to the narrowest interpretations of the Qur'an on war and the broadest interpretations on peace. It can also prepare leaders to counter those adversaries who will try to use the Qur'an's most violent passages as broadly as possible in order to suit their own purposes.

Several caveats should be kept in mind as I explain these six opportunities and elaborate on this thesis.

SEVERAL CAVEATS TO KEEP IN MIND

1. RELEVANCE TO CURRENT POLICY OF THE U.S. GOVERNMENT

Neither this chapter nor this book is intended to be a criticism of current U.S. policy or procedures. In fact, as of the publication date of this book, many U.S. government policies and procedures in fighting the al-Qaeda and the Taliban in and around Afghanistan appear to have avoided obvious violations of the Qur'an. A good example of this is that U.S. air and ground forces in Afghanistan have destroyed few mosques. The same was true of U.S. ground and air campaigns during the Persian Gulf War of 1991 and in the invasion of Iraq in 2003. Apparently few Muslim holy places were damaged. Another example of an enlightened policy is that al-Qaeda and Taliban prisoners that are being detained at the U.S. detention center in Guantanamo Bay, Cuba, are being allowed to practice many aspects of their religion without reducing the security of the center. Prisoners in individual cells are allowed to participate in the five daily prayer services and they are given prayer mats and copies of the Qur'an in Arabic, Urdu, or Pashtun.[5] However, there is also some criticism that the more than 3,000 al-Qaeda and Taliban detainees have been held secretly for more than one year and are being denied the status of POW that would afford them protection under the Geneva Conventions. Some of the detainees are reported to be subjected to very harsh "stress and duress" techniques that are marginal or disallowed by the Third Geneva Convention of 1949. It has also been reported that some of the more important detainees are "rendered" over to foreign intelligence services of Jordan, Egypt, and Morocco that are notorious for using extremely draconian forms of torture on their captives.[6]

Current government policy also has been criticized for not being especially effective in reducing criticism and hostility towards America and some of its allies in many Muslim nations and organizations that are predominantly Muslim. Even among some of the closest allies in Europe, complaints emerge about the U.S. trying to become a monolithic world empire. The monetary and political costs to the U.S. are rapidly mounting and they will take many years to be fully realized. The creation of the U.S. Department of Homeland Security underscores the fact that domestic security remains problematic and that the U.S. population no longer feels very secure. U.S. soldiers are still being attacked, wounded and killed in Iraq and in Afghanistan more than one year after the Taliban and al-Qaeda supposedly were defeated. They have not surrendered, and their danger as an irregular fighting force remains subject to debate and serious concern.[7]

**"Paratrooper from New Jersey Dies in Afghan Firefight:
A Recent Flurry of Attacks on U.S. Allied Forces."**

"Kandahar Airfield, Afghanistan, Dec. 21 — An Army paratrooper was killed in a firefight with gunmen in an eastern border area near Pakistan today, in the most serious of a string of recent attacks against United States and allied forces in Afghanistan.... The number of attacks against American forces here has risen sharply in recent months, spiking at about 60 in November, officials said. Most have not involved injuries, but early Friday morning, a Special Forces soldier was seriously wounded when a rocket exploded outside his tent in Kunar Province, also on the Pakistani border....'This place is just as dangerous as when I got here six months ago,' said Col. James Huggins, commander of the 82nd Airborne's 505th Parachute Infantry Regiment here. 'This morning is evidence of that.'"[8]

"Rebel Fighting Leaves 40 Taliban Dead"

"Peshawar, Pakistan, June 6, 2003 — Afghan government soldiers killed 40 Taliban fighters in three southern border villages in one of the deadliest instances of increased rebel activity this year, officials said yesterday. Seven government soldiers were also killed in the battle, they said.... During a visit to Kabul last month, Secretary of Defense Donald H. Rumsfeld announced the end of major combat operations and a shift to 'a period of stability and stabilization and reconstruction activities' for U.S. troops in Afghanistan. But this week alone there were two major responses to Taliban resistance. In addition to the fighting Wednesday, U.S. troops led a major airborne assault operation on Monday featuring 500 coalition soldiers in Paktia Province, one of the more troublesome regions."[9]

2. ISLAM AND THE QUR'AN'S INFLUENCES ON INTERNATIONAL RELATIONS ARE GROWING

There are many reasons why the Qur'an's influence on international relations is growing and will probably continue to grow for decades. First, as described in Chapter 1, there is widespread proliferation of many types of Islamic entities whose members are Muslims: nations, societies, social movements, sects, interest groups, and organizations. It is probably an oversimplification to say that Islam was once centered in Turkey under the Ottomans prior to the end of WWI, and that it existed in only two main sects, Sunni and Shiite. Since then, however, and especially with the decolonialization in Africa and the Middle East that accelerated after WWII, the number of Islamic entities has grown enormously, and they have dispersed through many areas of Europe, North and South America. Even small organizations and cells, such as splinter groups of al-Qaeda and Hezbollah, can muster enough resources to occasionally perpetrate an incident that grabs international press coverage. Second, many of these new Islamic entities use the Qur'an in imaginative and potent new ways to suit their own agendas, regardless of the Imams and traditional scholars. They exemplify what James Piscatori has called the "fragmentation of Islamic religious

313

authority" (as discussed in Chapter 1). Third, the enormous influence and worldwide notoriety that Qur'an-quoting proponents like Khomeini, bin Laden, Zawahiri, and Mullah Omar have had on world affairs has increased worldwide concern about the Qur'an. More people are paying attention to statements from and about the Qur'an. Fourth, cultural relativism in the West probably has increased to the point that there is a willingness to tolerate, if not accept, many of the sacred beliefs and practices of most religions — at least of those religions that do not espouse violence and human degradation as a matter of course. Islam is questioned and criticized by some people such as Reverend Franklin Graham, Reverend Pat Robertson, journalist James Buckley, and novelist Salman Rushdie on the grounds that it is, or has been, too often guilty of just these kinds of offenses.[10]

3. PAST AND CURRENT SUCCESSES
COULD JEOPARDIZE FUTURE SUCCESSES

"Don't prepare to fight past wars," is a longstanding warning in military academies, war colleges, and numerous research and consulting firms that cater to the mammoth, global defense industry. Many well-publicized efforts are underway to transform U.S. military forces for "Fourth Generation Warfare," "asymmetrical warfare," hostilities other than warfare, and many other contingencies. There can be little doubt that future armed conflicts are likely to be much more complex and less fortuitous to U.S. forces than was the 1991 Gulf War and the ongoing campaign in and around Afghanistan against the Taliban and al-Qaeda. The majority of nations and organizations with predominantly Muslim populations supported the U.N. and U.S. efforts, remained neutral, or remained ambiguous. Fortuitously, another Muslim entity, The Northern Alliance, already existed in Afghanistan. It had been fighting against the Taliban for years. It readily accepted U.S. and U.N. aid that converted it into a surprisingly aggressive fighting force when it was joined with U.S. Special Forces on the ground and with tactical air forces. Few if any wars have ever had a gap in technological superiority so great as this war. Total air superiority, laser guided smart bombs and drones, and a diverse array of helicopter borne ground forces opposed enemy forces that had no air force and whose most sophisticated weapons had been captured from Soviet forces ten years earlier. Many enemy forces were killed, although many others escaped into Pakistan and surrounding countries. Also very fortuitous for the U.N. forces was the open, arid terrain that often afforded superb visibility to the attacking forces and poor cover and concealment for the defenders, unless they hid in deep caves and tunnels (which then rendered them ineffective both offensively and defensively. They became hiders, rather than fighters).

The defenders were not strongly supported by the civilian populations in most areas, in part because the Taliban were oppressive and because of longstanding antagonisms among warlords, tribes, and sects. The enemy failed to defend Kabul and other built-up areas very tenaciously, although when they did so, they caused considerable problems for the U.N. forces, as was the case in the prison uprising at Kandahar in which a CIA agent was killed. This incident made it all the more obvious that U.N. forces suffered very few casualties due to enemy fire. Apparently no combatants were taken prisoner by enemy combatants or hostile civilians despite thousands of bombing missions by U.N. aircraft — situations which, had they occurred, could quickly have made the campaign much more controversial and difficult to resolve. U.N. combat operations apparently did not destroy many Muslim holy places or interfere with Muslim religious practices. They did not incite very much unrest or violence in the general civilian populations, although quite a few tribal warlords have continued to engage in violent attacks against a variety of targets from time-to-time, including attacks against U.N. forces.

Finally, Muslims in the U.N. and U.S. armed forces apparently did not pose problems. They did not balk. Some evidence exists that they were able to discriminate among their loyalties and understand that the campaign was not a campaign against Islam or against mainstream Muslims. Consider the case of Sergeant Mahmuti, a U.S. Army soldier who was interviewed by journalist John Sacks.

> "It wasn't the Muslim side, Mahmuti sincerely believed. He believed he could aim, fire, and kill a Muslim even if, as he also believed, the Muslim would go to paradise while all Mahmuti's fellow soldiers went to Muslim hell. In his own pocket, the Koran said, 'Lo! The worst of beasts in Allah's sight are the Unbelievers,' but also the Koran told how Muslims killed Muslims without the Koran's complaint. Nor did Mahmuti's parents demur at Mahmuti's killing another defender of Allah. 'Don't sweat it,' Mahmuti's father phoned him. 'To say this isn't easy for me, but if you must kill him, kill him.'"[11]

Overall, the campaign in and around Afghanistan has been a remarkably favorable situation in which the enemy's poorly trained, paramilitary forces for the most part fought vigorously for a few weeks, but then they were destroyed in place or escaped to fight another day. On the other hand (as shown in Chapter 5), there is only a limited amount of evidence that significant numbers of Taliban and al-Qaeda fought, or ceased fighting, because of the Qur'an. Naji, Aukai Collins, Mullah Omar and, of course, Osama bin Laden have been among them, however, and their fighting has been of considerable consequence (as described in Chapters 1 and 5).

4. THE QUR'AN COULD BECOME A MUCH GREATER INFLUENCE IN FUTURE HOSTILITIES

There are at least three reasons why the Qur'an could become much more influential in future hostilities. First, the fabric and nature of future hostilities probably will be influenced by more than one of the five major categories of combatants who advocate for the Qur'an or use it opportunistically:

1. Muslim proponents in the U.S. and allied armed forces.

2. Unaffiliated Muslim proponents who engage in violence against non-Muslims, such as the U.S. civilian who attacked the El Al passenger desk at Los Angeles International Airport in June 2002.

3. Long-established Islamic terrorist organizations such as Al-Qaeda, Fatah/Black September, Al-Gama al-Islamiyya, Hamas, Hizballah, Al-Jiha, Palestine Islamic Jihad, Popular Front for the Liberation of Palestine, as well as splinter groups, affiliates, and newly emerging organizations.[12]

4. Revolutionary guards of transitory, coercive regimes, such as the Taliban, and what have been called "ethno-nationalist paramilitary bands" that are organized into small dispersed units.[13]

5. Standing armed forces of nation states that are either formal Islamic states like Iran or that are secular states in which the armed forces are Islamic in their composition and doctrine, such as Pakistan.

Second, as mentioned several times throughout this book, the Qur'an is being distributed throughout the World in many different forms (CDs, tapes, Internet access, inexpensive paperback editions, capsule quotations) and in many different languages, dialects, and bilingual "side-by-side" editions. Such easy availability in so many media enhances the likelihood that tens of millions of new consumers will gain some familiarity with the Qur'an each year and that they will relate it to issues of peace and war that concern them. Third, as discussed in Chapter 1, the organization, style, and content of the Qur'an render it vulnerable to misuse, misinterpretation, and reinterpretation in ways that can both benefit or threaten peace-making efforts. It is highly evocative, connotative, repetitive and, at times, contradictory. There is plenty of material in the Qur'an to comfort, inspire, astound, confound, aggravate, intimidate, and even infuriate almost anyone who reads and studies most of it, including dozens of Muslims that I have conversed with and interviewed about these matters, from arch-conservatives to fairly liberal people.

These, then, are some of the considerations to keep in mind as I review next what the Qur'an and the history of Muslim warfare revealed to us in Chapters 2-5 about peace and war between and among nations.

REVIEW OF THE QUR'AN REGARDING PEACE, TERROR, AND WAR

REGARDING PEACE AND TREATIES

Government and military leaders should keep in mind that international peace is not described, promised, or expected in the Qur'an. Rather, the emphasis is on how spiritual peace can be attained by individual Muslims. Some attention also is given to how conflict can be minimized and resolved between and among individual Muslims and different communities of Muslims. Strict compliance to the tenets of Islam, as specified in the Qur'an, is the path, the "straight path" — the only path — for achieving both individual spiritual peace and social harmony between and among Muslim communities. The search for peace on Earth is a constant struggle against the devil, one's own temptation to self-indulgence, and offenses by non-believers. The Qur'an does not describe, promise, or predict a period of sustained peace on earth for Muslims, although some passages imply that worldwide peace might endure if all nations and people convert to Islam. This interpretation, sometimes called the "expansionist-universalist" interpretation, can be contrasted to the "separatist" interpretation, which contends that Muslim nations can be at peace (i.e. free from religious persecution) only when they are totally separated from non-Muslim nations in all of their institutions and activities: cultural, social, political, and economic. Even then, some passages of the Qur'an suggest that peace will endure only if all nations practice Islam. Islam is necessary for international peace. And yet, nothing in the Qur'an describes or predicts that international peace will ever be attained through worldwide conversion to Islam, other than that Muslim nations will no longer have a need to engage in war against non-Muslim nations if all other nations have converted to Islam. This might be a goal or an implied possibility, but it is not consistently predicted or promised in the Qur'an.

Regarding treaties, the Qur'an does not portray treaties as being permanent solutions for attaining everlasting peace among nations. They are temporary stopgaps that Muslims should enter into only for honorable purposes, to reduce religious persecution, and to enhance the likelihood of a period of relative peace that lasts several years. Treaties should not be used to jockey for more favorable advantage before war erupts. Muslims are warned to be suspicious of the motives of their treaty partners and to break treaties with partners whom they suspect of treachery.

THE NATURE AND CAUSES OF WAR, ACCORDING TO THE QUR'AN

The Qur'an only describes warfare between Muslim and non-Muslim nations and groups. It is almost as if war does not exist among non-Muslims or between and among Muslim nations and groups. According to the Qur'an, those nations and groups that initiate warfare against Muslims do so because they have been duped by the devil into wanting to persecute Muslims because of their practice of Islam. The Qur'an does not identify any other causes for non-Muslims attacking Muslims such as hatred, non-religious prejudice, border disputes, economic exploitation, ideological dominance, or retaliation for previous attacks. Muslims are to invest heavily in defending their far borders when they are threatened by non-Muslim armed forces. All Muslims must be willing to support the war effort in some way, although not necessarily by serving as armed combatants. In many passages the Qur'an explicitly prohibits Muslims from initiating hostilities and from fighting during sacred periods of time and in sacred places unless they are attacked first and further fighting is unavoidable. Muslims must not attack pacifists, those who offer peace, those with whom they have honorable treaties, and those who seek refuge with them or with their allies.

In the Qur'an the wartime enemies of Muslim armies are bands, tribes, coalitions, cities, and nations of disbelievers, hypocrites, polytheists, and others who persecute Muslims, who are alleged to be plotting against Muslims, or who are objectionable in other ways — primarily that their lifestyles and institutional practices, such as "devouring of illicit gain," are abominable by Muslim standards. Muslim armies are not restricted to fighting only the armed forces of non-believers who persecute Muslims because of Islam. Muslim armies are not compelled to fight all non-believers who persecute Muslims because of Islam, at least not until the persecution becomes intolerable and it includes physical attacks by the enemy's armed forces upon Muslim communities and holy places.

GOALS AND GENERAL ORDERS FOR MUSLIM BATTLES

The Qur'an does not restrict Muslims to fighting only to end religious persecution against them. Nor does it specify at what point religious persecution becomes so intolerable that war is imperative. It does instruct Muslims to attack and to slay "wherever ye find them" those enemy forces who have attacked and occupied Muslim lands and holy places. However, it does not address the issue of whether Muslims are allowed to plan and execute slayings or engage in offensive military campaigns in the distant foreign lands of enemies. The Qur'an certainly allows Muslims — and possibly even compels them at times — to ambush, wound, slay, capture, ransom, and release enemy combatants who are occupying Muslim lands and holy places. Muslim combatants must "fight in the way of Allah" and cease hostilities "except against wrongdoers," once the enemy desists, persecution has ended, and "religion is for Allah." Unfortunately the Qur'an is rather ambiguous about who is a "wrongdoer" besides those who persecute Muslims because of their religion. It is also ambiguous as to whether the phrase "religion is for Allah" means simply that Muslims are now free again to practice Islam in their homeland, that only Islam is allowed to be practiced in Muslim communities, or that only Islam is allowed to be practiced everywhere in the world.

Another seeming ambiguity in the Qur'an is that some passages instruct Muslim armed forces to "retaliate" by fighting the enemy "in like manner," while other passages instruct them to fight "in the way of Allah," without addressing the possibility that these directives could lead to the commission of very different behaviors in warfare. "In the way of Allah" would seem to manifest the principle of "righteous intention" and would discourage Muslims from abusing, mutilating, and executing enemy prisoners who are unarmed or wounded. Yet, if enemy forces have fought Muslims in these ways, the principle of

319

"proportionality" would seem to allow Muslim combatants to retaliate just like this — "in like manner." Additionally, while some passages mention that Muslims are allowed to be charitable towards their enemies and not retaliate against them, other passages seem to indicate that this license only applies to enemies who are also "believers" — other Muslims. Thus it seems that these ambiguities are a permanent feature of the Qur'an that cannot be clarified based on reading the Qur'an alone. They probably will be debated by scholars and clerics forevermore. But it can be helpful for military and government leaders to know that these ambiguities exist so as not to fall under the influence of over-simplifiers from one persuasion or the other. It also is appropriate to advocate on the side of the most humane interpretations of the Qur'an, in keeping with modern international laws including the Geneva Conventions.

SOME THEMES AND FORMS OF MUSLIM WARFARE

The Qur'an does not identify specific forms of organization, chains of command, weapons, strategies, or tactics that Muslim armed forces should use in warfare other than to insist repeatedly that Muslims join together and "fight in closed ranks as a solid unit." It does not describe situations in which Muslims fight in decentralized units as guerrillas, or as detached or self-appointed teams, cells, or "free agents." It also insists that, even though enemy forces will probably outnumber the Muslim forces by a ratio of at least 2:1 and possibly by as much as 10:1, Muslim armed forces must fight steadfastly, obediently, and loyally even if it means death for many of them. Muslims so engaged are prohibited from calling out for peace, even if they are winning. Instead, unless the enemy calls out for peace and surrenders, the enemy must be routed so decisively that fear and terror will be struck into the enemy's rear guard, support personnel, and anyone who supports the enemy forces in any way. This does not mean that the Qur'an endorses what is now widely considered to be terrorism (i.e. violent, surprise attacks on civilian populations that are intended primarily to inflict terror, fear, and panic upon them) — for it does not. However, there are several passages in the Qur'an that explicitly describe Muslim armed forces extending their routing of enemy military forces into the home bases, communities, and civilian populations of the enemy in foreign lands to the point that all of these are utterly destroyed and annihilated. Muslim ambushes, raids, and surprise attacks on communities whose residents are asleep at night and at noontime are described in the Qur'an in very direct, unapologetic and perhaps even in boastful ways. In some cases the Qur'an mentions that Muslim forces have sometimes first sent "commandment" to the residents of a township before they attack and destroy it. But, if the residents ignore the commandment and continue to "commit abomination," then the Muslim forces attack the township and wreck upon it "complete annihilation." Several passages in the Qur'an mention that Muslim forces used "slaves of Ours" in the attacks on enemy countries and that these attacks were so devastating that enemy communities were made extinct.[14]

SUPRESS DISSENT AT HOME

The principle of "discrimination" (that Muslims must distinguish among various targets of opportunity so as to exempt from attack those targets that are inappropriate by Qur'anic standards) is reflected in many passages of the Qur'an. These include passages that encourage tolerance towards non-Muslims who are pacifists, who desist from fighting, who become prisoners, and who seek refuge among allies. The discrimination principle is also reflected in passages that espouse that, during times of war, Muslims should suppress and punish pacifists, alarmists, dissenters, and hypocrites within their communities, including Muslim females and the allies of Muslims. Anyone who does not support the war effort fully and whose lack of support could sow dissension within the ranks of Muslim armed forces should be silenced. Thus it should not be surprising to read that some proponents of the Qur'an in Baghdad, Kandahar, Riyadh, Cairo, and Istanbul attack Muslims whom they consider to be dissenters, pacifists, and hypocrites because of their attitudes toward non-Muslims.

MOTIVATIONS AND JUSTIFICATION FOR MUSLIMS ENGAGING IN COMBAT

Certainly the primary reason and lawful motive for Muslims engaging in warfare is to end religious persecution against Muslims and the destruction of Muslim holy places and communities by enemy armed forces. There are many other motives in addition to this however. These other motives are secondary in that they are mentioned less frequently in the Qur'an and often they are qualified. While the Qur'an repeatedly assures Muslims combatants that Allah will reward them with eternal paradise if they are slain by enemy forces while fighting "in the way of Allah," (thus making them "martyrs" or "witnesses" in Islam), the Qur'an does not offer this incentive to Muslims who behave recklessly, independently from their commanders, or who intentionally allow themselves to be slain in combat simply in order to attain paradise. Other secondary motives include: proving that one actually is a believer and is worthy of becoming a martyr, to oppose the devil, and to provide an agent (the Muslim combatant) through which Allah actually does the killing and takes responsibility for it. Other secondary motives are to protect Muslims who are unable to defend themselves, including feeble people, women, and children; to avenge wrongs against Muslims, such as those who have been "driven from their homes unjustly;" to punish the enemy for breaking treaties; and for acts of duplicity and trickery. There are even more secondary motives. Allah promises to restrain the combat effectiveness of the enemy forces despite their numerical superiority. There will be plenteous spoils of war that are to be fully relished by the Muslim combatants (so long as one-fifth of the booty is allotted to Allah and his "messenger" Muhammad for the social welfare of needy Muslims). Other motivations that are highly controversial (and that often are denied by some apologists) include punishing those Jews and Christians who have become bellicose, sacrilegious, and who "commit abomination," and because Muslims who help in conquering other religions will have their sins forgiven and will gain eternal paradise. Some of these prescribed reasons for Muslims to fight seem to be unrelated to religious persecution of Muslims. They might even encourage religious persecution of non-Muslims by Muslims because of their alleged "devouring of illicit gain."[15]

OTHER PRESCRIPTIONS AND PROSCRIPTIONS FOR MUSLIMS IN COMBAT

There are many other instructions to Muslim combatants to be found throughout the Qur'an besides an insistence that they are to be steadfast, loyal, and obedient in combat. Special honors are to be given to those Muslims who are first to fight. Latecomers are to be accorded less honor or to be rejected if the course of battle already has been determined. Muslims are instructed to be willing to commit their wealth and lives to long expeditions against enemies in "distant" lands (not necessarily meaning foreign lands). Occasionally, situations might require Muslims to take the offensive and to fight very aggressively — even "harshly." At times this might include degradation and mutilation of enemy combatants until the enemy is "expelled out of the land" or is "annihilated." Muslim combatants are instructed to "kill those who don't offer peace." They must not retreat or allow others to do so under threat of eternal doom from Allah. Persecuted refugees must be protected by Muslim combatants and they should be given special rewards if they join in the fight. At the same time, however, Muslim leaders are to avoid mobilizing all Muslim people into the armed forces. The blind, lame, and sick should be exempted from combat, and other Muslims should be kept behind in Muslim settlements to pray, act as sentries, and perform other necessary services. The Qur'an insists that feeble people, women, and children should be protected by Muslim armed forces, but it does not explicitly prohibit elderly men, women, and children from being allowed to serve as combatants. Muslim combatants are warned not to call out for peace even if they are winning in combat. They are instructed to be willing to consider ceasing the fighting if the enemy forces offer peace and are willing to end all persecuting and wrongdoing against Muslims. Also, Muslims are instructed not to reject peace offerings just because enemy combatants do not believe in Allah or because Muslim combatants could capture more booty from their enemies if they continued to fight until the enemy was totally vanquished.

SPOILS OF WAR, CAPTIVES AND PRISONERS

Throughout the Qur'an many passages promise steadfast Muslim warriors that their courageous efforts in warfare will reward them with many spoils of war including valuable material objects and possibly even civilian captives. It leaves considerable ambiguity as to how the spoils are to be acquired, distributed, and managed. Some passages remind Muslim warriors that they should allot one-fifth of their booty to Allah, the Messenger (Muhammad), and for needy members of Muslim communities, even as they enjoy fully their remaining spoils of war. Enemy military personnel who become prisoners of war to Muslim forces apparently are not to be treated as the personal property of individual Muslim warriors, although this is not unequivocal in the Qur'an. Rather, POWs are to be firmly secured. Eventually they are to be ransomed or, if they repent, they might be converted to Islam, allowed to remain in Muslim communities as taxpaying non-Muslim residents, or possibly even freed as a charitable gesture on the part of the leader of the Muslim forces. Nothing in the Qur'an explicitly proscribes or prescribes that Muslim combatants harass, abuse, torture, or execute enemy prisoners, although there are passages that describe how Muslims have occasionally inflicted great pain, suffering, and even death upon some of their captives. However, it is not clear that these captives had been combatants in the armed forces of the enemy and that they were captured as a result of warfare. The Qur'an makes no mention of Muslims who are captured and who become prisoners of war. Nor does it mention Muslim property

323

that becomes spoils of war by falling into enemy hands. The general assumption seems to be that Muslim forces will respond so quickly and successfully to the enemy's incursions into the Muslim home-lands that the enemy forces will not have enough time to capture Muslim property and people as booty of their own.

ENDING BATTLES AND WARS

The Qur'an does not specify unconditional surrender, enemy retreat, paying of bribes, poor weather, nightfall, or any other specif-ic action or condition as being sufficient grounds for Muslims to end a particular battle. Rather, it portrays battles as ending only when the Muslim forces have prevailed over the enemy forces by routing them, capturing them, or forcing them to abandon the battlefield. As far as ending an entire war, passages in the Qur'an mention one or more of the following conditions or events that must occur before Muslim forces stop their war against enemy forces: the enemy offers peace, there is an end to the religious persecution of Muslims, religion is "for Allah," Muslims conquer all other religions, tribute is paid by the enemy, wrongdoers are punished or cease to exist, the enemy desists, or the enemy surrenders. Without further elaboration in the Qur'an, it seems that Muslim military leaders are allowed the latitude to determine which of these conditions are sufficient to end any partic-ular war and in ways that are acceptable in Islam. Unfortunately, pas-sages in the Qur'an do not establish whether Muslims are to try to achieve each and every condition sequentially, through negotiations, or as part of a process to end other types of conflicts among nations and to establish permanent peace.

Beyond human agency as a way of ending wars, the Qur'an also refers to some documented historical events in which sandstorms, heat waves, rain storms, plagues, and other dramatic natural events occurred so suddenly and miraculously that enemy forces became so confused, damaged, or discouraged that they lifted their sieges against Muslim forces and retreated back to their homelands. In one such instance (described in Chapter 2) that is taught to many Muslim schoolchildren, Mecca was saved in or about the year of Muhammad's birth there, about 570, when swarms of flying creatures suddenly appeared and attacked the army of the Abyssinian ruler, Abraha. So too, sandstorms and extreme heat waves had similar consequences. They allowed Muhammad to claim victory over the attacking Quraysh at the famous Battle of the Trench (described in Chapter 3). Thus it would not be surprising to find that many contemporary and recent proponents of the Qur'an who are inclined towards armed conflict, including Saddam Hussein, Osama bin Laden, and Mullah Omar, would encourage their followers to believe in "miracles" as ways for eventually defeating opponents who, otherwise, have overwhelming military forces. Historically, especially during Muhammad's life and in the first few decades afterwards, Muslim armies often have achieved rather stunning victories over numerically superior coalitions of enemy forces, often without much bloodshed, and sometimes by simply confounding the enemy forces with protracted negotiations, machinations, and sleight-of-hand maneuvers.

THE HISTORY OF MUSLIM WARFARE IN LIGHT OF THE QUR'AN

As we saw in Chapters 3-5, English language sources only disclose mixed and episodic evidence of the Qur'an's direct influence on the combat behavior of its proponents in more than a fraction of the most significant Muslim battles going back to Muhammad's battles at Badr, Uhud, The Trench, and Hudaybiya. There is plenty of evidence that passages of the Qur'an were recited to and by Muslim combatants before some of the battles since Muhammad's death in 632, but there is little direct evidence as to which passages were recited. There is little direct evidence as to whether the passages about war, terror, and peace directly influenced Muslim combatants once they were engaged in combat. There is no evidence that a specific Muslim combatant killed or did not kill another combatant in a battle because he felt compelled to do so by the passages of the Qur'an that are presented in Chapter 2 of this book. And yet, there is some direct if imperfect evidence that passages of the Qur'an were consulted by some military leaders before they decided to fight the battles of Siffin in 657, Simancas in 934, Las Navas de Tolosa in 1212, Kosovo in 1389, and Gallipoli in 1915. There also is strong circumstantial evidence that passages of the Qur'an were required reading for the perpetrators of the September 11, 2001, attacks on the World Trade Center in New York and the Pentagon in Washington, DC.

MAJOR PATTERNS IN MUSLIN BATTLES SINCE 624

While it is not obvious that the Qur'an directly and significantly influenced most Muslim battles and combat behaviors, there are several patterns in the overall history of Muslim warfare that are very con-

325

gruent with the Qur'an's directives and that could have been provoked by the Qur'an. These passages and patterns should not be overlooked by current and future military and government leaders. Undoubtedly, many Muslim political and military leaders in the world today know about them and could be tempted to take advantage of them.

1. The Qur'an's prescriptions about war, terror, and peace seem to have been obeyed much more often than were its prohibitions about these subjects. For example, Muslim combatants usually have defended their far borders quite rigorously, at least initially. They have been willing to retaliate in kind, just as they are instructed by the Qur'an. However, contrary to the Qur'an's prohibitions, Muslim combatants often have withdrawn under fire. They have signed peace treaties while they were losing in battle. They have initiated warfare many times. They have fought offensively and very far from their own borders.

2. Muslim armed forces often have defended far borders and they have invested heavily in defending their religious sites. Often they have fought as cohesive units, at least for short periods of time. Rarely have they joined with non-Muslims in waging offensive actions. They have been somewhat more willing to form coalitions with non-Muslims when they are in defensive positions and they are under duress. However, these coalitions usually have been dominated by the non-Muslim leaders and they have not been particularly effective.

3. Muslim armed forces have been willing to use every kind of weapon that was available to them in order to discourage their adversaries. These weapons have included poisons and dead animals for contaminating the water and the air and for spreading diseases, the use of phosphorous and other chemicals to incinerate their enemies, and virtually any other type of weapons that they have been able to acquire from their allies and their enemies.

4. Starting with the Prophet Muhammad himself, Muslim combatants have been willing and able to conduct offensive operations against non-Muslim armed forces far from the religious and political centers of the Muslim forces and deep into non-Muslim territories including the Far East as well as the European sub-continent.

5. Muslim armed forces have occupied distant "foreign" lands of non-Muslims for hundreds of years at a time, often adapting rather well to local customs and often without very much reliance on military violence to maintain their political control.

6. Muslim armed forces have been particularly adept at launching raids and surprise attacks (in apparent violation of some of the passages in the Qur'an), as well as envelopments and sieges of enemy defensive positions and cities. Often these operations have been directed in the field by the most senior Islamic religious leaders, starting with Muhammad. For several hundred years Muslim naval forces aggressively patrolled and controlled the Mediterranean Sea.

7. When they have been victorious in battle, Muslim forces often have been very destructive and brutal for several days against some of their captives, including non-combatant women, children, and the aged. Yet there have been many noteworthy exceptions, as presented in Chapters 3-5. Victorious Muslim forces have tended to be especially brutal against vanquished non-Muslim forces when the battles were quickly decided, rather than protracted; when the battles had been especially bloody to both sides; when they were battles of revenge; and when Muslim leaders and combatants believed that their adversaries had been excessively insulting, sacrilegious, and vicious towards Muslim combatants or civilian populations in recent campaigns. Under these circumstances and perceptions, Muslim treatment of non-Muslim POWs often was particularly ghastly. It included beheadings, ceremonial displays of decapitated leaders of the opposition forces, and the transporting of enemy body parts back to the ceremonial capitals of the Muslim forces.

8. When Muslim forces have been beaten on the battlefields, often they have done whatever was necessary in order to retreat to safe havens and to "lick their wounds" for years or even decades to come. They have almost never "fallen on their swords" out of a sense of dishonor. They have not readily and willingly been integrated into non-Muslim communities. Only rarely did they observe and honor truces and treaties that were imposed on them for more than a few years. Rarely have they accepted defeat as permanent. Rarely have they compromised and accepted non-Muslim domina-

tion of lands that they had contested. As combatants, their collective memories of insult and defeat embitter them for many generations, if not centuries on end.

SOME SUGGESTIONS FOR DEALING WITH THE QUR'AN'S PROPONENTS IN PEACE, CONFLICT, AND WAR

There are many ways in which familiarity with the Qur'an and with some aspects of popular renditions of Islamic military history can help in dealing with the Qur'an's proponents (coalitions, nations, other groups, and individuals who espouse the Qur'an and Islam as their doctrine and cause) regarding peace, conflict, and war. For convenience I will present these in categories such as diplomatic relations, international communications, preparations for armed conflict, conducting armed conflicts, dealing with prisoners, and re-establishing peaceful relations. Many of the recommendations apply across many if not all of these categories. Some of these suggestions are reinforcements for how government and military leaders are operating currently. Few of these suggestions contradict current policies, but some of them certainly go well beyond current policies in terms of advocating for greater awareness of the Qur'an and of Islamic military history as ways to help deal with the Qur'an's proponents in the future.

DIPLOMATIC RELATIONS

Provide Positive Reinforcement for Peaceful Relations Grounded on Historical Realism

This book has presented plenty of evidence that, despite the unfortunate abundance of social conflict and both civil and foreign wars in much of Islamic history and in much of the Qur'an, there is considerable precedent in both upon which to build more peaceful relations in the future. Here are some of the kinds of positive attitudes, dispositions, and measures that government and military leaders should take in dealing with proponents of the Qur'an. All of these are based on the likelihood that many of the Qur'an's proponents, from government leaders to the average women and men in the streets, villages, and hinterlands, have heard a lot more about social conflict and wars than about peace between and among nations. They need reassurances that what "was" need not be the present or the future in terms of how others regard them or deal with them.

Government and military leaders also should realize that, ever since Muhammad, Muslim leaders and armed forces often have been willing to face and fight numerically superior adversaries. Usually they have expected victory not only because the Qur'an repeatedly tells them that "Allah wills it," but also because they expected fate, sudden changes in weather, and other possible divine interventions from Allah to frustrate and confuse their adversaries enough to turn the tide of battle to the Muslims.

Leaders should not expect proponents of the Qur'an to be scared-off by threats or shows of force. Historically this has almost never happened — not during Muhammad's life, not during the 214 battles and wars from 632-1984, and not during the nine recent wars of the last twenty years that were considered in Chapter 5.

Encourage and Monitor Compliance with the Qur'an

Leaders should continually remind hostile regimes that they are aware that the Qur'an addresses issues about war and peace and that they will hold them to the most restrictive standards regarding behaviors in war. Be discreet, informed, and timely in pointing out to adversaries the ways in which their policies and actions are at odds with the Qur'an and with the more restrained behaviors of Muhammad's armies at the famous battles of Badr, Uhud, Hudaybiya, the Trench, and the occupation of Mecca. Encourage allies, neutrals, undecided regimes, and the world press to do the same thing. They should be encouraged to put subtle but fair pressure on hostile regimes to abide by the Qur'an and the most tolerant examples of Muslim warfare. For example, Muslim forces should not use disproportionate force or attack communities of non-combatants (despite some historical cases where Muslim forces did so, such as the massacre at Khaybar that is described in detail in Chapter 3). If appropriate, remind adversaries that Muhammad did not often allow his military forces to behave in these ways. Only in a few instances did Muhammad allow the mass slaughter of enemy soldiers and POWs. Much of the spirit and content of the Qur'an discourages these kinds of behaviors.

Very carefully and sensitively acknowledge some of the discrepancies between some of the Qur'an pronouncements and modern international conventions, including the ones that are endorsed by other nations whose populations, if not whose governments, are primarily Muslims. This can be done on topics such as the use of spoils of war and on efforts by adversaries to excuse or ignore their war criminals on the grounds that they were commanded by a higher authority (e.g. "Allah wills it"). However, leaders should try to do this in a way that encourages allegiance to the international standards by pointing-out that the Qur'an does not require Muslims to take spoils of war or to take prisoners. It simply allows them to do so under certain conditions. The Qur'an does not require the actual killing of disbelievers so much as it requires Muslims to use appropriate methods (that might include warfare, under certain conditions) to assure that disbelievers cease their persecution of Muslims on Muslim homelands.

Of course, along with monitoring and critiquing of Muslim adversaries, leaders should also provide reassurances that they are trying their best to avoid disturbing Islamic religious practices and are observing the sanctity of Muslim holy places and events that are not being used as covers for belligerent actions against us.

THEMES FOR INTERNATIONAL COMMUNICATIONS

Especially since the attacks on 9-11-2001, many Muslim leaders in the U.S. and elsewhere have taken to the public airwaves to tell non-Muslims that they don't know anything about the Qur'an or about the true nature of Islam, let alone have respect for them. While these often are overstatements in some ways, surely it is worthwhile to communicate to the Qur'an's proponents that many non-Muslims are trying to understand more fully the Qur'an and Islam. Respect for many aspects of the Qur'an and of Islam can grow, especially as non-Muslims see evidence that proponents of the Qur'an actually behave according to its most humane and tolerant provisions. Leaders should frequently and discreetly demonstrate that they are aware of the Qur'an's pronouncements regarding peace, conflict, and war, but that they certainly are not experts on these matters. Leaders can acknowledge that they respect the Qur'an's most tolerant pronouncements on these topics that are congruent with U.N. standards. They can announce that they encourage the Qur'an's proponents to observe the most tolerant and non-violent pronouncements in the Qur'an and indicate that efforts are being made to respect many of the Qur'an's pronouncements in their own policies and deployments, in so far as possible. For example, the Qur'an instructs its proponents to abide by their treaties with all other nations and groups, without mentioning any qualifications as to religious orientation, so long as they are not persecuting Muslims. The Qur'an also portrays peaceful relations as being far more desirable than warfare, except possibly in the event of a massive invasion of Muslim homelands by non-Muslim forces. As mentioned several times in earlier chapters, the Qur'an does <u>not</u> insist that its proponents engage in <u>military</u> jihad (i.e. warfare by established military forces) as only one of the four forms of jihad. Nor does the Qur'an insist that dying in battle against non-believers is the only way, or the best way, for believers to attain paradise. There are other ways for believers to attain paradise that are less violent and destructive than becoming a martyr in war. Reminding proponents of the Qur'an that government and military leaders are aware of these features of the Qur'an, and that these features are respected, might help to sustain peaceful relations.

There are a number of honest themes and messages that should be considered for international communications via press conferences, public speeches, and government websites.

Avoidance of Wars of Religion in U.S. History

In more than 225 years of its history, the U.S. has never engaged in wars of religion in which the motives were to eliminate a particular religion or to advance the status of one religion over another, either at home or abroad. The U.S. government and military have never attempted to convert adversaries to Christianity or to any other religion. The U.S. has had very few wars with Muslim countries. The most notable exception until recently was the so-called "war against the Barbary Pirates" more than two hundred years ago (as discussed in Chapter 5). And that encounter was relatively benign in terms of lives lost, damage to property, and disruption of world geopolitics. It had nothing to do with religious persecution. The U.S. often has been reluctant to engage in foreign wars, contrary to distorted impressions abroad. U.S. foreign wars have never been primarily in the form of a non-Muslim nation versus a Muslim nation. In WWI, for example, the United States joined the allies late in the war and did so primarily because German naval forces had been attacking U.S. merchant shipping for years. U.S. forces did not participate in the allied attacks against the Ottoman forces at the Battles of Gallipoli and the Dardanelles (as described in Chapter 4).

U.S. Government and Military Assistance to Muslim Societies

Strong cases can be made that the U.S. government often has provided financial aid, military assistance, and humanitarian aid to Muslim societies. For example, in WWII the U.S. (with the British and other Allied forces) was instrumental in freeing Morocco, Algeria, Tunisia, Libya, and Egypt from military occupation by Axis forces and in freeing Indonesia from Japanese occupation. U.S. financial and military aid occasionally assisted Turkey, Iran, and Iraq from being dominated by the Soviet Union during the "Cold War" and it was crucial in supporting some Afghanistan nationalists and tribes in their war against the Soviet occupation forces in the 1980s (as described in Chapter 5). The U.S. joined other U.N. forces in bringing an end to Serbian "ethnic-cleansing" attacks against Muslims in Croatia and Bosnia when the former state of Yugoslavia dissolved. These efforts remain crucial to the peace in that region and they probably will continue to be necessary for many more years. Leaders might remind proponents of the Qur'an that in all of these instances the U.S. government was helping societies that were predominantly Muslim gain freedom from forces that were predominantly non-Muslim. Clearly then, the U.S. was not engaging in religious persecution of Muslim societies in these campaigns. These campaigns were very costly to the U.S., they were very far from U.S. borders and included humanitarian aid to Muslim populations, and they did not lead to sustained U.S. occupation or exploitation of the liberated Muslim societies.

U.S. Laws Protect Religious Freedoms and Provide Freedom for Many Muslims

Leaders should emphasize that protections for religious freedoms abound and are long established in the U.S., going back beyond the First Amendment. "Congress shall make no law respecting an establishment of religion, or prohibiting the free exercise thereof." It can be worthwhile to explain honestly what laws like this mean, how they have been interpreted, and how they have been applied in the U.S. both to U.S. citizens, native born and naturalized, as well as to visitors, resident aliens, and visitors to the U.S. Leaders can explain clearly and often why Americans and the U.S. government try to extend these principles throughout the world. Draw attention to the fact that immigration and requested immigration to the U.S. by Muslims throughout many areas of the world has increased greatly during the past thirty years and that, despite some recent reversals since and because of 9/11, the prospects for Muslim immigration to the U.S. are strong. Muslims in the U.S. are free to return to their countries of origin. Many return to visit. Relatively few return permanently to their countries of origin. These are some of the reasons why non-native born Muslims are increasingly integrated into U.S. society.

The Increasing Muslim Population and its Integration into U.S. Institutions

As discussed in Chapter 1, the Muslim population in the U.S. has grown rapidly during the last thirty years due primarily to voluntary immigration to the U.S. from Arab states. Nearly 7,000,000 Muslims reside in the U.S., more than 500,000 in the Chicago area. Muslim mosques are found in most U.S. cities. They have been protected very well despite the international turmoil of the past few years. Muslims serve as full time employees in all U.S. government agencies and the U.S. military without violating their religious beliefs (as indicated in the case of U.S. Army Sergeant Mahmuti, earlier in this chapter). An estimated 4,000 Muslims serve in the U.S. military, which is an all-volunteer service.

EDUCATION

Educate People Worldwide about the Constraints that the Qur'an Imposes on War and the Encouragements that It Offers Regarding Peace

Certainly it will be very challenging to educate people throughout the world about the Qur'an's many constraints on war in a fair and positive way that does not inflame negative reactions. New international coalitions of organizations might be needed to do this effectively. To select from just a few of the dozens of insights that have been presented throughout this book, some of the messages to convey about the Qur'an are as follows.

- The majority of the verses in the Qur'an instruct Muslims about how to achieve individual spiritual peace. Most verses do not espouse social conflict and war between nations. Therefore the Qur'an should not be used to justify war, terror, and social conflict between nations.

- None of the people, societies, or nations that existed during Muhammad's life and during his recitation of the Qur'an exist today. Therefore, no current people, societies, governments, or nations, should be blamed for the events that are referred to in the Qur'an.

- The Qur'an does not tell its followers that they will be persecuted forever because of religion. In fact, the Qur'an often implies that Muslims will be able to cease hostilities with non-Muslims because Muslims will have succeeded in peace negotiations and in warning their adversaries to desist. The Qur'an also indicates that Muslims often have been and will be so successful in battles that their enemies will stop persecuting them.

- The Qur'an instructs its followers to accept peace offerings from adversaries.

- The Qur'an instructs its followers to send emissaries and envoys before attacking.

- The Qur'an instructs its followers not to initiate hostilities.

- The Qur'an instructs its followers to honor honorable treaties.

- The Qur'an instructs its followers to engage in defensive wars on their homelands and to protect their borders.

- The Qur'an often instructs its followers to behave according to what some Islamic scholars have called the principles of righteous intention, discrimination, proportionality, and transgression avoidance. These principles are generally compatible with some of the principles of war in many Western nations and with the spirit of many international laws, including the Geneva Conventions.

- The Qur'an does not instruct its followers to attack civilian populations, to execute, torture, and abuse enemy POWs, or to engage in violent activities such as the attacks of 9-11-2001 on the World Trade Center.

Educate People about the Historical Variability of Muslim Warfare

There are also honest and fair messages to be conveyed about Muslim military history that can be used to encourage the Qur'an's proponents to avoid the most brutal forms of violence. As a military commander at Uhud, the Trench, Hudaybiya, and the acquisition of Mecca, Muhammad did not use all means of violence possible in order to subjugate his adversaries. He did not attempt to totally rout, terrorize, and humiliate all of his adversaries. He did not order the execution of all prisoners, allow total destruction or confiscation of all of the dwellings and material possessions of all members of the adversary's communities, or force all captives into slavery. Undeniably, Muslim military history certainly has many examples of brutal and unprovoked military violence by some Muslim forces against other military forces and civilian populations, both Muslim and non-Muslim. And yet there certainly are many cases in which Muslim forces were less thoroughly destructive than they could have been. The post-war conditions that some Muslim regimes imposed on their opponents led to periods of extended absence of military warfare against their opponents and the communities that they conquered, even if the defeated people were never fully free or equal to their Muslim victors. In essence, Muslim military forces often were less destructive and vengeful than they might have been.

Educate Citizens throughout the World about Violence-Oriented Opportunists

Non-government institutions should be encouraged to alert and educate populations throughout the world, through TV, radio, and the Internet, about specific examples of misuses of the "holy books," including the Qur'an, and to misrepresentations of military history by violence-oriented opportunists and selectivists. I have called attention to some of these misrepresentations in the preceding chapters. Some of the pronouncements of Osama bin Laden and Mullah Omar certainly are among the most unfortunate examples of misuse of the Qur'an.

IF WAR BECOMES IMMINENT

If it is deemed necessary to engage in warfare against proponents of the Qur'an, government and military leaders should keep in mind the patterns that have been found in both the recent and distant history of Muslim warfare dating back to Muhammad's own record as a military commander.

- It is highly likely that significant numbers of hostile government and military leaders and combat personnel who espouse the Qur'an will be inclined to behave in accordance with the Qur'an regarding peace, conflict, and war, insofar as possible, unless they are motivated or forced to behave otherwise by their peers or they are somehow relieved of the Qur'an's constraints.

- It is highly likely that proponents of the Qur'an will be more likely to fight according to the Qur'an's constraints regarding excessive violence towards their adversaries under some conditions more than others. For example, the Qur'an is likely to have more of a constraining influence on its proponents when they are fighting for long periods of time in foreign lands that are far from their own homelands and against adversaries who do not provoke animosities or suspicions related to religion. As long as this is the case, the Qur'an's proponents are more likely to accept peace offerings, to enter into and abide by treaties, to withdraw back to their homelands without achieving victory, to desert, or to be less than steadfast and cohesive during combat.

- Conversely, the Qur'an's proponents are more likely to ignore and violate its many constraints when they are engaged in warfare against foreign invaders on Muslim homelands and close to the most sacred sites of Islam in Medina, Mecca, Jerusalem, Damascus, Istanbul, Cairo, Baghdad, Isfahan, and Kabul (as discussed in Chapter 4). The Qur'an's constraints on its proponents' use of excessive violence will diminish appreciably the longer that non-Muslim armed forces remain in and around these ancient capital cities of Muslim empires. Many of the Qur'an's proponents will become less likely to call for and abide by cease-fires and treaties, to surrender, or to disarm. They will become more willing to ignore the Qur'an's principles of righteous intention, proportionality, discrimination, and transgression avoidance. It is also highly likely that hostile military and political leaders who espouse the Qur'an will be willing to incur heavy casualties and costs until they are decisively defeated, they are victorious, their forces are outnumbered by far more than 2:1, or they are persuaded to disengage by more powerful coalitions of the Qur'an's proponents.

PREPARING MILITARY FORCES TO FIGHT HOSTILE ARMED FORCES THAT ARE PROPONENTS OF THE QUR'AN

If warfare becomes necessary, then government and military leaders should prepare combat personnel for warfare against proponents of the Qur'an in several new ways. Personnel in combat units might be alerted to expect that opposition will be particularly intense in and around Muslim holy places, especially when Muslim political and religious leaders are present. Opposition also will be especially intense whenever Muslim units are in close formations with few escape routes and many of the Muslim combat personnel can actually see their adversaries advancing overland towards them or in prepared defensive positions that appear to be vulnerable to Muslim attack by infantry and armor. These are the kinds of situations that are similar to the situations that Muslim forces faced under Muhammad at the famous battles of Badr, Uhud, the Trench, Hudaybiya, and Mecca. These are the kinds of situations that are apt to motivate Muslim combatants to fight steadfastly and cohesively.

Military leaders should be sensitive to special concerns that Muslim troops, officers, and chaplains in non-Muslim military forces might have about fighting against other Muslims (as was the case with Sergeant Mahmuti that was presented earlier in this chapter). Counseling services should be readily available, but care must be taken not to make Muslim personnel feel conspicuous even if they have some special needs.

Leaders might also consider presenting objective and informed lectures on the actual combat operations and behaviors of Muslim armed forces in the famous battles of Muhammad's life, including Uhud and Hudaybiya, in order to dispel myths about Muslim armies always using excessive violence during battles and committing war crimes against prisoners and civilians.

Although this could be very controversial, it might be appropriate to have some passages from the Qur'an (such as passages 12, 89, 97-100, 102, 108, and 109 in Chapter 2) recited to military personnel who will have direct contact with hostile Muslim combatants and civilian populations, especially if they become POWs. Passage #89 in Chapter 2 might be particularly useful because it encourages Muslims to "be careful to discriminate" by not refusing peace offers and by not using undue force against adversaries. It is repeated here for convenience:

> 89. (88/4: 94) "O ye who believe! When ye go forth (to fight) in the way of Allah, be careful to discriminate, and say not unto one who offereth you peace: 'Thou are not a believer,' seeking the chance profits of this like (so that ye may despoil him). With Allah are plenteous spoils. Even thus (as he now is) were ye before; but Allah hath since then been gracious unto you. Therefore take care to discriminate. Allah is ever Informed of what ye do."

Besides revealing what the passages do say (for example, that Muslim combatants who fight honorably are allowed to capture prisoners and take booty after the battle is won) it is also important to call attention to what the Qur'an does not say. For example, the Qur'an does not tell followers to execute POWs or to force their conversion to

Islam, contrary to rumors that might circulate among troops. However, troops also should be warned not to depend on their adversaries obeying the Qur'an in actual combat, but they should not be surprised the Qur'an is obeyed even under situations of great duress including the proverbial "heat and fog" of battle.

PREPARING COMBAT PERSONNEL TO SURVIVE AS POWs

Passages from the Qur'an that are presented in Chapter 2 show us that the Qur'an often instructs its followers on how to deal with enemy combatants who become prisoners. Government and military leaders should consider informing combat personnel about these instructions in the Qur'an and about the ways that Muslim military forces have actually treated their captives historically and in recent wars (subjects that are described in Chapters 3-5). Doing this can help combat personnel anticipate how they might be treated if they are captured by hostile Muslim forces. This can enable them to be better prepared psychologically and physically for the deprivations and humiliations of captivity.

As presented in Chapter 2, passages in the Qur'an emphasize that Muslim combatants should capture enemy combatants after the battles have been won. POWs are to be shackled and secured until Muslim leaders can decide how to deal with them. There seems to be a preference for ransoming POWs for a profit when possible. But Muslim leaders might also decide to release some POWs as a charitable gesture "for grace." They might encourage POWs to convert to Islam, without using force, and become an integral part of the Islamic community. They might even allow some POWs to remain in Muslim settlements as relatively free members so long as they pay the required taxes and are non-disruptive.

The history of Muslim warfare shows that all of these procedures often were used by Muslim leaders to process POWs. However the historical record (as recounted in Chapters 3 and 4) also shows that Muslim leaders, including Muhammad, sometimes allowed or ordered their followers to treat some of their POWs in more abusive ways that included summary executions on the battlefield and mutilations of the bodies of executed POWs. In several instances the bodies of enemy military commanders were beheaded and their heads were treated as trophies of war. Enemy captives who had been insulting towards Muslim leaders or who had been suspected of committing atrocities tended to be the ones who were executed and mutilated. Sometimes they were tortured beforehand. Therefore, as an additional precaution, military leaders might warn their combat personnel to avoid taunting or belittling their adversaries on the battlefield and, even more so, in captivity. Other procedures, including selling POWs into slavery, retaining POWs as personal slaves within Muslim communities, and using slaves as combatants in Muslim armies, sometimes occurred as a consequence of Muslim victories on the battlefield during Muhammad's life and well into the 17th century. The Qur'an does not explicitly prescribe or proscribe many of these more extreme treatments of POWs. Chapter 4 shows us that these more extreme behaviors by Muslim military forces have been relatively infrequent and that their non-Muslim adversaries also mistreated Muslim POWs in these ways with similar frequency (or even more frequently in the case of victorious Mongol armies under Genghis Khan and some of his successors).

In more recent wars and battles including the nine that were examined in Chapter 5, Muslim forces captured only small numbers of non-Muslim combatants. They treated these POWs rather well compared with historical standards. While it is still too early to provide definitive statements on these matters, it appears that all or almost all non-Muslim POWs eventually were released outright or they were exchanged for Muslim POWs. Military and government leaders might consider disseminating appropriate factual information on these matters to combat personnel several weeks before they are sent into battle so that they can prepare realistically for the contingency of becoming POWs. Useful in this regard might be the case materials in Chapter 5 about three former POWs: U.S. Air Force Colonel David Eberly, British Special Forces Sergeant Andy McNab, and U.S. Army Chief Warrant Officer Mike Durant.

Along with case materials like these on POWs, military leaders might provide combat personnel with field-tested POW support packets along with the Code of Conduct cards that are issued to them before they go into combat zones. The packets could contain plastic-coated "friendship cards" that have key passages from the Qur'an (such as passages 102, 108, and 109 in Chapter 2) in English and Arabic script or in other languages and dialects that might be appropriate. These should emphasize the humane treatment of POWs. Plastic-coated cards might also have several reassuring and polite phrases that can be spoken or displayed in Arabic or other languages by POWs to their Muslim captors.

رَعِبَادُ الرَّحْمَنِ الَّذِينَ يَمْشُونَ عَلَى الْأَرْضِ
هَوْنًا وَإِذَا خَاطَبَهُمُ الْجَاهِلُونَ قَالُوا سَلَامًا

كُلِّ الذَّبَلَاتِ الْأَكْبَرِ فِي الْعَالَمِ تَبـ
تَكُونُ أَحْسَنَ إِلَى حَنَتْ عَلَى السَّلَمِ
وَالسَّلَامُ هُمْ

رُضِّيَ عَنِ الَّذِينَ يَسْعَابَنْشُونَ مَعَ أُنَاسٍ
مُخْتَلِفِينَ وَالَّذِينَ يُجِّدُونَ عَمَلٍ صَلَاحِ
وَالَّذِينَ يَسْعَوْنَ إِلَى السَّلَمِ

Friendship Card

"I respect you, your country, and your religion. Please respect me and my religion."

"We are not harming Muslim POWs. Please do not harm us."

"Please be Merciful, as the Qur'an says."

"Thank you."

Finally, the POW support packet might also contain several miniature Qur'ans or excerpts from the Qur'an. Two of the Qur'anic passages that might be mollifying would be passages #7 and #13 in Chapter 2, when translated into Arabic or local dialects:

> 7. (53/2:224) "And make not Allah, by your oaths, a hindrance to your being righteous and observing your duty unto Him and making peace among mankind. Allah is Hearer, Knower."

> 13. (143/8:61) "And if they incline to peace, incline thou also to it, and trust in Allah. Lo! He is the Hearer, the Knower."

POWs could distribute these excerpts from the Qur'an to their captors at opportune times. Of course it is quite likely that these materials would be confiscated as booty by the Muslim captors of POWs. This might be even more beneficial to both the captors and the POWs if the captors read through the materials and contemplate them. As a precautionary note, proposals like this should be field-tested by Muslim psychologists and social scientists before they are put into practice in order to assure that they would be beneficial rather than counter-productive or even dangerous to POWs. These proposals also should be examined in the light of the Geneva Conventions on POW procedures. If they pass close scrutiny, then government and military leaders can use them to increase the likelihood that POWs will survive their captivity, remain as healthy as possible, and still remain faithful to the spirit of the Code of Conduct.

SOME STRATEGIC AND TACTICAL CONSIDERATIONS

If Muslim combatants fight strictly according to the Qur'an, they would be fighting primarily if not exclusively in their own homeland either defending their borders or trying to expel foreign forces from their homelands, particularly from Muslim holy places and residential communities in their homelands. For this reason, leaders should try to minimize placing their forces in situations like these. They should not mass their forces at the borders of Muslim nations unless they really do want their adversaries to fight aggressively at these places. Leaders also should try to cooperate with like-minded allied forces including proponents of the Qur'an in order to avoid one-on-one confrontations with hostile Muslim forces. At the same time, leaders should realize that while descriptions of battles in the Qur'an usually portray one unified Muslim military force facing only one enemy force at a time (e.g. the Medinans versus the Quraysh from Mecca), certainly there have been occasions in Muslim military history, especially in the late-middle period (1500-1920), when Muslim forces joined with non-Muslim forces and fought against coalitions of adversaries that represented several other nations and religions. In general, however, Muslim military leaders since Muhammad seem to have a great preference for fighting as one unified Muslim army or navy against only one non-Muslim army or navy at a time, in one place at a time. Therefore, strong consideration should be given to using strategies that frustrate this preference. The same can be said regarding warfare conducted at night. Few, if any, of the more than 225 battles and wars that have been analyzed in this book featured Muslim forces fighting voluntarily and effectively at night. Included here are nine of the most recent wars since 1984. Military operations against U.S. and British forces in Afghanistan and Iraq in 2003 are among them.

Through both diplomatic and military channels leaders should try to arrange to have allied forces, preferably including allies with heavy Muslim representation, ready to replace and relieve their non-Muslim troops as soon as possible after the war has been decided. Discreet efforts should be made to bring supportive and moderate Muslim nations, factions, and leaders into the allied coalition. Allies that have been most effective in the past in dealing with hostile Muslim regimes might be willing to provide relief forces that include Muslim chaplains, military, and police personnel who can provide appropriate levels of security and access to Muslim holy places in the homelands of hostile Muslim regimes.

Strategically, leaders also should anticipate that hostile Muslim combatants might use every type of weapon that is available, including poisons and chemicals. As mentioned several times in Chapters 2-5, the Qur'an does not explicitly proscribe or prescribe these kinds of weapons. Poisons and contaminated substances were significant weapons of war that were used by and against Muslims, including Muhammad (who barely survived being poisoned by Zanab after the sacking of Khaybar). The history of Muslim warfare provides few if any instances where Muslim armed forces were reluctant to use any type of weapon that was available to them in order to frustrate and weaken adversaries. Unfortunately the same thing can be said about many non-Muslim armed forces over the course of history — at least until 1946.

AN ASIDE TO OPERATIONAL UNIT COMMANDERS IN COMBAT ZONES: OVERCOMING CULTURAL RESISTANCE BY INDIGENOUS PEOPLE[16]

SOME OBSERVATIONS ABOUT CULTURE-BASED RESISTANCE

How can commanders of brigade, regiment, battalion, and company sized units that are deployed in combat zones overcome culture-based resistance by indigenous people, who are "hostiles," "friendlies," and everything in between, including undecideds and vacillators? One way to start is to distinguish culture-based resistance from other kinds of forces that can frustrate the good intentions of highly skilled field commanders.

Like all human beings everywhere, people that are indigenous members of social groups that reside in a particular geographical area that happens to become a combat zone often behave as they do because of a number of different reasons or forces, only one of which is primarily cultural. Consider an example derived from some of my experiences as an infantry, civil affairs, and ground reconnaissance officer in Viet-Nam, 1965-66, and as a sociologist who returned to Vietnam in 2000 in order to study the after effects of that war on villages I had known as a combatant. Village "V" (as I will call it for convenience and anonymity), was a traditional peasant community of about 1,200 tenant rice growers, fishermen and their families and kin groups. The commanding officer of Battalion "A" ordered that the village should be evacuated within three days so that his battalion could destroy the bunkers and tunnels that the Viet Cong had built throughout the village, without injuring the villagers. After three days, however, the villagers gave no sign of leaving the village. Why? Consider the many possible reasons why they remained there.

One reason might have been because the battalion commander's order did not get through to the *de facto* village chief, to all of the members of the council of elders who customarily decided on how to react to such an order, and to the senior males that headed each kin group. Or possibly the order was received by the chief and the council members, but they decided to wait, they could not reach consensus, or they did not understand the order — not because they resisted it. They and the villagers might have believed, mistakenly or not, that they would be captured or killed by Battalion A if they left the protective cover of their village. Possibly the Viet Cong cadre in the village had warned them about this prospect. Or the villagers might have believed that they would be attacked and killed by some other battalion, perhaps by a North Vietnamese battalion, "X," that was hidden in a densely forested ridgeline on the opposite side of the village from Battalion A, without detection by Battalion A. Another reason might be that Viet Cong cadre already had control over the village and held its elders hostage. The villagers might have been too intimidated, too sick, and too weak to evacuate the village. They might have feared they would lose their entire crop of rice, which was ripe and ready to harvest in the dry paddies, if they left, even for only a few days. Many villagers might have remained simply because they did not know where to go or how to go about it. They had never left their village before. They had heard that the war was even more dangerous everywhere else.

These are just a few of the reasons why indigenous people may or may not follow the orders of an operational commander who has their best interests in mind. These reasons might or might not have had much to do with the *culture* of the indigenous groups when we consider that many professional anthropologists consider *culture* to consist of the core beliefs, behaviors, and values of a group of people that are passed on from generation to generation through a process of social learning, imitation, and reinforcement.[17] In the case of village V, *culture-based resistance* could take a variety of forms. One form would be an unwillingness of the villagers to evacuate their village because all of the villagers had learned and internalized the belief, as they were growing up, that leaving their village would dishonor them and their ancestors who are buried there. They might have internalized this belief from passages of "holy books" that were recited to them, from lessons taught to them by their parents, revered uncles, village elders and from other sources, such as the monks at the nearby Buddhist temple. Probably they learned these beliefs from all of these sources and from many others, given that their culture was so traditional and homogenous. In any event, the villagers may have come to believe that if they evacuated their village they would be condemned to become just like the *bui doi*. These are the ghostly souls of dead thieves and prostitutes that are condemned to search forever for a final resting-place because they dishonored their villages and their ancestral burial grounds. If so, then this would exemplify the essence of *culture*. And if so, then the unwillingness of the villagers to abandon village V would constitute *cultural resistance* to the order that was issued by the commanding officer of Battalion A.

We will focus on cultural resistance in the sections that follow because many military officers and troops understandably have more difficulty detecting and dealing with this type of resistance than with the other types of problems that are identified above. These other types usually are dealt with extensively in military schools and training exercises. Additionally, cultural resistance often is harder to detect and to overcome, even for professional anthropologists, in part because its forms vary so much from one society to another and from one subcultural group to the next.

A Success Story

Let us now consider a celebrated success story of an U.S. military officer who overcame a puzzling case of cultural resistance by indigenous groups. In 1991 he was assigned responsibility for feeding and housing, aiding, and protecting some of the Kurdish tribes in northern Iraq after the formal cessation of the Kuwait Gulf War.[18] U.S. military forces and government contractors erected tent camps in the valleys beneath mountain ranges where many Kurds had fled in order to avoid reprisal attacks by Saddam Hussein's army and air forces.

Predictably the tent camps were laid out in orderly matrices of blocks of tents that were separated by evenly spaced streets. They resembled typical U.S. military tent camps in Virginia in WWII, or in the U.S. Civil War, for that matter. After several weeks of waiting, the Kurds still had not come down out of the hills to occupy the tent camps and to benefit from the security and the massive amounts of food and medical supplies that were available to them.

Perplexed by this lack of a positive response by the Kurds, the U.S. commander in charge of the relocation asked a Kurdish-speaking Turkish-American staff officer to help him understand the mindset and culture of the tribesmen. The staff officer went into one of the tribal camps in the hills and found a Kurdish schoolteacher who was willing to serve as what anthropologists sometimes refer to as a "culture informant" — someone who knows both the "inside" and the "outside" of a culture well enough to be able to help outsiders understand some of its core elements. The schoolteacher was willing to help the U.S. commander gain some insight into the thinking of the tribal chiefs and into how the Kurdish culture operates. She explained that the most powerful tribal chiefs will not make themselves known to you. They will not come "down" to you. Rather, you must go "up" and find them on their own terrain. You must establish rapport with them on their own terms. The U.S. commander patiently began doing just these things. Slowly he was able to gain the trust of the Kurdish chiefs and their people. He learned that these Kurdish tribes traditionally live in convoluted clusters of shelters that are arrayed around the residences of the chiefs of different kin groups according to a complex status hierarchy that would be unfathomable to outsiders without access to cultural informants. He learned that he should allow the Kurds to re-construct the tent camps in their own fashion, according to their own "culture maps," rather than try to force them into the linear tent camps that the allies had built for them in the valleys. By doing this the Kurds would preserve their traditional sense of order, place, and internal security. They would gain a sense of personal and communal ownership of the camps. Even then, with these insights and the changes that followed, it was many months before all of the tribesmen relocated into their new tent camps in the valley.

Surely a case like this one shows us the value that patient and astute "culture-sensing," combined with cultural sensitivity, can have for operational success of missions in combat zones that contain many indigenous people. Anthropologists often tell us that culture-sensing is an arduous but fascinating process that is part of what they refer to as the "anthropological perspective."

ACQUIRING AN ANTHROPOLOGICAL PERSPECTIVE

Without realizing it, the field commander acquired a rudimentary anthropological perspective on the Kurdish tribes. This is similar to what anthropologists, especially ethnographers, must acquire whenever they try to understand the deep patterns of culture in isolated, traditional societies such as the !Kung of the Kalahari Desert and the Aborigines in New Zealand, whose customs and ways of thinking might seem to be hopelessly undecipherable to many outsiders. Acquiring an anthropological perspective can make it easier to deal with almost all indigenous people, except perhaps those who suffer from severe mental illness or those whose society has suffered a profound catastrophe such as a devastating earthquake or widespread genocide. This perspective can even be useful in dealing with allies and with one's own troops and government workers who were raised in societies whose culture and subculture groups are very different from the primary culture of one's own nation. Yet it is also true that an anthropological perspective is not a panacea for many of the problems faced by unit commanders in the field, especially the necessity of finding and destroying enemy forces as expeditiously as possible. There is no doubt that advanced warfighting techniques and abundant resources, rather than an anthropological perspective, will be a much more decisive factor in dealing with enemy combatants in highly indoctrinated and disciplined military units that are closely controlled by their superiors. But in peacekeeping missions and in situations other than conventional warfare, an anthropological perspective can be very useful.

Acquiring this perspective takes time and patience, even for highly trained anthropologists who spend their professional careers trying to understand one or two native societies or a few subcultures in modern societies. Often they have had at least three years of graduate school in ethnographic theory, methods and area studies. Yet it still takes them more than a year of full "immersion" in a remote indigenous society before they get enough of a sense of its culture that they can publish their insights in scholarly journals. Even then, they often focus on a few specific aspects of the society, such as family structure, food gathering techniques, or beliefs about outsiders, the weather, or warfare, rather than try to understand everything about the society. Fortunately there are some procedures that you can use, as unit commanders in combat zones, that can help you and your forces gain enough of an anthropological perspective to be able to reduce some forms of cultural resistance. Besides, as a field commander, you are not trying to become a professional anthropologist. Probably you are "only" trying to complete your assigned mission as professionally as possible.

SOME PROCEDURES THAT CAN REDUCE CULTURAL RESISTANCE

First, ask yourself, "Why are 'they' (the indigenous people) behaving like 'this' in ways that might be dictated by their culture, rather than because of other things such as 'weird' individual idiosyncrasies of their leaders, external threats, sickness, ignorance, xenophobia, or disdain towards outsiders?"

Second, ask other informed and trustworthy people the same

question. Ask others who might be able and willing to serve as intermediaries and as culture informants (not to be confused with spies or intelligence agents). The U.S. commander in northern Iraq used the Kurdish schoolteacher as an intermediary. Often a person who can be a useful intermediary is not able to serve as well as a cultural informant. Usually the most insightful culture informants are people who were born and raised as a member of the indigenous population, in the same culture area. They were "insiders." But it is even better if they are not *just* insiders. It is even better if they have lived elsewhere and gained familiarity with several other societies, including modern nation states such as the U.S. and members of the European Union. Besides knowing several languages, these kinds of people are more likely to be able to function simultaneously both as insiders and outsiders to the indigenous culture that is of interest. They are likely to know more about why the indigenous people believe and behave as they do. And they are more likely to know how to explain these insights to you.

Third, be willing to experiment a little and to use trial and error until you gain the insights that you need. Often it takes trial and error and considerable experimentation until you can identify the intermediaries who can find trustworthy and talented culture informants who will not jeopardize their own security, your security, and the integrity of your mission. And of course it is important to assure that intermediaries and culture informants are not misused as spies.

Fourth, don't overlook the possible value of interpreters who are assigned to your units as intermediaries or as culture informants, especially if they understand the nuances of local dialects and customs. Keep sifting through the interpreters who are available to your unit until you find those who can interpret the native culture as well as the language.

Fifth, consider requesting that at least one trustworthy allied officer who has familiarity with the indigenous people is assigned to your unit long enough to help you gain a better understanding of the "locals." At the same time, however, do not assume that decidedly cosmopolitan or elitist allied officers who have become thoroughly "Westernized" will be able to provide many insights into the culture of the indigenous people. If they once had insights into the local culture, they might well have lost them in the process of becoming "professional" military and government officers.

Sixth, consider conferring with mature and trustworthy anthropologists who have established their expertise in understanding the indigenous people. It is true that many anthropologists, especially those who are still in the early phase of their careers, are reluctant to serve as consultants to military units and to government agencies. Often this reluctance stems from their general distrust of military institutions in modern societies and their sense that anthropology must remain a "pure" science of human cultures, rather than an application of scientific knowledge to those cultures. On the other hand, mature anthropologists who also have had positive experiences in military and public service can be valuable consultants who will help you find intermediaries and culture informants even if they cannot serve in those capacities themselves. Even when this is not the case, their published ethnographies and monographs on the indigenous people in your combat zone can be very useful sources of insights. Published materials can be identified quickly through Internet search engines on your laptop computer and they can be purchased readily through commercial Websites.

Seventh, if time permits, once you have identified the probable forms of culture-based resistance, try to reduce that resistance on a small scale, using one or two pilot projects, before you try them on a larger scale. For example, the U.S. commander in northern Iraq focused on getting one Kurdish tribe at a time to reconstruct one tent camp at a time. When the first test case succeeded, the commander cautiously extended the program to another tribe, rather than risk failure by assuming that all tribes would respond the same way to his new initiative.

APPLICATIONS TO OPERATIONS IN THE MIDDLE EAST?

As of the time of this writing, field operations by Coalition forces in Afghanistan and Iraq are in a state of flux. Considerable success in the first months of the occupations has been tempered by some highly publicized setbacks since then. Controversy and heated debates abound. Not all of these setbacks can be attributed to culture-based resistance by indigenous people. Nor is it possible to determine how much of culture-based resistance is attributable to deeply held beliefs that originate out of the Qur'an, the Hadith, or any other single source. Nonetheless, here are some tentative suggestions for unit commanders in the field that are derived from an anthropological perspective. Hopefully these suggestions can help reduce culture-based resistance by some of the indigenous groups in these countries and in other countries with predominantly Muslim populations in the Middle East.

Attitudes Can Be As Important As Behaviors

The basic starting attitudes that your forces hold towards indigenous groups can be as important as their subsequent behaviors towards them. Often, perceptions about an outsider's general attitude towards others are more important than how that person actually behaves in the presence of others. Therefore it is important to adopt an attitude of cultural sensitivity and respect towards individual members of an indigenous society and to their culture as a whole — not just behave that way. Insult comes easily in many cultures and subcultures in the Middle East. Any perception or misperception of mockery, ridicule, or "Western" superiority on your part or the part of your troops can be forever damning. Unfortunately, appropriate ways of projecting an attitude of respect vary somewhat from one society to another in the Middle East, but often they are quite different than in Western societies. Shaking hands and making sustained eye contact is not as widely accepted in some Middle Eastern societies as it is in Western societies. This is particularly true in rural areas and when people of unequal social statuses are meeting for the first time in public places. At the same time, be prepared that locals might try to get much closer (face-to-face) during personal conversations with outsiders as a way of getting acquainted. "Conversational distance" customarily is closer in some Middle Eastern groups than in many Western societies.

Respect The Importance Of Modesty And Subtlety
In Islamic Cultures

Try to discourage troops from eating and playing in the presence of locals. Discourage troops from removing any personal or military equipment or clothing in the presence of locals, particularly around schools, mosques, or residences that contain women and children. Sometimes doing so is misinterpreted as "undressing" in preparation for sexual activities. Also discourage troops from revealing their skin other than on their hands and faces, and from displaying "muscles," tattoos, body piercings, and adornments. Consider whether you should encourage troops who are required to be in public places around local people to "wash" their hands and faces frequently with water, sand, or other materials in order to signify that they value personal cleanliness.

Distinguish Between Public And Private Situations

Attitudes and behaviors witnessed in public places can be far more embarrassing and aggravating to some indigenous groups than when they are witnessed in private settings. Therefore it is advisable to try to take advantage of opportunities for voluntary contact with locals, especially when it occurs at safe distances from your own defensive positions, in comfortable, fairly private places rather than at large, open, public places such as public parks and highway intersections. Do not allow troops to expose locals to sensationalistic, erotic, and pornographic material, or to alcoholic beverages or drugs of any sort, including prescription drugs, even if these kinds of materials are available to the locals in their own marketplaces. Understand that the widespread availability of digital cameras, and video cameras, cell phones, recording machines and access to the Internet can turn "private" events and encounters into inflammatory worldwide "public" spectacles within a matter of a few hours.

Encourage Subdued Rather Than Demonstrative Behaviors

In keeping with widespread customs in much of the Middle East that are reinforced repeatedly in the Qur'an and the Hadith, encourage your forces to be rather subdued but pleasant whenever they are visible to indigenous people. Discourage them from being overly affective and demonstrative. Gesturing with arms and feet towards locals or towards other troops is likely to be misinterpreted and despised by locals. Show authority and respect through a firm, but measured professional presence. Do not greet locals too enthusiastically. Avoid needless insults by removing gloves, sunglasses and jewelry. Avoid pointing with fingers or with feet. Do not allow troops to use their feet to gesture or draw maps. Discourage troops from using their left hands, if possible, in public, because the left hand often is associated with personal hygiene for excretory functions in some societies in the Middle East. Be very discreet about personal hygiene and bodily functions. Avoid witnessing locals when they are performing personal hygiene.

Try To Accommodate The Status And Gender Expectations Of "Locals," Insofar As Possible

Generally, many indigenous groups in the Middle East frown upon social interactions in public between people who are perceived to be of unequal social status. One implication of this is that, if it is necessary to conduct body searches of sheiks, females, or other locals in special statuses, the searches should be conducted as quickly, privately, and discreetly as possible by people of similar status (and gender). This is even more important when locals with special social status must be arrested and detained.

If Physical Contact Is Necessary

Forceful arrests, inspections, or "take-downs" of locals should be limited to young males, if possible. These should be conducted out of public sight, if possible, and they should not involve kicking, mocking, or blindfolding of the detainees unless blindfolding is absolutely necessary for security purposes.

If Armed Conflict Is Necessary

Recall from earlier chapters of this book that "proportionality" is one of the four key principles of warfare in Islam. With this in mind, if it becomes necessary to use weapons, consider using weapons that dispense water, sticky foam, lubricants, or non-lethal projectiles rather than metal projectiles. Doing so will not only save lives, but it will tend to temper the reactions of some locals by demonstrating to them a sense of moderation. However, if lethal force becomes necessary, it should be delivered as quickly, discreetly, and conclusively as possible. Do not broadcast it by allowing unauthorized photographs or media coverage. Immediately remove POWs, casualties, and KIAs to safer locations, consistent with accepted local customs, if possible. At the same time, keep in mind that local customs often require the closest relatives of the deceased to prepare the body and to bury or dispose of it within a matter of hours or one day, at most. Protests can escalate into mob violence when these customs are violated. As shown many times in earlier chapters of this book, although prisoners sometimes are detained for years, there is a longstanding tradition in many Muslim societies for prisoners to be released, exchanged for other prisoners, or ransomed within a few weeks. Many indigenous people will hold these expectations of you as a unit commander if they believe that you authorized the capture of their own relatives. They can become very troublesome if their expectations are not met within a few weeks.

These, then, are just a few of the possible suggestions to be derived from applying an anthropological perspective to various forms of cultural resistance in combat zones in the Middle East. Fortunately, it seems as though many of these suggestions already are being observed by many members of the Coalition forces. Yet it is also abundantly clear that lapses have occurred. Hopefully they will not be repeated in future military and government operations.

ENDING BATTLES AND WARS AND RE-ESTABLISHING A DURABLE PEACE

As mentioned several times already in this book, government and military leaders should keep in mind that the Qur'an does not have many passages that deal directly with how battles and wars should be concluded or with how peace should be re-established between Muslim and non-Muslim nations. The paucity of directions in the Qur'an on these topics potentially can be beneficial to government and military leaders who deal with proponents of the Qur'an. This is because, while the Qur'an does not offer much guidance on these matters, it also does not impose many constraints upon Muslims who are inclined to end battles and wars and enter into honorable and equitable peace treaties. Mainly the Qur'an prohibits its followers from calling-out for peace while they are winning on the battlefield but before they have achieved a decisive victory, and before they have retaliated for past damages and injustices to the point that they will no longer be persecuted because of their religion. Regarding treaties, the Qur'an does not portray treaties as being permanent solutions for attaining everlasting peace among nations. Treaties are temporary stopgaps that Muslims should enter into only for honorable purposes, to reduce religious persecution and to enhance the likelihood of a period of relative peace that lasts several years. Treaties should not be used to jockey for more favorable advantage before war erupts. Muslims are warned to be suspicious of the motives of their treaty partners and to break treaties with partners whom they suspect of treachery.

Therefore, government and military leaders should anticipate that hostile Muslim forces might withdraw from battles, surrender, or behave in a variety of other ways that will essentially end a particular battle without necessarily ending the war. The "war" might or might not end formally, with a written peace treaty; but the hostilities might well continue on indefinitely. It might be wise for government and military leaders to be prepared to refresh and renegotiate peace treaties every four or five years. Projecting from the historical record of Muslim warfare and diplomacy, peace treaties with Muslim leaders are more effective in sustaining a modicum of peace for at least several years when they are entered into voluntarily and the provisions are mutually beneficial both politically and economically. The viability of treaties and truces with Muslim leaders often has been diminished by the presence of non-Muslim military, "peacekeeping," and police forces in Muslim lands before, during, and after the peace negotiations. Said another way, peace negotiations and treaties with Muslim leaders, just as with non-Muslim leaders, are more likely to prevent future wars to the extent that they are based on mutual understanding rather than on military force alone. This insight is hardly original. It has been expressed by many intelligent and compassionate people over the years. Among these people was a rather eccentric theoretical physicist who had no experience as a government or military leader but who cared deeply about the fate of humankind.

"Peace cannot be kept by force. It can only be achieved by understanding."[19]

---

[1] Adam Davidson, "Loves Microsoft, Hates America." *The Sunday New York Times Magazine*, March 9, 2003, p. 20. Reporter Adam Davidson witnessed this exchange between three educated Jordanians in Amman, Jordan, February 2003. They were in a restaurant discussing the Qur'an and their personal dispositions about waging violent jihad against U.S. soldiers in their country or on their way to Iraq.

[2] "Anti-American Sentiment Grows in Philippines." *Los Angeles Times*, February 27, 2003, p. 13. According to this article, this sentiment is widespread among the 95% of Jolo Island's inhabitants that are Tausig, an Islamic tribe that fought aggressively against the Spanish colonizers, the American "liberators," in the early 1900s, and the Japanese Occupation forces in the 1940s.

[3] James Risen, "Voice Heard on New Tape Might be bin Laden's." *The New York Times.* November 13, 2002. p.1.

[4] "Bush Slips, Bin Laden Gains in Poll." *The Providence Journal*, June 4, 2003, p. A4 (quoting from *The Washington Post*).

[5] Personal e-mail correspondence with a career Marine Corps NCO, Gy/Sgt. Julio Chang, who served six months as a security guard over Taliban prisoners at Guantanamo Bay in 2002.

[6] Dana Priest and Barton Gellman, "Terrorism Detainees Face Harsh Treatment." *The Washington Post.* December 26, 2002. p. 1.

[7] Eric Schmidt, "Paratrooper from New Jersey Dies in Afghan Firefight." *The New York Times*, December 22, 2002, p. 8.

[8] Eric Schmitt, "Paratrooper from New Jersey Dies in Afghan Firefight." *The Sunday New York Times.* December 22, 2002, p. 6.

[9] "Rebel Fighting Leaves 40 Taliban Dead." *The Providence Journal.* June 6, 2003, p. A8 (quoting *The New York Times*).

[10] On this point, I hope that readers understand clearly by now that I have not tried to address the subject of the moral integrity of the Qur'an or of Islam in this book.

[11] John Sack, "Anaconda." *Esquire.* August 2002, pp. 135-136.

[12] *The Wall Street Journal*, Monday, September 17, 2002, p. A5.

[13] These are the kinds of units that were the targets of U.S. "battle swarm" tactics in Afghanistan, as described in *The New York Times Sunday Magazine*, December 9, 2001, pp. 56-57.

[14] Although there are only a few passages like this in the entire Qur'an, I cannot help but wonder if these passages have been taken by proponents of the Qur'an, such as Osama bin Laden, to justify suicide bombings in non-Muslim countries.

[15] See the passages #74 and #75 in Chapter 2 for examples of possible encouragements to Muslims to persecute some, but not all, Jews and Christians by waging war against them because of refusal to convert to Islam, until they "pay the tribute readily" and are "brought low."

[16] This section is informed by personal conversations that I have had with several distinguished military officers who had direct experience dealing with Islamic military and political leaders in the field in Bosnia, Iraq, Somalia, and other places. I am especially indebted to General Anthony C. Zinni, USMC (Ret.) for his conversations with me on these matters. Errors in fact and interpretations are mine alone.

[17] Peacock, 1986, p. 7; Lenski and Nolan, 1999, p. 14.

[18] This case is based on my conversation with retired General Anthony C. Zinni, USMC, about his personal experiences, for which I am very grateful. Also see Chris Seiple's account of these events in his book, *The U.S. Military/NGO Relationship in Humanitarian Interventions*, pp. 21-62.

[19] Nobel laureate Albert Einstein. "Peace," as quoted in George Seldes (ed.), *The Great Quotations*. NY: Simon and Schuster, Inc. 1972. p. 719.

كُلُّ الدِّيَانَاتِ الكُبْرَى فِي العَالَمِ قَـدْ
تَكُونُ أَحْسَنَ إِلَى حَدٍّ بُعِثَتْ عَلَى السَّلْمِ
وَالتَّفَاهُمِ .

"The great religions of the world
would be much greater if they brought us
more peace and understanding."

Istanbul residents, many of them new arrivals in this 10-million city which gets 200,000 migrants from the countryside annually, crowd a street lined with street vendors in downtown Eminonu on May 19, 1996. Despite the crowding, people of different ages, genders, religions, and ethnicities interact peacefully. (AP Photo/Burhan Ozbilici)

EPILOGUE:

TOWARDS PEACE
AND UNDERSTANDING

"The great religions of the world would be much greater
if they brought more peace and understanding to us
along with spiritual guidance and hope for salvation."[1]

"At a time when foundational assumptions of all kinds, including religious ones, are underwriting the self-righteousness, triumphalism and contempt for the Other that threaten the world with mass violence, the urgent need is for nations—and especially for religions—to re-examine those assumptions in the light of what they lead to, and where necessary to correct them. Jewish settlers who invoke a divine sanction for a claim to disputed land have this obligation. Roman Catholics who put clerical power above the safety of children have this obligation. Hindus who justify a nuclear threat in the language of apocalypse have this obligation. And so do Muslims when suicidal murderers act in the name of God."[2]

For the moment, let us assume that the preceding quote by James Carroll is correct: that at least a few of the "foundational assumptions" of all contemporary religions are "underwriting the self-righteousness, triumphalism, and contempt" that "threaten the world with mass violence." What can we do about these problems?

Admittedly, I am not an expert on the "foundational assumptions" of contemporary religions. And yet, I feel obliged to end this book by suggesting some ways that all of us — not just government and military leaders — can help reduce unintended adverse consequences of some aspects of contemporary religions, including Christianity, Judaism, and Islam. I do this while realizing fully that some people from very different religious and political orientations probably can take offense at one or more of the following suggestions, especially if they have not read this book with an open mind.

357

SOME WAYS TO REDUCE RELIGION-BASED MASS VIOLENCE, SELF-RIGHTEOUSNESS, TRIUMPHALISM, AND "CONTEMPT FOR THE OTHER"

FOR ALL OF US

First, we should try harder to realize that peace, conflict, terror, and war existed among many human societies before the major world religions emerged and that they have often occurred since then quite independently of the major world religions.

Second, we should try harder to realize that all of the major world religions originated long ago in types of human societies that were very different from the majority of the societies in the world today. All of these religions are struggling to adjust to contemporary challenges from within and among societies. Admittedly, some religions are struggling more than others. Rather than disparage them or ignore them, we should try to encourage them to adjust in ways that will contribute to peace, understanding, and an adequate standard of living for all people in the world — not just their own members.

Third, all of us can try a little harder to accept the fact that the major religions of the world are not going to disappear in our lifetimes and that billions of people are going to continue to be influenced by the major religions of the world. Therefore, as "citizens of the world," we should try a little harder to understand the world's religions and the behaviors of their proponents. Hopefully, this book can help in this regard.

Fourth, all of us can try a little harder to realize that all major ideologies and religions have some self-righteous and often ignorant proponents who try to advance their own beliefs despite the costs to others. We should not stereotype ideologies and religions based on the behaviors and statements of their most extreme proponents, or those of their most extreme opponents.

Fifth, we should try harder to realize how all of the major religions and their "holy books" have contributed in some ways to peace, understanding, and adequate living standards for their members, rather than just focus upon the excesses, errors, and adverse consequences of the religions and their holy books. Hopefully, this book has helped in this regard.

Sixth, we should realize that government and military leaders alone cannot solve all of the problems of mass violence, self-righteousness, triumphalism, and "contempt for the other" that exist in the world today. We should also admit that government and military leaders are not necessarily the major sources of these problems although, over the course of human history, some government and military leaders certainly have created more of these problems than they have solved. Surely, there is no need to name names and provide examples at this point. Rather, these problems will require concerted efforts by informed and committed individuals and groups in all of the institutions within and across human societies including families, schools, communities, religions, and international organizations.

For Non-Muslims

First, try harder to realize that all ideologies and religions — not just Islam — have been malpracticed at times by some of their proponents, and particularly by opportunists.

Second, try harder to acknowledge that historically (as shown in Chapters 3-5) some Muslim leaders, regimes, sects, societies, and empires have been much more peaceful and tolerant than others in their relations with non-Muslims. Not surprisingly, these more peaceful Muslim entities often have been more concordant with the spirit and content of the Qur'an when it is taken as a whole.

Third, try harder to realize the special predicament of many Muslims, especially those who were born Muslim, and try to sympathize with them rather than ridicule and ostracize them. Theirs is a particularly demanding and absolutist religion. For many of them the Qur'an is the final, unalterable, and complete "word of God." For them the Qur'an reveals the one, single "Straight Path" that must be followed religiously, each day, in order for them to gain eternal paradise. Unfortunately, the Qur'an also reveals that they will be condemned to hell forever — *if* they fail to follow the one Straight Path. That Straight Path does *not* require them to engage in violence and warfare against non-Muslims except under the most extreme circumstances and under some very strict constraints. This is a singularly compelling reason why non-Muslims should try harder to understand the Qur'an and Islam. It is also a compelling reason to sympathize with Muslims who try to live according to the constraints of the Qur'an, rather than condemn them here on earth. The Straight Path that has been laid out in front of them is a very difficult one, indeed. What is more, their Straight Path need not conflict with the paths of non-Muslims. Non-Muslims can try harder to assure that their own paths do not interfere with the Straight Path of Islam.

Fourth, try harder to understand that, as shown repeatedly in this book, the Qur'an does not encourage or allow Muslims to engage in violence against non-Muslims except under a few rather specific conditions. As a community (*umma*), but not as individuals, the Muslim community is required to use violence in the form of warfare, as a last resort, in order to defend the community against non-Muslims who repeatedly interfere with Muslims practicing their religion. This one situation is most consistently identified in the Qur'an as requiring warfare on the part of the Muslim community against non-Muslims.

Fifth, try harder to avoid putting Muslims in the situation (just identified) that requires the Muslim community to engage in warfare.

Sixth, try harder to allow Muslim people to create Muslim governments, societies, and nations that are of their own choosing, regardless of the economic and political systems that they choose, and independent of outside influence, so long as they do not intentionally, directly, and significantly threaten many people in other nations.

Seventh, try harder to enable Muslims of different social classes and ideologies to interact with non-Muslims of different social classes and ideologies in equitable and non-threatening ways, especially in non-Muslim environments. Make it easier for Muslims to see for themselves those non-Muslims and those often understated elements in non-Muslim societies that embrace modesty, self-restraint, concern for the welfare of others, non-violence, understanding, and peace.

FOR MUSLIMS

First, try harder to understand and acknowledge that there are some ambiguities, if not omissions and oversights, in all ideologies, religions, and "holy books," including Islam and the Qur'an. Recognizing that ambiguities exist in holy books does not invalidate those books or make them less useful. Ambiguities can encourage people to think and feel more deeply, and to be less self-righteous, triumphal, and contemptuous of other people. Ambiguities can discourage violence and war — if they are allowed to do so.

Second, try harder to be a little more circumspect about any and all human beings alive today who try to convince you that your religion and its holy books demand that you or other Muslims behave violently against non-Muslims. Closer examination of your religion and its holy books might reveal some ambiguities and quite a few constraints about when, where, how, and why violence can be used against others.

Third, try harder to at least consider the possibility that the Prophet Muhammad went through many changes after witnessing his first revelation on Mt. Hira. At times he was a rather peaceful man and he promoted peaceful relations with non-Muslims. At other times this was less true. Nonetheless, in the battles that he led, Muhammad often could have been much more violent, punitive, and destructive towards his adversaries. Muhammad was less violent and bellicose than were many of the caliphs, sultans, and imams who followed him. It is also true that some of the most distinguished leaders of Islam over the centuries have been as steadfast in avoiding war and in fostering peace as was Muhammad — if not even more so.

Fourth, try harder to realize that while the Qur'an's messages are considered complete and eternal, the Qur'an's organization has been altered from time to time by very distinguished imams and scholars of Islam. Currently the Qur'an is organized mainly according to the length of the suras, from longest to shortest, although there are some exceptions. In the future the Qur'an might be re-organized and recited in other ways that can be very revealing, such as by the historical chronology of the suras, or by certain topics, such as instructions for making peace or for waging war. Doing so might be very worthwhile. Furthermore, no verse in the Qur'an explicitly prohibits reciting it or re-organizing it in other ways.

Fifth, try harder to consider the possibility that the content and the intent of Allah's revelations to Muhammad evolved between the time of the first and the last revelations. Consider the possibility that Allah's revelations to Muhammad became more tolerant and encouraging, rather than demanding, as Muhammad and his followers gained fuller understanding of the recitations and as they demonstrated increased understanding of the Straight Path.

Sixth, try harder to consider the possibility that the Qur'an and Islam are primarily guides to you as Muslims for finding *spiritual* peace. They also might provide more guidance to you on how to behave towards other Muslims than towards non-Muslims. Perhaps the Qur'an is somewhat less complete as a guide to relationships between Muslim societies and non-Muslim societies. If so, then additional sources of guidance might be appropriate for contemporary international relations among Muslim and non-Muslim groups and nations.

Seventh, try harder to realize that while the Qur'an certainly gives the Muslim community (*umma*), rather than individual Muslims, the right to defend itself against outsiders who interfere with the practice of Islam, it does not unequivocally demand that Muslims convert to Islam all human beings throughout the world. Also, try harder to acknowledge that only one of the forms of *jihad* requires military warfare by the Muslim community and that military *jihad* can only be authorized by the Muslim community under very limited conditions.

Eighth, try harder to acknowledge that Islam has already spread throughout the world (as described in Chapter 1). Muslim people now live voluntarily and quite freely in all continents and in many nations of the modern world. Islam already *is* a "world" religion, and it will continue to grow as a world religion without having to rely on warfare and forced conversions.

Ninth, try harder to acknowledge that there are many compatibilities between Islamic and non-Islamic principles of world order, as well as warfare, such as righteous intent, proportionality, discrimination, and transgression avoidance. Try to add to these compatibilities. Placing more emphasis on international peace, understanding, and adequate living standards for all people would be worthy additions.

Finally, try harder to appreciate the fact that many Muslims and non-Muslims, including the author of this book, are trying very hard to find better ways to foster peace and understanding across all religions, groups, and nations. Please try to forgive us for any oversights and ambiguities.

"Blessed are those who communicate with others
who are unlike them, those who do good works,
those who make peace."

---

[1] Anonymous, 2003.

[2] James Carroll's review of Seyyed Hossein Nasr, "The Heart of Islam." *The New York Times Book Review*, Sunday, September 7, 2002, p. 23.

APPENDIX A:
214 MUSLIM BATTLES

Battle #	Place name	Year begun	Attacker	Outcome
84	Hira	633	Muslims	win
11	Ajnadain	634	Muslims	win
60	Damascus I	635	Muslims	win
150	Pella	635	Muslims of Walid	win
207	Yarmuk River	636	Muslims of Walid	win
88	Jalula	637	Muslims	win
89	Jerusalem VI	637	Muslims	win
96	Kadisiya	637	Muslims	win
15	Aleppo	638	Muslims	win
19	Al-Fustat	641	Muslims	win
139	Nihawand	641	Persians	lose
17	Alexandria II	642	Muslims	win
197	Tripoli I	643	Muslims	win
122	Lycia	655	Egyptian Muslim navy	win
40	Basra	656	Caliph Ali's Muslims	win
178	Siffin	657	Muslim rebels in Syria	draw
54	Constantinople III	673	Caliph Muawiyah	lose
100	Kerbela	680	Arab Muslims	lose
50	Carthage III	698	Muslims	win
94	Kabul I	709	Arab Muslims	win
58	Covadonga	711	Muslims	lose
163	Rio Barbate	711	Moors	win
55	Constantinople IV	717	Muslims	lose
195	Toulouse I	721	Franks	win
196	Tours	732	Moors	lose
99	Kashgar	736	Tsung and Chinese	win
6	Acroinum	739	Muslims	lose
208	Zab al Kabir	750	Abbasid Muslims	win
81	Heraclea-Pontica	806	Muslims	win
22	Amorium	838	Muslims	win
169	Samosata	873	Byzantines	win
28	Apulia	875	Byzantines	win
189	Taormina	902	Moors	win
74	Erzurum	928	Byzantines	win
130	Melitene II	934	Byzantines	win
180	Simancas	934	Spaniards	win

Attacked	Outcome	Congruence with the Qur'an
Persians	lose	Muslims invade Persia, extract tribute
Byzantines	lose	Muslims invade
Byzantines	lose	Muslims invade Syria and win decisively
Byzantines	lose	Muslims invade and rout enemy
Byzantines	lose	Muslims invade and move on to Damascus
Persians	lose	Muslims invade Persia
Sophronius and residents	lose	Muslims invade city
Persians	lose	Muslims massacre survivors, behead Rustam, sack city
Syrians	lose	Muslims invade Syria
Byzantines	lose	Muslims invade Egypt
Muslims of Omar	win	Muslims invade and conquer
Byzantines	lose	Muslims invade, but allow a truce with provisions congruent with the Qur'an
Byzantines	lose	Muslims invade Tripoli, siege and kill many.
Byzantine navy	lose	undetermined
Muslim rebels in Basra	lose	(Civil war) Suppress dissent, but kill some POWs
Muslims of Ali	draw	(Civil war) Famous truce based on the presence of the Qur'an
Byzantines	win	Muslims invade but fail in five year siege
Persian Muslims	win	(Civil war) Controversial "civil war" that starts the Shite-Sunni split
Byzantines	lose	Muslims invade and destroy city
Afghan tribes	lose	Muslims invade Afghanistan
Spaniards	win	Muslims invade, attack, but are thrown back
Visigoths	lose	Moors invade Spain, win battle, behead some POWs
Byzantines	win	Muslims invade but fail again
Moors	lose	Muslims invade France, plunder and slay city dwellers before losing
Charles Martel and Franks	win	Muslims invade, plunder and enslave before battle; winners massacre many POWs
Arab Muslims	lose	Muslims invade China but are repulsed
Byzantines	win	undetermined
Ommiad Muslims	lose	(Civil war) Power shifts from Damascus to Baghdad
Byzantines	lose	Muslims invade, attack, force humiliating peace
Byzantines	lose	Muslims massacre the garrison
Muslims	lose	undetermined
Muslim garrison	lose	undetermined
Byzantines	lose	Moors invade Sicily, burn city
Muslim garrison	lose	undetermined
Muslims	lose	undetermined
Moors	lose	undetermined

Battle #	Place name	Year begun	Attacker	Outcome
210	Zamora	939	Moors	lose
48	Candia I	960	Byzantines	win
7	Adana	964	Byzantines	win
16	Aleppo-Antioch	969	Byzantines	win
61	Damascus II	976	Byzantines	win
151	Peshawar	1001	Persian Muslims	win
184	Somnath	1024	Persian Muslims	win
140	Nishapur	1038	Seljuk Muslims	win
126	Manzikert	1071	Byzantines	lose
194	Toledo I	1085	Spaniards	win
209	Zallaka	1086	Spaniards	lose
85	Huesca	1096	Spaniards	win
24	Antioch I	1097	Crusaders	win
191	Tarsus	1097	Crusaders	win
30	Ashkelon I	1099	Crusaders	win
90	Jerusalem VII	1099	Crusaders	win
131	Melitene III	1100	Crusaders	lose
71	Eregli I	1101	Crusaders	lose
72	Eregli II	1101	Crusaders	lose
132	Mersivan	1101	Crusaders	lose
159	Ramleh I	1102	Egyptian Muslims	lose
153	Philomelion	1116	Byzantines	win
171	Saragossa I	1118	Spaniards	win
25	Antioch II	1119	Muslims	win
145	Ourique	1139	Portugal	win
66	Edessa II	1144	Muslims	win
119	Lisbon	1147	Portugal and others	win
62	Damascus III	1148	Crusaders	lose
31	Ashkelon II	1153	Crusaders	win
170	Santarem I	1171	Portuguese	win
135	Myriocephalon	1176	Byzantines	lose
160	Ramleh II	1177	Mamelukes	lose
91	Jerusalem VIII	1187	Turkish Muslims	win
193	Tiberias	1187	Muslim Turks	win
2	Acre I	1189	Crusaders	win
29	Arsouf	1191	Crusaders	win
190	Taraori	1192	Persian Muslims	win
12	Alarcos	1195	Moors	win
116	Las Navas de Tolosa	1212	Spaniards and others	win
13	Alcacer	1217	Portuguese	win

Attacked	Outcome	Congruence with the Qur'an
Spaniards	win	Muslims invade but lose during siege
Muslims	lose	undetermined
Muslims	lose	undetermined
Muslims	lose	undetermined
Muslims	lose	undetermined
Punjabs	lose	Muslims invade, rout enemy and plunder the region
Afghans	lose	Muslims invade, sack city, covert residents to Islam
Persian Muslims	lose	(Intra-Muslim war) Winners invade and overrun Persia
Turkish Muslims	win	Muslims ransom and release some POWs
Moors	lose	undetermined
Berbers	win	Muslims behead many prisoners
Moors	lose	undetermined
Muslims	lose	Crusaders slay POWs; many Muslims desert
Turkish Muslims	lose	undetermined
Egyptian Muslims	lose	undetermined
Muslims and Jews	lose	Crusaders massacre both Muslim and Jewish inhabitants
Turkish Muslims	win	Muslims defend, kill some POWs but ransom others"
Muslims	win	undetermined
Muslims	win	undetermined
Turkish Muslims	win	Muslims win again and massacre clergy, women and children in the Crusader column
Crusaders	win	Muslims try to oust Crusaders from Palestine
Seljuk Muslims	lose	Muslims lose and accept truce
Moors	lose	undetermined
Crusaders	lose	Muslims invade, sack city, torture and slay many POWs"
Moors	lose	undetermined
Franks	lose	Muslims execute POWs and sell inhabitants into slavery
Moors	lose	Winners massacre Muslim POWs
Muslims	win	Muslims vigorously defend the city against huge Christian armies
Egyptian Muslims	lose	undetermined
Moors	lose	undetermined
Turkish Muslims	win	undetermined
Crusaders	win	Mamelukes retreat back to Egypt
Crusaders	lose	Saladin accepts truce, ransoms some POWs
Crusaders	lose	Muslims defend homelands, win, execute, ransack, behead and enslave losers
Saladin	lose	Crusaders execute 2700 Muslim captives
Muslims	lose	Muslims accept truce
Hindu army	lose	Muslims invade India, go on to take Delhi
Spaniards	lose	Muslims invade but also release thousands of POWs
Moors	lose	Truce had been broken; winners massacre many Moors
Moors	lose	undetermined

Battle #	Place name	Year begun	Attacker	Outcome
63	Damietta	1218	Crusaders	draw
103	Khojead	1219	Mongols	win
44	Bukhara	1220	Mongols	win
82	Herat I	1220	Mongols	win
168	Samarkand	1220	Mongols	win
39	Bamian	1221	Mongols	win
133	Merv	1221	Mongols	win
73	Erzincan	1230	Seljuk Turks	win
57	Cordova	1236	Spaniards	win
115	La Forbie	1244	Crusaders and Turkish Muslims	lose
67	El Mansura	1250	Crusaders	lose
35	Baghdad I	1258	Mongols	win
10	Ain Jalut	1260	Mamelukes	win
26	Antioch III	1268	Ottomans	win
200	Tunis II	1270	Crusaders	lose
198	Tripoli in Lebanon	1289	Mamelukes	win
3	Acre II	1291	Ottomans	win
45	Bursa	1317	Ottomans	win
164	Rio Salado	1340	Portuguese and Spaniards	win
20	Algeciras	1344	Spaniards	win
8	Adrianople VI	1365	Ottomans	win
127	Maritsa River	1371	Serbs and others	lose
109	Kosovo I	1389	Ottomans	win
138	Nicopolis	1396	Balkans and many allies	lose
65	Delhi I	1398	Mongols and Muslims	win
36	Baghdad II	1401	Mongols	win
23	Angora	1402	Mongols	win
52	Ceuta	1415	Portugal	win
167	Salonika I	1430	Ottomans	win
203	Varna I	1444	Hungarians and others	lose
110	Kosovo II	1448	Ottomans	win
56	Constantinople VII	1453	Ottomans	win
42	Belgrade I	1456	Ottomans	lose
137	Negroponte	1470	Ottomans	win
176	Shkoder I	1478	Ottomans	lose
21	Alhama de Granada	1482	Spaniards	win

Attacked	Outcome	Congruence with the Qur'an
Egyptian Muslims	draw	Crusaders capture then lose the city; Sultan allows a truce
Persian Muslims	lose	Muslims defend homeland, but Mongols execute most POWs
Muslims	lose	Mongols sack city and slaughter residents
Afghan Muslims	lose	Mongols slay virtually all inhabitants
Persian Muslims	lose	Muslims defend city but are slaughtered
Persian Muslims	lose	Mongols massacre Muslims and burn city
Persian Muslims	lose	Mongols invade, siege and burn city, massacre inhabitants
Persian Muslims	lose	(Intra-Muslim war) undetermined
Moors	lose	undetermined
Egyptian and Persian Muslims	win	Winners slaughter many losers; truces had been broken
Egyptian Muslims	win	Muslims defend stoutly, win, ransom some POWs, and arrange treaty, but also execute some POWs
Muslims	lose	Mongols sack city and brutalize people
Mongols	lose	undetermined
Franks and others	lose	Muslims invade, destroy city, slay or expel residents
Tunisian Muslims	win	Muslims defend land, win and negotiate an agreement
Franks and others	lose	Mamelukes defend lands, win, execute and enslave many
Franks	lose	Muslims sell some Franks as slaves
Byzantines	lose	undetermined
Moors	lose	undetermined
Moors	lose	undetermined
Serbians, Greeks, others	lose	Muslims invade
Ottomans	win	Muslims invade Balkans, kill three Serb princes
Serbs and others	lose	Muslims invade, use Qur'an, massacre, create vassal state
Ottomans	win	Ottomans ransom some POWs, execute others, pillage villages, massacre many
Indians	lose	Victors invade, execute POWs, raze city
Ottomans	lose	Mongols lay waste to Baghdad
Ottomans	lose	Ottoman vassals desert as Mongols massacre survivors
Moors	lose	undetermined
Venetians, Byzantines	lose	Ottomans invade, enslave and execute survivors
Ottomans	win	Ottomans massacre and decapitate some losers
Hungarians	lose	Muslims invade Hungarian lands
Venetians, Genoese	lose	Muslims invade, massacre POWs, pillage, and enslave inhabitants
Hungarians	win	Muslims invade and attack but lose
Venetians	lose	Ottoman navy invades and attacks
Venetians	win	Ottoman siege of town fails but wins in a treaty
Moors	lose	undetermined

Battle #	Place name	Year begun	Attacker	Outcome
120	Loja	1486	Spain	win
124	Malaga I	1487	Spain	win
41	Baza	1489	Spaniards	win
78	Granada	1491	Spaniards	win
117	Lepanto I	1499	Ottomans	win
144	Oran I	1509	Spain	win
53	Chaldiran	1514	Ottomans	win
128	Marj-Dabik	1516	Ottomans	win
46	Cairo	1517	Ottomans	win
43	Belgrade II	1521	Ottomans	win
161	Rhodes	1522	Ottomans	win
134	Mohacs I	1526	Ottomans	win
146	Panipat I	1526	Mogols	win
205	Vienna I	1529	Ottomans	lose
37	Baghdad III	1534	Ottomans	win
201	Tunis III	1535	Holy Roman Empire	win
156	Preveza	1538	Holy Roman fleet	win
147	Panipat II	1556	Mogols	win
125	Malta	1565	Ottomans	lose
188	Talikota	1565	Muslims and Moguls	win
187	Szigetvar	1566	Ottomans	win
32	Astrakan II	1569	Ottomans	lose
59	Cyprus	1570	Ottomans	win
118	Lepanto II	1571	Holy League states	win
14	Alacazarqvivir	1578	Portuguese	lose
101	Keresztes	1596	Ottomans	win
104	Khotin I	1621	Ottomans	lose
49	Candia II	1646	Ottomans	win
186	Szentgotthard	1664	Ottomans	lose
105	Khotin II	1673	Ottomans and Cossacks	lose
206	Vienna II	1683	Ottomans	lose
80	Harkany	1687	Austrians	win
183	Slankamen	1691	Austrians	win
34	Azov	1696	Russians	draw
173	Senta	1697	Ottomans	lose

Attacked	Outcome	Congruence with the Qur'an
Moors	lose	undetermined
Moors	lose	Winners sold most Muslim captives into slavery
Moors	lose	Moors surrender the city
Moors	lose	Muslims agree to peaceful capitulation
Venetians	lose	undetermined
Moors	lose	Spain invades, sacks Oran, kills thousands
Heretic Shites of Persia	lose	(Civil war) Ottomans execute thousands of POWs
Egyptian and Persian Muslims	lose	(Intra-Muslim war) Winners invade Syria, losers stoutly defend
Mamelukes	lose	(Intra-Muslim war) Ottomans invade, sack city, execute some POWs
Hungarians	lose	Muslims invade, massacre, and decapitate some POWs
Holy Roman Empire	lose	Ottomans invade, win siege, accept surrender
Hungarians and others	lose	Ottomans invade, massacre and enslave many soldiers and inhabitants
(Intra-Muslim war) Afghan Muslims	lose	undetermined
Holy Roman Empire	win	Ottomans invade, lose but massacre many villagers and POWs
Persians	lose	(Intra-Muslim war) undetermined
Moors	lose	Moors defend city but lose "in a three day orgy
Ottoman fleet	lose	undetermined
Hindus	lose	Mogols invade and suppress Hindu revolt
Holy Roman Empire	win	Muslims invade, lose, but massacre many opponents
Hindus	lose	Winners invade and destroy Hindu kingdom
Croats and others	lose	Ottomans invade Hungary
Russians	win	Ottomans invade Russia
Venetians, Cypriots	lose	Ottomans invade, massacre, torture, and execute leaders
Ottomans	lose	undetermined
Moors	win	Portuguese invade Morocco
Austrians	lose	Ottomans invade Austria and Hungary
Poles	win	Ottomans invade, lose, and some Janissaries revolt and kill Osman
Venetians	lose	Ottomans invade Crete
Austrians and others	win	Ottomans invade, lose and withdraw
Poles	win	Muslims invade, eventually lose, but accept truce
Austrians and others	win	Ottomans invade but siege fails
Ottomans	lose	undetermined
Ottomans	lose	undetermined
Ottomans	draw	undetermined
Holy Roman Empire	win	Ottomans invade, lose, but agree to truce

Battle #	Place name	Year begun	Attacker	Outcome
152	Peterwardein	1716	Austrians	win
47	Calcutta	1756	Muslims of Bengal	win
148	Panipat III	1761	Afghan Muslims	win
51	Cesme	1770	Ottomans	lose
162	Rimnik	1780	Russians and Austrians	win
157	Pyramids	1798	Napoleon	win
1	Abukir	1799	Ottomans	lose
4	Acre III	1799	Napoleon	lose
199	Tripoli II	1804	U.S. Navy	win
107	Kirovabad	1826	Russians	win
136	Navarino	1827	British, Greeks, and allies	win
204	Varna II	1828	Russians	win
111	Kulevcha	1829	Russians	win
108	Konya	1832	Egyptian Muslims	win
83	Herat II	1837	Persian Muslims	lose
141	Nizib	1839	Ottomans	lose
5	Acre IV	1840	British, Ottomans	win
95	Kabul II	1842	British and Indians	draw
86	Isly River	1844	Algerian Muslims	lose
142	Oltenita	1853	Ottomans	win
143	Omdurmna	1853	British	win
182	Sinope	1853	Russians	win
179	Silistra	1854	Russians	lose
154	Plevna	1877	Russians	win
175	Shipka Pass	1877	Russians	win
185	Svistov	1877	Russians and others	win
149	Peiwar Pass	1878	British and Indians	win
155	Plovdin	1878	Russians	win
97	Kandahar	1880	British	win
123	Maiwand	1880	Afghan Muslims	win
18	Alexandria IV	1882	Muslim revolt	win
192	Tell el-Kebir	1882	British	win
68	El Obeid	1883	British and Egyptians	lose
69	El Teb I	1884	British and Indians	lose
70	El Teb II	1884	Sudanese Mahdists	lose
102	Khartoum	1884	Sudanese Mahdists	win
98	Kars II	1887	Russians	win
202	Tyrnavos	1897	Ottomans	win
33	Atbara	1898	British and Egyptians	win
106	Kirk-Kilissa	1912	Ottomans	lose

Attacked	Outcome	Congruence with the Qur'an
Ottomans	lose	undetermined
British and Indians	lose	Muslims allow many POWs to die
Maranthas and Sikhs	lose	Muslims invade and shatter Maranthas
Russians and others	win	undetermined
Ottomans	lose	undetermined
Egyptian Muslims	lose	Both sides execute POWs and civilians before and after the battle
Napoleon	win	undecided
Ottomans, British	win	undecided
Barbary "pirates"	lose	Pirates steal and plunder ships, take prisoners, but defend their ports and abide by treaties and some rules
Persian Muslims	lose	undetermined
Egyptian Muslims	lose	Muslim naval forces invaded and massacred many civilians
Ottomans	lose	undetermined
Ottomans	lose	undetermined
Ottomans	lose	(Intra-Muslim war) Muslims versus Muslims
Afghan Muslims and British	win	(Intra-Muslim war) undetermined
Egyptian Muslims and others	win	(Intra-Muslim war) Egyptian Muslims revolt against Ottoman domination
Egyptian Muslim rebels	lose	Egyptian Muslim rebels are forced out of Acre
Afghan Muslims	draw	Afghans repulse attack, then lose Kabul briefly
French	win	undetermined
Russians and others	lose	Ottomans declare war and invade
Sudanese Mahdists	lose	Mahdists defend vigorously but lose
Ottomans	lose	undetermined
Ottomans	win	undetermined
Ottomans	lose	undetermined
Ottomans	lose	Ottomans surrender
Ottomans	lose	Ottomans lose and sign peace treaty
Afghan Muslims and others	lose	undetermined
Ottomans	lose	undetermined
Afghan Muslims	lose	Muslims resist, revolt, defend, but lose
British and Indians	lose	undetermined
British, French	lose	undetermined
Egyptian Muslims	lose	Muslims defend homeland
Sudanese Mahdists	win	Mahdists defend Sudan but massacre many POWs
Sudanese Mahdists	win	undetermined
British and Indians	win	undetermined
British	lose	Muslims defend homeland, execute many POWs
Ottomans	lose	Ottomans surrender
Greeks	lose	undetermined
Sudanese Mahdists	lose	undetermined
Bulgarians	win	undetermined

Battle #	Place name	Year begun	Attacker	Outcome
112	Kumanovo	1912	Serbians	win
121	Luleburgaz	1912	Bulgarians	win
9	Adrianople VII	1913	Bulgarians	win
177	Shkoder II	1913	Greeks and Balkans	win
172	Sarikamis	1914	Russians	win
64	Dardanelles	1915	British, French	lose
76	Gallipoli	1915	British, French	lose
113	Kut-al-Imara I	1915	British	win
114	Kut-al-Imara II	1915	Ottomans	win
75	Erzurum	1916	Russians	win
165	Rumani	1916	Ottomans and Germans	lose
38	Baghdad IV	1917	British	win
77	Gaza III	1917	British, Anzacs	win
158	Ramadi	1917	British and Indians	win
129	Megiddo III	1918	British and Egyptian Muslims	win
174	Sharqat	1918	British and Indians	win
27	Anual	1921	Moors	win
166	Sakarya River	1921	Greeks	lose
93	Jidda	1925	Wahabi factions	win
79	Habbaniya	1941	Iraqi Muslims and Germans	lose
92	Jerusalem IX	1948	Syria, Jordan, others	draw
181	Sinai Peninsula	1956	Israel and others	win
87	Israeli-Arab War	1967	Israelis	win
211	Yom Kippur War	1973	Egypt and others	draw
212	Afghanistan	1979	Soviets	lose
213	Iraq-Iran War	1980	Iraq	draw - lose
214	Beirut, Lebanon	1982	Israelis	draw - win

Attacked	Outcome	Congruence with the Qur'an
Ottomans	lose	undetermined
Ottomans	lose	undetermined
Ottomans	lose	undetermined
Ottomans	lose	undetermined
Ottomans	lose	undetermined
Ottomans, Germans	win	Ottomans stoutly defend their homeland
Ottomans, Germans	win	Stout defense by Ottomans of homeland
Ottomans	lose	Ottomans defend stoutly but lose; many escape
British	lose	Muslims reverse earlier defeat, accept surrender of British forces
Ottomans	lose	undetermined
British, French, Anzacs	win	undetermined
Ottomans	lose	Many Muslim combatants do not fight
Ottomans, Germans	lose	undetermined
Ottomans	lose	undetermined
German led Ottomans	lose	Ottomans defend, lose, ask for armistice
Ottomans	lose	undetermined
Spaniards	lose	undetermined
Ottomans	win	Ottomans defend and win under Kemal Ataturk
Husein factions	lose	(Civil war) House of Saud captures Mecca, Jidda, and gains monarchy
British	win	Iraqis try to expel British but fail
Israelis	draw	Israelis eventually gain statehood; other controversies continue about attackers and outcomes
Egypt	lose	undetermined
Egypt, Jordan, Syria	lose	Arab allies observe cease fire (but only Egypt accepts peace)
Israel	draw	Egypt and allies use surprise invasions with mixed results
Afghan rebels and others	win	Muslims defend stoutly but also execute prisoners and others
Iran	draw - win	(Intra-Muslim war) Iraq invades, executes POWs and others; Iran defends stoutly; controversies continue
PLO, Syrians and others	draw - lose	Stout defense of Beirut with executions and many controversies

BIBLIOGRAPHY

Ali, Maulawi Sher. *The Holy Qur'an*. Rabwah, West Pakistan: The Oriental and Religious Publishing Corporation Ltd. 1955.

Andrews, Edmund L., and Patrick E. Tyler. "Muslim Cleric Issues Call for Jihad Against U.S." *The New York Times*, Saturday, June 7, 2003, p. 1. (as quoted in *The Providence Journal*, June 7, 2003, p. A-1).

"Anti-American Sentiment Grows in Philippines," *Los Angeles Times*, February 27, 2003, p. 13.

Appleby, L. Scott and Martin E. Marty. "Fundamentalism." *Foreign Policy*, January/February 2002. pp. 16-22.

Arberry, A.J. *The Koran Interpreted*. Oxford: Oxford University Press. 1964.

Associated Press, "Bin Laden on Tape: We Calculated in Advance." Published in *The Providence Journal*, December 14, 2001, p. A17.

"Basic Principles of the Law of War," The Center for Law and Military Operations. *Marine Corps Gazette*. October, 2002, pp. 36-37.

Bell, Richard. *The Quran*. Edinburgh: Edinburgh University Press. 1937.

Bergen, Peter L. *Holy War, Inc. Inside the Secret World of Osama bin Laden*. NY: The Free Press, 2001.

"Bin Laden on Tape: We Calculated in Advance." *The Providence Journal*. December 14, 2001, p. A17 (quoting from the Associated Press).

Bonner, Raymond. "Gunmen Kill Seven Shiite Worshippers in Pakistan." *The New York Times International Sunday Edition*. February 23, 2003, p. 10.

Bowden, Mark. *Black Hawk Down*. New York: Signet: New American Library. 1999.

_____. "Centerpiece: The Kabul-Ki Dance" *The Atlantic Monthly*. November, 2002. Vol. 290 #4.

_____. "Tales of the Tyrant." *The Atlantic Monthly*. May, 2002. pp. 35-51.

Bullock, John, and Harvey Morris. *The Gulf War: Its Origins, History, and Consequences*. London: Methuen. 1989.

"Bush Slips, Bin Laden Gains in Poll." *The Providence Journal*, June 4, 2003, p. A4 (quoting from *The Washington Post*).

Caplow, Theodore, and Louis Hicks. *Systems of War and Peace*. Lanham, MD: University Press of America, Inc. 1995. p. 3.

Carroll, James. Review of Seyyed Hossein Nasr. "The Heart of Islam." *The New York Times Book Review*, Sunday, September 7, 2002, p. 23.

Chang, Gy/Sgt. Julio. Personal e-mail correspondence with a career Marine Corps NCO who served six months as a security guard over Taliban prisoners at Guantanamo Bay in 2002.

Clancy, Tom, and General Fred Franks, Jr. *Into the Storm*. NY: Berkey Books. 1996.

Collins, Aukai. *My Jihad*. Guilford, CT: The Lyons Press (and imprint of The Globe Pequot Press). 2002.

Cushman, John H., Jr. et al. "War in Afghanistan Evolves Into a Race to Impose Law and Order." *The New York Times*. December 9, 2001, p. B3.

Davidson, Adam. "Loves Microsoft, Hates America," *The Sunday New York Times Magazine*, March 9, 2003, p. 20.

Dellios, Hugh, and E.A. Torriero. "Questions Raised over POW's Rescue." *The Providence Journal*. May 28, 2003, p. A9.

Eberly, David. *Faith Beyond Belief: A Journey to Freedom*. Richmond, VA: Brandylane Publishers, Inc. 2002

Eggenberger, David. *An Encyclopedia of Battles: Accounts of Over 1,560 Battles from 1479 B.C. to the Present*. NY: Dover Publications, Inc. 1985.

Einstein, Albert. "Peace." in George Seldes (ed.). *The Great Quotations*. NY: Simon and Schuster, Inc. 1972.

Encyclopedia Britannica, Volume 12. "Islam." London: Encyclopedia Britannica, Inc., 1973, pp. 663-671.

_____, Volume 13. London: Encyclopedia Britannica, Inc., 1973, p. 454.

_____, Volume 15. "Mohammad." London: Encyclopedia Britannica, Inc., 1973, p. 639-642.

Esposito, John L. *Islam: The Straight Path (Third Edition)*. New York: Oxford University Press. 1998.

Finkel, Michael. "Naji's Taliban Phase: The Making and Unmaking of a Holy Warrior". *The New York Times Sunday Magazine*, December 16, 2001: pp. 78-81.

Freedman, Lawrence, and Efriam Karsh. *The Gulf Conflict 1990-1991: Diplomacy and War in the New World Order*. Princeton, NJ: Princeton University Press. 1993.

Fregosi, Paul. *Jihad in the West: Muslim Conquests from the 7th to the 21st Centuries*. Amherst, New York: Prometheus Books. 1998.

The Gesta Francorum. Anonymous. Edited by R. Hill, London. 1962 (as reported in *Chronicles of the Crusades: Eyewitness Accounts of the Wars Between Christianity and Islam*," edited by Elizabeth Hallam, NY: Welcome Rain, 2000.

Gopin, Marc. *Between Eden and Armageddon: The Future of World Religions, Violence, and Peacemaking*. Berkeley, CA: University of California Press. 2000.

_____. *Holy War, Holy Peace: How Religion Can Bring Peace to the Middle East*. Berkeley, CA: University of California Press. 2002

Graham, Franklin (with Bruce Nygren). *The Name*. Nashville, TN: Thomas Nelson Publishing 2002.

Groom, Winston, and Duncan Spencer. *Conversations with the Enemy: The Story of Pfc. Robert Garwood*. New York. G.P. Putnam's Sons. 1983.

Gutman, Roy, and David Rieff (editors). *Crimes of War: What the Public Should Know*. New York: W.W. Norton & Company. 1999.

Haleem, Muhammad Abdel. *Understanding The Qur'an: Themes and Style*. London: I.B. Taurus Publishers, 1999.

Hitti, Philip K. *History of the Arabs*. NY: St. Martin's Press. 1967.

_____. *Islam: A Way of Life*. New York: Henry Regnery. 1971.

Holbrooke, Richard. *To End a War, Revised Edition*. New York. The Modern Library. 1999.

Holy Bible. King James Version. Gideon's International, 1978.

Huntington, Samuel. *The Clash of Civilizations and the Remaking of the World Order.* NY: Touchstone, Simon & Schuster. 1996.

Hylton, Wil S. "Mazar-I-Sharif," *Esquire,* August, 2002. pp. 108-109.

"Iraq Rewards Family of Suicide Attacker." *The Providence Journal.* March 31, 2003, pp. A5, A14.

Khan, Dr. Muhammad Muhsin. *The Translation of the Meanings of "Sahîh Al-Bukhâri."* Volumes 1-9 Arabic-English. Riyadh-Saudi Arabia: Darussalam Publishers & Distributors.

_____. *The Translation of the Meanings of Summarized "Sahîh Al-Bukhâri."* Volumes 1-9 Arabic-English. Riyadh-Saudi Arabia: Maktaba Dar-ús-Salam.

Kaplan, Robert D. *Soldiers of God: With Islamic Warriors in Afghanistan and Pakistan.* Boston: Houghton Mifflin Co. 1990

Karsh, Efriam. *The Iran-Iraq War, 1980-88.* Oxford, England: Osprey Publishing, 2002.

Kassis, Hanna E. *A Concordance of the Qur'an.* Berkeley, CA: University of California Press.1983.

Khadduri, Majid. *War and Peace in the Law of Islam.* Baltimore: Johns Hopkins Press. 1955.

Kushner, Harvey W. (editor/author). *Essential Readings on Political Terrorism: Analyses of Problems and Prospects for the 21st Century.* Gordian Knot Books. 2002.

Laber, Jeri, and Barnett R. Rubin. *A Nation Dying: Afghanistan Under the Soviets, 1979-87.* Evanston, IL: Northwestern University Press. 1993.

Lapidus, Ira M. *A History of Islamic Societies.* Cambridge: Cambridge University Press. 1988.

Lazar, Najih, a member of the Rhode Island Islamic Center, Wakefield, Rhode Island. Personal conversations with the author. 2001-2003.

Lehrer, James. "A Summary of the News." Public Broadcasting Station. May 28, 2003.

Lenski, Gerhard and Patrick Nolan. *Human Societies: An Introduction to Macrosociology, 8th Ed.* New York: McGraw-Hill. 1999.

Lewis, Bernard (ed. and trans.). *Islam: From the Prophet Muhammad to the Capture of Constantinople.* New York: Harper & Row. 1974.

_____. *The Arabs in History.* New York: Harper & Row. 1966.

Maass, Peter. "Cultural Property and Historical Monuments," pp. 110-112 in Roy Gutman and David Rieff (eds.), *Crimes of War: What the Public Should Know.* NY: W.W. Norton & Company. 1999.

_____. "Good Kills," *The New York Times Magazine*, April 20, 2003. pp. 32-37.

Marsden, Peter. *The Taliban: War, Religion and the New Order in Afghanistan.* London: Oxford University Press (Zed Books). 1998.

McNab, Andy. *Bravo Two Zero.* New York: Dell. 1993.

"Military Studies in the Jihad Against Tyrants." Translated as "Terrorist Training Manual." U.S. Department of Justice. Federal Bureau of Investigation. Washington, DC: November, 2001.

"Mohammed." *Encyclopedia Britannica*, Volume 15. 1973, pp. 639-642

Murray, Williamson and Robert H. Scales, Jr. *The Iraq War: A Military History.* Cambridge, MA: The Belknap Press/Harvard University Press. 2004.

Nasr, Seyyed Hossein. *The Heart of Islam: Enduring Values for Humanity.* San Francisco: Harper San Francisco. 2002.

Nawawi, Riyadh as-Salihin of Imam. *Gardens of the Righteous* (Hadith). Translated from the Arabic by Muhammed Zafrulla Khan. London. Curzon Press. 1975.

"A Nation at War." *The New York Times.* March 30, 2003, pp. B1-B16.

"A Nation at War." *The New York Times.* April 13, 2003, pp. B1-B11.

"A Nation Challenged: Life in bin Laden's Army." *The New York Times.* Sunday, March 17, 2002, pp. 18-20.

O'Neill, Helen. Associated Press. "Killed in Action." *The Providence Sunday Journal.* May 26, 2002, pp. 1, A22.

Overby, Paul. *Holy Blood: An Inside View of the Afghan War.* Westport, Conn. Praeger. 1995.

Peacock, James L. *The Anthropological Lens: Harsh Light, Soft Focus.* Cambridge, UK: Cambridge University Press. 1986, 1997.

Perry, Joellen. "Rhonda Cornum: The Iraqi Army Couldn't Quash Her Fighting Spirit." pp. 37-42 in *U.S. News and World Report.* "Heroes." August 20/ August 27, 2001.

Pickthall, Mohammed Marmaduke. *The Meaning of the Glorious Koran.* NY: The New American Library, Inc. 1955.

Piscatori, James. "The Turmoil Within: The Struggle for the Future of the Islamic World." *Foreign Affairs*: Volume 81 No. 3. May/June 2002, p. 146.

Priest, Dana, and Barton Gellman. "Terrorism Detainees Face Harsh Treatment." *The Washington Post.* December 26, 2002, p. 1.

Rapoport, David C. "Sacred Terror: A Contemporary Example from Islam." pp. 103-130 in Walter Reich (ed.). *Origins of Terrorism: Psychologies, Ideologies, Theologies, State of Mind.* Washington, DC: Woodrow Wilson Center Press. 1990.

Rashid, Ahmed. *Taliban: Militant Islam, Oil, and Fundamentalism in Central Asia.* New Haven: Yale University Press, 2000.

"Rebel Fighting Leaves 40 Taliban Dead." *The Providence Journal,* June 6, 2003, p. A8 (quoting *The New York Times*).

Reich, Walter (ed.). *Origins of Terrorism: Psychologies, Ideologies, Theologies, State of Mind.* Washington, DC: Woodrow Wilson Center Press. 1990.

_____. "Understanding Terrorist Behavior: The Limits and Opportunities of Psychological Inquiry." pp. 261-280 in Walter Reich (ed.). *Origins of Terrorism: Psychologies, Ideologies, Theologies, State of Mind.* Washington, DC: Woodrow Wilson Center Press. 1990.

"Religion, War are All Omar Knows." *The New York Times.* December 7, 2001, p. 4.

"Restoring Iraq." *The Providence Journal.* Tuesday, May 27, 2003, p. A9 (quoting the *Los Angeles Times*).

Risen, James. "Voice Heard on New Tape Might be bin Laden's." *The New York Times,* November 13, 2002, p. 1.

Riyadh as-Salihin of Imam Nawawi. *Gardens of the Righteous* (Hadith). Translated from the Arabic by Muhammed Zafrulla Khan. London. Curzon Press. 1975.

Roberts, Gwynne. "Poisonous Weapons." pp. 279-281 in Roy Guttman and David Rieff (eds.). *Crimes of War: What the Public Should Know.* NY: W.W. Norton & Company. 1999.

Rochester, Stuart I., and Frederick Kiley. *Honor Bound: The History of American Prisoners of War in Southeast Asia*, 1961-1973. Washington, DC: Office of the Secretary of Defense. 1998.

Rodinson, Maxime. *Mohammed.* Translated by Anne Carter. New York: Pantheon Books. 1971.

Roy, Oliver. *Islam and Resistance in Afghanistan.* Cambridge: Cambridge University Press, 1986.

Sack, John, "Anaconda," *Esquire*, August, 2002, pp. 18-36, 135-136.

Said, Edward W. *Orientalism.* New York: Vintage House. 1979.

Schmitt, Eric. "Surprise. War Works After All." pp. 1, 4 in *The New York Times Sunday Week in Review.* November 18, 2001. .

_____. "Paratrooper from New Jersey Dies in Afghan Firefight." *The New York Times*, December 22, 2002, p. 8.

Schwartz, T. P. "Terror and Terrorism in the Koran," pp. 22-34 in Harvey W. Kushner (ed.). *Essential Readings in Political Terrorism: Analysis of Problems and Prospects for the 21st Century.* Lincoln, NE: University of Nebraska Press. 2002.

_____. "The Qur'an as a Guide to Conduct of and in War, Including Treatment of Prisoners of War." *Marine Corps Gazette.* February, 2002. pp. 43 - 48.

_____. "Waging War Against Hostile Combat Units That Fight According to al-Qur'an (The Koran)." *Marine Corps Gazette.* September, 2002. pp. 75-79.

Seiple, Chris. *The U.S. Military/NGO Relationship in Humanitarian Interventions.* U.S. Army War College Peacekeeping Institute. Center for Strategic Leadership. 1996.

Seldes, George. *The Great Quotations.* NY: Simon and Schuster. 1972.

Sharif, Mohammed. Professor of Management, University of Rhode Island. Personal conversations with the author. 2001-2004.

"Shifting Missions Come with Rising Risks." *The New York Times.* December 9, 2001, p. B2.

Shlaim, Avi. *War and Peace in the Middle East: A Critique of American Policy.* New York: Viking. 1994.

Smith, Dan. *The State of War and Peace Atlas.* Oslo. 1997.

_____. The Penguin Atlas of War and Peace. 4th edition. NY: Penguin Putnam Inc. 2003.

Sprinzak, Ehud. "Rational Fanatics." pp. 66-73 in *Foreign Policy.* September/October 2000.

Stack, Megan K. "Suicide Bomber Kills 15 in Israel." p. 1 in *Los Angeles Times.* March 6, 2003.

Stern, Jessica. *Terror in the Name of God. Why Religious Militants Kill.* New York: Ecco/Harper Collins Publishers. 2003.

Tanakh. The Holy Scriptures. The New JPS Translation According to the Traditional Hebrew Text. Philadelphia & Jerusalem: The Jewish Publication Society. 1985.

"Terrorism Detainees Face Harsh Treatment." *The Washington Post.* December 26, 2002, p.1.

Urban, Mark. *War in Afghanistan, 2nd Edition.* New York. St. Martin's Press, 1999.

U.S. Department of Justice. "Terrorist Training Manual" ("Military studies in the Jihad Against Tyrants"). Washington, DC: Federal Bureau of Investigation. November, 2001.

Van Natta, Dan Jr., and Daniel Johnston. "Attacks Sow Fears of al-Qaida Resurgence." *The New York Times,* October 1, 2002. p. 1.

Vick, Karl. "Rout in the Desert Marked Turning Point of War." *The Washington Post.* December 31, 2001. pp. 1, A13.

Wansbrough, John. *Qur'anic Studies.* 1977. .

Watanabe, Teresa. "Understanding Islam." *Los Angeles Times,* as quoted in *The Providence Sunday Journal,* September 30, 2001, p. B-1.

WGBH, Boston, "Morning News." May 25, 2002.

The World Almanac and Book of Facts, 2001. NY: World Almanac Books.

The World Almanac and Book of Facts, 2003.
NY: World Almanac Books.

Wright, Lawrence. "The Man Behind Bin Laden." pp. 43-55 in
The New Yorker. September 16, 2002.

Zaman, Muhammad Qasim, Professor in the Islamic Studies
Department, Brown University, Providence, RI. Personal
conversations with the author. 2001-2003.

Zinni, General Anthony C. USMC (Ret.). Personal communications
with the author. 2004.

INDEX

A

Abbasid Muslims, 142, 146, 147, 288, 289, 366

Abderman, 156

Abukir, battle of, 194, 374

Abyssinia, Abyssinian(s), 81, 97-99, 114, 285, 324

Acre I, battle of, 368

Acre II, battle of, 191, 370

Acre III, battle of, 374

Acre IV, battle of, 189, 374

Acroinum, battle of, 366

Adana, battle of, 368

Adrianople VI, battle of, 195, 370

Adrianople VII, battle of, 196, 376

Afghan(s), 16, 17, 178, 197, 199, 212-214, 250, 260, 261, 312, 313, 353, 367, 369, 371, 373-375, 377

    Muslims, 199, 371, 373-375, 377

    Rebels, 213, 377

    Tribes, 16, 212, 213, 367

Afghanistan, 2, 14-18, 20, 21, 26, 35, 36, 69, 144, 165-167, 180, 199, 206, 212-214, 242-244, 246-250, 260, 261, 263, 309, 311-315, 332, 341, 348, 354, 367, 376

Aidid, Mohamed Farrah, 239-241

Ain Jalut, battle of, 168, 370

Air Force, U.S., 233, 245, 247, 339

Ajnadain, battle of, 150, 191, 366

Alacazarqvivir, battle of, 372

Alarcos, battle of, 368

Alcacer, battle of, 199, 368

Aleppo, battle of, 181, 366, 368

Aleppo-Antioch, battle of, 368

Alexandria II, battle of, 366

Alexandria IV, battle of, 374

Al-Fustat, battle of, 366

Algeciras, battle of, 370

Algeria, Algerian(s), 331, 374

Algerian Muslims, 374

Alhama de Granada, battle of, 370

Ali Pasha, 183, 184

Ali, Maulawi Sher, 266, 292, 294, 300

Al-Qaeda, xix, 2, 14, 18, 69, 242-245, 247-251, 260, 309, 311-314, 316

Amorium, battle of, 366

Angora, battle of, 370

Anthropological perspective, 345, 346, 348, 351

Antioch I, battle of, 368

Antioch II, battle of, 368

Antioch III, battle of, 370

Anual, battle of, 376

Anzac(s), 177, 179, 233, 376, 377

Apulia, battle of, 366

Arab Muslims, 37, 38, 146, 366, 367

Arafat, Yassar, 2

Army

    Hindu, 166, 369

    Kuwaiti, 225, 226, 232

    Ottoman, 148, 168, 170, 171, 173, 177, 181, 189

    U.S., 231, 245, 247, 251, 255, 315, 333, 339

Arsouf, battle of, 368

Ashkelon I, battle of, 368

Ashkelon II, battle of, 368

Astrakan II, battle of, 372

Atbara, battle of, 199, 374

Aukai Collins, 15, 18-24, 29, 32, 37, 243, 244, 308, 316

Austria, Austrian(s), 172, 174, 177, 182, 183, 195, 372-374

Azov, battle of, 372

B

Badr, the victory at, 6, 12, 51, 85, 100, 106-112, 116, 117, 122, 123, 136, 138, 142, 190, 206, 277, 278, 285, 304, 325, 329, 337

Baghdad I, battle of, 165, 167, 168, 173, 370, 372

Baghdad II , battle of, 370

Baghdad III, battle of, 372

Baghdad IV, battle of, 376

Bainbridge, Capt. William, 185, 186

Balkan(s), 149, 158, 160, 167-174, 195, 196, 370, 371, 376

Bamian, battle of, 165, 167, 173, 370

Barbary pirates, 185-187, 197, 239, 331, 375

Basra, battle of, 143, 231, 232, 251-254, 257, 366, 367

Battle of the Black Sea, Somalia (1993), 182, 238-242

Baza, battle of, 372

Beheading(s), 110, 125-127, 137, 151, 153, 160, 171, 174, 176, 184, 202, 209, 327, 338, 367, 369

Beirut, Lebanon, 150, 197, 219-221, 376, 377

Beirut, Lebanon War, 150, 197, 376

Belgrade I, battle of, 370

Belgrade II, battle of, 195, 372

Berber(s), 155, 164, 195, 369

Bible, 5, 10, 29, 30, 38, 47, 92, 183, 242

bin Laden, Osama, xix, 2, 3, 10, 15, 18, 20, 31, 36, 59, 69, 84, 93, 243-245, 247, 263, 307-310, 314, 316, 325, 335, 353, 354

Black Sea, battle of (1993), 182, 238-242

Bosnia, 19, 20, 26, 222, 223, 332, 354

Bowden, Mark, 3, 35, 242, 263

Britain, British, 35, 41, 174, 175, 177-182, 189, 195-197, 199, 200, 206, 212, 214, 216, 221, 230, 233, 235, 236, 252, 253, 256-258, 331, 339, 341, 374-377

Bukhara, battle of, 370

Bulgaria, Bulgarian(s), 169, 375, 376

Bursa, battle of, 370

Bush, George W. (President), xix, 14, 229, 251, 252, 307, 309, 310, 353

Byzantine(s), 51, 90, 93, 97-100, 131, 132, 134, 144, 159, 182, 191, 193, 197, 287, 366-368, 371

Navy, 367

C

Cairo, battle of, 372

Calcutta, battle of, 374

Caliph Ali's Muslims, 366

Caliph Muawiyah, 143, 144, 154, 155, 366

Candia I, battle of, 368

Candia II, battle of, 372

Carthage III, battle of, 366

Cesme, battle of, 182, 374

Ceuta, battle of, 370

Chaldiran, battle of, 372

Charles Martel, 31, 144, 151, 157, 158, 163, 367

Charles V, 172-174

Chechneya, 15, 21-24, 243

China, Chinese, 165, 167, 197, 216, 263, 366, 367

Coalition, The, 5, 112, 122, 124, 127, 129, 176-179, 181, 195, 226-235,

237-239, 251, 313, 341, 348, 352

Code of conduct, 339, 340

Collateral damage, 89, 276

Collins, Aukai, 15, 18-24, 29, 32, 37, 243, 244, 308, 316

Constantinople III, battle of, 366

Constantinople IV, battle of, 182, 366

Constantinople VII, battle of, 370

Cordova, battle of, 155, 370

Cossack(s), 372

Covadonga, battle of, 366

Croat(s), Croatians(s), 222, 373

Crusader(s), 159-162, 194, 195, 197, 198, 201, 289, 368-371

Culture-based resistance, 342, 343, 348

Cypriot(s), 373

Cyprus, battle of, 183, 372

D

Damascus I, battle of, 366

Damascus II, battle of, 368

Damascus III, battle of, 368

Damietta, battle of, 370

dar al-harb, 270, 282, 299

dar al-Islam, 149, 270, 275, 282, 299

Dardanelles, battle of, 169, 176-182, 187, 331, 376

Dayton Peace Accords, 224

Defendent, Muslim- (stereotype), 151, 192, 200

Delhi I, battle of, 370

dhimmis, 270

Diplomatic relations, 328

Discrimination, principle of, 42, 69, 72, 152, 157, 162, 219, 241, 250, 259, 296, 297, 311, 321, 334, 336, 362

Diyala Bridge, battle of (2003), 254, 255

Dominant, Muslim- (stereotype), 150, 151, 192, 194, 196, 200, 203

Durant, Mike CWO, 239, 241, 242, 339

E

Eberly, Colonel David, 233-236, 262, 339

Edessa II, battle of, 368

Eggenberger, David, 138, 149, 150, 171, 185, 189, 190

Egypt, Egyptian(s), 3, 11, 143, 144, 147, 159, 162, 168, 172, 174-177, 181, 182, 188, 189, 194, 196-201, 285, 287, 289-291, 306, 312, 331, 366-369, 371, 373-377

Egyptian Muslim navy, 366

Egyptian Muslim rebels, 375

Egyptian Muslims, 181, 189, 368, 369, 371, 374-376

Einstein, Albert, 354, 380

El Mansura, battle of, 201, 370

El Obeid, battle of, 374

El Teb I, battle of, 374

El Teb II, battle of, 374

Eregli I, battle of, 368

Eregli II, battle of, 368

Erzincan, battle of, 370

Erzurum, battles of (928, 1916), 366, 376

Esposito, John, xix, 8, 28, 36, 141, 143, 146, 149, 266, 284-286, 289-291, 300, 301

F

Farr, 276

Fath (Wars of Conquest), 287

376, 377

Iraq, Iraqi(s), 1, 3, 140, 143, 144, 190, 197, 199, 206, 210-212, 214-219, 224-235, 237, 238, 250-262, 264, 287, 307, 308-312, 332, 341, 344, 347, 348, 353, 354, 376, 377

Iraqi Muslims, 376

Iraq-Iran War (1980-1988), 190, 214-219, 238, 376

Islam, 1-3, 5, 7, 8, 10, 15-20, 24, 25, 28, 30, 33-35, 37, 38, 41, 43, 46, 48, 50, 51, 53, 55, 59, 69, 70, 76, 82-86, 91-93, 95, 96, 102, 106, 108, 110, 112, 120, 124-126, 131, 132, 134, 137, 139, 142-147, 149, 151, 152, 154, 163, 172, 175, 177, 180, 187, 191, 197-200, 203, 206, 207, 212-215, 223, 224, 227, 236, 238, 240, 242-244, 260, 263, 265-273, 275, 278-280, 282-286, 288, 289, 291, 292, 295, 297, 299-301, 303, 308, 313-315, 317-319, 321, 323, 324, 328, 330, 336, 338, 351, 354, 357, 359-362, 369

Islamic, 2, 3, 5-10, 14, 15, 17, 20, 22, 23, 26, 28, 32, 34-37, 41, 42, 75, 82, 83, 86, 93, 95, 100, 127, 133-135, 137, 138, 140, 142, 143, 145, 146, 148, 149, 151, 176, 177, 185, 200, 214, 215, 218, 221, 224, 238, 239, 242, 243, 248, 260, 265-270, 272-275, 277-284, 287-291, 295, 297, 299, 301, 302, 307, 313, 316, 327, 328, 330, 334, 338, 349, 353, 354, 362

Islamic Law (*Sharia* or *Shar'ia*), 10, 15, 95, 142, 145, 265, 268-270, 272, 273, 275, 278-284, 289, 295, 297, 301

Isly River, battle of, 374

Israel, Israeli(s), 1, 5, 10, 34, 67, 130, 194, 196, 197, 216, 219-222, 227-229, 234, 238, 251, 252, 306, 307, 376, 377

Israeli-Arab War, 376

Israeli invasion of Lebanon (1982-

1993), 150, 197, 219-222, 238, 376

J

Jalula, battle of, 197, 366

Jerusalem IX, battle of, 376

Jerusalem VI, battle of, 366

Jerusalem VII, battle of, 159, 162, 197, 368

Jerusalem VIII, battle of, 162, 368

Jews, Jewish, 5, 6, 9, 14, 38, 48, 50, 60, 66, 67, 68, 82, 83, 88, 92, 98, 99, 102, 112, 113, 116, 119, 120, 122,-125, 127, 129, 130, 136, 139, 151, 152, 159-162, 193, 196-198, 209, 234, 248, 277, 285, 287, 300, 306, 322, 354, 357, 369

Jidda, battle of, 190, 194, 200, 376, 377

Jihad, xix, 1, 11, 12, 15, 20, 34, 36, 37, 85, 149, 164, 172, 176, 178, 179, 219, 238, 256, 263, 271, 290, 297, 305, 316

  jahada (variant), 271, 283

  juhd (variant), 271

  Military *jihad*, 85-88, 270-274, 277, 281, 282, 331, 362

Jordan, Jordanian(s), 28, 181, 197, 256, 307, 312, 353, 376, 377

K

Kabul I, battle of, 197, 366

Kabul II, battle of, 374

Kadisiya, battle of, 153, 154, 197, 366

Kandahar, battle of, 15-17, 245, 247, 249, 312, 315, 321, 374

Karr, 276

Kars II, battle of, 374

Kashgar, battle of, 366

Kerbela, battle of, 366

L

M

152, 219, 261, 266, 306, 333, 353, 354

Diplomatic relations, 91, 224, 227, 272, 310, 328-330

Peacekeeping missions, 3, 24, 224, 227, 241, 349, 356

Pearl, Daniel (*New York Times* reporter), 3, 21, 145

Peiwar Pass, battle of, 199, 374

Pella, battle of, 366

Pentagon (September 11, 2001 attack),
2, 11, 22, 84, 244, 251, 297, 298, 325

Persian Muslims, 367-369, 371-375

Persian(s), 51, 93, 97-99, 123, 134, 142, 144, 146-148, 152, 153, 155, 159, 165, 167, 193, 197, 215, 225, 228, 231, 251, 252, 285, 287, 311, 366-369, 371, 373-375

Peshawar, battle of, 313, 368

Peterwardein, battle of, 374

Philomelion, battle of, 368

Pickthall, Mohammed Marmaduke, 4, 5, 8, 32-36, 38, 39, 41, 48, 55, 56, 58-60, 69, 70, 81, 82, 92, 93, 101, 111, 139, 140, 142, 266, 285, 286, 292, 294, 298, 304

Piscatori, James, 9, 10, 313

Plevna, battle of, 374

PLO (Palestine Liberation Organization), 2, 220, 377

Plovdin, battle of, 196, 374

poison(s), 11, 83, 217-219, 279, 326, 341

Poles, Polish, 171, 373

Population, Muslim, 25, 26, 28, 60, 97, 126, 156, 164, 166, 170, 171, 176, 177, 202, 203, 210, 214, 215, 217-219, 222, 224, 238, 250, 252, 253, 256, 257, 277, 279, 287, 288, 291, 311, 312, 314, 315, 320, 327,

329, 332-335, 337, 347, 348

Portugal, Portuguese, 144, 155, 158, 195, 197-199, 216, 368, 370, 372, 373

POW(s), Prisoner(s) of war, 21, 76-79, 126, 188, 201, 213, 222, 226, 233-238, 253, 257-260, 262, 264, 278, 312, 323, 327, 329, 334, 337-340, 351, 367, 369, 371, 373, 375, 377

Preveza, battle of, 182, 372

Principle(s) of

Discrimination, 42, 69, 72, 152, 157, 162, 219, 241, 250, 259, 296, 297, 311, 321, 334, 336, 362

Proportionality, 42, 56, 93, 152, 157, 162, 238, 241, 250, 259, 293, 296, 297, 311, 320, 334, 336, 351, 362

Righteous intention, 42, 157, 162, 219, 238, 250, 259, 296, 311, 319, 334, 336

Transgression avoidance, 42, 152, 157, 162, 219, 250, 259, 293, 296, 311, 334, 336, 362

Prisoner(s), 9, 12, 14, 41, 62, 72, 74-79, 86, 105-111, 126, 130, 131, 135, 137, 151, 153, 154, 158, 161-164, 167, 170, 171, 173, 174, 176, 180-183, 186, 187, 202, 216, 217, 221, 230-236, 238, 241, 242, 252, 263, 275, 278-280, 283, 292, 293, 298, 300, 302, 310, 312, 315, 319, 323, 328, 330, 334, 337, 338, 351, 353, 369, 375, 377

Proportionality, principle of, 42, 56, 93, 152, 157, 162, 238, 241, 250, 259, 293, 296, 297, 311, 320, 334, 336, 351, 362

Punjabs, 369

Pyramids, battle of, 169, 175-177, 188, 196, 374

Q

Qaddafi, Colonel Kuammar al-, 2

Quotations from the Qur'an, xxvi, 42-83, 337, 340

Regarding ending wars, 79-84

Regarding enemies, 50, 56-58

Regarding motivation to fight, 64-69

Regarding peace, 6, 42-46, 340

Regarding peace treaties, 45-46

Regarding POWs, 76-79

Regarding spoils of war, 74-81

Regarding war, 47-74, 337

Qur'an, Koran, xix, xx, xxi, xxv, 1, 3, 4, 7, 9, 12, 13, 14, 15, 17, 25, 33, 35, 38, 93, 95, 141, 143, 169, 175, 178, 249, 289, 315

As a holy book, xxiv, 4-7

Correspondence/congruence with, 107, 110-112, 116-118, 125-127, 133, 134, 149, 150, 160, 168, 173, 225

Interpretations

Khadduri's, 266-284

John Esposito's, 284-292

Ali's, 292-295

Haleem's, 295-300

Its importance, 7-10

Muhammad as reciter of, 136-138

R

Rahman, 156, 157

Ramadi, battle of, 376

Ramleh I, battle of, 368

Ramleh II, battle of, 368

Research procedures (methods), xxiii, 309, 310, 399

Retaliation, 57

Rhodes, battle of, 182, 372

Rimnik, battle of, 374

Rio Barbate, battle of, 156, 195, 207, 366

Rio Salado, battle of, 370

Roderick, 155

Rodinson, Maxime, 35, 83, 92, 97, 103, 104, 106, 111, 116, 125, 138-140, 207, 266, 285, 286, 304

Rumani, battle of, 376

Rumsfeld, Donald H. (Secretary of Defense), 313

Russia, Russian(s), 20-23, 149, 177, 180, 182, 195-197, 206, 213, 244, 372-376

S

Sakarya River, battle of, 376

Salaatul Fajr, 20, 244

Saladin, 147, 162, 163, 289, 290, 369

Shows restraint, 147, 162, 163, 289, 290, 369

salat, 48

Salonika I, battle of, 370

Samarkand, battle of, 370

Samosata, battle of, 366

Santarem I, battle of, 368

Saragossa I, battle of, 368

Sarikamis, battle of, 376

Seljuk Muslims, 368, 369

Seljuk Turks, 370

Senta, battle of, 372

September 11, 2001 (attack), xix, 2, 69, 244, 325

Pentagon, xix, 2, 11, 22, 84, 244, 251, 297, 298, 325

World Trade Center, xix, 1, 2, 11, 22, 84, 244, 251, 297, 325, 334

ABOUT THE AUTHOR

T. P. Schwartz-Barcott was raised in Latrobe, Pennsylvania, and graduated from Miami University, Oxford, Ohio, USA. He is a former Captain in the United States Marine Corps who served as an infantry, ground reconnaissance, and civil affairs officer in Viet Nam, 1965-66. He is a sociologist (Ph.D., University of North Carolina, Chapel Hill), who has taught at Brown University, Providence College, the University of Connecticut, and the University of Delaware. His articles about warfare and international affairs have been published in *The Journal of Political and Military Sociology*, the *Marine Corps Gazette*, and *Essential Readings in Political Terrorism*. Currently he is the Director of Social Research Services, a consulting and research organization in East Greenwich, Rhode Island, USA.